ARTICULATING RIGHTS

RIGHTS

NINETEENTH-CENTURY

AMERICAN WOMEN

ON RACE, REFORM,

AND THE STATE

ALISON M. PARKER

NORTHERN ILLINOIS UNIVERSITY PRESS *DeKalb*

© 2010 by Northern Illinois University Press

Published by the Northern Illinois University Press, DeKalb, Illinois 60115

Manufactured in the United States using postconsumer-recycled, acid-free paper.

All Rights Reserved

Design by Julia Fauci

The images that appear on pp. 53, 64, 98, 178, and 204 are courtesy of the Library of Congress.

The image that appears on p. 133 is courtesy of Manuscrpts, Archives and Rare Books Division, Schomburg Center for Research in Black Culture, The New York Public Library, Astor, Lenox and Tilden Foundations.

The images that apear on pp. 140 and 163 are from Anna Gordon's book, *The Life of Frances Willard* (Evanston, IL: National Woman's Christian Temperance Union, 1912).

Library of Congress Cataloging-in-Publication Data

Parker, Alison M. (Alison Marie), 1965-

Articulating rights: nineteenth-century American women on race, reform, and the state / Alison M. Parker.

    p.   cm.

Includes bibliographical references and index.

ISBN 978-0-87580-416-3 (clothbound : alk. paper)

1. Women political activists—United States—Biography. 2. Women social reformers—United States—Biography. 3. United States—Race relations—Political aspects—History—19th century. 4. African Americans—Civil rights—History—19th century. 5. Social movements—United States—History—19th century. 6. Federal government—United States—History—19th century. 7. Women—Political activity—United States—History—19th century. 8. Women—United States—Intellectual life—19th century. 9. United States—Politics and government—19th century. 10. United States—Social conditions—19th century. I. Title.

HQ1236.5.U6P37 2010

323.092'273—dc22

2009038442

WITH LOVE TO FRANCES AND GEOFFREY

Contents

Illustrations

Acknowledgments

This book has been a long time in the making. I appreciate the support I've received along the way from family, friends, colleagues, archivists, and librarians.

I'd like to thank my colleagues at the University of Texas at Arlington, where I began work on this project as well as all of my supportive colleagues at the College at Brockport, State University of New York, where I completed it.

The members of RUSH (the Rochester area United States History working-papers draft group) were particularly helpful in reading one or more draft chapters over the years, especially John Daly, Jon-Paul Dyson, Alicia Chase, Peter Eisenstadt, Carol Faulkner, Greg Garvey, Susan Goodier, Jennifer Haytock, Owen (Steve) Ireland, Bruce Leslie, Jennifer Lloyd, Ken O'Brien, Michael Oberg, Meghan Obourn, Dorinda Outram, Mark Rice, Joan Shelly Rubin, Joan Saab, James Spiller, and Victoria Wolcott.

I appreciate the constructive criticisms of the various anonymous reviewers who have read book proposals or parts or all of this manuscript. While I may not have answered all their concerns, I certainly benefited from their close readings. Also helpful have been the critiques from commentators on my papers at conferences, NEH seminars, or invited talks, including Catherine Allgor, Sheri Browne, Lori Ginzberg, Sarah Barringer Gordon, Lisa Materson,Karen Offen, and Ula Taylor. In addition, Toby Ditz, Nancy Hewitt, and Ronald G. Walters have been consistently supportive.

Robert Gilliam, our wonderful interlibrary loan librarian, provided invaluable service in tracking down many difficult-to-locate items. In addition, I'd like to thank the librarians at the William L. Clements Library at the University of Michigan, the Mooreland-Spingarn Research Center at Howard University, the New Harmony Working-men's Institute and Library in Indiana, Columbia University, and the Library of Congress. The entire staff at Northern Illinois University Press has been a pleasure to work with. I appreciate the support of

Sara Hoerdeman and Susan Bean, as well as the creative design work of Julia Fauci.

Family and friends make all the difference. In my case, I'm lucky to have a great support network. I'd especially like to thank Valeria Chapman-Sinclair, Tina Chung, Amy Hsi, Caterina Falli, Alison Fletcher, Marilyn Lee, Alexis McCrossen, Jyothsna Ponnuri, Cristina Saenz de Tejada, and Tracy Wilborn. My dear friends Kimberley Healey and Cynthia Rogers selflessly and generously read my entire manuscript for me and provided crucial moral support.

My family has been equally generous and supportive. My loving mother, Joanne Johnson Parker, is my role model and inspiration, especially in her longtime dedication to excellent teaching and her support for women's studies. Geoffrey Hale has provided me with twenty wonderful years of love and kindness. His personal and intellectual support is invaluable, sustaining, and always appreciated. What can I say about the other love of my life? Frances, you are my best hope for a fabulous future!

ARTICULATING RIGHTS

Introduction

My book examines the public lives of six nineteenth-century American women who were producers of ideas as well as leaders of social movements and whose lives span the entire century. I chart their ideas and activism at the intersection of the nineteenth century's profound transformations in ideas about race, citizenship, and the state. The public lives of Fanny Wright, Sarah Grimké, Angelina Grimké Weld, Frances Watkins Harper, Frances Willard, and Mary Church Terrell stretched across decades and movements that were central to the nation's political and intellectual culture, including abolition, temperance, suffrage, and civil rights. This study brings to the fore the intellectual thought of women who have been disregarded as political thinkers by most historians. I offer a synthetic narrative of nineteenth-century women's politics that connects these women, all of them political thinkers engaged in reconceptualizing the relationship between the state and its citizens—rather than considering them separately, as is often the case in histories of individual women, antislavery, black women's clubs, temperance, or the WCTU. To examine these women collectively disrupts dichotomies such as those between the pre– and post–Civil War periods or between black and white women. I begin with two women born in the 1790s, Fanny Wright and Sarah Grimké, and end with Mary Church Terrell, who was born during the Civil War and lived into the 1950s.

Each woman featured in this book fought for a range of interrelated reforms, not just one. They explicitly contemplated the role of the federal government in achieving the reforms they desired. Thus, as a criterion for inclusion in this work, they not only had to discuss the merits of federal regulation but also had to engage actively in the larger societal debate concerning the status and rights of African Americans— concerning both race and gender in American society. In this context, race is both a social construction being manufactured by way of racial projects, including abolitionism and temperance, and also a social fact around which women vied for power and tried to negotiate difference.[1] I aim to shed new light on just how broad and complex were the everyday debates articulated by activist women over race, gender, and the role of the federal government in reform.

Over the course of the nineteenth century, increasing numbers of black and white women identified themselves as full citizens who deserved voting rights and a role in public political reform debates. They saw citizenship both as a right and as a set of obligations. Women believed that full citizenship would include voting rights, expanded social and political influence, snd possibly even improvements in women's economic status (from married women's property rights to greater access to education and to wage-earning work). The political, legal, economic, and social dimensions of citizenship underwent a sea change during the nineteenth century. Activist women recognized that they remained outside these expanded definitions of citizenship, especially expanded voting rights.[2] First, in the early decades of the nineteenth century, white men without property holdings were granted the right to vote by the states. Then, black men gained the vote with the passage of the Fourteenth and Fifteenth Amendments during Reconstruction. Finally, in 1890, white women mounted a more unified fight for a constitutional amendment for woman suffrage in the new National American Woman Suffrage Association (NAWSA) and by 1896 had gained federal voting rights in four states.[3]

As many other abolitionist, temperance, and civil rights activists did, these women worked out their reform agenda through strategies aimed at a variety of levels of government and at nongovernmental reforms. Overall, however, over time they demonstrated a progressively greater level of confidence in an expanded role for the central state in reform, by demanding more federal laws and constitutional amendments. American women's political thought evolved from relying on moral suasion and a states' rights perspective toward a wholesale embrace of an expansion of federal power and the state. By "the state," I refer to the federal government. Historian William Novak argues that "the state" was centered in state and local governments for most of the nineteenth century and that America was not unregulated during the antebellum era but, rather, was highly regulated at the local (and sometimes the state) level. Although I accept his general point about the amount of local regulations in the early national and antebellum eras, Novak agrees, it is important to note, that the central government itself was comparatively weak and that the American public was generally wary of federal power.[4] It is women's path toward a greater acceptance of the federal government that interests me here. Placing women reformers' ideas within a changing historical context—from the Jacksonian era to the turn of the century—allows us to see more fully how women claimed a role for the government and for themselves in political reform, as well as how their race and sex shaped those claims. In the early decades of the nineteenth century, women reformers more often used combinations of moral suasion, direct action, and/or advocacy of local and state legislation as the best means to produce social change. By the second half of the century, they more consistently demanded federal regulation. They participated in and helped to influence the development of reform proposals that relied increasingly on the federal government to achieve their goals.[5]

To hold black and white women in the same frame is to bring the complexity of nineteenth-century American political culture into full view. White and black women must be included in the same analysis. From earlier works on antebellum abolitionist culture to recent works on late-nineteenth-century women's activism, historians have begun to adjust their lenses. The result is an increasingly complex picture of how women both cooperated and clashed across lines of race.[6] Yet, in much of American women's history and political history, black women still tend to fade into the background unless they are the sole subjects of the study. Black women had to fight for their rights both as women and as blacks; this double burden encouraged them to develop a broad range of reform strategies and to articulate and work for them separately as well as in unison with others. Especially since the advent of the Civil War, black women fought for constitutional amendments to advance and protect their civil rights and then for federal legislation to enforce those rights. In spite of their efforts, they found that their race and sex led to significant denials of their citizenship rights, particularly the right to vote.

Race and gender were not the only salient lines of difference at play in nineteenth-century American reform movements. Class and religion also influenced patterns of reform. Gender, religion, and reform were crucial to the making of the white middle class at the beginning of the century and to the making of the black middle class at the end of the century.[7] Each woman in this study can be classified as middle-class or above, with the classification based on her family background, income, and educational achievements. In spite of their middle-class status, black women found themselves fighting to assert their own respectability even as they advocated their legislative agenda. To be heard and to be taken seriously in the public political sphere, they articulated a maternalist rhetoric similar to that of white women reformers—but one that built on a long tradition of the heightened importance of mothering under the system of slavery rather than the white middle-class "cult of domesticity."[8] In addition, most of these black and white women reformers (with the exception of the anti-clerical skeptic, Fanny Wright) frequently envisioned themselves as working to realize a truly moral Christian nation on earth. From this perspective, they saw themselves as missionaries whose role it was to convert others to their reform cause.

Each woman reformer featured here shared in a transatlantic reform culture, reading journals and books that published the works of important political thinkers such as John Locke, Jeremy Bentham, Mary Wollstonecraft, Thomas Jefferson, and William Lloyd Garrison. Whereas only Fanny Wright was born abroad, and Frances Willard and Mary Church Terrell were the only American women featured here to travel to Europe (several times and extensively), even those women who never left the North American continent, such as the Grimké sisters and Frances Harper, immersed themselves in a vibrant transatlantic dialogue with other antislavery and anti-lynching activists abroad. Even though several of the women featured in this book were not contemporaries and never met, those who were born later or whose lives overlapped all knew of each other by reputation and often had read speeches, articles, letters, or poems by the others. In most cases they participated in a conversation about political reform built on shared Christian values and a willingness to engage in questions about what their ideal nation should look like. This ongoing question of national identity formation was important to each woman as she tried to define the appropriate limits of the state, the basis of its authority, and the role that women could play in shaping their government.

Even in periods of increased tension, racial conflict, and disaffection such as during Reconstruction, when some women objected to the Fifteenth Amendment because it did not extend voting rights equally to women as well as to men, or in the 1890s, when Jim Crow segregation gained official sanction from the U.S. Supreme Court, black and white women reformers remained in contact with and aware of one another. In all cases female activists drew upon a shared wellspring of ideas to craft their views of gender, race, reform, and the role of the state. Against the background of the contributions of these particular six women reformers, it becomes possible to see more complex dynamics regarding the interplay of race and gender among black and white women. Divisions among women, especially those based on differing ideas concerning race and civil rights, posed a consistent and considerable problem for interracial reform activism and sometimes led to divergences in reform priorities or to the creation of separate organizations. Although these reformers shared the belief that legislative reform and constitutional amendments were the most effective ways to achieve lasting reforms, at some moments they found themselves organizing separately in order to achieve their different reform agendas. African American women, for instance, found that most white women would not join them in an anti-lynching movement or in efforts to improve public schools for all children through a national education bill.

The political thought of women such as Elizabeth Cady Stanton, Susan B. Anthony, Lucy Stone, Victoria Woodhull, and Ida B. Wells has been well documented.[9] Instead, I intentionally turn to six other nineteenth-century women reformers—Fanny Wright, Angelina Grimké Weld, Sarah Grimké, Frances Watkins Harper, Frances Willard, and Mary Church Terrell—who were better known as stirring public speakers, activist poets, or women's club organizers and who have generally not been taken seriously enough as political thinkers.[10] My argument is not that these six women were more significant or more serious than the likes of Stanton or Anthony but that we can find in a much broader range of contemporary women's speeches and writings ideas about reform and the federal government that are both clearly articulated and important.[11] These six women are not unique. Rather, they are representative of larger trends in political thought and reform over the course of the nineteenth century. This book uncovers a robust ongoing conversation about politics—about difference and equality, about state action and individual rights, about citizenship and identity—taking place among black and white women activists who are less studied than the luminary feminists Stanton, Anthony, and Stone, or the educator Catharine Beecher.

Although some engaged directly with the ideas of John Locke, Thomas Jefferson, Jeremy Bentham, or Edmund Burke, the women featured here were not primarily political theorists. Yet in the process of speaking and writing about critical sociopolitical problems such as slavery, woman's rights, temperance, education reform, and lynching, each woman articulated a clear political theory—a vision of the proper role of government in reform and the place of women in American politics. Each woman featured here was a political actor whose work and ideas illuminate the major transformations of her era, particularly women's increasing conception of themselves as having a right to participate in politics and reform as well as their growing belief that the federal government must be encouraged to legislate for women's political and social reform goals.

My first chapter focuses on freethinker Fanny Wright (1795–1852), a woman acknowledged by Ernestine Rose, Stanton, and Anthony as a path breaker for woman's rights.[12] Born in Scotland in 1795, by the 1820s Wright had become a reformer in the United States. She was immersed in the intellectual traditions of the Scottish Enlightenment. Wright spent her formative teenage years living with her uncle James Mylne, a professor of natural philosophy at the University of Glasgow. Mylne and his colleagues were products of the Scottish Enlightenment; during social engagements at the Mylne home Wright heard them espouse the ideas of the famed philosophers David Hume and Adam Smith. Largely self-taught, the teenaged Wright mined her uncle's library and the university library, reading a large number of classical and contemporary texts and engaging in philosophical and political discussions with her uncle's friends and colleagues. After publishing an account of her first trip to America in 1821, Wright gained access to other prominent thinkers, including the English philosopher Jeremy Bentham, who exposed her to utilitarianism. Wright returned to America in 1824 with another friend and mentor, General Lafayette. In the United States she met a fellow Scot, the famed industrialist and utopian socialist Robert Owen, who was promoting his plan for a new utopian socialist community in New Harmony, Indiana. Wright's subsequent plans for her own experimental reform community in Nashoba, Tennessee, were informed by her personal relationships with these prominent thinkers and reformers of her era, who nurtured (sometimes inadvertently) her reform spirit and her utopian idealism.

Fanny Wright's opposition to the system of slavery and her support of woman's rights link her to the other women in this book, even though their solutions to these problems were sometimes quite different. Viewing Wright as an inspiration for the woman's rights movement, activist Ernestine Rose, after she visited Wright's grave in Cincinnati, Ohio, considered her legacy in an 1855 letter to the *Boston Investigator*: "The place, the remembrance of the high-minded woman that rested there, her devotion to the race, her noble efforts to benefit society by the spread of useful knowledge, her love of human freedom and human rights, her opposition to superstition and intolerance, and the bitter persecutions she suffered in consequence . . . called up . . . a stronger devotion to the cause of freedom and of right for which she had to suffer so much."[13]

Wright debated the appropriate level of governmental intervention in reform, whether local, state, or federal. Her life and ideas best represent democratic thought in the age of revolution and enlightenment. Women reformers in the early national and antebellum eras had relatively less faith in the federal government as a site or an agent of reform than those activists working at the turn of the twentieth century. They relied less on legislation than on voluntary measures such as moral suasion. Wright adopted a variety of radical ideas and experiments in the 1820s and 1830s, all unified by her belief in moral suasion and her states' rights perspective. Out of the six women in this study, Wright placed the least faith in the federal government as an agent of change. Drawing on the ideas of Thomas Jefferson, she viewed the main purpose of the U.S. Constitution to be, as Jefferson put it, "the preservation of State rights," and she created her reform ideas according to these principles.[14]

Fanny Wright firmly rejected federal intrusion into the affairs and laws of the separate states. Thus, when she decided to fight to end slavery in the American republic, she chose to do so through moral suasion and direct action. Her antislavery experiment at Nashoba, Tennessee (1825–1829), provided what she hoped would be a practical model for reform. Problematically, Wright tried to end slavery indirectly by educating slaves in the evening and having them work during the day to pay for their freedom from the money earned by their labor. The slaves would be motivated to work hard, she believed, since they would be working for their own emancipation. Wright hoped that once white Southerners came to see that slavery could profitably be replaced by free labor, they would pass their own state-level antislavery laws. Wright's commune was one of over a hundred communitarian living experiments that were founded in the first half of the nineteenth century by Americans eager to change their world. Rather than simply withdrawing from the world, those who participated in communitarian experiments often hoped to influence the outside society by drawing more Americans into their way of life by the positive power of example.[15] Communitarian examples, they hoped, could lead to a series of personal transformations that could, in turn, transform society as a whole. Believing that moral suasion and state and local reform best represented the collective will of the people, throughout her reform career Wright maintained her suspicion of the federal government.

Wright's utopian idealism was shared by many Americans. Although her proposals were radical, she was less of an aberration in the antebellum era than has previously been thought. Wright's suspicion of a strong federal government found a sympathetic audience with those who feared the potentially unchecked power of the central government. She also supported colonization and opposed William Lloyd Garrison and other radical abolitionists who favored the immediate abolition of slavery. Wright argued that white slave owners must not be stripped of slaves, their valuable property, without due compensation or consent. Throughout the antebellum era, colonization had many supporters, especially among members of the Democratic Party, including white Northerners, ministers, and politicians, as well as white Southerners.[16] Like many white Americans, Wright held racist beliefs, including the idea that the current generation of whites was superior to black slaves. Accordingly, she could not conceive of immediately freeing slave men and women and giving them equal citizenship. Wright took the slaves she had purchased for her (by then failed) Nashoba experiment and freed them in 1829 in Haiti, rather than on U.S. soil. In 1835 Wright again advocated colonization as she campaigned for the Democrats. White working-class men who had cheered Wright's speeches for the Working Men's Party in the 1820s likely overlapped with her intended audience in the 1830s and 1840s—Jacksonian Democrats in the North. White Democrats feared economic competition from free blacks and favored colonization and limits on the expansion of slavery rather than immediate emancipation as a way to protect their jobs.[17]

A pioneering feminist and woman's rights activist who tackled issues of slavery and educational reform, Wright was the first woman in nineteenth-century America to become famous by speaking to large mixed audiences of men and women on controversial political topics.[18]

She is a precursor to women who criticized organized religion for its patriarchal oppression of women, such as critics of mainstream Christian denominations and clergy Elizabeth Cady Stanton and Matilda Joslyn Gage. Wright's radical critique of religion is compatible with the views of other female activists who challenged organized religion. Even the deeply religious Sarah and Angelina Grimké had to defend themselves against Christian ministers who challenged women's right to participate in public moral reform efforts. WCTU president Frances Willard, moreover, maintained her strong Methodist faith even as she fought against strictures that prohibited women from being preachers. Challenges to patriarchal religion and to the right of the clergy to control access both to religious authority and to reform agendas were an important aspect of the nineteenth-century women's rights movement that Fanny Wright helped to ignite.[19]

Fanny Wright's greatest fame during her own time and among subsequent women reformers was based on her public speaking and on the fact that she was an early strong advocate for woman's rights. In the late 1820s when Wright became co-editor with Robert Dale Owen of the *New Harmony Gazette* (later, the *Free Enquirer*), for instance, she established her woman's rights agenda and encouraged a transatlantic communication of women's rights ideas by publishing, in serial form and for the first time in a U.S. newspaper, Mary Wollstonecraft's *Vindication of the Rights of Woman*. Wright's stances on marriage, sex outside of marriage, and illegitimacy as well as her advocacy of equal education for males and females made her a precursor to the mid-nineteenth-century women's rights movement. Even if subsequent women reformers did not want to be caricatured as "Fanny Wrightists" simply because they chose to speak in public (a problem most directly confronted by the Grimké sisters), they recognized her to be a pathbreaking role model, an early advocate for woman's rights, and a pioneer who had fought hard to resolve the problem of slavery. Wright's status as a barrier-breaking woman led Anthony, Stanton, and Gage to choose her portrait for the frontispiece of the first volume of their *History of Woman Suffrage*.[20]

Chapter 2 moves from Fanny Wright to Angelina and Sarah Grimké who, when they became abolitionists in the 1830s, found themselves immediately confronted with the difficult legacy of the freethinking

Wright, who by that time was trying to find audiences still interested in hearing her speak. In contrast, the Grimké sisters were drawing large crowds as they lectured on immediate emancipation. In spite of their status as respectable southern ladies, their role as prominent public speakers generated anxiety and criticism among their fellow abolitionists and especially among members of the clergy. They were strongly condemned as "Fanny Wrightists," and their sex influenced the way the Grimkés were received and the ways in which they could acceptably broach their ideas to a wider public.[21] Like Wright before them, the Grimkés and female antislavery activists more generally had to confront questions about the proper role of women as they strove to exercise social and political authority. Sarah (1792–1873) and Angelina (1805–1879) Grimké insisted on the legitimacy of women's participation as political actors in the public arena of abolitionist work.[22] Meeting resistance, the sisters were forced to negotiate between radical abolitionism and their newfound women's rights ideas. The Grimké sisters maintained a strong personal commitment not just to antislavery but to practical antiracism work and to practicing their views on interracial equality by developing intimate friendships with women such as the free black Philadelphia-based Douglass family, especially the educator and abolitionist Sarah Mapps Douglass. Later in their lives, in 1868 when they discovered the existence of their mixed-race nephews (sons of their brother and one of his female slaves), they openly embraced and acknowledged them as family.[23] Their antislavery stance was enhanced by their antiracism work and informed the way they argued for securing the citizenship rights of all black Americans.

The Grimkés realized that for women to be accepted as agents of social change, they must articulate explicit intellectual and moral justifications for women's full participation in politics and reform movements.[24] Both Angelina and Sarah Grimké were well versed in contemporary abolitionist literature. They regularly read and contributed to William Lloyd Garrison's *Liberator* and, like many Americans, had a sound foundation in the Bible. Neither sister was as widely read as Wright was, yet as they became more involved in the struggle for women's rights, Sarah especially began to read more European women writers such as Florence Nightingale, Anna Jameson, George Sand, and Jeanne Deroin, a leader of working-class women's rights during the 1848 revolution in France. Both sisters maintained a long-term transatlantic dialogue with several antislavery and women's rights activists as they sought to influence the debates over slavery, racial prejudice within the Society of Friends, and women's rights in the United States.

Along with other antebellum abolitionists and woman's rights advocates who struggled against slavery and for expanded political rights for women, the Grimké sisters grappled with questions about where to locate change: In the conversion of individuals? In open debate? In federal- or state-level legislation? In intimate discourse? In a marriage of religion, law, and politics? In institutions such as medical colleges? In moral suasion or political action? These were basic questions for American reformers in an era when it was not at all clear how individuals could foster change in a dynamic, highly decentralized society, especially in a society where gender set the terms of political participation. Abolitionists in the 1830s often put their faith in moral suasion as the best way to solve social problems; they believed in a Christian perfectionist obligation of individuals to recognize their sins and change their behavior. Angelina and Sarah Grimké were religious perfectionists who embraced moral suasion, believing that the best way to make change would be for each person to undergo a conversion that would lead him or her from sin to righteousness.[25] The Grimkés echoed Fanny Wright when they appealed directly to slaveholders to emancipate their slaves voluntarily. They hoped emancipation would happen through moral suasion, ideally without governmental force or laws.

The Grimké sisters temporarily adopted the Garrisonian perfectionist stance of avoiding interaction with a tainted government that condoned slavery.[26] While maintaining their core moral beliefs they soon became more flexible about how to achieve their goals, however, and urged the federal government to repeal the Fugitive Slave Acts, keep slavery out of the territories, or abolish slavery altogether. In the decades leading up to the Civil War, female abolitionists moved episodically toward holding the federal government responsible for the problem of slavery and toward seeing it as part of the solution to ending slavery. Abolitionists who adopted the strategy of moral suasion—including the Grimké sisters—simultaneously petitioned the government to change its laws and/or the U.S. Constitution. By the 1850s some perfectionists participated in partisan politics, abandoning their earlier strategy of boycotting what they perceived to be a corrupt political system.[27]

Angelina and Sarah Grimké ultimately concluded that women must engage with the federal government through petitioning and by demanding the right to vote. Social change required human agency, and women, they argued, must be participants in bringing about change. More radically, the Grimkés suggested that women must become part of the federal government. Sarah Grimké's advocacy of the theory of "co-equality" provided a rationale for women's public activism based on their physical and moral differences from men, especially their unique status as mothers or potential mothers. By bringing their greater morality into politics, especially into state and federal governments as legislators, women would change government for the better. Using the doctrine of co-equality as her guide, Sarah Grimké insisted on parity—that women must not only vote but also serve as half of all legislators in order to see that their priorities were enacted into law as well as to fulfill their responsibilities and duties as full citizens.[28]

Considerably younger than the Grimkés, the African American abolitionist, poet, fiction writer, and woman's rights activist Frances Ellen Watkins Harper (1825–1911) campaigned for several social and political reform causes of her lifetime, including abolition, temperance, woman suffrage, and anti-lynching. With a career that began in the antebellum era and continued into the early years of the twentieth century, she became a well-known writer, activist, and speaker in the interracial transatlantic abolitionist movement beginning in the 1850s, more than a decade after the Grimkés had ceased their public lectures.[29] Frances Watkins grew up in a vibrant free black community in Baltimore, in the southern slave state of Maryland. She received a good education at a school for free blacks run by her uncle, the Reverend William Watkins. Her literary style was informed by her reading of poetry, fiction, and news articles in the secular and religious African American press, as well as by antislavery, temperance, and other reform papers that she read.[30] This engagement with a variety of journals, many of which she contributed to from the 1850s onward, informed her political thought, including her evolving stance on the role of the government in reform.

As she assessed the import of historic developments such as the Civil War on the potential for expanded political and civil rights for African

Americans and women, Frances Watkins's reform strategies expanded. During the antebellum era she was cool to calls for federal intervention on behalf of slaves, since she noted that the government—indeed, clauses of the U.S. Constitution itself—had white slave owners' interests at heart. During the antebellum era Watkins used moral suasion in her poetry, fiction, and speeches to try to persuade white Americans of the evils of slavery and of racial prejudice. She engaged in direct action by defying state and national laws forbidding assistance to fugitive slaves on the Underground Railroad.

With the advent of the Civil War, black and white reformers turned more definitively to the federal government, demanding legislation to end slavery and ensure universal suffrage. Frances Watkins Harper (now married) made a clear shift toward supporting a strong federal government when President Lincoln issued the Emancipation Proclamation of 1863. When Lincoln made the abolition of slavery in occupied territory part of the Union's plan for winning the war, Harper recognized that African Americans could make substantial gains with the help of a strong federal government. The executive branch and Congress might be persuaded to use their great powers to remedy rather than perpetuate evils in American society. Also at that point, thousands of northern women abolitionists joined the Women's National Loyal League, newly established by Stanton, Stone, and Anthony. The league organized a petition campaign to demand a constitutional ban on slavery throughout the United States and its territories. Its members successfully collected hundreds of thousands of signatures on petitions and sent them to the U.S. Congress.[31]

After the Civil War, Frances Harper, Charlotte Forten, Sarah Remond, and many other black women activists supported a strengthened role for the federal government and its troops. They rejected states' rights as a reform approach that they knew would benefit southern whites to the detriment of the newly freed slaves.[32] Historian Amy Dru Stanley points out that the "Civil Rights Act linked equal contract rights to the sovereignty of the national state" and provided black activists with another argument against states' rights. African Americans' pursuit of federally protected civil rights now clearly depended upon the strength of the national government.[33]

Radical Reconstruction, undertaken by the U.S. Congress, was particularly vital to the success of former slaves who needed the support of U.S. troops and federal laws in order to become full citizens by exercising their right to vote and the obligation to serve on juries. Once Congress passed the Thirteenth, Fourteenth, and Fifteenth Amendments guaranteeing citizenship to all African Americans and voting rights to black men, black women reformers called on the federal government to enforce the legal rights and protections it had constitutionally guaranteed. Always viewing both racial and gender equality as necessary for the progress of all African Americans, Frances Harper joined Lucy Stone and the American Woman Suffrage Association in endorsing the Fifteenth Amendment, which enfranchised black men, while immediately calling for another constitutional amendment granting women the right to vote. During Reconstruction, Harper traveled throughout the South as a lecturer, hoping to help build viable futures for the newly freed slaves.

By the mid-1870s Harper and many other African Americans had become sorely discouraged by the failure of the federal government to protect blacks' civil rights, despairing about the situation in the South. Even as the promise of Reconstruction faded, Harper never abandoned her faith in the power—if not the will—of the federal government to enact reform. Constitutional amendments for women's voting rights and the prohibition of alcohol, she concluded, could best promote civil rights for all African Americans. Several prominent black women activists such as Frances Harper and Lucy Thurman turned their attention to achieving civil rights, including women's voting rights, from within a national white-dominated women's reform organization, the Woman's Christian Temperance Union (WCTU), which, under the leadership of its president, Frances Willard, developed well-organized national campaigns for constitutional amendments enforcing prohibition and granting woman suffrage.[34] Hoping to solve the problem of black women's comparative lack of access and influence at the national level and noting its power as the preeminent women's organization of its day, black women began joining the WCTU in the late 1870s and early 1880s. Continuing the interracial work she had begun in the abolitionist movement, Harper became a member of the WCTU in order to pursue her agenda of federal legislative reforms.

When Harper, already a famous activist and writer, was appointed the national superintendent of the department "Work Among the Colored People" in 1883, black women gained symbolic prominence within the WCTU. In this leadership position Harper pursued her goal of increasing grassroots activism by helping to form local black WCTU chapters across the country. Black WCTU members articulated what they hoped could be an expanded legislative agenda that white women could also agree upon, such as federal protection of voting rights, national educational reform laws, or anti-lynching legislation. Yet Harper and other black WCTU members often found their efforts dismissed or actively thwarted by white women generally disinterested in including black members as equals within the organization or in working together on issues of special concern to African Americans. To be black in America often meant being expected to accept the limited social and political status assigned by whites to blacks; to be white in America carried a presumptive acceptance of both race and self. Over time Harper and Willard disagreed on the level of WCTU commitment to African Americans and their rights. Frustrated by persistent racism within the WCTU, Harper left her leadership role in the organization in 1891 but remained an active member.

In 1896 Harper joined the younger Mary Church Terrell to unite black women in a new organization, the National Association of Colored Women (NACW), which became a national forum for a network of local clubwomen dedicated to grassroots activism on behalf of both local and federal reforms. The WCTU (founded in 1874) was active at the local, state, and federal levels and offered a variety of reform options to its grassroots members. NACW members adopted their own version of the WCTU's expansive and inclusive "Do Everything Policy" as the best way to reach out to the widest possible number of black clubwomen, who had varying levels of political and reform interests, including literary, sewing, or prayer societies. NACW leaders like Harper and Terrell fought for federal laws—including anti-lynching legislation, woman suffrage, a ban on the convict labor system in the South—and for a renewed federal commitment to enforcing civil rights. While consistently against states' rights initiatives and in favor of federal reform legislation, during the 1890s, when lynchings were at their peak and when the political climate was particularly hostile to assertions of black rights, the NACW simultaneously promoted localized and individualistic self-help options. The organization emphasized what black women could do at the local level, such as establishing kindergartens and day nurseries, to improve life immediately for themselves, their families, and for more disadvantaged black families.

*B*orn fourteen years after Frances Watkins Harper, Frances Elizabeth Willard (1839–1898), the future WCTU president and the subject of chapter 4, was a teenager in the years leading up to the Civil War. She grew up on the Wisconsin frontier where her father farmed and served one term as a state legislator. The Willards supported the Free Soil and then the Republican Party and were members of the Methodist Episcopal Church. In her 1889 autobiography, *Glimpses of Fifty Years,* Willard highlighted her antislavery genealogy, remembering a tract published by the Anti-Slavery Society, called *The Slave's Friend,* as the "earliest book of all my reading, [which] stamped upon me the purpose to help humanity, the sense of brotherhood, of all nations as really one, and of God as the equal Father of all races."[35] At age twenty in 1859, in her diary Willard revealed her commitment to antislavery ideals when John Brown was hanged for his attempted slave rebellion in Harper's Ferry, Virginia. In her diary entry, Willard reflected that "I have been reared a believer in Anti Slavery doctrines. At first, I received them on faith—afterwards on evidence." She pointed to Thomas Jefferson as lending these antislavery ideas concrete meaning. "Thomas Jefferson's memorable words: 'All men are born free and equal' lie at the foundation of our noble Declaration of Independence." Not only was antislavery a fundamental American value, the government's perpetuation of slavery damaged its international reform reputation: "American slavery—the absolute control of one body and soul over another body and soul—is a . . . lie told by the people of the United States to the world. . . . John Brown saw this. He thought it possible that he might wipe this monstrous Falsehood from the land. . . . I do not believe him to have been insane or fanatical. I believe him to have been a Christian man of strong, unwavering mind."[36] Cherishing a view of the United States as having the potential to be a Christian nation, Willard sympathized deeply with Brown's motivations. In these ways the young Frances Willard would have sanctioned and understood the adult Frances Harper's contemporaneous decision to reach out and provide comfort to John Brown and his wife after his arrest. The reform careers of Frances Watkins Harper and Frances Willard became linked by their work, after Reconstruction, in the WCTU.

Although Frances Willard is recognized as the most influential president of the WCTU, the largest women's organization of the nineteenth century, she has rarely been taken seriously as a political thinker. Not only was she a prominent leader in American reform, she viewed herself and her organization as engaging in international missionary work to spread women's rights, pro-temperance, and Christian values throughout the world. The World's WCTU had branches in European countries and also in Japan, Mexico, and Nepal.[37] Willard spent time traveling abroad, and she encouraged a whole network of WCTU women reformers to set out across the globe to act as missionaries for their cause. On the home front, she aptly represents the generation of women reformers who came of age during and after the Civil War and who believed that grassroots organizing could be an effective tool to achieve federal legislative reforms.[38]

An examination of her political thought shows how and why she advocated increased power for the federal government as the best agent of and site for reform. Drawing especially on the ideas of Edmund Burke, Willard convinced a large number of middle-class women of the need for government regulations to protect the interests of the entire society over the potentially selfish desires of individuals. She argued that legal and governmental restrictions against "lawless individuality" were an accepted part of all civilized countries, and thus she embraced "restricted liberty" as the basis for a well-run society.[39]

Frances Willard created a "Do Everything Policy" that allowed WCTU members to try to achieve their goals through campaigns for local- or state-level reform laws as well as federal legislation. State and local WCTU chapters responded by urging officials and legislators to pass reform legislation at every level of government. While many started by initiating local campaigns, by the 1880s Willard had convinced many thousands of WCTU members to campaign for federal amendments for prohibition and woman suffrage. Those who had participated in grassroots organizing for local dry laws, for example, now supported federal prohibition and, accordingly, a government with a regulatory arm strong enough to enforce it. Willard's ideas about women's citizenship and politics represent how women's confidence, abilities, and both political and reform strategies grew exponentially in the last decades of the nineteenth century.

Although the welfare state did not fully develop until the New Deal, the shift toward support for a welfare state began in the late nineteenth century. Legal scholar Jane Larson describes Willard's WCTU as engaging in a "turn towards the state. . . . In the closing decades of the century, reformers were coming to abandon a limited conception of the state as responsible only for restraining one person's interference with another's rights, and embracing the emerging notion of a welfare state responsible for nurturing a prosperous, just, healthful, and moral social environment. This new conception of the state would reach full flower in the Progressive Era." Willard's WCTU represents the highpoint of nineteenth-century women reformers' embrace of federal legislation to solve a wide variety of problems ranging from alcohol abuse to women's access to the vote, age-of-consent laws to protect girls and young women from rape, and even the question of how to keep "impure literature" from children.[40] In the early decades of the twentieth century, progressive reformers continued to push for more federal regulation, and eventually they achieved prohibition and woman suffrage. Most other legislative changes, especially regarding federal labor protections, had to wait until the New Deal, when Congress stepped in to help solve the crisis of the Great Depression under the Democratic president Franklin Delano Roosevelt. We can see in nineteenth-century American women reformers' campaigns the impetus for the view of the federal government as an agent for reform.

Although Frances Willard supported a wide variety of federal reforms, she refused to launch a campaign for anti-lynching legislation. Willard and Harper had shared an early sympathy for John Brown, and in the 1880s and 1890s for other federal legislative reform goals, yet they fundamentally disagreed on the need for federal anti-lynching laws. The WCTU was one of the only interracial national women's organizations of the late nineteenth century, yet when its black members tried to get it to campaign for federal anti-lynching legislation (a strategy that seemed like a logical fit for the organization, given its consistent focus on federal reform laws to solve moral and social problems), they met with intransigent resistance. Although Willard had initially invited northern and southern black women into the organization, by the 1890s she was more invested in promoting the growing popularity of the WCTU among southern white women than in building up black membership.[41] Willard's initial willingness to build a union of white and black American women conflicted with her desire to be recognized as a major force in the national reconciliation of whites in the last decade of the nineteenth century.

In the 1890s (after Harper had been removed from her leadership positions but was still a member of the WCTU), Willard became embroiled in a bitter controversy over lynching and civil rights for African Americans. From 1893 to 1895, anti-lynching activist Ida B. Wells publicly condemned Willard and the WCTU for refusing to protest or to move to protect black families from the ravages of lynch mobs. Focused on recruiting and sustaining significant white membership in the South, Willard and her national organization repeated white Southerners' claims that lynchings were understandable responses to the "outrages" to white southern women by black men.[42] White WCTU members privileged their whiteness over connections based on sex. Black and white women faced persistent difficulties in creating sustainable dialogues and partnerships on reform issues that mattered to each.

The last chapter focuses on Mary Church Terrell (1863–1954), whose political thought and activism serves as a bridge from the women's rights and civil rights movements of the last decade of the nineteenth century to those same campaigns in the twentieth century. Born during the Civil War, this child of former slaves spent her early years in Memphis, Tennessee, during the turbulent time of Reconstruction. Mary Church Terrell lived out her reform career in the United States, directly addressing race and sex. In the late 1880s, as a young woman, Mary Church studied and traveled in Europe, often thinking about how her race and sex modified her ability to claim full citizenship in the United States. She found Europeans to be more welcoming and less racist than white Americans, yet she chose not to live permanently abroad. Her transatlantic experiences forced her to confront the question of citizenship for black Americans, and she vowed to return to the United States to gain full citizenship rights for her race and to secure voting rights for her sex. Terrell's subsequent European trips—to speak, in 1904, at the International Congress of Women in Berlin or, in 1919, at the Women's International League for Peace and Freedom (WILPF) in Zurich—reaffirmed her desire to fight on U.S. soil for the full social and political rights so blatantly denied to African Americans.[43] Mary Church Terrell became a committed reformer and activist, helping to found the Colored Woman's League of Washington, D.C., in 1892, which offered services from which African Americans were often excluded, such as day nurseries and kindergartens as well as night classes for adults. In 1896 Terrell was elected the first president of a new national organization that united black women's clubs, the National Association of Colored Women (NACW).

Black women reformers advanced their political agenda by favoring federal reforms that would finally accord full citizenship to all Americans, without restrictions based on race or sex. The NACW, with Mary Church Terrell at its helm and Frances Watkins Harper as one of several vice presidents, from the very start endorsed a strong federalism and constitutionalism by calling for laws against the leasing of convicts' labor, for woman suffrage, and for anti-lynching legislation at the federal level. The NACW, like the WCTU, used grassroots organizing to pursue both local and national reform campaigns. It was not so much that these two groups' strategies of lobbying for and achieving federal legislative reforms, were so different but, rather, that the NACW was the first race-based, national, secular organization for black women.

Collectively and individually, black women made a significant contribution to the shift toward an activist central state by strongly supporting a federal government with expanded authority to protect and enforce civil rights. Like Harper, Terrell viewed federal legislation and constitutional amendments (properly enforced) as the best means to improve civil rights and to protect African Americans from the extralegal violence condoned by so many white local and state officials. Both Harper and Terrell protested the legal and social barriers that kept black Americans in their subordinate place in the social order. Arguing that all women of color should unite and work for racial uplift, they campaigned against the Jim Crow laws that mandated segregation of the races and outlawed interracial marriages, calling instead for laws based on equal rights for all. Only equality for all citizens—black and white, male and female—would lead to the better society they were striving for. Especially in the North, black women worked tirelessly and for generations to make good on the Republican Party's enforcement of the Reconstruction Amendments; they also fought for the Eighteenth and Nineteenth Amendments and for federal anti-lynching legislation, well into the twentieth century. Terrell herself joined other black women engaging in partisan politics, working as an organizer for the Republican Party, especially in the first few decades of the twentieth century.[44]

In addition to their national reform agenda, from a combination of commitment, necessity, and exclusionary racism, NACW women also pursued self-help and local solutions to social problems. As NACW president at the turn of the century, Terrell supported local self-help initiatives that black women could work on within their homes, clubs, and churches to help improve the lives of their families and local communities. Black women in their local communities focused on training mothers to raise healthy, morally upright youths—by holding mothers' meetings and by founding local daycare facilities for black wage-earning mothers. National political campaigns by black women, moreover, could lead to violent reprisals against them for entering into a political world from which black men were already effectively excluded. The federal government had turned its back on African Americans by ignoring or condoning the violence, segregation, disfranchisement, and other violations of civil rights that were occurring throughout the South and the rest of the nation. The Compromise of 1877 and the hostile U.S. Supreme Court decision in *Plessy v. Ferguson* (1896) are clear examples of this trend. These legal and political changes were accompanied by a rise in lynchings, which reached a peak in the 1890s, as white racism became even more open and virulent.[45] In the South especially, where Jim Crow, race prejudice, and terrorist violence against blacks were now virtually condoned by the federal government, self-help and mothers' meetings were the most practical and sometimes the safest way to start building and strengthening black communities.

Terrell's participation in the NACW, an all-black organization, did not limit her support of interracial alliance building. Instead, her leadership of the NACW allowed her to act as an ambassador for her race, enabling her to claim to speak for thousands of other black women. A lifetime member of the National American Woman Suffrage Association, Terrell was also a member of the National Women's Party, the Women's International League for Peace and Freedom, and the League of Women Voters, among other white-dominated women's organizations. Terrell became a founding member of the interracial National Association for the Advancement of Colored People (NAACP) in 1909 and served on its board of directors. On the lecture circuit in the early decades of the twentieth century, Terrell characterized herself as a missionary who could save white Americans from their own ignorance and racism, and especially from their willingness to allow and condone the desecration of the U.S. Constitution. She knew she would have to persuade her white audiences of the depth of the problems facing blacks in order to generate enough support beyond the African American community for political campaigns that would lead to real legislative change. To point out to whites the injustice of the convict lease labor system, she drew on *Clyatt v. United States,* a largely unenforced U.S. Supreme Court decision of 1905 that ruled that convict labor violated the Thirteenth Amendment's prohibition of slave labor or peonage. Decrying "white lawlessness," she urged whites to join blacks in calling on Congress to pass additional laws to protect all individuals' civil rights.

This book charts black and white women's changing approach to the state, politics, and reform over the course of the nineteenth century. Women activists increasingly demanded more roles and responsibilities for women as full citizens. They also demanded a significantly expanded regulatory role for the federal government. Collectively, nineteenth-century women reformers' expanding reform agenda helped to change expectations of what government could and should do to accomplish women's most cherished reform goals.

Chapter One

Frances Wright

MORAL SUASION AND STATES' RIGHTS

From her original vantage point as a European intellectual and radical, Fanny Wright (1795–1852) was deeply impressed by the promise of the American Revolution and the U.S. Constitution. Vowing to visit the United States, she did so as soon as her sister reached the legal age of independence and could travel with her. Just four days before her twenty-third birthday, on September 2, 1818, Fanny Wright and her sister, Camilla, sailed into the harbor at New York City, beginning a two-and-a-half-year tour of the young republic she had so admired from afar.[1] This unchaperoned tour was not her first break with convention—Fanny had already written a play called *Altorf,* a tragedy set during the Swiss wars of independence against Austria, which she hoped to produce in America (it was performed in 1819 in New York and then in Philadelphia).[2] Its publication provided Wright with a rationale for writing to one of her intellectual heroes, Thomas Jefferson, in order to give him a copy. He responded, "Th. Jefferson presents his compliments. . . . he has read it with great pleasure and sees in it that excellent moral which gives dignity and usefulness to poetry. [T]he character of Altorf the father is a model of patriotism and virtue well worthy of the imitation of our republican citizens: and that of Giovanna is a proper study for both sexes." Thrilled to receive his praise, Fanny replied, "mingled with the affection I feel for the young and free America, and the deep interest with which I

Indicating her importance to the nineteenth-century woman's rights movement, this image of Fanny Wright appeared on the frontispiece of the first volume of the *History of Woman Suffrage*, by Susan B. Anthony, Elizabeth Cady Stanton, and Matilda Joslyn Gage (1881).

regard her amazing progress in all that renders a nation important in its foreign relations, and happy in its internal arrangement, is the reverence I feel for the name of Mr. Jefferson, to whose enlightened, active and disinterested patriotism of his country owes much of its glory, its virtue, and its happiness."[3] As she thought about how this American democratic experiment could be improved, Wright frequently turned to Jefferson's writings to inform her theories and reform positions.

Based on her interpretation of Jefferson's ideas, Wright upheld states' rights and state-level legislation as the best ways to transform American society. She specifically viewed the U.S. Constitution as guaranteeing states' rights as a guard against the potential tyranny of the federal government. Wright championed the Constitution for allowing power to be located in popular politics and state laws rather than in a strong central state.[4] The structural flexibility and democratic potential inherent in the American Revolution and in the nation's founding documents inspired Wright; her challenges to America's laws and politics derived from her profound faith in their potential to represent the will of the people.[5]

Describing the history of the "establishment of the federal Constitution," Wright explained that, after its ratification, "the people were yet apprehensive lest they might have delegated too much power to the new government."[6] She praised the first U.S. president, George Washington, therefore, for moderating rather than expanding the power of the new government. Wright was particularly impressed by Jefferson's commitment, as president, to shrinking the power of the federal government. She described his terms in office as follows: "The most rigid economy was carried into every department of government, some useless offices were done away, the slender army was farther reduced, obnoxious acts, passed by the former Congress, repealed, and the American Constitution administered in all its simplicity and purity." What some saw as a weakness, she viewed as a strength: "The government of the United States has been denominated weak; but that only by those who are accustomed to consider a government as arrayed against a people. It is quite another thing here; the government acts with the people; is part of the people; is in short the people themselves."[7] The relative lack of power of the central state, she asserted, was a positive manifestation of the will of the people.

Rejecting the federal government as a vehicle for reform, Wright joined many Americans of the 1820s and 1830s in viewing the central

state as being more dangerous as well as more distant and less responsive to the average citizen than state and local governments.[8] Wright's
emphasis on state-level legislation found a sympathetic audience with
Jacksonian Democrats who wanted to expand the power of average
citizens by encouraging states, for instance, to enfranchise all adult
white men. Wright supported states' rights in order to ensure that federally mandated solutions would not be imposed on unwilling states.
Her reliance on moral suasion and on state-level legislation reflects the
more limited nature of governmental power at the federal level, as well
as citizens' continued suspicions of a powerful central government.
Historian William Novak insists that there was in fact a significant
governmental regulatory and legal presence in the nineteenth-century
United States. In order to destroy what he sees as the myth of the
absence of government during this time, he details numerous local laws
and the extensive duties of police departments and city councils. Yet
Novak acknowledges that a strong centralized federal government did
not exist. He confirms that the modern state with its "monopoly in the
use of force," its "system of order," and its bureaucratic structure was
not present before the Civil War. Therefore, his convincing documenta-
tion of the pervasiveness of local regulation does not substantially alter
the fact that the central state was a less dominant presence in the early
national and antebellum eras.[9]

Fanny Wright's ideas concerning legislation, governmental power,
and moral suasion link her to the democratizing impulses and popular
concerns and priorities of the Jacksonian era.[10] In the late 1820s Wright
became a radical freethinker and a public speaker. Ignoring gender
prescriptions against women's involvement in politics, she publicly
campaigned for the Working Men's Party and shaped its platform to
include state legislation for education reform. Her calls for universal
equal education were given serious consideration by the working
classes and by middle-class freethinkers. Wright's public speaking, early
support of women's rights, and opposition to slavery made her a role
model for those who participated in the antebellum woman's rights
movement and beyond. Although her reform approaches differed from
those of other reformers (especially her insistence upon a strict states'
rights approach), Wright's interest in both ending slavery and promoting women's rights connects her to the other women in this study and
to the women's rights movement more generally. Thus, when Stanton,
Anthony, and Gage wrote their *History of Woman Suffrage* in 1881, they

characterized Fanny Wright as an important pioneer, ahead of her time: "Her radical ideas on theology, slavery, and the social degradation of woman, now generally accepted by the best minds of the ages, were then denounced by both press and pulpit, and maintained by her at the risk of her life."[11] Lionizing Wright as a martyr, they paid tribute to her courageous attacks on conventional ideas.

"A PEOPLE VOLUNTARILY SUBMITTING TO LAWS OF THEIR OWN IMPOSING"—WRIGHT'S *VIEWS OF SOCIETY*

Emboldened in part by the publication of *Altorf* and by Jefferson's praise, Wright soon published another book, the first British travelogue about the New Republic. *Views of Society and Manners in America* (1821) was based on a series of letters to a Scottish friend during her travels. Young Fanny Wright's *Views of Society* lauded America's revolutionary possibilities. Ignoring her own alien status as a Scot, she claimed the United States as her newly adopted country. Using the term "we" to include herself as an American, she celebrated the United States as having the necessary elements to make up a successful government by and for the people: "[W]e should distinguish the advantage we possess over other nations, to be—*not that our form of government is republican, or democratic, or federative, but that it possesses the power of silent adaptation to the altering views of the governing and the governed people.*"[12] The Constitution could be the basis for more profound and radical change because it guaranteed that the people could both amend it and pass new laws in their own states to suit changing mores, needs, and priorities.

The central and state governments, according to Wright, existed purely as representatives of the will of the people, acting only on the behalf and in the interest of the people. Wright pointed out that, after the American Revolution, the founders of the New Republic instead of creating an administratively centralized state in fact set up a system whereby politics and legislation became the means by which public welfare was debated and decided: "When the *Federal Constitution* superseded these articles [of Confederation], the people parted with no new powers, but transferred some of those, before delegated to their representatives in their own houses of assembly, to their representatives in the general congress." Wright understood a central tenet of the Constitution, as described by historian John Murrin: "By so institutionalizing the premise that the people alone are sovereign, and not government at any level, Americans made it possible for a sovereign citizenry to delegate some powers to the states, others to the central government."[13]

Praising the nation's decentralized system that ensured states' rights, Wright presented the U.S. political system as an excellent model for other countries in need of reform.[14] Elaborating on what she saw as the crucial differences between England and the United States, Wright argued that Parliament had too much power in England. In contrast, the American Congress was carefully limited by the constitutional principle of states' rights, as exemplified in the Tenth Amendment. Wright agreed with Jacksonian era political activists who, for instance, wanted U.S. senators to be selected directly by the citizens of each state in order to ensure that they represented state rather than national interests. The right to vote and participate in politics restricted the dangerous power of the central government. Later, in 1836, she praised the founders of the United States for devising a more balanced political system than that of England:

> America's first political fathers had evidently deeply studied the machinery of British government, and distinguished where the shoe pinched. The Puritans of New England . . . determined to establish popular power in its substance; and to them we are indebted for that first organization or systematic division of the parts of government, together with the sectioning of the territory so as to facilitate the action of the population, which, in its whole, will constitute, in the progress of its development and sound action, the definitive state of human society.[15]

Strong local and state governments ensured that power would stay in the hands of average citizens. Wright highlighted what made the United States different from European governments: "Its powers in short extend to all matters connected with the common defense and general welfare of the confederacy; and these powers being clearly defined, it may make laws necessary and proper for rendering them effective. For the just administration of these powers, it is directly responsible to the people."[16] In the United States, no monarch or parliament reigned supreme; instead, the people were sovereign.

Wright's *Views of Society* engaged the ideas of other thinkers and politicians who wrote at the time of the American Revolution. In addition to Thomas Jefferson, she cited Benjamin Franklin, David Ramsay, and Edmund Burke. Wright quoted, for instance, from Burke's 1775 "Speech on Conciliation with America" as well as his discussions of the "popular" nature of colonial governments. She quoted from a passage in David Ramsay's two-volume *History of the American Revolution* (1789) that echoed Burke's ideas about the need for citizens to "surrender" their liberties to create a civil society (we will see that Frances Willard, as WCTU president, also made extensive use of Burke's ideas). Wright commented:

> The remarks made by Ramsay on the adoption of the federal constitution are so apposite that I cannot resist quoting them: "The adoption of this constitution was a triumph of virtue and good sense over the vices and follies of human nature. . . . [h]igher grades of virtue are requisite to induce freemen, in the possession of a limited sovereignty, voluntarily to surrender a portion of their natural liberties; to impose on themselves those restraints of good government which bridle the ferocity of man, compel him to respect the claims of others, and to submit his rights and his wrongs to be decided upon by the voices of his fellow-citizens."[17]

As Novak argues, Americans in the early 1800s accepted restrictive state and local regulations in order to ensure public safety, economy, and morals. Wright celebrated Americans as "a people voluntarily submitting to laws of their own imposing, with arms in their hands respecting the voice of a government which their breath created, and which their breath could in a moment destroy!" More radically than many of her contemporaries, Wright then extended these ideas on the authority and rights of the people to examine and challenge the condition of free white and black women in the United States.[18]

On her first visit to the United States, Wright viewed the condition of women in the New Republic more positively than she did a few years later. At this point she provided a neutral description of the role of American women after the Revolution, as republican mothers "in a country where a mother is charged with the formation of an infant mind that is to be called in future to judge of the laws and support the liberties of a republic, the mother herself should well understand those laws, and estimate those liberties." For this reason, Wright reported, women were getting better basic educations than

ever before. She challenged Americans to abandon some of the nice-
ties of a European-style education for elite women (focusing on music,
foreign languages, and embroidery) in order to allow them more time
to study "philosophy, history, political economy, and the exact sci-
ences." In the North, she observed approvingly, the "child of every
citizen, male or female, white or black, is entitled, by right, to a plain
education." Wright's interest in universal, equal education became a
central reform goal for her. More radically, she suggested, "Alas for the
morals of a country when female dignity is confounded with helplessness, and the guardianship of a woman's virtue transferred from
herself to others!" Women, she explained, must be in control of their
own bodies, and thus they must be able to leave unhappy or abusive
marriages. She advised other American states and European countries
to adopt divorce laws similar to those of Rhode Island, which allowed
for an annulment of a marriage after a two-year separation based on
"incompatibilities." This law, she suggested, would "cement rather
than weaken the marriage tie throughout the world" by giving women
control of their destinies.[19]

In *Views of Society* Wright also explored the subject of slavery, which
she labeled a "revolting" and unmitigated "evil." Not wanting to fully
condemn this young republic she so admired, Wright awkwardly
argued that the "history of African slavery is at once the disgrace and
honor of America"—a disgrace because it existed there but an honor
because it "was the first country to abolish the [international] trade;
first by the laws of her separate states, among which Virginia led the
way, and secondly by the law of her federal government." Wright
pointed out that the Southern state of Virginia had taken the initiative
and that the U.S. Congress "composed, in great part, of representatives
from slave-holding states, *themselves slave-holders*" had complied with
the wishes of the people in their states (and, she implied, nobly voted
against their own self-interest).[20] Wright ignored the fact that these
slave owners were not making any real sacrifice by passing a ban on
the international slave trade. After all, slaves in the United States were
now reproducing at a rate that allowed for the perpetuation and even
expansion of slavery and of the internal slave trade without any new
influx of slaves from Africa or the Caribbean. Historian Gail Bederman argues that Wright blamed her own country, Britain, for having
imposed the system of slavery on colonial America. Bederman suggests

that, by doing so, Wright "misrecognized slavery as a vestigial remnant of British colonial tyranny rather than an intrinsic part of U.S. political culture." She therefore falsely believed that most American slaveholders hated and feared the slave system and longed for a way to rid themselves of this burdensome colonial legacy.[21]

On her first visit to America, Wright was already thinking about how she might help to end slavery there. She conceded that it "is not for a young and inexperienced foreigner to suggest remedies for an evil which has engaged the attention of native philanthropists and statesmen, and hitherto baffled their efforts," yet she did ponder remedies. Informed by her support for states' rights, she believed that only white male voters within a state could eliminate slavery. Rather than focusing on the plight or rights of the slaves themselves, Wright expressed more concern about the "American planters," whose economic interests "must be sacrificed" if slavery were to be abolished. She sanctioned an earlier committee report of Virginia's first assembly after the American Revolution that had proposed "a plan of colonization" to achieve "the removal of such a proportion of the slave population, as shall render practicable the emancipation of the remainder." Not all freed blacks would have to leave the United States, but she agreed with pro-colonization slaveholders that a large number of slaves would have to do so in order for the rest to be more easily assimilated. Following the lead of a New York representative who had made a recent motion in Congress "to purchase the slaves from their owners at a regulated price," Wright proposed that "before such a system [of slavery] can be productive of any national benefit, it must be made a national concern." The U.S. Congress should "educate the whole black population at the public expense," pay to equip them for colonization abroad, and reimburse slave owners. She also endorsed a proposal she had heard of to use "money arising from the sale of the national lands" to pay for this: "I am led to think that this measure is neither visionary nor impracticable, especially as it finds supporters among the slaveholders of the South." From the start she believed that the consent and participation of Southern slaveholders was necessary in all plans to remove slavery. (In the last pages of *Views of Society,* Wright proposed an alternative plan that did not involve colonization: "Were the whole race emancipated, their education would necessarily become a national object, the white population would be constrained to hire their service, and they themselves be under the necessity of selling it."[22] Universal education of all freed blacks would bolster the status of all wage laborers.)

"THE PRESERVATION OF STATE RIGHTS"—JEFFERSON, LAFAYETTE, AND WRIGHT

Not surprisingly, Fanny Wright's *Views of Society and Manners in America* (1821) was generally appreciated by American reviewers and by some British and French supporters of revolutionary ideals but was dismissed by other Britons as fawning and overstated.[23] Overall, its publication gained Wright a great deal of attention in European intellectual circles. Her newfound fame enabled her to meet and befriend some important thinkers such as the famous English utilitarian philosopher Jeremy Bentham, who read her work enthusiastically. He did not mind her correction, in *Views of Society,* of his misstatement that the president of the United States was also the "President of Congress." To Wright, this was a serious "error" because it ignored the balance of power that kept the U.S. Congress free from the direct pressure or undue influence of the president.[24] Bentham appreciated her book. After meeting and befriending her, he appreciated Wright as well, declaring, "She is the Sweetest and Strongest Mind that ever was Cased in a female Body." Wright returned the favor on the acknowledgments page of her book *A Few Days in Athens,* where she wrote, "To JEREMY BENTHAM, As a testimony of her admiration of his enlightened sentiments, useful labors, and active philanthropy, and of her gratitude for his friendship, THIS WORK, is respectfully and affectionately inscribed by Frances Wright."[25]

Her book *Views of Society* also attracted the attention of the aging French hero of the American Revolution, the Marquis de Lafayette, who described it to his close friend Thomas Jefferson, "the elder Miss Wright did for the first time Give me the pleasure to Read the praise of America from an English pen. On that ground Began an Acquaintance which soon Became affectionate Mutual friendship." Indeed, Lafayette became her friend, mentor, and substitute father figure (she had been orphaned at age two). Fanny and her sister lived with Lafayette and his family at his home, La Grange, in France during most of 1821 until 1824. At La Grange, Lafayette helped Wright edit her *Views of Society* for a second edition and encouraged her to publish another book, *A Few Days in Athens*, in 1822, which purported to be a translation of a "Greek manuscript discovered in Herculaneum." In this work she defended Epicurean philosophy and provided a secular critique of the Theists. Lafayette recommended the revised edition of her *Views on Society* to Jefferson: "I Much want to know Your opinion of that work, which Has Been translated in German, French, and Modern Greek, and if favorable, as I Hope it will Be the Case, I am sure no greater Gratification Can Be offered to My Young friend." Just as Wright had sent Jefferson a copy of *Altorf,* Lafayette sent Jefferson copies of *Views of Society* and *A Few Days in Athens* in 1823. In response, Jefferson sent the praise that Lafayette had been hoping for: "her *'A Few Days in Athens,'* was entirely new, and has been a treat to me of the highest order. The matter and manner of the dialogue is strictly ancient; and the principles of the sects are beautifully and candidly explained and contrasted; and the scenery and portraiture of the interlocutors are of higher finish than anything in that line left us by the ancients; and . . . is equal to the best morsel of antiquity. I augur, from this instance, that Herculaneum is likely to furnish better specimens of modern than of ancient genius; and may we not hope more from this same pen?" Lafayette responded, "She is very Happy in Your Approbation; for, You and I are the two Men in the World the Esteem of whom she values the Most."[26]

At La Grange, Lafayette shared his personal correspondence with Wright. She learned from these letters just how much Jefferson valued states' rights and feared what he termed "a consolidated government." In 1822, already thinking of the upcoming 1824 presidential election, Jefferson noted caustically that all the candidates called themselves "Republicans," but some were really former Federalists "endeavouring to break down the barriers of the state rights provided by the constitution against a consolidation." Jefferson's letters confirmed Wright's developing view of the U.S. Constitution. In another letter to Lafayette, Jefferson explained the different partisan positions being staked out in American politics: "The line of division now, is the preservation of State rights as reserved in the constitution, or by strained constructions of that instrument, to merge all into a consolidated government. The tories are for strengthening the executive and general Government; the whigs cherish the representative branch, and the rights reserved by the States, as the bulwark against consolidation, which must immediately generate monarchy." From his perspective, strong states would prevent a monarchical form of government from being imposed in America.[27]

The correspondence between Jefferson and Lafayette also included an extended debate over how to end American slavery, and Lafayette engaged Wright in this debate, enabling her to refine her own ideas about how to end slavery. Jefferson declared to Lafayette that he favored expanding slavery into new states and territories: "All know that permitting the slaves of the South to spread into the west will not add one being to that unfortunate condition, that it will increase the happiness of those existing, and by spreading them over a larger surface, will dilute the evil everywhere, and facilitate the means of getting finally rid of it." An incredulous Lafayette wrote a series of letters to Jefferson asking, "Are You Sure, My dear friend, that Extending the principle of slavery to the New Raised States is a Method to facilitate the Means of Getting Rid of it? I would Have thought that By Spreading the prejudices, Habits, and Calculations of planters over a larger Surface You Rather Encrease the difficulties of final liberation." As he and Wright discussed the stain of slavery on the international reputation of the New Republic they agreed, as Lafayette put it, that "Was it not for that deplorable Circumstance of Negro Slavery in the Southern States, Not a word Could Be objected, when we present American doctrines and Constitutions as an example to old Europe."[28]

When General Lafayette set off on a triumphal return visit to the United States from 1824 to 1825, Fanny and Camilla Wright joined him. For the sake of respectability, they traveled separately from his entourage, sometimes meeting up with him on his travels and always using his letters of introduction to correspond with or meet with famous American political leaders, from Thomas Jefferson and James Madison to Andrew Jackson.[29] Most important, Lafayette secured an invitation for Fanny and Camilla to join him in visiting Jefferson at Monticello. Thus, when the two men met and continued their debate over the merits of colonization or the emancipation of slaves on U.S. soil, Wright was there with them.[30] Fanny Wright's conversations with Jefferson confirmed her states' rights perspective, while her long discussions with Lafayette confirmed her conviction that slavery damaged the international reputation of the new United States. When she developed a plan to end slavery, however, we will see that her proposal was uniquely her own.

On this her second trip to the United States, Wright criticized more consistently those state and federal laws that subordinated women and slaves. Observing that most laws affecting women were not the work of this newly liberated people but were instead based on English common law, Wright asked Americans to rid themselves of the evils of the English legal system. She regretted that it had been thought-lessly adopted in full: "Every part and parcel of that absurd, cruel, ignorant, inconsistent, incomprehensible jumble, styled the common law of England . . . is at this hour the law of revolutionized America." Anticipating antebellum era reformers who lobbied states to expand the property rights of married women, Wright objected to marriage laws that denied married women their inheritances, wages, and joint guardianship of their children. Wright also criticized organized religion as irrational, charging that the clergy helped prop up the unfair legal institution of marriage in order to reinforce women's subordination in all aspects of their lives. Challenges to women's subordinate place within organized religion were an important aspect of the nineteenth-century women's rights movement and connect Wright to the women who came after her.[31]

Fanny Wright further observed that the ideals of the Declaration of Independence with its promises of equality and freedom were bla-tantly denied to those who were enslaved. She boldly decided that she personally wanted to help eliminate slavery in the United States. An introduction from Lafayette gained Wright access to Andrew Jackson, the hero of the battle of New Orleans during the War of 1812. He had recently won the greatest number of popular and electoral votes in a four-way contest for president in the election of 1824 but then lost the presidency when the House of Representatives chose John Quincy Adams. Ironically, to start her project to help end slavery, Jackson helped Wright purchase "recently confiscated Native American land" that he had, as historian Gail Bederman points out, wrested from the Chickasaw Indians at Nashoba, near Memphis, Tennessee.[32]

At this time most colonization societies were still in the South, not in the North. White planters who feared slave rebellion and ques-tioned slavery as a permanent labor solution for the South advocated colonization as the ultimate solution to the problem of slavery. Yet, since the Revolution, Southern antislavery ideas had not translated into widespread emancipation or colonization for slaves. Wright envisioned Nashoba as the first of many working farms where slaves would be motivated by a (vague) promise of future freedom to produce enough profits through their labor to compensate their owners and free themselves. Seemingly more concerned about the economic welfare of slave owners than about the liberty of the slaves themselves, Wright anticipated the Free Soil, Free Labor ideology of the 1840s by focusing on the economic benefits that would come to whites by ending the system of slavery.[33]

Acting on her states' rights principles, Wright argued that white Southerners must take the initiative to end slavery. Taking this point literally she concluded that, in order to effect change, she herself had to become a "southern citizen, and, even, a slaveholder."[34] Thus, Wright purchased slaves to start her experiment, with the plan of having them work for their eventual freedom. Unconcerned that black slaves would have to earn the freedom that whites had by birthright, she asserted that they were not yet ready for freedom. Because the "public mind" must make its own state-level laws, Wright declared herself unwilling to violate existing state laws on slavery. She reported that, before beginning her experiment, she carefully read "all the laws of the slave states, bearing directly upon the labor and the government of the negro."[35] She explained, "As it was the object of the founder to attempt the *peaceful* influence of example, and *silently* to correct the practice, and reach the laws through the feelings and the reason of the American people, she carefully forebore from outraging any of the legal provisions in the slave state in which she ventured to attempt her experiment, or those of any of the slave states with which she is acquainted."[36] Because each slaveholder must come to understand that slavery was wrong and ultimately economically unproductive, only legislative change at the state level would show that "human opinion" had changed and was now "righteous."[37]

Taking from Thomas Jefferson the notion that "the people" could transform their nation, Wright argued that Southern slavery was and should remain outside the sphere of national legislation—no revolution in the ideas of Northerners alone would suffice.[38] Slavery must be dealt with as "a sectional question," for Wright claimed it was "unprovided for in the national constitution." By this, she meant that slavery was not outlawed at the time of the nation's founding. Therefore, it was a system of labor that each state could regulate at will: "I have stated southern slavery to be, at this existing point of time, without the pale of effective and beneficent legislation. . . . [B]efore legislation may be effective and beneficent in its action, public opinion must be in unison with its statutes. . . .Where and when constitutional law doth not speak, but the public mind is prepared to make it speak, the people have to supply its deficiencies or to rectify its errors." In an overture to white woutherners, Wright argued that slavery could only be abolished by "the future decision of our southern fellow-citizens themselves acting constitutionally within their own states' jurisdictions."[39]

Wright's communal experiment at Nashoba was based on her antislavery principles and her commitment to moral suasion—a model of reform whereby individuals' values would be transformed by moral example. Once white Southerners objectively observed her experiment, she imagined, they would see that slavery could be eliminated without undue financial hardship on their part. Speaking of herself in the third person, Wright explained that she "had observed that the step between theory and practice is usually great . . . mankind must reasonably hesitate to receive as truths, theories, however ingenious, if unsupported by experiment. . . . She determined to apply all her energies . . . to the building up of an institution which should have those principles for its base, and whose destinies, she fondly hoped, might tend to convince mankind of their moral beauty and practical utility." Although she admitted that her premise for Nashoba was "opposed to all existing opinions and practice," Wright anticipated that her antislavery ideas would seem less threatening and more of a real possibility for the future if she tried to enact rather than just assert them. While she insisted that "the founder of Nashoba looks not for the conversion of the existing generation; she looks not even for its sympathy," Wright clearly hoped that slave owners would follow her lead and move toward emancipation and colonization once they saw the success of her experiment. Nashoba, she insisted, was founded "not in a spirit of hostility to the practice of the world, but with a strong moral conviction of [its] superior truth and beauty." Personal example, moral suasion, and a respect for states' rights would lead white Southerners to decide to end slavery.[40]

Wright's interest in founding a communal experiment was not unique at the time; there were over a hundred secular and religious utopian communitarian living societies in the first half of the nineteenth century. Wright was particularly inspired by her visit to George Rapp's religious community at New Harmonie, Indiana, where she heard the successful industrialist-turned-utopian-socialist Robert

Owen explain how he intended to purchase this prospering religious village and transform it into New Harmony, a secular communitarian living experiment.[41] Just as her advocacy of states' rights reflects the influence of Thomas Jefferson, so Wright also espoused a variant of white supremacist opposition to slavery that Jefferson subscribed to. Although opposed to slavery, Jefferson did not believe in the equality of the races at that point in time (although he left open the possibility of their future advancement, as did Wright). In conceiving of Nashoba as a necessary stage before emancipation, Wright shared the conviction of most white Southerners, including Jefferson, that slaves could not immediately be freed because they first needed to be schooled in liberty.[42] Even if some planters were ready, slaves themselves were not prepared for immediate emancipation: "Human enfranchisement," Wright explained, "is but another name for civilization." Slaves would have to be civilized before they were freed. An "apprenticeship," like that at Nashoba, would provide them with an education and teach them to be civilized prior to emancipation. Even then, former slaves could not automatically be given political citizenship, because, in her estimation, the first generation would lack moral and mental elevation. They must be guided, Wright determined, by the white "master race," which was "superior in knowledge" and "therefore necessarily the sovereign disposer of their destinies." Wright's language about white supremacy reveals her commonality with most white Americans who believed in a racial hierarchy in which whites were, in her words, "the master race." Her acceptance of racial hierarchies reinforced Wright's connection to the era's racially divisive politics, including Andrew Jackson's Indian Removal policies.[43]

Although she did not embrace colonization, Wright made a concession to slave owners by declaring that all slaves emancipated from Nashoba would be colonized abroad: "the founder judged that she should best conciliate the laws of the southern states and the popular feeling of the whole union, as well as the interests of the emancipated negro, by providing for the colonization of all slaves emancipated by the Society." Colonization would serve as a safety valve by sending some freed blacks to live outside the borders of the United States; white laborers would therefore not object to the end of slavery (based on their fears that free blacks would compete against them in a tight labor market). Wright's acceptance of and immersion in the prejudices of her era foreclosed the radical possibilities of Nashoba.[44]

After visiting Monticello, Wright wrote to Jefferson in 1825 about her antislavery experiment at Nashoba, hoping to gain his endorsement. Jefferson replied to her request with a long, kind letter telling her that he could not officially endorse her plan. He began with a self-deprecating humorous reference to his advanced age and declining health: "At the age of eighty-two, with one foot in the grave, and the other uplifted to follow it, I do not permit myself to take part in any new enterprises, even for bettering the condition of man, not even in the great one which is the subject of your letter, and which has been through life that of my greatest anxieties." (Jefferson's health was indeed failing; he died the next year on July 4, 1826.) He continued, "I leave its [the abolition of slavery] accomplishment as the work of another generation. And I am cheered when I see that on which it is devolved, taking it up with so much good will. . . . The abolition of the evil is not impossible; it ought never therefore to be despaired of. Every plan should be adopted, every experiment tried, which may do something towards the ultimate object."[45] Jefferson acknowledged that slavery was an evil that must somehow be abolished, while confessing that he had not yet figured out a practical way to end it.

Then, Jefferson addressed the specifics of Wright's proposal. Based on his belief in a hierarchy of the races, he feared her plan might falter on its notion that blacks would work to improve their own condition without "physical coercion":

That which you propose is well worthy of trial. It has succeeded with certain portions of our white brethren, under the case of a Rapp and an Owen; and why may it not succeed with the man of color? An opinion is hazarded by some, but proved by none, that moral urgencies are not sufficient to induce him to labor; that nothing can do this but physical coercion. But this is a problem which the present age alone is prepared to solve by experiment. It would be a solecism to suppose that a race of animals created, without sufficient foresight and energy to preserve their own existence. It is disproved, too, by the fact that they exist, and have existed through all the ages of history. We are not sufficiently acquainted with all the nations of Africa, to say that there may be some in which habits of industry are established, and the arts practiced which are necessary to render life comfortable.

Believing that whites were inherently superior to blacks, Jefferson told Wright that he could not imagine a case where blacks would work without coercion (and unfortunately, when her experiment began to go awry, Nashoba's trustees did, indeed, resort to physical coercion). Anticipating a Social Darwinist "survival of the fittest" argument, Jefferson then tried to disprove his own misgivings by suggesting that although he did not know of any specific examples, some Africans or people of African descent must share with whites the "habits of industry"—otherwise the whole race would have died out already. Jefferson also observed that "The experiment now in progress in St. Domingo, those of Sierra Leone and Cape Mesurado, are but beginning. Your proposition has its aspects of promise also; and should it not answer fully to calculations in figures, it may yet, in its developments, lead to happy results." Jefferson did not provide Wright with the ringing endorsement she had hoped for. This was a disappointment to her because she admired him so greatly, but she took heart perhaps from his last words: "You are young, dear Madam, and have powers of mind which may do much in exciting others in this arduous task. I am confident they will be so exerted, and I pray to heaven for their success, and that you may be rewarded with the blessings which such efforts merit." Although acknowledging her enthusiasm and good intentions, he declined to lend his prestige to her experiment.[46]

In one of Lafayette's last letters to Jefferson before the latter's death, he wrote again of Fanny Wright: "You Have, No doubt, Heard of My Young philanthropic friends now at Memphis West Tennessee. They write that they find in that part of the Country Better dispositions than is Generally thought in the North. I ever thought the feelings, and interest of the people of the South were to be immediately applied to without Recurrence to Northern influence." Lafayette had also declined to endorse Wright's plan but now condoned a states' rights approach that it seems he had resisted prior to Fanny's experiment. He concluded, "My dear Jefferson, the more I see, I Hear, I think, and I feel on the subject the greater Appears to me, for the white still more if possible than the Colored population of the Southern States, the importance and Urgency of Measures pointing towards the Gradual Emancipation of Slavery. Could not Mexico, and those American wide Republics of South America offer an additional vent for liberated

Negroes?"[47] A combination of emancipation and colonization, Lafayette hoped, might save white Southerners from the evils of slave owning.

"THE FORCE OF ITS OWN PRINCIPLES"—RACE AND SEX AT NASHOBA

Fanny Wright's article "Nashoba: Explanatory Notes, Respecting the Nature and Objects of the Institution of Nashoba, and of the Principles Upon Which it is Founded" (1828) reads as if it were a blueprint for her experiment, but it was, in fact, written and published after Nashoba's inception, at a point when her experiment was on the brink of failure. The "Explanatory Notes" were written in response to the extremely negative publicity her community received as a result of the publication of entries from the trustees' journal detailing the internal workings of Nashoba. These journal entries were sent by a resident trustee of Nashoba, James Richardson (a freethinking anticlerical Scotsman who had joined Wright in Tennessee), to the antislavery paper published by Quaker Benjamin Lundy, the *Genius of Universal Emancipation.* Published in July 1827 under the title "Frances Wright's Establishment," the entries revealed Nashoba to be exceedingly radical in terms of its ideas and practices regarding sex, marriage, and the amalgamation of the races. The entries also revealed that the trustees at Nashoba were cruel in their treatment of Nashoba's slaves. Most controversial at the time was its report that Richardson and a free black woman, Josephine Prevot, were living together at Nashoba as an interracial unmarried couple.

The uproar and scandal caused by the publication of the trustees' journal entries initiated an overwhelming series of attacks against Wright and her community. She could have renounced Richardson— and did privately reprove him for his indiscretion. However, Wright felt that she had no choice but to acknowledge the fundamental veracity of the entries and explain her principles to the public. Her "Explanatory Notes," first published in the *Memphis Advocate* in December 1827 and then reprinted in January and February of 1828 in *The New Harmony Gazette,* went far beyond her own initial antislavery goals for Nashoba and expressed her most radical ideas regarding free love and racial amalgamation.[48]

She began, predictably, by criticizing American slavery, stating that the "*more especial object*" of Nashoba was "*the protection and regeneration of the race of color, universally oppressed and despised in a country self-denominated free.*" Although she initially purchased slaves for her experiment, Wright soon decided not to buy any more slaves, aiming instead to admit "*free citizens of color*" and "mixed race" people "on the same principles of equality which guide the admission of all members." She hoped that this, in addition to the equal "education of the race of color" at Nashoba, would lead to positive social interactions and communication between blacks and whites that would break down racial barriers. Wright viewed free blacks as "respectable" and equal to whites but held no such views of slaves. The current generation of slaves she deemed to be "unfit . . . for incorporation into the society as a free proprietor"; thus, they could not become full citizens in the United States. Differentiating between free blacks and slaves, she explained, "It is not supposed that (with some rare exceptions) human beings raised under the benumbing influence of brutal slavery can be elevated to the level of a society based upon the principles of moral liberty and voluntary cooperation."[49] Whereas the wider white society lumped free blacks and slaves together as inferior beings, she made a new hierarchy based on an individual's current condition of servitude or freedom.

Fanny Wright and her free-thought compatriot Robert Dale Owen (the son of Robert Owen, the utopian socialist founder of New Harmony, Indiana) left for a trip to Europe in May of 1827 to recover her health and to recruit more European intellectuals to join Nashoba. Two days before they left, she gathered the slaves together to announce a new decision of the resident trustees who were Fanny Wright, Camilla Wright, Robert Dale Owen, Richesson Whitbey (a former Quaker and Camilla's future husband), and James Richardson: "if any of the slaves neglect their duty, and thus retard the object of the plan, we will . . . treat them, according to the slave system, until it shall appear that their habits are changed for the better." Echoing Jefferson's disbelief in blacks' willingness to labor without physical coercion, Wright thus threatened her slaves. The trustees concluded that drastic measures were needed since, according to their expectations, the slaves were not working hard enough. They had hoped that Nashoba's slaves would work hard in order to avoid being treated "according to the slave system," understanding instead, as Robert Dale Owen put it, the "direct and uniform bearing which our regulations had on their happiness." When the white resident trustees and their slave managers discovered that they could not convince Nashoba's slaves to work hard enough to turn a profit (or even to sustain those living there), they resorted to threats and punishments to force them to do so. Maintaining the system of slavery, Nashoba's trustees implemented different rules, punishments, and privileges for free versus enslaved residents. The journal entries revealed that the slaves were treated as harshly in this "utopian" commune as they would have been in the hands of a merciless master who unapologetically embraced the slave system.[50]

The contrast is stark between Wright's most radical beliefs, as expressed in her "Explanatory Notes," and their reality when put into practice at Nashoba. While she viewed adults as permanently "warped" by "prejudice," she more optimistically believed that "of children we may make what we please." To do so, however, she believed that children needed to be removed from the influence of parents and trained in a carefully controlled environment. A May 1827 journal entry—"Mamselle Lolotte, a free colored woman, and family, arrived from New Orleans"—signaled Wright's first attempt to organize a school for slaves and free blacks at Nashoba by bringing in Charlotte Larieu as a future teacher (they had no books, paper, or classroom space as yet). Wright envisioned a "school for children of color," where free blacks would send their children to be educated at the cost of a hundred dollars a year. Her "Explanatory Notes" suggested that if parents could not afford the cost they could send their children "without payment, upon condition that the parents or guardians of such children shall transfer to the institution *all rights* over the children so received. Such children in all things to be treated and cared for, the same as those born in the institution." Parents would have to relinquish their role as primary guardians of their children, with only a vague promise of gaining for their children an ostensibly equal education in return.[51]

Even before a school was ready for the slaves, Camilla Wright called them together and "informed them that to-morrow, the children, Delila, Lucy, Julia, and Alfred, will be taken altogether from under the management of their parents, and will be placed until our school is organized, under the management of Mamselle Lolotte; that all communication between the parents and children shall, in future, *be prevented*, except such as may take place by the permission, and in the presence, of the manager of the children." Through this order,

Nashoba's trustees participated in another bitter standard aspect of the slave system—the forced separation of parents from their children. This new rule was not easily accepted by the slave parents, as evidenced by entries from the trustees' log, such as "Reprimanded Willis for having tried to interfere between Lolotte and one of his children." At Nashoba, the parents were in close proximity with their children but were not able to communicate with or nurture them without fear of punishment.[52]

In addition to her ideas about education, Wright's "Explanatory Notes" also revealed her radical ideas about sexuality and marriage. These ideas formed an important component of her multifaceted reform agenda at Nashoba and, unfortunately, contributed to the problems facing the enslaved women who lived there. Moving from radical theory to shocking practice, Wright further isolated herself from mainstream society and guaranteed the condemnation of Nashoba by declaring that "without disputing the established laws of the country, the institution [Nashoba] recognizes *only within its bosom*, the force of its own principles." Specifically, she announced that "the marriage law existing without the pale of the Institution, is of no force within that pale."[53] Her willingness to defy state marriage laws in this case drew on the intellectual tradition of Scottish common sense philosophy, which stressed that the only valid laws were those that upheld each individual's rational, moral sense.[54] Whereas she had accepted the arbitrary power of laws that enslaved blacks (until white slave owners agreed to overturn them), Wright summarily rejected the arbitrary power of marriage laws at Nashoba. Her uncompromising, assertive, and openly defiant stance on marriage contrasts with her explanations for why she became a slave owner, bought slaves, and did not immediately free them. The difference seems to be that, in Wright's mind, white women ranked higher in her racial hierarchy and were already prepared for their freedom whereas black slaves were not.

Current state laws on marriage and illegitimacy (in her opinion biased against women) should be replaced with what Wright termed "nonlegalized bonds of 'free and voluntary affections.'"[55] Partnerships based on mutual respect as well as love, she boldly insisted, need not be officially regulated or sanctioned by either legal or religious authorities.[56] Wright focused her critique on marriage because of its powerful symbolic value as a legal institution, a religious commitment, and a privileged site of human emotions. She protested the United States' reliance on English common law, especially in its unfair marriage laws and its restrictions on divorce (along with its allowance of the death penalty, which she opposed as cruel and inhumane). Wright had probably discussed these ideas with Jeremy Bentham, who was critical of America's adoption of the vague and uncertain common law system and, in 1811, had even written to President James Madison, offering to write a clear legal code for the United States.[57]

Young and unmarried, Fanny Wright then shockingly affirmed sexual experience as a source of human happiness even outside of marriage. In her "Explanatory Notes," she claimed that "existing institutions and existing opinions . . . have perverted the best source of human happiness—the intercourse of the sexes—into the deepest source of human misery." Wright lamented "the dying health of daughters condemned to the unnatural repression of feelings and desires inherent in their very organization and necessary alike to their moral and physical well-being." To her, prohibitions against sex outside of marriage were unhealthy and cruel to young women whose sexual "passions . . . supply the best joys of our existence." Wright noted that women who, like herself, were "cultivated, talented, and independent women . . . shrink equally from the servitude of marriage, and from the opprobrium stamped upon unlegalized connexions."[58]

Elite women, she declared, often decided to refrain from marriage because they cherished their independence but also felt that they had to forgo sex. She questioned why these "childless females" must become "devoted victims to unnatural restraints." In order to escape the two evils of either subservience in marriage or condemnation as immoral loose women, elite educated women often had no choice but to live unnaturally barren lives. Wright wanted women to be able to fulfill their sexual passions. She urged her readers, "Let us not attach ideas of purity to monastic chastity, impossible to man or woman without consequences fraught with evil, nor ideas of vice to connections formed under the auspices of kind feelings." Wright's strong advocacy of sex and love "either with or without the sanction of a legal or religious permit" made her a genuine advocate of free love, thereby giving women real control over their bodies and their lives. Her free love views also made her a prime target for those wishing to discredit her and her experiment at Nashoba, as well as any other woman coming after her who held woman's rights or antislavery sentiments.[59]

Fanny Wright's ideas of free love were put into practice, in a distorted form, at Nashoba. Explicit details regarding sexual and interracial alliances at Nashoba were revealed to the public when Richardson published the trustees' log. Two entries proved particularly shocking and damaging in this regard. First was the report of an attempted rape of an enslaved woman by a male slave. New rules implemented by trustees Camilla Wright and James Richardson while Fanny was away highlight the vulnerability of enslaved women at Nashoba. As the log recounted:

> Met the slaves at dinner time—Isabel had laid a complaint against Roderick, for coming during the night of Wednesday to her bedroom, uninvited; and endeavoring, without her consent, to take liberties with her person. Our views of the sexual relation had been repeatedly given to the slaves: Camilla Wright again stated it, and informed the slaves that, as the conduct of Roderick, which he did not deny, was a gross infringement of that view, a repetition of such conduct, by him, or by any other of the men, ought in her opinion, to be punished by flogging. She repeated, that we consider the proper basis of the sexual intercourse to be the unconstrained and unrestrained choice of *both* parties. Nelly having requested a lock for the door of the room in which she and Isabel sleep, with the view of preventing the future uninvited entrance of any man; the lock was refused, as being, in its proposed use, inconsistent with the doctrine just explained; a doctrine which we are determined to enforce, and which will give to every woman a much greater security, than any lock can possibly do.[60]

This entry combined a report of an attempted sexual assault with an endorsement of sex outside of marriage and a refusal to protect defenseless enslaved women from sexual attack. When Fanny Wright subsequently railed against "those ignorant laws . . . [and an] ignorant code of morals, which condemn one portion of the female sex to vicious excess, another to as vicious restraint, and all to defenceless helplessness and slavery," she did not connect her comments to the helplessness of the black women enslaved at Nashoba.[61] They had no recourse against the trustees, who irresponsibly insisted that the slaves would be protected only by internalizing the trustees' belief that "the proper basis of the sexual intercourse . . . the unconstrained and unrestrained choice of *both* parties . . . will give to every woman a much greater security, than any lock can possibly do." Nelly's request for a lock for the room she shared with Isabel was cavalierly dismissed. Both women clearly preferred the protection of a lock to the promise of security the trustees insisted could come from internalizing their free love doctrine.[62]

The most controversial log entry published in the *Genius of Universal Emancipation* announced: "Met the slaves—James Richardson informed them that, last night, Mamselle Josephine* and he began to live together; and he took this occasion of repeating to them our views on color, and on the sexual relation. *A Quarteroon, daughter of Mamselle Lolotte." This public revelation—that an unmarried interracial couple were choosing to live together openly at Nashoba—inspired an outraged correspondent, in the next issue of the *Genius,* to condemn the establishment as "one great brothel." Richardson wrote a reply to the *Genius* that served only to exacerbate the situation; he freely admitted to the correspondent's charge that he was "libidinous," insisting that it was the natural state of all humans.[63]

Wright's "Explanatory Notes" did not try to deny or downplay the situation. Rather, she challenged whites to admit that interracial sex and relationships were common throughout the South. She highlighted the fact that "no natural antipathy blinds the white Louisianian to the charms of the graceful quadroon—however the force of prejudice or the fear of public censure makes of her his mistress, and of the white-skinned, but often not more accomplished or more attractive female, his wife."[64] Unlike most Southern white men, James Richardson had done the honorable thing, Wright implied, by openly acknowledging his attraction and connection to Charlotte's daughter, Josephine Prevot. Wright might also have been thinking of Thomas Jefferson, who publicly opposed the racial amalgamation of blacks and whites, having stated in his "Notes on the State of Virginia," for instance, that "Among the Romans emancipation required but one effort. The [white] slave, when made free, might mix with, without staining the blood of his master. But with us a second is necessary, unknown to history. When freed, he is to be removed beyond the reach of mixture." The white race would be stained by intermixture with the black race, he feared.[65] Wright had visited Monticello, however, and most probably had met Sally Hemings and inferred the nature of their relationship (especially if she had met any of Hemings's sons or grandchildren, who resembled Jefferson), in spite of these statements.[66]

Not only did Wright openly sanction an interracial unmarried couple's decision to live together at Nashoba, she also endorsed racial amalgamation. She worked her way into the topic by first mildly envisioning a future wherein there would be no profit motive for continuing slavery. Southern planters could then abandon colonization schemes and favor her ultimate goal—the emancipation of slaves within the borders of the United States. She then stepped back from her frequent contention that reformers should not offend the sensibilities and laws of the white South. Although she reassuringly reiterated a states' rights position, that "the emancipation of the colored population cannot be *progressive thro' the laws*. It must and can only *be progressive through the feelings*," she continued with a surprising conclusion: "through that medium [the feelings], be finally complete and entire, involving at once political equality and the amalgamation of the races." Blacks and whites, she predicted, would blend into one politically and socially equal "American" race.[67] In contrast to her colonization ideas and belief in moral suasion, both of which were advocated (in different ways, of course) by various other early nineteenth-century reformers, Wright's support for miscegenation and out-of-wedlock relationships set her apart.[68]

Her open advocacy of amalgamation in her "Explanatory Notes" led to great public censure and attacks upon Wright's sexual morality and upon Nashoba. The great majority of white Americans insisted on maintaining clear distinctions between the races, labeling as "black" all children who were in fact the products of interracial unions (often the rape of black female slaves by their white masters and overseers).[69] Wright called their bluff, suggesting that the already large number of mixed race children in the South showed how easily the eventual erasure of visible racial differences into one new blended race of Americans could take place. She believed that "the olive [branch] of peace and brotherhood [will] be embraced by the white man and the black, and their children, approached in feeling and education,[will] gradually blend into one their blood and their hue."[70] Amalgamation, she imagined, would finally end the divisive issue of race in U.S. society. Rejecting the argument "that the mixture of the races is not in nature," Wright pointed out that it must be natural if healthy children can be born as a result of interracial sex. She concluded that "since it *does* happen, the only question is whether it shall take place in good taste and good feeling and be made at once the means of sealing the tranquility, and perfecting the liberty of the country, and of peopling it with a race more suited to its southern climate than the pure European,—or whether it shall proceed, as it now does, viciously and degradingly, mingling hatred and fear with the ties of blood—denied indeed, but stamped by nature herself upon the skin." Here, she rightly noted that race mixing already did happen—but in a secretive, often violent way that produced shame and denial and increased racial hatred by "mingling hatred and fear with the ties of blood." This shame and hatred allowed white men not to feel remorse even when, for example, "the child is the marketable slave of its father." Wright's support of "rapid" and open amalgamation of the races was based on the idea that white Americans must "raise the man of color to the level of the white." Once this happened, they could stop enforcing false barriers between the races and "leave the affections of future generations to the dictates of free choice."[71] On the ground at Nashoba, choices made by the white residents and by Charlotte Larieu and her family contrasted starkly with the severely restricted options available to the black slaves.

As if determined to confront openly every controversial issue, Wright's "Explanatory Notes" also critiqued the legal and social prejudices against "illegitimate" children. Terming them "helpless innocents," she sympathetically characterized them as persecuted by a society eager to "disown and stigmatize" them. Legal and social concepts of illegitimacy punished women and children, Wright charged, while exonerating and even condoning men's behavior: "The children denominated illegitimate, or *natural,* (as if in contradiction of others who should be *out of nature,* because *under law*) may be multiplied to any number by an unprincipled father, easily exonerated by law and custom from the duties of paternity, while these duties, and their accompanying shame, are left to a mother but too often rendered desperate by misfortune!"[72] Defying society's valorization of white women's sexual purity, Wright condemned the legally endorsed double standard that forced unwed mothers and their children to live in poverty and infamy and allowed men to avoid all financial, legal, and social responsibility for their children. In her own life, Wright found it difficult to flout laws affecting women—even those she strongly disagreed with. She did have sex outside of marriage, but when she found herself pregnant she clearly understood the opprobrium she would face. Ironically, she felt obliged to enter into the institution of marriage, although she knew full well that by doing so she would lose legal control over her property, herself, and her child.[73]

Questioning the rationale that forced couples into unhappy marriages simply because the woman had become pregnant, Wright speculated, "The tyranny usurped by the matrimonial law over . . . the noblest of the human passions, had probably its source in religious prejudice, or priestly rapacity, while it has found its plausible and more philosophical apology in the apparent dependence of children on the union of the parents." Dismissing the real issue of child support, she concluded that restrictive marriage laws were designed by clerics who intended to control women and inculcate their own notions of sin by positing marriage as the only acceptable union between a man and a woman. To Wright, this insistence on marriage at all costs ignored the fact that "the forcible union of unsuitable and unsuited parents can little promote the happiness of the offspring." Since divorce was so hard to attain and women almost always had more to lose, men could threaten to gain sole custody of the children in a divorce, since at that time it was men's legal right to have control over their offspring. Wright observed that the threat of losing their children kept many women chained to men in terrible marriages, whereby the "fond mother" was held hostage "as a galley slave, to the oar." Although she used the metaphor of slavery when discussing white women, Wright was clearly less concerned with the sexual exploitation of enslaved women at Nashoba than with that of white women.[74]

Looking back and assessing the problems at Nashoba, Wright concluded that they resulted from her excessive optimism and a lack of information, claiming that she was "ever prone to underestimate difficulties . . . partly (and there I believe lay the main root of the error) to my then imperfect acquaintance with the character and condition of the American people, and to my ignorance of the immense distance between the theory of American government and its development in practice." The United States was more racist and farther from its revolutionary potential than she had hoped. Wright's exploitation of her slaves demonstrates that she was, as well. Indeed, Wright's observation that the "step between theory and practice is usually great" certainly held true for her own experiment at Nashoba.[75]

Both practically and ideologically, Wright and Nashoba had many flaws. In practice, she was not prepared for the difficulties of setting up and maintaining a farm-based experiment. Neither a farmer nor a

Fanny Wright's bold public speaking was subjected to unrelenting caricatures in the press, especially as she gained greater popularity among working-class audiences in 1828 and 1829. This image also draws on Wright's anti-clerical stance by having her engaging in what could be construed as liturgical rites.

businessperson, she had hoped to create a productive working farm that would sell its excess crops. Neither the slave families (with several young children) nor the white idealists who joined her at Nashoba were prepared or trained to do this work. In addition, this malaria-prone land outside of Memphis increased all residents' susceptibility to illness, malnutrition, and economic crisis. Wright exploited her slaves at Nashoba; the white residents could and did exempt themselves from physical labor by contributing money, whereas the labor of the slaves was required. Overworked, disciplined by overseers, and still enslaved, they were unconvinced by Wright's promises of eventual emancipation and colonization. After the scandal caused by Richardson's publication and her own "Explanatory Notes," Wright conceded that Nashoba would not succeed, but she did not give up her radical public activism. In 1828, her sister, Camilla (now married to trustee Richesson Whitbey), left Nashoba in poor health for Robert Owen's commune in New Harmony, Indiana, and Fanny followed within six weeks, leaving the slaves and an overseer at Nashoba to struggle on for another year before she emancipated them and took them to Haiti.[76]

Deciding in retrospect that she had begun her experiment "at the wrong end," Wright concluded that the "degradation of [all] human labor" was the real problem. Slavery was simply the institutionalization of that degradation, which would naturally be eliminated once all labor was elevated and rewarded.[77] This perspective enabled Wright to turn her attention from slavery toward the plight of the white urban working classes. Her goal of elevating free white labor depended upon colonization, which would improve wage labor by eliminating the unfair competition of slavery. Wright began contributing to the *New Harmony Gazette,* a free-thought journal edited by Robert Dale Owen that was read by radical urban workers and middle-class intellectuals. Soon she became the co-owner and co-editor of the paper, which was renamed the *Free Enquirer.* Together, Wright and Owen announced that they would write about and promote any worthy secular experiment.[78]

"PRIESTESS OF BEELZEBUB"—FANNY WRIGHT AS
A PUBLIC LECTURER

In 1828, defying conventional behavior yet again, Fanny Wright became the first woman in the United States to speak publicly to large audiences of men and women on secular and political topics.[79] At this time the simple act of a woman giving a public speech was charged with meaning; conservative contemporaries feared that Wright's words and actions might inspire other women to challenge limitations on their participation in the public sphere, especially in politics. Wright's radical ideas earned her the enmity of many newspaper editors, who slandered her with gendered insults. Most frequently she was charged with being a free lover, a loose woman, and a "priestess of Beelzebub."[80] Wright's public speeches became the most significant source of her fame; thousands of people attended her lectures, from Indiana to the eastern seaboard, in part for the novel and "sensational" phenomenon of hearing a woman speaker and in part because of their attraction to her ideas. Some radical Hicksite Quaker women, for instance, were drawn to her women's rights stance (including the right of women to speak publicly, for the Society of Friends allowed women to minister) and her ideas about equal education for all children. Quaker women in their plain dress sometimes sat on stage at her public lectures, providing moral support. In spite of her anticlerical secularism, Wright had long been sympathetic to the Society of Friends. In her *Views of Society and Manners in America,* for instance, she stated, "To the society of Friends also is humanity indebted for a continued opposition to the odious traffic in the African race."[81]

In her new role as a public speaker, she now moved the problems and needs of the white working classes to the forefront of her concerns. Speaking to the fears and desires of those artisans and mechanics whose skilled jobs were threatened, Wright criticized industrialists, lawyers, and members of the clergy for their undue influence in American society.[82] Rewarded by strong support from her working-class audiences, Wright decided to open a Hall of Science in a former church in New York City to serve as a permanent site for herself and other radical freethinkers to find and build an audience. Anticlerical speakers, in particular, often found it hard to find a venue in which to speak. Churches, not surprisingly, refused to give them a forum, and prudent businessmen who feared protests or mob violence often refused to rent their halls to them. Abolitionists later encountered similar difficulties.[83]

Wright's very first public address before a mixed audience of men and women was at Robert Owen's New Harmony, Indiana, communitarian living society on July 4, 1828. Reminding her audience of their revolutionary heritage, she appropriated the meaning of the Fourth of July, the celebration of which many Americans considered "a reenactment of republican faith," and warned that the Revolution had been left incomplete. Drawing upon a long-established tradition among popular lecturers of celebrating the nation's founding documents, she dramatically flourished a copy of the Declaration of Independence from the podium, maintaining that it provided a practical basis for change.[84] Speaking to audiences in packed lecture halls from 1828 to 1830, Wright encouraged her audiences to work for profound social change through constitutional means—by voting for new state-level education laws, for example. Arguing for a more politically involved citizenry, she directed her enthusiasm to the process of democratization and to a new political party, the Working Men's Party, which welcomed her interest and adopted her call for universal equal education as part of its platform.[85]

A RADICAL PLAN FOR STATE-LEVEL "REPUBLICAN EDUCATION"

State-level legislation had always been part of Wright's antislavery solution. Now education laws became her primary focus. Insisting that legislative reform was consistent with the need for individual moral transformation, Wright argued that if legislation passed in any state, it was because the people had taken to heart the necessity of change. Any enacted legislation, therefore, directly reflected the changed beliefs of the citizens. She urged her audiences to adhere "firmly to the constitutional principle, of effecting wholesome changes *peacefully through their legislatures,* and that, not by hastily subverting the existing *forms* of society, however unwise or unjust, but by preparing a change in the *very soul* of society." Wright embraced state-level legislation as the embodiment of the will of the people: "What we *do expect the people legislatively to effect,* and what we do think, for the honor of the nation, for the realization of its republican professions and for the salvation of the human race, they *ought* and *must* so effect, is to organize a system of education as shall facilitate that universal correct training of the human mind from which all things may be expected, without which nothing." Individual independence and the common good would not be in conflict but, rather, in harmony: "The American people shall present, in another generation, but one class, and, as it were but one family—each independent in his and her own thoughts, actions, rights, person, and possessions, and all cooperating, according to their individual taste and ability, to the promotion of the common weal." According to Wright's logic, if citizens supported legislation for equal education, this would prove they had already undergone the necessary moral change and were enacting their will.[86]

The "national" education advocated by Wright would be enacted by every state legislature, not by the U.S. Congress. It was from this perspective that Wright argued in 1829 that the solution to society's ills "IS NATIONAL, RATIONAL, REPUBLICAN EDUCATION; FREE FOR ALL,

AT THE EXPENSE OF ALL; CONDUCTED UNDER THE GUARDIANSHIP OF THE STATE, AT THE EXPENSE OF THE STATE, AND FOR THE HONOR, THE HAPPINESS, THE VIRTUE, THE SALVATION OF THE STATE." Although language such as the "salvation of the state" might suggest a focus on a strong central government, Wright did not equate the two. Instead she contended that "the state" meant "the people," represented by each state in the union.[87]

Wright then took this idea of equal education further than other reformers by proposing that the states set up boarding schools to replace all existing schools or reformatories for youths: "I would suggest that the state legislatures be directed (after laying off the whole in townships or hundreds) to organize, at suitable distances, and in convenient and healthy situations, establishments for the general reception of all the children resident within the said school district." From the young age of two years old, all children—boys and girls, rich and poor—would be educated together, away from their parents, without reminders of their class, sex, or race-based disadvantages or advantages.[88] Envisioning equal educations for children in state-run boarding schools, she imagined that the schools would produce citizens trained to think more of the collectivity than of their own selfish interests: "a nation to be strong, must be united; to be united, must be equal in condition; to be equal in condition, must be similar in habits and in feeling; to be similar in habits and in feeling, must be raised in national institutions, as the children of a common family, and citizens of a common country." This type of education would reinforce the fundamental principles of the Declaration of Independence—that "all men are free and equal."[89] Citizen taxpayers would fund education reform through new state taxes, such as a progressive tax on all incomes, with the wealthiest paying more and an extra tax to be paid by all parents. "When two years old," she proposed, "the parental tax should be payable, and the juvenile institution open for the child's reception; from which time forward it [the child] would be under the protective care and guardianship of the state, while it need never be removed from the daily, weekly, or frequent inspection of the parents."[90] For Wright, states had a consistency and an ability to enforce equality that average parents could not be trusted to have.

Intolerant of anything less than her own vision of a perfect society, Wright, just as she had at Nashoba, viewed parents as obstacles to progress, whose rights to determine or influence their children's futures must be limited so that class, race, and gender biases could be eliminated. She had no sentimental fears of breaking family bonds. After all, she had been orphaned at age two (exactly the age she proposed to move all children from their homes into boarding schools) and raised by an emotionally distant and conservative aunt.[91] Wright imagined that "the parents who would necessarily be resident in their close neighborhood, could visit the children at suitable hours, but, in no case, interfere with or interrupt the rules of the institution." Her plan was, as historian Sean Wilentz points out, "authoritarian and moralistic." Wright illogically denied the possibility that an authoritarian state would take from parents their treasured responsibility of producing good citizens, reasoning that citizens collectively made up the states and so would authorize the states to train their children and thereby produce a better nation.[92]

Comfort with authoritarian control—epitomized by her idea of national boarding schools—was tempered by Wright's concurrent and often contradictory dream of creating a society based on minimal laws and regulations. With universal education in place, Wright imagined, penal codes would no longer be necessary because a better-trained and classless populace would not turn to crime. Thus, she could envision a society with *fewer* rules: "The people who shall once organize and carry into universal effect, a system of enlightened, industrial and protective education may lay aside their penal and their civil codes, their statutes and enactments, and confine their legislative operations to the simple regulation of such matters as shall be found positively and immediately to regard the comforts and convenience of the whole mass of society." Once the people passed universal education laws, other regulatory laws would become gradually obsolete and government itself would be dismantled: "Let government do this, and, for aught we care, it may then wind up business."[93]

Even as she toured the nation championing her educational reform ideas, Wright could not ignore the plight of those still in residence at Nashoba. From the start she had claimed that the reality of violent racism in the United States made colonization the only reasonable option for any slave freed from Nashoba: "it appeared consistent with justice and humanity to enforce his being sent to a country of safety for his color when ejected from the protection of the Institution." In 1829, after only four years, Wright officially dissolved the experiment and fulfilled her promise to colonize the slaves; she accompanied thirty-one freed slaves to the new black republic of Haiti, where they were offered asylum and liberty, as well as cabins, gardens, water, tools, and provisions.[94] This trip marked the end of Wright's brief years of fame as a popular, often notorious, public speaker. During the trip she began a sexual relationship with William Phiquepal d'Arusmont, a Pestalozzian teacher and the printer of the *Free Enquirer*. When Wright found herself unwed and pregnant, she herself was in the mortifying, difficult dilemma of many of the women she had spoken and written about when she had publicly condemned the bitter prejudices against illegitimate children and their mothers. She knew just how harshly society treated those who deviated from its norms—and just how much she wanted to achieve a more tolerant society. Given the already vicious attacks against her, she felt she had no option but to marry. Her sense of humiliation and defeat was so great that, after a series of speeches before large crowds in New York and Philadelphia upon her return from Haiti, in 1830 she fled to Paris with Phiquepal before any news of her pregnancy was revealed. She lived a life of secrecy and obscurity until she gained the courage to return to the United States as Frances Wright d'Arusmont in late 1835.[95]

FIGHTING "FEDERAL DESIGN"—FANNY WRIGHT AND THE JACKSONIAN DEMOCRATS IN THE MID-1830S

Upon her return to the United States, Wright engaged anew in partisan politics, this time turning her sympathies to the Democratic Party (which, unlike the Working Men's Party, was not particularly grateful for the endorsement of such a notorious woman). She embraced the Jacksonian Democrats' fight for decentralized institutions and for the direct election of legislators who would truly represent the will of the people in each state. Like many working-class Jacksonians, Wright focused her anti-monopoly rhetoric on the Second Bank of the United States. Suspicious of the credit and national banking system, she strongly supported President Andrew Jackson's decision not to reissue to the bank the charter that gave it monopoly control of banking in exchange for handling federal deposits. She condemned the arbitrary power of such a "consolidated national monopoly" as "an enemy to the country."[96] The Second Bank of the United States as well as the monied elites' domination of Congress represented to Wright and others the potentially dangerous and increasing strength of the central government. Endorsing Democrat Martin Van Buren for president in 1836, Wright smeared the new Whig Party by linking it to Alexander Hamilton and the Federalists.[97] She charged that "those leaders first tried their scheme of despotism under the form of one central strong government with obliterancy of state divisions," had failed, and now turned to a national bank as their "Federal design." In this, Wright echoed Thomas Jefferson's view of "the States, as the bulwark against consolidation."[98]

Colonization of freed slaves still appeared to Wright to be the way to create a more equal republic based on free white labor. Colonization had many supporters in both the South and the North in the 1830s. Indeed, William Lloyd Garrison wrote a substantive pamphlet against colonization in 1832 precisely because of its continued popularity. Historian Alisse Portnoy points out, "In 1837, most Americans considered abolitionists fanatics. In contrast, colonizationists were led and supported by former presidents of the United States, national and state legislators, U.S. Supreme Court justices, respected clergymen from all of the major Christian religions, and influential editors of secular newspapers." As late as 1852, the famous antislavery author Harriet Beecher Stowe advocated colonization at the end of *Uncle Tom's Cabin*.[99] Wright tapped into this popular sentiment, therefore, when she argued that colonization would effect "simultaneously the civilization and removal of its slave population, and the introduction of free, enlightened, and, as it ever should be, honorable and honored labor, by immigration from the Northern states." The removal of black slaves and their degraded labor from the United States could make way for the elevation of manual labor by white agricultural workers. The "African race" would be "leaving behind it a country prepared for facile cultivation by the white race."[100] Less crowded conditions in the North would raise the status of industrial laborers, as white workers moved south to replace black slaves; the new white agricultural workforce would benefit from healthy, virtuous farm work.

In spite of the fact that Fanny Wright's support of the Democrats, endorsement of colonization, and opposition to the national bank were relatively mainstream ideas compared to her reform ideas of the 1820s, her return to partisan politics and to the lecture platform in the mid-1830s did not go smoothly. Wright found it difficult to raise and enthuse audiences the way she once had. Hounded by those who issued fierce denunciations of her as a female public speaker and a loose woman, Wright faced diminishing audiences that were hostile or, worse, indifferent.[101]

*O*n issues regarding marriage and sexuality, Fanny Wright presented serious—often radical—alternatives to the values and practices of mainstream antebellum America. When she called for an acceptance of sex and love outside of the legal bonds of matrimony, for instance, Wright challenged a fundamental aspect of most Americans' sense of social stability. Although she took her critique of marriage farther than most, Wright inspired other women's rights activists like Ernestine Rose to fight for legal reforms such as married women's property rights acts in the mid-1830s.[102] On issues of race, Wright was less radical. She wanted to rid the United States of slavery but maintained her belief in white racial superiority. In the case of unfair and inequitable marriage laws, she was willing to engage in a form of civil disobedience by ignoring their validity among the white and free black residents of Nashoba. In contrast, in the case of laws maintaining slavery and upholding the property rights of white slaveholders, Wright insisted that she and the Nashoba trustees must not disobey these laws and must defer to the will of Southern slaveholders. Her different positions can be explained only by her greater estimation of white women as compared to black men and women. By founding an antislavery experiment and by becoming a public lecturer, Wright pushed the boundaries of acceptable female behavior and became a notorious public figure. Her defiance of social conventions led subsequent generations of women's rights reformers to admire her for her courage in the face of often vicious attacks upon her morality and character.

In spite of these very real challenges to contemporary social norms, overall Fanny Wright's reform ideas remained within the tradition of the American Revolution and the nation's founding documents. Idealizing the founding documents and the corresponding concept of "the nation," Wright embraced the power invested in the people by the U.S. Constitution while simultaneously opposing increased powers for the central government. Throughout her reform career, Wright rejected the role of the central government in making change and hoped that government as an oppressive entity would somehow be abolished or disappear.[103] Even as she pushed for state-run boarding schools for all children, for instance, she expressed concerns about governments with too much power over citizens. In the case of slavery and her experiment at Nashoba, she relied on moral suasion and state-level legislation, rejecting any proposal for immediate emancipation of the slaves that involved the federal government's imposing its will upon the white South. Her insistence on the power of moral example to transform society went hand in hand with her insistence that only the white male voters in Southern states could legislate slavery out of existence. Because of her privileging moral suasion and her rejecting reforms imposed by Congress on the states, Wright can be counted among the majority of American citizens in the early decades of the nineteenth century who championed the Constitution's recognition of states' rights as "the only bulwark of a free constitution."[104]

Wright believed that through moral suasion and personal action she, as an individual, could profoundly shape the direction and the character of the nation. She represents an earlier era of reformers' suspicion toward the federal government and reliance on moral suasion that was gradually displaced. In the antebellum era some reformers abandoned their suspicions of the central state, calling on it to act immediately to ban slavery. Antebellum activists, perfectionist abolitionists, and women's rights advocates such as Angelina and Sarah Grimké believed that moral suasion could change society. By the decade leading up to the Civil War, they also advocated national legislation to promote their goals. Wright, in contrast, maintained her states' rights and moral suasion positions, viewing national legislation as wrongly mandating reforms before the people were ready for them.

Sarah and Angelina Grimké

WOMEN'S POLITICAL ENGAGEMENT

In 1839 abolitionists Sarah Grimké and Angelina Grimké Weld wrote their close friend Sarah Mapps Douglass, a black woman who ran a school for free blacks in Philadelphia whom they had first met at the Society of Friends' Fourth and Arch Street Meeting. Angelina added a postscript to the letter with a message from her husband, the abolitionist Theodore Weld: "Theodore . . . desires me to send his love to thee and asks thee whether thou art willing to write off those facts about thy brother being refused a passport as a citizen of the United States in order that he may publish them as a proof of our prejudice against color."[1] Douglass's brother Robert had tried to travel abroad in 1839 to study painting in Europe. However, since he and all free blacks were denied the right to vote under Pennsylvania's new constitution, the secretary of state, equating voting rights and citizenship, concluded he was not a citizen and thus could not be issued a passport. Firsthand testimony like this could force northern whites to recognize the tenuous and circumscribed citizenship status of free black Americans.[2] The question of who could be a citizen and how one's citizenship could be acted upon and truly realized was one that had engaged the Grimké sisters from the start of their reform work in the mid-1830s. Their intimate friendships with the Douglass family and other free black activists enabled the sisters to enter into serious conversations about the evils

Sarah Grimké   *Angelina Grimké*

These wood-engraved portraits of Sarah M. Grimké and Angelina E. Grimké depict the sisters in simple Quaker garb. Note that Sarah Grimké is holding a book, perhaps a sign of her desire to be taken seriously as an educated woman and an intellectual.

of slavery, but also about the nature and extent of racial prejudice and of the constricted citizenship then available to free blacks in the North. Their friends Grace Bustill Douglass and Sarah Mapps Douglass, mother and daughter of a prominent free black family from Philadelphia, for instance, were founding members of the Philadelphia Female Anti-Slavery Society in 1833 and of the Female Vigilance Association, a literary society that raised funds for fugitive slaves.[3] In an earlier letter written in 1837, Sarah Grimké told Sarah Douglass, "See too in Penn[sylvania] the desperate effort made against the colored citizens to deprive them of the right of voting." Defining free black men as "citizens" who must maintain their voting rights, Grimké despaired that they were being "unrighteously oppressed" by whites who wanted to deny them their rights through violence and by changing the voting laws in each state. Yet Grimké believed that citizenship rights should not just be expected and guaranteed to free blacks; fugitive slaves who managed to escape to the North should also be guaranteed their constitutional rights, including the right to have a jury hear the case against them: "In New York oppression reigns. The fugitive there as well as in Pennsylvania is hunted like a partridge on the mountain and denied the right of jury trial."[4] Throughout their reform careers, Angelina and Sarah Grimké worked also to expand black and white women's citizenship rights, arguing for women's participation in reform, legislative change, politics, and voting.

From petitioning to public speaking, Angelina and Sarah Grimké were at the forefront of the effort to allow black and white women a full voice in abolitionism as equal citizens. Daughters of South Carolina slaveholders, the Grimké sisters became abolitionists in the North and became involved in national political and legislative reform as well as in international antislavery and reform movements.[5] Like other abolitionists, they advocated moral suasion and the development of individual conscience as the best way to achieve change; they also accepted a role for the federal government in enacting legislation and passing constitutional amendments that could promote the changes they sought. They called on Congress to find a legislative end to slavery. Fanny Wright's experiment at Nashoba was based on moral suasion and was meant to end the system of slavery through nonlegislative means: the power of example at her communal experiment, Nashoba, would show white Southerners how they could organize labor differently. Unlike Wright, the Grimkés combined their belief in moral suasion with an engagement with the federal government. Their involvement in petition campaigns, for instance, was based on their understanding of the U.S. Constitution and the First Amendment as offering protections and rights to blacks and women, including the right of all citizens to protest to the laws and policies of the federal government. The sisters' doubts about the legitimacy of the federal government did not come from a states' rights perspective like Wright's but grew out of the uncomfortable reality that the Constitution sanctioned slavery. This fact caused a significant minority of perfectionist abolitionists, led by William Lloyd Garrison, to pull away from what they perceived to be the sinful federal government and to speak of "disunion" with the corrupt southern slaveholding states. Although the sisters were briefly interested in this nonresistance, disunionist philosophy, with the encouragement of abolitionist Theodore Weld (Angelina's future husband), the Grimkés joined the majority of abolitionists who identified lobbying the federal government and participating in partisan party politics as offering better prospects for overturning slavery. In the decade before the Civil War, the sisters also campaigned for moral reform through the passage of regulatory laws that would increase the power of local and state governments to restrict the behavior of individuals, such as pro-temperance dry laws. During the war and Reconstruction, they supported federal amendments to the U.S. Constitution to abolish slavery and to enfranchise black men and black and white women, thereby ensuring their status as true citizens.

The two sisters spent their adult lives together, so their biographies are closely intertwined. As Gerda Lerner's classic biography tells the tale, in her youth Sarah M. Grimké (1792–1873) at her own insistence acted as a surrogate mother for her youngest sister, Angelina (1805–1879), exerting a powerful influence on her sister's development. In her late twenties, after the death of her father, Judge John Grimké, Sarah gained the courage to move out of the South, and away from her family. Sarah Grimké's spiritual quest led her from Charleston to Philadelphia where she was welcomed by the Society of Friends at the Fourth and Arch Street Meeting and converted in 1821. She was attracted to the Quakers because of their pacifist ideology, their emancipation of their slaves, and the greater role accorded to women within their meetings. The Society of Friends inspired many abolitionists because they believed that slavery was a sin, but they also generally rejected political activism and direct engagement with "the world." Their prohibition on members' participation in social movements, including immediate abolitionism, eventually led to problems for the sisters.[6] Sarah joined the Society of Friends before the 1827 Hicksite split; when Angelina joined Sarah in Philadelphia in 1829, she converted to the Orthodox branch of Quakerism, with which Sarah was affiliated.[7] At that point, the Hicksites might have been a better fit for the sisters because of Elias Hicks's antislavery Free Produce stance and that sect's "belief in the primacy of individual conscience." Individual Hicksites such as James and Lucretia Mott became prominent activists in immediate abolition societies.[8]

Sarah believed that she was called on by God to be a preacher and tried to use her gift during Quaker meetings. Although women were generally allowed to speak in meetings, in the mid-1830s Sarah was discouraged from doing so by the male elders at the meeting. This hurtful silencing alienated Sarah from the Friends at the same moment that Angelina was embracing immediate abolitionism.

Reversing the process of their religious conversion, Sarah followed Angelina into the antislavery movement just as Angelina had followed her into Quakerism. Angelina committed herself to the immediate abolition of slavery in an 1835 letter to William Lloyd Garrison, which he published in *The Liberator.* Although Sarah resisted initially, both sisters became Garrisonian abolitionists, embracing the moral argument that slavery was a sin that needed to be recognized as evil and eradicated without delay.[9] Arguing that each individual must reexamine his or her conscience before broad social change would be possible, the Grimkés acted on their faith in the persuasive power of moral example by transforming themselves from members of a prominent southern slaveholding family into northern abolitionists. Since individuals were free agents in the deepest sense, radical abolitionists believed that each person could virtually perfect himself or herself through an act of will and eventually make society perfect as well. Personally testifying to the brutalizing impact of slavery on both slaves and slaveholders alike, the sisters appealed to the consciences of slave owners and northern whites. The sisters hoped that immediate abolitionist arguments, rooted in Christian theology and perfectionist ideas, would function as moral suasion, converting Southerners and Northerners alike to the belief that the institution of slavery was a sin that must be abolished at once.[10]

In 1837, drawing in part on the Quaker tradition of sanctioning women preachers, Angelina and Sarah Grimké became the first women to speak widely—to large mixed audiences of women and men—on political topics since Fanny Wright had begun lecturing in 1828 and since Maria Stewart, a free black woman reformer, had lectured from 1831 to 1833. Resistance to women's lecturing remained strong. Catharine Beecher, the prominent educator and authority on domesticity, for instance, wrote a scathing denunciation of women's public speaking after attending a lecture by Fanny Wright, who had returned to the United States to launch a lecture tour in 1836: "who can look without disgust and abhorrence upon such an one as Fanny Wright, with her great masculine person . . . feeling no need of protection, mingling with men in stormy debate, and standing up with bare-faced impudence, to lecture to a public assembly."[11]

The strong and persistent condemnations of Wright as an impure "infidel" and free lover damaged the Grimkés. Deploring attempts by conservatives to damage the sisters' reputations and silence them by linking them, as public speakers, to Wright, Angelina complained in 1837 that, "If we dare to stand upright & do our duty according to the dictates of *our own* consciences, why then we are compared to Fanny Wright, &c."[12] The sisters' status as respectable Southern ladies did not spare them from sustained attack from both inside and outside the antislavery movement for speaking to "promiscuous" audiences of men and women.[13] By engaging in public speaking tours and in debates about the rights of blacks and women from 1836 to 1838, Angelina and Sarah Grimké challenged proper gender norms and found support within the Garrisonian wing of the movement. Prominent female abolitionists such as Maria Weston Chapman, Abby Kelley, and Lydia Maria Child joined the Grimkés in calling "for women's rights from abolition platforms."[14]

Later, in essays she wrote in the 1850s, Sarah Grimké called for women's political activism and advancement based on their right to representation and their responsibilities as citizens. Demanding full political power for women, Grimké's expansive view of citizenship now mandated that women vote and serve as legislators in order to fulfill their responsibilities and duties as citizens. She emphasized that women must improve their access to education and change the laws that kept them economically dependent and subordinate in marriage.[15]

"AMERICA IS AWFULLY GUILTY"—LEGISLATIVE ENDS TO SLAVERY

More comfortable than Fanny Wright with making direct demands upon the central state, the Grimké sisters believed that the federal government could be a positive agent of social reform. Drawing upon the democratic principles of the nation's founding documents, the sisters formulated a patriotic antislavery rhetoric. Like Frederick Douglass, Alvan Stewart, and other abolitionists they highlighted the difference between the noble principles articulated in America's strong founding documents and the nation's inhumane practices.[16] In an 1837 letter to Queen Victoria they declared, "America is awfully guilty; she has professed herself a Republic, whilst cherishing in her bosom a confederacy of petty tyrants [slaveholders] who are not exceeded in power, nor surpassed in cruelty, by any despots whose blood stained annals disgrace the page of history." America's position as a republic, founded on the democratic participation of its (white male) citizens, made it more vulnerable to critique than monarchical forms of government that made no such pretenses to republicanism. The United States was an imperfect republic, the sisters suggested, for it denied full citizenship rights to slaves and white women alike. Similarly appropriating the country's founding documents for abolitionism, the Philadelphia Female Anti-Slavery Society (of which the sisters were members) claimed that "slavery and prejudice are contrary to the laws of God and the principles of our Declaration of Independence."[17]

For the abolitionist movement to be effective, the Grimkés asserted, a more forceful U.S. Congress must legislate against slavery, and states' rights would consequently have to be diminished. A correspondent named "Clarkson" argued in the *New Haven Religious Intelligencer* in 1837 that the sisters had convinced many Northerners of the evils of slavery but now needed to offer *"definite practicable"* suggestions about how to end it. Taking up the challenge in the *Friend of Man,* the sisters insisted that women as well as men should attack the problem of slavery with moral arguments and petitions for legislative reform. Acknowledging the unfortunate fact that both the federal government and the U.S. Constitution sanctioned slavery, the Grimkés outlined the various things Congress could do immediately to restrict slavery. Joining Gerrit Smith and other radical abolitionists, they noted that "slavery now exists in the District of Columbia, over which, according to the Constitution of the United States, Congress has power 'to exercise exclusive legislation in all cases whatsoever.'"[18] Therefore, they suggested that petitions should be directed to Congress asking it to ban the slave trade in the nation's capital immediately.

Congress should also be encouraged to amend the U.S. Constitution, the sisters suggested. They implored Northerners "respectfully [to] ask for an alteration in that part of the constitution by which they are bound to assist the South in quelling servile insurrections."[19] As increasingly large numbers of Americans, with the help of the abolitionists, recognized that slavery was morally wrong, the Grimkés predicted that Congress would feel compelled to amend the Constitution to reflect their constituents' abhorrence of the institution. Perhaps because they thought it impractical at this point (1837), the Grimkés did not explicitly suggest that abolitionists should petition for an amendment to abolish slavery altogether. Later, during the Civil War, the sisters fought for this more sweeping constitutional amendment. In 1863 Angelina Grimké Weld agreed to serve as a vice president of Anthony and Stanton's Women's National Loyal League, which successfully gathered hundreds of thousands of petitions for an amendment to the Constitution that would immediately outlaw slavery.[20]

"WOMAN HAS NO POLITICAL EXISTENCE"—ABOLITIONIST PETITIONS AND WOMEN'S CITIZENSHIP

During the antebellum era, growing numbers of American women asserted their citizenship rights, especially the right to petition, as the best way to participate in reform.[21] Directly engaging the federal government, the Grimkés supported women's First Amendment right to petition the federal government to change its unjust laws. Angelina characterized petitioning as central to women's political identity and as a moral form of public speech: "the right of petition is the only political right that women have: why not let them exercise it when they are aggrieved?" Julie Jeffrey asserts, "The ambitious scope of women's petitioning activities represented their entry into the world of mass democratic politics and . . . a voice in the civic sphere." Women were at the forefront of the abolitionists' coordinated national petition campaign, demonstrating their political virtue and civic abilities. Historian Susan Zaeske conservatively estimates that "the total number of female signatures gathered from 1836 to 1863 would amount to almost 3 million."[22]

Petitioning was only the beginning of women's political engagement. In a section entitled "Legal Disabilities of Women," from her 1837 *Letters on the Equality of the Sexes and the Condition of Woman*, Sarah Grimké characterized women's right to petition as important but insufficient: "Woman has no political existence. With the single exception of presenting a petition to the legislative body, she is a cipher in the nation." As she canvassed for signatures, Grimké encountered married women's persistent fears about defying their husbands. She complained :

I have known some women sign petitions for the abolition of slavery in the District of Columbia, secretly, because their husbands forbade their doing it, or disapprove of it. . . . Deception gives a mortal stab to moral rectitude. The moment we admit the idea, that we may do evil that good may come, we lose our self-respect, and adopt policy as our rule, instead of righteousness. Never deceive a man by a *show* of submission. Tell him that you cannot obey him, rather than God, and that it is your intention to sign that petition.[23]

Women must have pride and confidence in themselves and not allow themselves to be governed by men, only by God, Grimké insisted. She pushed women to take responsibility for their actions, to admit that they signed these petitions, and to act openly as independent political beings.

The large number of signatures collected by abolitionists made petitioning more controversial and, in the eyes of proslavery politicians, potentially dangerous. Starting in 1836 congressional "gag" rules tabled all antislavery petitions, which were studiously ignored by the very legislators they were meant to influence.[24] Once significant numbers of women became involved in the abolitionist movement, women's seemingly clear and uncontested constitutional right to petition was challenged by conservative ministers, educators, and politicians as an inappropriate entry into politics.[25] Characterizing petitioning as men's proper domain because it was a political act, conservatives outside the movement argued that women should not insert themselves in such an unladylike manner into the political sphere. In her *Essay on Slavery and Abolitionism, with Reference to the Duty of American Females* (1837), for instance, Catharine Beecher argued that women could best influence society indirectly through their moral teachings to their fathers and brothers, husbands and sons, rather than through petition campaigns and public speaking, which she criticized as inappropriate direct political action. (Ironically, Beecher herself had participated in the 1829 petition drive against the removal of the Cherokee from Georgia.)[26]

As petitioning by women became more prevalent, some men within the abolitionist movement also began to express discomfort with it as a political device. They now characterized petitioning as an ineffective tool that was used as a last resort by white women and slaves who could not participate directly at the polls. These men favored forming an antislavery political party instead. In a critique with fascinating gender implications, the *Massachusetts Abolitionist* editorialized in 1839 that to rely on petitions was "to throw away *power* and use *weakness.*" This publication represented the male-dominated clerical and political branch of abolitionism then contending against the Garrisonians, who rejected partisan politics and welcomed women's participation in the movement. Attempting to gain support for an antislavery political party (implicitly men's domain), the paper labeled petitioning a strategy of "weakness"—a trait often negatively characterized as female.[27] The Grimkés' defense of black and white women's right to petition led to their broader call for women's rights.

THE "LEGAL DISABILITIES" OF WOMEN AND SLAVES— THE CASE FOR REFORM

Breaking across boundaries that women were not supposed to cross, in her first major essay, *Epistle to the Clergy of the Southern States* (1836), Sarah Grimké critiqued contemporary laws and state-level legislative debates about slavery as if she were a male legislator. She also quoted from and interpreted the Bible with as much assurance and authority as if she were a male minister. Unlike Fanny Wright, whose skeptical secularism did not leave room for God or organized religion, Grimké maintained a deep Christian faith even as she moved from Episcopalianism to Presbyterianism, then to the Society of Friends, and finally to a nonclerical nondenominational Protestantism.[28] Faith could lead women not just to salvation after death, she believed, but to an awareness of their equality and rights in this world. Grimké challenged women's constricted roles in the church and the state by daringly presenting her own biblical argument against slaveholding to the male "experts," the Southern ministers, who condemned both abolitionism and women's political activism. God could not accept woman's legal or social subordination to man; Grimké's religious faith confirmed woman's necessary participation in politics and government.

By critiquing specific laws on slavery, Grimké challenged men's control of the public political sphere. Boldly highlighting her moral and legislative priorities, she attempted to persuade Southern ministers of their duty to oppose slavery from the pulpit and to emancipate their own slaves. Sarah contrasted a passage in the Bible, for instance, to a passage from the laws of South Carolina to argue that, whereas Christ viewed all humans as his "brethren," South Carolina laws wrongly denied slaves their humanity by explicitly defining them as "chattels personal"—as property, not people. She rejected states' rights and immoral human-made laws, insisting, "But can 'legislative enactments' annul the laws of Jehovah, or sanctify the crimes of theft and oppression? 'Woe unto them that decree unrighteous decrees . . . to take away the *right* from the poor of my people.'"[29] Congressional laws could not annul the laws of God or take away the God-given rights of even the poorest, most subordinate people, including slaves and black and white women. The Bible provided the moral example that should inform all laws and help reformers decide how to change them.

Grimké's *Epistle to the Clergy of the Southern States* explicitly claimed politics and the law as appropriate topics for women's political speech. Always regretting the fact that she had been blocked from becoming a judge or a lawyer like her father and brothers, she approached her task of persuading the ministers in a lawyerly fashion. Specifically, she read in their entirety the transcribed debates of the Virginia legislature after Nat Turner's 1831 rebellion and used them to bolster her antislavery argument. Sarah quoted from these legislative debates to prove that Southern lawmakers themselves openly admitted slavery was an unnatural condition that slaves would always resist, either psychologically or physically. She pointed out that slavery and rebellions against it were "the result of laws enacted in a free and enlightened republic." She declared that no matter whether women had been given the legal right to vote, they had an ethical duty to act as politically engaged citizens. The records of the Virginia legislature included an antislavery "memorial of the female citizens of Fluvanna Co., Va. to the General Assembly of that commonwealth in 1832." This document helped Sarah Grimké argue that some Southern white women, at least, were against slavery: "the daughters of Virginia have borne their testimony to the evils of slavery, and have pleaded for its extinction." If Southern ministers and their congregants could view slavery as a sin, Grimké confidently asserted, it could be abolished.[30]

Sarah Grimké's *Letters on the Equality of the Sexes and the Condition of Woman* published in 1837 also pointed to laws as the central part of the governing system in the United States that oppressed slaves as well as white and black women. Turning her attention to enslaved women, Grimké examined the significance of the intersection of race and gender in enslaved women's lives. Her discussion of black women under the system of slavery identified the ways in which sexual and racial oppression were separate but linked sets of inequalities. Noting the unique problems faced by slave women, Grimké recognized their particular legal status and their double subordination by both race and sex. A member of a Southern slave-owning family, Grimké knew from personal observation that "the virtue of female slaves is wholly at the mercy of irresponsible tyrants, and women are bought and sold in our slave markets, to gratify the brutal lust of those who bear the name of Christians."[31] Rather than seeing interracial sex as, at least sometimes, a matter of choice (as Fanny Wright did when referring to James Richardson and his free black companion, Josephine Prevot, for example), Grimké exposed interracial sex within the slave system as inherently coercive and nonconsensual.

Contributing to the budding women's rights movement, Grimké systematically critiqued women's "legal disabilities" by interspersing her own commentary between quotes from William Blackstone's summary of the status of married women under English common law.[32] Linking the plight of enslaved women to free black and white women, Grimké argued that these unfair laws must be exposed and reformed: "women should certainly know the laws by which they are governed, and from which they frequently suffer; yet they are kept in ignorance, nearly as profound, of their legal rights, and of the legislative enactments which are to regulate their actions, as slaves." Like Fanny Wright and the other women featured here, Sarah Grimké lamented that English common law was the foundation of marriage laws in the American states. For Grimké, Blackstone's infamous interpretation of coverture—"By marriage . . . the very being, or legal existence of the woman is suspended"—was most problematic. As historian Amy Dru Stanley confirms, "no other contract contained a rule obliterating the identity and autonomy of one party to the contract." Marriage laws enabled reformers to argue that slaves and (putatively) free black and white women lived in the United States without legal autonomy or full citizenship.[33]

Complaining that male legislators kept women not only legally subordinated but also "in ignorance of those very laws by which we are governed," Sarah Grimké informed American women of their unequal legal status, hoping to inspiring them to press for change.[34] Significantly, the denial of women's legal and political rights amounted to an implicit refusal to acknowledge women's *responsibilities* as citizens.[35] Citing a particularly egregious common law principle that "a wife is excused from punishment for theft committed in the presence, or by the command of her husband," Grimké charged that "it would be difficult to frame a law better calculated to destroy the responsibility of a woman as a moral being, or a free agent." Laws that treated married women as less culpable of crimes than their husbands were not, in fact, acts of mercy or greater leniency, for they robbed women of ethical responsibility for their own actions. For activists such as Grimké who wanted to enact their moral vision in the public sphere, the abolition of slavery and other changes in the legal status of all women, especially married women, were crucial.[36]

CONFLICTING IDEAS—AMEND THE U.S. CONSTITUTION OR REJECT ALL HUMAN GOVERNMENT?

Even as they critiqued American laws, petitioned the U.S. Congress, and worked to amend and improve the U.S. Constitution, the Grimké sisters joined in a debate among antislavery activists over whether to privilege political engagement, fully reject the corrupt U.S. government, or find a way both to criticize and to engage it. Given the terrors of violence against abolitionists such as the 1837 murder of the abolitionist newspaper editor Elijah Lovejoy, the impact of Congress's "gag rule" against abolitionist petitions, and the rise of political antislavery in the late 1830s, the abolitionist movement as a whole was sorting through the demands of religious perfectionism on the one hand and political engagement on the other.[37]

Abolitionists were debating how to approach and understand the U.S. Constitution. Some claimed it was a reform document, construing it as already against slavery. Alvan Stewart, for instance, cited the Preamble and the Fifth Amendment's protection of "life, liberty, or property" to bolster his antislavery argument. In contrast, nonresistant abolitionists and peace advocates such as Henry C. Wright and William Lloyd Garrison prioritized an uncompromised morality over all else and condemned the U.S. Constitution's support for slavery, as seen in its pledge to return fugitive slaves to their masters, in its counting of a slave as three-fifths of a person for purposes of representation, and in its pledge to suppress insurrections in the states. They went further than most antislavery advocates by demanding nonrecognition of and noncompliance with corrupt human governments. Their version of perfectionism was variously labeled as "nonresistance," or "no-human-government."[38] Informed by their perfectionist and Quaker beliefs, the Grimké sisters briefly sympathized with "ultra" Garrisonian arguments that conscience and Christianity provided a higher law than the flawed U.S. Constitution.[39] The Grimkés were also attracted to this strain of perfectionism because of their friendship with Henry Wright, a Massachusetts agent of the American Anti-Slavery Society who, in 1837, was in charge of scheduling the Grimkés' speaking engagements. He had the opportunity to converse with them extensively about nonresistance; the sisters appreciated Wright in part because of his willingness to broaden the scope of the Anti-Slavery Society to include issues such as woman's rights and nonresistance, rather than continue its more narrow focus on abolition alone.

Soon, however, the sisters were torn by the question, as Lewis Perry puts it, "[W]as the Constitution a moral covenant to be won back from the hands of political hypocrites or was it contractual evidence of human depravity?"[40] In letters to the Grimké sisters, abolitionist Theodore Weld wrote scathingly of nonresistance and of Henry Wright—in part because Theodore was jealous of Wright's close friendship with the sisters at a point when he was falling in love with Angelina. Responding to Weld's harsh attacks, Sarah Grimké advocated no-human-government principles in an 1837 letter to her future brother-in-law. She puzzled: "I wonder that thou canst not perceive the simplicity and beauty and consistency of the doctrine that all government, whether civil or ecclesiastical, conflicts with the govt. of Jehovah and, that by the Christian, no other government can be acknowledged without leaning more or less on an arm of flesh." Unknowingly aggravating Weld's jealousy by praising Wright, she concluded, "Would God all abolitionists put their trust where I believe H.C.W. [Wright] has placed his, in God alone." Asserting that "the arm of the law for retaliation" should be rejected in favor of "turning the other cheek, as Jesus commands," she supported pacifist nonresistance even in the face of violence.[41] Weld responded, "*Practically* I have always been a 'peace man' in *my* sense of the word. Not a 'no government' man—*that* doctrine fills me with *shuddering.*" Favoring political engagement by antislavery activists, he condemned their "*conclusion* . . . that what *you* call human government is *forbidden* by the Bible." Also in love, Angelina responded more defensively than Sarah had, insisting to Theodore, "In writing, I think I never have *committed myself.*" Angelina tried, however, to state "our premises" for

Weld: "Civil Government is based on physical force, physical force is forbidden by the Law of Love. . . . Now, the puzzle in my mind is this. If these things ARE SO, then God *has changed* the moral government of his people, and yet *my* favorite theory has been the *unchangeableness* of this government."[42]

The tensions between Angelina's conceptions of moral versus political authority are revealed in an 1837 letter to her friend Jane Smith: "my own mind is all in a mist, & I desire earnestly to know what is truth about it; whether *all* civil government is an usurpation of God's authority or not." Ultimately, Angelina Grimké could not reject all laws and government; rather, she insisted that unjust laws should be revoked and replaced by morally right legislation. Angelina's greater skepticism of no-human-government ideas, in addition to her recognition of the limited effectiveness of petitioning, led her to argue for increased political rights and participation for women. She advocated women's direct involvement in voting and partisan politics before Sarah was ready to do so, insisting on women's rightful place in politics and the governance of the nation: "Now, I believe that it is woman's right to have a voice in all the laws and regulations by which she is to be *governed,* whether in Church or State; and that the present arrangements of society, on these points, are *a violation of human rights, a rank usurpation of power,* a violent seizure and confiscation of what is sacredly and inalienably hers." Angelina argued in favor of woman suffrage, and even women's political leadership of nations, as the most direct way to ensure their "right to have a voice in all laws." Women should be allowed to sit as full members of all reform societies and legislatures, she argued, and then she made the bold proposal that women had equal rights to sit "in the Presidential chair of the United States."[43]

In contrast, in the 1830s Sarah Grimké's nonresistance, no-human-government ideas made her reject women's full political engagement. Contrasting fixed Christian morality to the unstable immoral world of politics, she wrote, "I had rather we suffer any injustice or oppression, than that my sex should have any voice in the political affairs of the nation." At this point, paradoxically, Sarah's desire for purity kept her from endorsing women's participation in what she perceived to be a flawed and corrupt human government. Sarah insisted on women's right to play a role in political debates and legislative reform, yet she also feared the corruption she perceived in antebellum politics. We will see that by the 1850s, Sarah Grimké advocated women's suffrage and went farther than many other woman's rights activists of her time by demanding that women should have literally equal representation in the state and federal legislatures.[44]

Convinced by Theodore Weld's arguments, both sisters had abandoned nonresistance doctrines by mid-1838, concerned that the Garrisonians' "ultra" belief in a supreme moral authority could delegitimize all political authority or human government. The Grimkés concluded that the need for and primacy of moral suasion did not preclude engagement with the government; they especially supported reformers' demands for legislative and constitutional solutions to end slavery and women's inequality. The sisters took what they saw as the most workable aspects of each faction, condemning the U.S. Constitution's support of slavery while also arguing that the Constitution, since it could be amended, had much unfulfilled potential. Angelina Grimké pointed to the obvious flaw in the logic of those who petitioned the government but then said government could not or should not exist. For women's right to petition to have any power or meaning, government itself would have to have some legitimacy. In her most pointed and insightful critique of no-government principles, Angelina in 1838 asked her friend Anne Warren Weston, a founder of the Boston Female Anti-Slavery Society, "But do tell me how you can consistently petition government to exercise a power which you believe to be usurped."[45]

The fact that women were already participating as responsible citizens in public campaigns for moral and social reform was an important factor in the Grimké sisters' acceptance of reformers' engagement with political and legal systems in order to reform government and society. Lori Ginzburg argues that, "during the antebellum decades, even the most passionate believers in moral suasion directed their attention to the state." Each sister called for a new, activist, public role for women in the abolitionist movement and for changes in state and federal laws to enact their reform agenda. The sisters' refusal to join Henry Wright and Maria Weston in the New England Non-Resistance Society after Angelina's 1838 marriage to Theodore Weld was a result of their continued discussions with Weld. Writing from their new home in Fort Lee, New Jersey, Sarah explained their position to the now-marginalized Henry Wright: "It is a solemn thing to come out in a public document and say that we believe Jehovah has abrogated his own laws." Disagreeing with Wright's ultra position, Sarah Grimké and the Welds declined to criticize publicly all human-made laws as being fundamentally in contradiction with the laws of God. Instead, they took the position that they could engage the political process and try to change those laws that they saw as being in contradiction with Christianity.[46]

In the decade before the Civil War, some radical abolitionists, including Frances Harper and William Wells Brown, began to sympathize openly with armed militancy on behalf of fugitive slaves and their rescuers and even condoned the violent actions of those who fought against the extension of slavery into new territories. The Welds, Sarah Grimké, Stephen and Abby Kelley Foster, Edmund Quincy, and Parker Pillsbury also moved away from pacifism. By 1854, for instance, Sarah's personal friends the abolitionists Augustus and Susan Wattles were defending themselves and free soil in Kansas. Explaining that, while she would certainly support them in nonresistance if they felt "called to endure rather than resist," Grimké now accepted violence as morally justifiable during a crisis. Struggling to imagine what she might do in the Wattles' situation, Sarah went so far as to sanction murder: "if you religiously believe that the best means is to settle it by the sword, to become yourself a bearer of the sword and with your own hand perhaps transfer a brother man to another sphere of existence—do it dear Augustus and God speed your efforts for the race." Here, Sarah Grimké worked to reconcile her moral ideals of peace, mercy, and nonviolence with the need to transform the country radically so that free and enslaved African Americans could take their place as full citizens. Taking a forceful and pragmatic approach to a specific set of circumstances in Kansas, she shifted the terms of her morality to adjust to the realities of what was virtually a civil war there.[47]

Even the self-described "'ultra' peace man," William Lloyd Garrison, condoned John Brown's violent resistance to slavery in 1859. Sarah Grimké expressed great "sympathy" for Brown during his imprisonment and trial and probably offered support to his wife, Mary Brown, when Mary visited their reform community at Raritan Bay, New Jersey, after her husband's arrest. (We will see that Frances Watkins Harper also supported John Brown after his attempted uprising. Harper wrote his wife, sent her money, and stayed with her in Philadelphia just before John Brown's execution.)[48] Once the war began, like most abolitionists, Sarah Grimké criticized President Lincoln for approaching the war as an issue concerning the centrality of the federal government and for focusing on national reunification rather than seizing on the moment for a moral battle against slavery. Both sisters hoped that the war could become a means to abolish slavery and, after Lincoln's 1863 Emancipation Proclamation, supported a constitutional amendment to abolish slavery throughout the entire nation.[49]

"UNRIGHTEOUS POWER"—LEGALLY DEFENSELESS FEMALE SLAVES

When Angelina Grimké married Theodore Weld in 1838, as prominent abolitionists they planned their wedding ceremony as a private event that would be widely publicized as a symbol of their love and of their radical politics.[50] Angelina rejected the official presence of a minister or magistrate and decided to defy social conventions by having an interracial wedding party. Among those who attended were their friends Grace and Sarah Douglass.[51] For the ceremony Angelina and Theodore wrote their own vows, and Theodore renounced "the unrighteous power vested in a husband by the laws of the United States over the person and property of his wife."[52] Before and after this wedding ceremony, both sisters linked the "unrighteous power" of the laws governing married women with laws governing slaves, especially enslaved women.

After the Welds' marriage, Angelina and Sarah worked intensively during the winter of 1838 and the spring of 1839 on a book entitled *American Slavery As It Is: Testimony of a Thousand Witnesses,* which was published under Theodore Weld's name in 1839 and became an abolitionist bestseller. Theodore had always thought that the sisters best served the abolition movement when they emphasized their status as former slaveholders who could testify firsthand against slavery. The sisters collaborated fully with him on this volume, which indicted the system of slavery by using only the words of Southern whites. Sarah and Angelina pored over Southern newspapers and state legislative debates to reveal the terrible condition of the slaves. Each sister also wrote her own testimonial on the horrors of slavery from her perspective as a member of a prominent Southern slaveholding family.[53]

Sarah Grimké's essay in *American Slavery As It Is* discussed the plight of slave women. She explained her earlier decision to leave her wealthy slave-owning family in Charleston, South Carolina: "I left my native state on account of slavery, and deserted the home of my fathers to escape the sound of the lash and the shrieks of tortured victims." Upon moving north she felt "impelled by a sacred sense of duty, by my obligations to my country, by sympathy for the bleeding victims of tyranny and lust, to give my testimony regarding the system of American slavery . . . most of which came under my *personal observation.*" Emphasizing in particular the sexual abuse of slave women, Sarah recounted an incident of an eighteen-year-old slave who was condemned to be whipped in the Charleston workhouse but who "pleaded in vain for a commutation of her sentence, not so much because she dreaded the actual suffering, as because her delicate mind shrunk from the shocking exposure of her person to the eyes of brutal and licentious men; she declared to me that death would be preferable." Here, Grimké sympathetically claimed for black slave women the purity, virtue, and delicacy so often reserved for white women in antebellum society.[54]

Grimké characterized white men as exercising a legal power over female slaves that was based on sexualized violence and domination. As historian Amy Stanley notes, "Dishonored, stripped bare, the bondswoman literally embodied the denial of property in the self, which for abolitionists counted as the ultimate wrong." Grimké recognized how hard it was for enslaved women to protect themselves: "In our slave States, if amid all her degradation and ignorance, a woman desires to preserve her virtue unsullied, she is either bribed or whipped into compliance, or if she dares resist her seducer, her life by the laws of some of the slave States, may be, and has actually been sacrificed to the fury of disappointed passion."[55] Female slaves were legally unable either to resist or to protest assaults upon them by white men. Not only could slave women be punished by death for resisting rape, Grimké recognized that slave owners had full legal control over their slaves: "the power which is necessarily vested in the master over his property, leaves the defenseless slave entirely at his mercy, and the sufferings of some females on this account, both physical and mental, are intense."[56] Negatively contrasting the laws of the American slave states to those of ancient Athens, which at least allowed slave women to ask for new owners if they were being abused, Grimké lamented that "even if any laws [to protect enslaved women from abuse and rape] existed in the United States . . . they would be null and void, because the evidence of a colored person is not admitted against a white, in any of our Courts of Justice in the slave States."[57] State and federal laws wrongly denied free blacks and slaves alike the legal protections granted to white citizens.

Condemning the widespread practice of Southern married white men purchasing mixed-race slave women in order to keep them as their mistresses, Grimké (as Fanny Wright had also) noted its unnatural result: "It is an occurrence of no uncommon nature to see a Christian father sell his own daughter, and the brother his own sister."[58] Sarah Grimké's position as the daughter of a prominent Charleston slave-owning family gave her a perspective that the British-born Wright did not have. As Sarah put it: "Nor does the colored woman suffer alone: the moral purity of the white woman is deeply contaminated. In the daily habit of seeing the virtue of her enslaved sister sacrificed without hesitancy or remorse, she looks upon the crimes of seduction and illicit intercourse without horror." White women who did not value or protect black women's purity and safety were complicit in the sins of their brothers, fathers, husbands, and sons. By blaming enslaved black women instead of their white male relatives (whose behavior, by law, they must tolerate and ignore), white mistresses directed their anger and jealousy at the powerless female slaves instead.[59] She explained that the white mistress "lives in habitual intercourse with men, whom she knows to be polluted by licentiousness, and often is she compelled to witness in her own domestic circle, those disgusting and heart-sickening jealousies and strifes which disgraced and distracted the family of Abraham." White mistresses' lack of compassion for black women, the victims of white male aggression, had terrible consequences. According to Grimké, white women condoned—and sometimes even perpetrated—violence: "the female slaves suffer every species of degradation and cruelty . . . they are indecently divested of their clothing, sometimes tied up and severely whipped, sometimes prostrated on the earth, while their naked bodies are torn by the scorpion lash. . . . Can any American woman look at these scenes of shocking licentiousness and cruelty, and fold her hands in apathy and say, 'I have nothing to do with slavery'? *She cannot and be guiltless.*"[60] White women condoned the violence against slave women, Grimké charged, by refusing to intervene and stop it; they must recognize their guilt in perpetuating an inherently evil system. Grimké's theoretical and practical approach to antislavery and woman's rights came from her determination to renounce her past life as a slave owner and from her understanding of the power of prejudice based on race and sex. Addressing the entwined issue of racial and sexual subordination, Sarah Grimké concluded that enslaved women had fewer chances than other women of exercising their free will. She understood that black slave women faced different and worse challenges than other women because of their subordinate status, recognizing that race and sex were two interconnecting systems of subordination that needed to be tackled together if all women were to achieve true equality.

"EQUALITY OF THE SEXES AT THE FAMILY ALTAR"— WOMEN'S DIFFERENCE AND EQUALITY

Once they completed *American Slavery As It Is,* Angelina and Sarah participated less directly in the antislavery and woman's rights movements. Mostly, they wrote supportive letters to be read aloud at reform conventions while keeping up an extensive correspondence with national and foreign activists.[61] After Angelina's marriage, Sarah lived with the Welds and helped with the housekeeping and then child care. The sisters hoped that their newfound commitment to domesticity would prove that granting American women expanded political roles and rights (including public lecturing) would not subvert their traditional domestic roles. Accordingly, Angelina Grimké Weld became a hardworking wife and mother, living with her husband and sister on a modest farm in New Jersey. In a letter to abolitionist and woman's rights advocate Anne Warren Weston, Angelina boasted in 1838 of making "very nice bread." She wrote, "I do not agree with thee that I can now be doing any thing of more importance than superintending my household affairs, because in doing so I am proving that public lecturing does not unfit woman for private duties. No one, then, but Sister & myself can do our work & demonstrate this for the benefit of our sex at large."[62] Their strategy of using the conduct of their own lives as an argument for the fitness of their cause, in order to prove that abolitionism and public speaking had not de-sexed them, resonates with the themes of the Second Great Awakening, where conduct could publicly testify to personal conversion.[63]

In an 1842 letter to the British abolitionist Elizabeth Pease, Sarah Grimké wrote that some activists were disappointed in the sisters, fearing that their commitment to woman's rights and abolition had waned with Angelina's marriage. Sarah herself worried that they would be unlikely "to satisfy those who insist on [continued] public action as the only satisfactory evidence" of their reform commitments. Instead, she politicized their private lives: "we believe that God calls now to other duties, to the living out of our anti slavery principles in every day life, to assert our unchanged opinions as to *equality of the sexes* at the family altar, around the social board and on all the occasions which may and do arise in domestic life." Grimké's assertion of women's necessarily different role as childbearers and breastfeeders was a defense of the sisters' more narrow focus on Angelina's children and family. In her letter to Pease, Sarah argued that women's physical differences from men were significant: "It is plainly the right of all human beings to cultivate the powers which God has given us; it is plainly the duty of woman to nurse her offspring; it cannot be the duty of man because God has not furnished him with the nourishment necessary for the infant." Here, Grimké discussed the fact of women's physical difference—their unique capacity to bear and nurse children—as the central difference between men and women. She characterized women's role as mothers as a God-given duty and power. Sarah also defensively mentioned to Pease that Angelina had sent a letter of support to a recent Pennsylvania Anti-Slavery Society meeting and that she herself had attended and spoken at a temperance meeting.[64]

The lengthy transatlantic correspondence between Pease and the sisters was not meant to be private. Pease circulated their letters, ideas, news, and pamphlets throughout Britain's antislavery community. Sarah's concurrent defense of domesticity and support of women's rights was written with this larger audience in mind. In her letter to Pease, Grimké adamantly condemned the sexism of the 1840 World's Anti-Slavery Convention, which had refused to seat the American women delegates, and supported women's equal rights to a full role within the antislavery movement: "That the London Committee had no right to reject the female delegates is perfectly clear. I think it was an unwarrantable assumption of power, and when they better understand the rights of women as human beings, they will see that they are *co-equal* with their own." Women's difference did not conflict with Sarah Grimké's support of their political equality. Women were not the same as men, yet as co-equals to men they were entitled to equal participation in the political process.[65]

In her 1850s essays, we will see that Sarah Grimké merged together a

natural rights discourse of equality with a discourse of women's difference, arguing that women should be the legal and political co-equals of
men and that the sexes were inherently different.[66] Her ideas are part of a
long line of transnational feminist thought based on complex and over-
lapping arguments concerning sameness (natural rights) and difference
(co-equality). Like European woman's rights activists, Grimké and other
antebellum women reformers linked women's special moral authority to
their right to demand changes in the laws and politics. Acknowledging
their physical difference, she refused to allow these differences to deny
women their rights as citizens. Instead, women's capacity as mothers,
along with their greater morality, required them to take political responsibility for social change. Gender difference did not lead her to want to
protect women within a sanctified domestic sphere; rejecting as false the
separation between private and public spheres, Sarah claimed: "we covet
an *enlarged sphere* of usefulness."[67]

After the Civil War, Angelina Grimké Weld and Sarah Grimké continued their fight for full citizenship of black and white women by
advocating their right to vote. In 1868 they served as vice presidents of
the Massachusetts Woman Suffrage Association, which was affiliated
with the American Woman Suffrage Association (AWSA). Founded by
Lucy Stone, Henry Blackwell, Julia Ward Howe, and Frederick Douglass, AWSA supported the Fourteenth and Fifteenth Amendments to
the Constitution, which gave citizenship to blacks and the right to
vote to black men (but not to black or white women). After the passage
of these amendments, AWSA chose to fight for woman suffrage on a
state-by-state basis, whereas Stanton and Anthony's organization, the
National Woman Suffrage Association (NWSA), fought against these
amendments, arguing that white women must be enfranchised at the
same time as (or even before) black men. The sisters joined woman's
rights activists in insisting that the language of the Fourteenth
Amendment automatically granted women the right to vote because
it acknowledged them as full citizens (the "New Departure" strategy).
Acting on this idea, they engaged in a theatrical form of public political protest: they committed civil disobedience by illegally voting with
a group of women in an 1870 Massachusetts town election. In a similar suffrage protest, Anthony was arrested for illegally voting in the
presidential election of 1872.[68] When the U.S. Supreme Court in *Minor
v. Happersett* (1875) denied that the Fourteenth Amendment already

enfranchised women, the sisters worked for the passage of a separate woman suffrage amendment.[69]

"LIVING OUT OUR ANTI SLAVERY PRINCIPLES"— INTERRACIAL FRIENDSHIPS AND ANTIRACISM WORK

When Sarah Grimké stated to Elizabeth Pease that she and the Welds were "living out our anti slavery principles," she referred to the fact that they were developing increasingly intimate friendships with African Americans, especially with Grace and Sarah Douglass. They also participated in antiracism (often anti-segregation) work in the North on behalf of and with free blacks before and after the Civil War.[70] Trying to break down customs and social barriers to interracial friendships, the sisters and Weld invited Sarah and Grace Douglass to come stay with them for extended visits and talked with them in-depth about their experiences of prejudice, segregation, and discrimination. The first time Sarah Douglass visited the Welds and Grimké at their home in Fort Lee, New Jersey, in 1839, she came for only one day. After the visit was over Sarah Grimké wrote her asking her why:

> As we put in a claim pretty early to a portion of thy vacation, it was a disappointment to see so little of thee—by the way dear, and I love frankness, I am going to tell thee what I have thought . . . and if I am mistaken tell me honestly—It seemed to me thy proposal "to spend a *day*" with us was made under a *little* feeling. . . . "Well after all I am not *quite certain* I shall be an acceptable visitor". . . . If this were so my sister, I can only say that it is no surprise to me that thou shouldst be beset with such temptations [Douglass's fears of racial prejudice]. . . . Now beloved it was in my heart just to say this, and to invite thee to equal candor that then thro' the blessing of God we may do each other good.

Continued letters and conversations like these helped Douglass feel certain of her welcome. Thus, by 1840, Sarah's mother, Grace Douglass, could write a letter to the Welds' young son, Charley (Charles Stuart): "Thou must tell dear Father & Mother & Aunt Sarah how grateful I feel to them for all their kindness to my daughter Sarah, she came home with a heart full of gratitude to God for permitting her to sojourn with you for a season."[71]

Intimate time spent together allowed their friendship to deepen over the years; Sarah Grimké wrote to Douglass about how she viewed their relationship as a step toward fostering real interracial communication and understanding between blacks and whites. She revealed that she viewed their friendship as her path to spiritual salvation: "Sarah, my intercourse with thee has been a great blessing to my soul. I regard it as a peculiar testimony of God's love to me. He gave me thy heart, he gave me a just appreciation of thy character, and deep sympathy for thy trials. . . . In giving me thy friendship God gave me an opportunity practically to demonstrate that *He* had delivered me from the odious and wicked prejudice which crushed thee to the earth." In the last year of her life, Grimké sent Douglass a letter and a handmade tidy, to which Douglass replied, "Thanks, for the love that has sweetened my life for so many years!" She predicted that after their deaths, their friendship would be "improved in a higher world."[72]

The tie between Sarah Douglass and the Grimké-Weld family is evidenced by the fact that she continued corresponding with Charles Stuart Weld and his father, Theodore Weld, in the late 1870s after both Sarah and Angelina had died.[73] Another example of the sisters' attempts to break through racial boundaries and prejudices is the fact that, in 1868, Sarah Grimké and Angelina Grimké Weld warmly embraced their newly discovered biracial nephews, Archibald and Francis Grimké, the children of their late brother and one of his slaves (Archie became a Harvard educated lawyer and Frank a minister and the husband of Charlotte Forten). The sisters initiated a relationship with them that lasted for the rest of their lives, openly and proudly claiming their nephews as legitimate members of the Grimké family, providing them with both emotional and financial support.[74]

The friendship between the Grimké sisters and the Douglass family, among others, enabled them to learn and communicate about manifestations of racial prejudice that were experienced by free blacks on a daily basis. As early as 1837, Sarah Grimké wrote Douglass asking her for accounts of her family's experiences with racism. When British abolitionist Elizabeth Pease wrote to Sarah Grimké in 1839 asking her to obtain firsthand accounts of "the prejudice against color which exists in this country" to send abroad, Grimké knew of a number of hurtful slights that Sarah Douglass had described to her in the past. She again asked her friend to recount them: "make any statements which will answer her [Pease's] purpose, such as thy mother's treatment at friend Snowden's funeral, the case of thy cousins at North meeting, and the facts whatever they may be relative to the 'bench for colored persons'. . . . Consider, too, whether you are prepared to have your own names published and the names of those who have manifested towards you this prejudice." Grimké specifically asked her to document the fact that the Society of Friends had betrayed its egalitarian rhetoric by maintaining segregated seating for blacks at their meetings. Douglass complied with the request, and Grimké then forwarded the account to Pease to distribute and publish abroad.[75] Douglass subsequently published versions of her complaints against the Friends in American publications, including the organ of Quaker Orthodoxy, *The Friend* (1840), and the *National Anti-Slavery Standard*.[76] Through their letters and essays, both Douglass and Grimké engaged in a transnational discussion of racial prejudice in the United States that went beyond a mere critique of slavery to include exposés of Northern white racism.

"LEGISLATION CAN DO MUCH"—MARRIAGE LAWS AND WOMAN'S RIGHTS

Sarah Grimké's 1850s essays expanded upon an issue of legal reform that she had first addressed in the 1830s, arguing that English common laws were relics of past unenlightened discrimination and must be abandoned. She particularly criticized the common law concept of coverture or the legal invisibility of the wife, which served as the basis for marriage laws throughout the United States.[77] Broadly stating that "the laws respecting married women are one of the greatest outrages that has been perpetrated against God and humanity," Grimké demanded their repeal.[78] New laws would give black and white women, whether married or single, their due place in government and make them equals to men:

> This exposition of the *principles* of the Woman's Rights movement I heartily accept. We do claim the absolute and indefeasible right of woman to an equality in all respects with man and to a complete sovereignty over her person and conduct. Human rights are *not* based upon sex, color, capacity, or condition. They are universal, inalienable and eternal, and none but despots will deny to woman that supreme sovereignty over her person and conduct which Law concedes to man.[79]

Emphasizing equality and self-sovereignty, Grimké's natural rights argument refused to allow difference (including color or sex) to signify inferiority.[80]

Whereas Fanny Wright advocated free love and an open defiance of laws on marriage and illegitimacy, Sarah Grimké advocated a single standard of sexual purity and formulated a pro-regulatory argument, demanding the passage of new laws to give equal rights and protections to married women.[81] Grimké conceded that men and women instinctively act from their passions but concluded that both sexes must learn to control their passions: "The Doctrine that human beings are to follow their attractions, which lies at the base of the miscalled 'free love' system, is fraught with infinite danger. We are too low down to listen for one moment to its syren voice." Because people were prone to follow their basest instincts, she asserted, they needed laws to regulate them and to protect them from themselves and others.[82]

Extending this pro-regulatory logic to another reform issue, both Angelina and Sarah supported temperance legislation that would allow localities or the state to restrict individuals' access to alcohol. In fact, the sisters adopted a pro-regulatory stance that would later be championed by temperance activists such as Frances Harper and Frances Willard. In the antebellum era, the emphasis of temperance advocates was on passing state and local dry laws rather than on national prohibition. Thus, in 1842, Angelina wrote a petition against licensing all alcohol in the township of Belleville, New Jersey, which she and Sarah then circulated door-to-door. Sarah and Angelina first joined a temperance society in the late 1830s. Theodore Weld continued to speak on temperance into his eighties.[83] Believing in government's duty to impose laws that would control individuals' passions and behaviors, the sisters and Theodore fought for local dry laws and attended and spoke at temperance meetings until the end of their lives. Had she been younger, Sarah Grimké might have traveled the same path as Frances Watkins Harper, who after the Civil War moved from antislavery activism into woman suffrage and pro-temperance work with the Woman's Christian Temperance Union.

Sarah Grimké's legal reform agenda included a feminist analysis of the real but hidden problem of marital rape, which she referred to as "legalized licentiousness." She framed her argument in terms of women's legal status because, as Gerda Lerner observes, she "sees male sexual dominance as the primary evil and legislated equality as the means to end it." In her 1850s *Sisters of Charity* essay, Sarah raised the taboo topic of marital rape and its place in the American legal system: "Legislation can do much towards producing that harmonious cooperation of the sexes by which the establishment of equal rights to person and to property will release woman from the horrors of forced maternity and teach her partner to subject his passions to the control of reason." Identifying marital rape as a problem that existed because husbands had legal right to and control over their wives' bodies, Sarah argued that new laws must be passed to ensure equality and rights for women.[84]

Comparing the legal institution of marriage to prostitution and slavery, Grimké continued and amplified the earlier critiques of marriage made by Mary Wollstonecraft and Fanny Wright. Decrying woman's enslavement in her private life, Grimké stated, "The existing laws can answer that she is your slave, the victim of your passions, the sharer willingly and unwillingly of your licentiousness." Sarah characterized Northern husbands as licentious—similar to those Southern white slave owners who raped their slaves. When thinking about the subordinate condition of women in marriage, she labeled all wives as slaves. By identifying each married woman under current law as "a legal prostitute, a chattel personal," Grimké linked the plight of white and free black women to the plight of black slaves. (Not coincidentally, abolitionist Frances Watkins Harper decided to join the woman's rights movement once she realized the legally subordinate position of all married women.) Grimké's discussion of marriage as legally sanctioned prostitution highlighted the inequalities resulting from the denial of rights to married women and anticipated arguments made by woman's rights activists of the 1870s, such as Victoria Woodhull, who focused on what historian Amy Dru Stanley calls "the symbolism of marriage as prostitution."[85]

"EDUCATION, SELF-SUPPORT, AND REPRESENTATION"— WOMEN'S POLITICAL AND EDUCATIONAL EQUALITY

The correspondence between Sarah Grimké and Elizabeth Pease is just one example of Grimké's transnational reform connections, and of the European intellectual thought that nourished her ideas. In the 1850s Grimké wrote letters to and composed essays in which she cited the works of contemporary European woman's rights advocates such as Anna Jameson, author of *Sisters of Charity, Catholic and Protestant, Abroad and at Home* of 1855; Jeanne Deroin, a French socialist and newspaper publisher active in the revolutions of 1830 and 1848; and novelist George Sand. During these years Grimké also published letters to the editor in Amelia Bloomer's temperance and woman's rights paper, *The Lily*, and discussed her ideas with close friends such as Dr. Harriot K. Hunt of Boston and Sarah Douglass.[86] Grimké's transnational feminist thought appears in her injunction to study the history of great women worldwide. Producing a progressive historical narrative with the rights of women at its core, she asserted that "another phase of humanity is now before us," a phase she defined as the summoning of women to the "theater of action."[87]

Grimké objected to the fact that American women were not granted full citizenship rights and obligations including suffrage, jury service, or the right to serve as representatives in the state and national legislatures. In her search for ways to change the legal and political system, she had come to realize that even a small number of women reformers could make change. Reminding her readers that only fifty-six men actually signed the Declaration of Independence, Grimké noted that, "Nevertheless, the grand and glorious words had been uttered 'Liberty or Death,' 'Taxation and Representation' and they rang through the land with magic power. . . . Will it not be so with the words which woman utters? Rights, Equality, Education, Self-support, and Representation." Women had a right to full representation in government and politics and to equal education.[88]

No longer hidden in the domestic sphere, educated women would take public, political action. Sarah Grimké's 1850s essay, *The Education of Women,* argued that unequal education for females led to the denial of other fundamental political and legal rights and so must be remedied.[89] By the antebellum era, laws in Northern states had opened up primary education to both sexes, but, she pointed out, taxes paid by men and women routinely funded higher education for males only. Indeed, before the Civil War, only a few private women's colleges existed. An even smaller number of institutions, such as Oberlin and Antioch colleges, accepted both female and male students. Society's refusal to educate females equally to males, she claimed, had inadvertently fostered the woman's rights movement: "It is doubtless the feeling of injury on the part of woman which has induced a few of us to claim the Rights so unjustly withheld. It is because we feel that we have powers which are crushed, responsibilities which we are not permitted to exercise, duties which we are not prepared to fulfill, rights vested in us as moral and intellectual beings, which are utterly ignored and trampled upon." Women's lack of access to higher education wrongly kept them from rewarding careers and from political citizenship.[90]

State and local laws that governed the availability of education, Grimké argued, ought to be amended. In a democracy, no one should have to accept "inequalities and injustice." The denial of equal education to women, she claimed, was grounds for the next American Revolution—what she termed the second, "greater Revolution.[91] Like Fanny Wright before her, Grimké sought "universal education" through reform legislation at the state level.[92] She suggested that states pass laws guaranteeing women full access to publicly funded higher education and, thus, to the range of professions and knowledge that men currently enjoyed. Only then could women become full citizens. Grimké challenged women to think about this question: "How many millions are invested in colleges, universities, theological seminaries for the education and exaltation of *men* to prepare them to fill offices of honor, trust, and emolument?" She asked women to "appeal then to the States in which we live to incorporate us among her citizens; to give us the same advantages she gives to her sons; to open to us the portals of science, art and literature."[93] Writing in Amelia Bloomer's reform paper *The Lily*, in 1852, Grimké again implored each individual woman to make history by challenging her current subordinate status: "Let woman appeal to Legislative and Ecclesiastical bodies, as well as to Medical Colleges. . . . Let her go herself before those public bodies, and set forth the difficulties under which she labors, the disabilities which are imposed upon her, the injustice of taxation without representation, and of not permitting her to be tried by a jury of her peers." Sarah's notable categorization of "Medical Colleges" as institutional powers similar to "Legislative and Ecclesiastical bodies" reflects her conviction that women needed access to the realms of professional and economic power in American life existing outside the domestic sphere and somewhat independent of politics and the state.[94]

Grimké's use of the word "women" in her writings on equal education implicitly included white and black women. She was always supportive, for instance, of the educational mission of her friend Sarah Douglass, whose Philadelphia school for free blacks was founded and partially supported by the Philadelphia Female Anti-Slavery Society from 1838 to 1849 (she continued to operate the school even after its funding was cut off). In an early letter to Douglass, Grimké approved of her attempts to increase her education by attending a set of lectures: "I am truly glad my dear friend that thou hast had the privilege of attending J. Simmons lectures. Knowledge is very valuable and I believe our heavenly father approves of our improving the intellectual faculty with which he has blest us, if we consecrate our talents to his service surely the more highly cultivated they are the more widely attended will be our sphere of usefulness."[95] Since Grimké tried to attend medical school (and inquired about the male-only field of the law) when she was in her sixties, she could appreciate Douglass's decision during the 1850s, when she was in her fifties, to take medical classes at the Female Medical College of Pennsylvania and the Pennsylvania Medical University. Douglass used this training to lecture on female health, hygiene, and physiology.[96] Later, in 1863, Grimké wrote letters to Douglass when she was trying to find boarding and a suitable school for a "colored girl about 12 years old" who was too young to attend Oberlin College but whose parents wanted to prepare her for higher education. Thinking of Charlotte Forten, who was educated in Salem, Massachusetts, and whose letters and essays about her experiences as a teacher in Port Royal, South Carolina, were being published in Northern papers, Grimké asked, "Do you know where Miss Forten . . . was educated? . . . Is there any school there where she ['my child'] would be received on an equality with white children?" Grimké also asked Douglass's opinion as to whether it would be profitable for the child to board with a sympathetic white family, in order to experience racial equality and harmony firsthand.[97] For Grimké women's higher education must be accomplished in order to achieve racial and sexual equality for all American citizens.

"LEGISLATE FOR A CHRISTIAN COMMUNITY"—
SARAH GRIMKÉ'S VISION OF A CHRISTIAN NATION

Grimké's 1850s essay on the *Condition of Women* argued that only women's full political citizenship could lead the country toward her goal of a nondenominational Christian state. Anticipating arguments made by WCTU president Frances Willard, she demanded women's full citizenship based on women's greater piety, their fundamental rights to equality under the law, and their physical and "affectional" differences from men.[98] She began by emphasizing that women's "affectional natures, by virtue of their office as *mothers* renders them peculiarly fit to *select* those who are to represent and watch over the interests and legislate for a Christian Community." Here, women's natural biological difference did not disqualify them from suffrage but, rather, increased their suitability for it. Men had historically pointed to women's physical difference as a way to deny them rights; Grimké pointed to women's moral and physical difference as a way to justify expanding their rights. Grimké believed that only with women's full political participation could an ideal nation be created, for their ability to mother ensured that their votes would be based on what was best for the entire community.[99] Certain of God's will, Grimké insisted that women carefully study the secular laws made by men and challenge those that denied them their God-given rights: "The laws respecting women are a blasphemy against God, they invade his right to decide on the equality of Human Rights and charge him with surrendering the duties and obligations, the conscience and the will of half his intelligent creation to the caprice, selfishness and physical superiority of the other."[100] God, she believed, created both men and women and prized them equally, so women had to fight to make the laws on earth more accurately reflect God's will.

Grimké argued that women's "purifying influence" meant that they should be laboring members of "every department of government." It was crucial, she said, to "let the moral character of the women of the U.S. bear testimony to their power of self-government, power more essential than any other to qualify . . . women to *reside* in our halls of legislation." Women with their higher "moral character" should literally constitute half of every field of government, including the state and national legislatures, she insisted, because only this would ensure that government would have a "healthy channel of reciprocal intercourse with one half the persons over whom it claims to exercise authority and for whom it enacts laws." In line with her idea that women needed to be jurors so that they could truly be tried by a jury of their peers, she reasoned that men could not legislate for women, who must represent themselves. Turning the conventional argument on its head, Grimké argued it was women's difference that necessitated their full inclusion in the world of politics. Women's political participation would ensure that legislatures effectively represented their concerns. Norma Basch suggests that "Only woman suffrage and (for the most radical) the concomitant right of women to serve on juries, hold political office, and be admitted to the bar, could begin to adjust the inequities of marital property." Sarah Grimké was among these "most radical" reformers who advanced an expansive definition of women's citizenship.[101]

Grimké concluded that women were more moral and religious than men *and* that governments must be founded on morality. Her attempts to resolve the perceived tensions between the supposedly female virtues of religion and morality versus the ostensibly male sphere of politics and law are revealed in a passage from her mid-1850s *Condition of Women:*

> I once heard a person in the House of Representatives in Washington declare that morality and law were divorced, that an attempt to govern political movements by moral right was an absurdity, but however this may have been the case I am persuaded that as the [human] race progresses the principle will become practically true that *law and religion are a unit,* and that the only stable foundation on which government can rest is morality. If this be true is it not manifest that the portion of the race which possesses *most* religion must form an element in government perfectly organized?

In this remarkable passage, Sarah links the conventionally male sphere of politics, government, and law to women, religion, and morality. Law and religion, she insisted, were not only compatible, they were indispensable to each other and could not be effectively combined without women's participation as full citizens.[102]

*T*hroughout their lives, Sarah and Angelina Grimké argued that women must be included in the world of politics in order to interject their moral sensibilities into the laws and to maintain the right of self-representation upon which the very morality of political institutions is based. Thus, they argued that women's exclusion from politics and the law, rather than protecting women's "purity" from the immoral world of politics, subjected them to a perhaps greater immorality—the denial of the right to self-representation. Moral truths remained the sisters' motivation for demanding legislative and political change.[103]

The Grimkés confronted antebellum critics of women's political activism by challenging the separation of women from politics, legislative reform, citizenship, and the state. They found support among abolitionists, woman's rights advocates, and those involved in temperance and other reform campaigns. From the mid-1830s through the Reconstruction era, Sarah and Angelina Grimké demanded legislative changes from the federal government, conceiving of it as an increasingly viable agent for reform. During the Civil War, Angelina and Sarah worked for the passage of a federal amendment to abolish slavery. Once Congress passed the Thirteenth Amendment, they supported the passage of the Fourteenth and Fifteenth Amendments, granting blacks citizenship and black men the right to vote. The sisters also worked to gain the right to vote for black and white women. The Grimké sisters championed the legitimacy of women's participation as citizens—as political actors who directly called upon the federal government to enact the necessary legislative changes to create a more righteous nation. Perceiving women's political activism to be part of their legitimate claims to full citizenship, both sisters emphasized the moral basis of women's political action and of their claims for the necessary power to change their government and its laws.

Frances Watkins Harper

CIVIL RIGHTS AND THE ROLE OF THE STATE

Frances Ellen Watkins Harper (1825–1911) was a free black woman who grew up in the slave state of Maryland. She moved north after 1851 but found herself "sorely oppressed with the thought of the condition of her people in Maryland." Referring to Maryland's free blacks, who had few rights and were not recognized as full citizens, Watkins described their status using the inclusive "we": "we are treated worse than aliens among a people whose language we speak, whose religion we profess, and whose blood flows and mingles in our veins. . . . Homeless in the land of our birth and worse off than strangers in the home of our nativity." Watkins emphasized the commonalities between whites and blacks but lamented that these commonalities had not yet guaranteed African Americans their rights as citizens. Instead, they were "treated worse than aliens." Their experience of being strangers in their own land—indeed, "worse off than strangers"—made their situation particularly painful and literally alienating. Watkins's strong sense that black Americans had a right to full citizenship contrasted painfully with their actual status as second-class citizens, subjected to racial segregation, discrimination in employment, and the denial of the right to vote, among other indignities.[1]

Frances Watkins Harper appears in this formal portrait as confident and serene. Although this image was probably taken around the time of the Civil War, Harper used it for the frontispiece of her novel *Iola Leroy, Or Shadows Uplifted* (1892) and in an 1898 collected volume of her poetry.

In 1853 the legal status of free blacks in Maryland worsened when the state passed a law forbidding all free blacks from entering its borders; those who did so were threatened with a suspension of their citizenship rights and with enslavement by state authorities. Since she was then teaching in Pennsylvania, Watkins became permanently exiled, an "alien" unable to return to her ancestral home. Her sense of alienation from her own state and nation informed Watkins's political thought and activism. Outraged at the terrible human consequences of this state law and profoundly moved by the report of a man who had escaped from slavery but was sent back to his death, she later recalled, "Upon that grave I pledged myself to the Anti-Slavery cause."

Watkins vowed to dedicate her life to fighting for human justice and against repressive state and federal laws such as the Maryland law and Congress's Fugitive Slave Act, which enforced racial inferiority and subordination on slaves and free blacks alike.[2]

Frances Ellen Watkins is recognized by scholars as a writer, a prominent abolitionist, and a woman's rights activist. Literary scholars have focused on her place in the canon, her strengths as a poet, and her status as a popular African American orator and poet in the nineteenth century. Many of her writings have been collected in edited volumes, yet there has been relatively little scholarship on her political thought. Throughout her life Watkins asserted that the federal government and the U.S. Constitution should apply equally to all citizens, black and white. Watkins's poetry, fiction, and speeches contain clear explications of her political thought. In the antebellum era she emphasized how profoundly the government and its founding documents had failed black Americans, and she called on the government to take on more responsibility for guaranteeing and enforcing civil rights. Highlighting the fact that the U.S. government was deeply implicated in the system of slavery, Watkins argued that either it needed to be part of a solution to end slavery or there should be disunion. Given that the U.S. Constitution was corrupted by the Southern "slave power," Watkins envisioned a new government—purged of slavery—that could be a real force for ensuring the freedom and rights of African Americans.[3]

During the Civil War and Reconstruction, Frances Watkins Harper (she married in 1860) advocated a stronger, pro-regulatory, and interventionist stance for the federal government. She supported the Reconstruction Amendments to the U.S. Constitution, which abolished slavery, gave civil rights to African Americans, granted the vote to black men, and strengthened the power of the federal government. After Reconstruction, black activists involved themselves with organizations that embraced the positive possibilities of federal reform legislation. In the late 1870s, for instance, Harper turned to the Woman's Christian Temperance Union as an organizational base.[4] The WCTU's commitment to the expansion of federal power explains much of its appeal to black women such as Harper, who agreed with its strategy of calling upon the government to help solve the country's social and moral problems—by passing, for example, constitutional amendments for woman suffrage and to prohibit the sale and distribution of alcohol. By the 1890s Harper had shifted her attention from the WCTU and helped form a new national organization, the National Association of Colored Women (NACW). The 1896 founding of the NACW represents black women's resourceful, hopeful response to their exclusion from (or experiences of racism within) predominantly white women's clubs. Harper's participation with this new group highlights her determination to find an organizing space for black women to pursue federal and local reforms in this more hostile racial climate.

GOVERNMENT AS A "BLOOD-STAINED RUFFIAN"—
WATKINS'S POLITICAL VIEWS IN THE ANTEBELLUM ERA

Frances Ellen Watkins lived her entire life in circles of educators and intellectuals. Orphaned before she was three, she was raised in a free black abolitionist household in Baltimore. The abolitionist William Still provided the only contemporary biographical sketch of her in his 1872 book, *The Underground Railroad,* which includes a number of excerpts of letters she sent him as well as some early speeches and poems. Watkins described her mother as a free black woman but did not discuss the identity of her father (some scholars have suggested that this silence and her skin tone—remarked upon as "copper" in news reports of her lectures—may indicate that he was a white man).[5] Frances was raised by her aunt Henrietta Watkins and uncle the Reverend William Watkins, a prominent black minister, journalist, teacher, immediate abolitionist, and temperance supporter. His newspaper articles argued against colonization schemes as well as against segregation and Northern white racism.[6] Her uncle ran the William Watkins Academy for Negro Youth, which Frances and her cousins attended until about age thirteen. At that point, she began to work for wages as a domestic servant, seamstress, and nanny (her cousins also left school at approximately the same age to work for wages). After entering the workforce, Watkins continued her self-education. Fortuitously, she wrote such a precocious article when she was fourteen that her employers, the Armstrongs, subsequently allowed her to borrow and read books from their bookstore. Writing in whatever spare time she could make for herself, Watkins published her first book of essays and poetry, *Forest Leaves,* in 1846 at age twenty-one.[7]

At age twenty-five, after the passage of the notorious 1850 Fugitive Slave Act, Frances Watkins left Maryland to teach sewing at the Union Seminary School, a school for free blacks in Ohio. She was uncertain that teaching was her true calling; her ambivalence about teaching is attributable to a problem that many educated black and white women faced. As woman's rights advocate Frances Willard later explained: "Not to be at all, or else to be a teacher, was the alternative presented to aspiring young women of intellectual proclivities when I was young."[8] Watkins wanted a different career from that of teaching—she hoped to be a successful writer. Although she greatly valued education for black children, she did not find it personally rewarding or an effective way to make change. In particular, she was dissatisfied with her overcrowded classes and lamented that they were not conducive to learning. Teaching large classes of "unruly" students, as she did in Little York, Pennsylvania, drained her energy and talents. Hoping to become a self-supporting writer and evangelical abolitionist, in 1854 she left her teaching job and moved to Philadelphia. Remarkably, while teaching she had managed to complete her second book of Christian antislavery poems and essays, *Poems on Miscellaneous Subjects,* for which she planned on finding a publisher in Philadelphia.[9]

When Watkins moved to Philadelphia in 1854, she lived with the abolitionists William and Letitia Still, just above the American Anti-Slavery office that William managed. To prepare herself for a career as an abolitionist writer, she regularly visited the office to "read Anti-Slavery documents with great avidity."[10] Among the books she read were Harriet Beecher Stowe's *Uncle Tom's Cabin* (1852) and Solomon Northrup's narrative, *Twelve Years a Slave* (1853). Stowe's novel so inspired Watkins that she wrote a poem based on Stowe's character Eliza Harris. Northrup inspired her to advocate "Free Produce," or the purchase by Northerners of goods produced by free laborers. Watkins agreed with Northrup that Free Produce would "strike at one of the principal roots of the matter" by economically depriving slave owners of profits from slave labor.[11] Her continuing self-education exposed Watkins to a broad range of ideas. Soon her activism brought her into intimate dialogue—in person and in print—with many of the era's most influential thinkers on questions of race, citizenship, and the state.

Watkins formally launched her abolitionist career by visiting the American Anti-Slavery Society in Boston in 1854. There, she secured the assistance of William Lloyd Garrison, who had lived in Baltimore and knew the Reverend William Watkins, who wrote anti-colonization articles for Garrison and Benjamin Lundy in the *Genius of Universal*

Emancipation and then for Garrison's *The Liberator,* launched in Boston in 1831. Reverend Watkins's articles exposed the racial prejudices and problems facing free blacks in the North and the South.[12] Garrison agreed to endorse Frances Watkins's new book of poetry, *Poems on Miscellaneous Subjects,* by writing a preface in which he vouched for her as having "always resided in a slave State." To Garrison, Watkins's close proximity to slavery lent authenticity to her antislavery positions. Somewhat patronizing but also sympathetic, Garrison asked that her volume be "criticised in a lenient spirit," for her poems were "written by one young in years, and identified in complexion and destiny with a depressed and outcast race, and who has had to contend with a thousand disadvantages from earliest life."[13]

Using her own experiences of prejudice and legal injustice to try to persuade whites that racial discrimination and slavery were morally wrong, Frances Watkins gave her first speech in 1854 under the auspices of the American Anti-Slavery Society in New Bedford, Massachusetts. It was entitled "Education and the Elevation of the Colored Race."[14] Addressing white Northerners who were convinced of the evils of white Southern slave owners but were often unwilling to acknowledge their own role in this "national sin," Watkins tried to make them see their role in the oppression of African Americans based on their own prejudices and perpetuation of racial injustice in the North. Black Americans could not testify on their own behalf, they were denied jury trials, Watkins noted, and black and white Northern supporters of fugitive slaves faced fines and imprisonment. Watkins's speeches were such a success that she was invited by the Maine Anti-Slavery Society to tour the state speaking on the injustices of slavery, white prejudice, and the federal government's complicity in upholding the institution of slavery. Watkins soon became part of a sophisticated intellectual circle of abolitionists, frequently appearing alongside other Garrisonian abolitionists such as Lucy Stone, Lucretia Mott, William Lloyd Garrison, and Frederick Douglass.[15] Watkins's literary and speaking career represent her commitment to public, political activism on behalf of black Americans.

By the time that Watkins gave her first antislavery lecture in 1854, female speakers were more accepted and expected within the abolitionist and woman's rights movements than when the Grimké sisters had lectured in the 1830s.[16] Whereas Fanny Wright had an outsider's perspective on reform as a Scot and as a radical free thinker, and whereas Angelina and Sarah Grimké were wealthy women from a slave-owning family who voluntarily left the South to become abolitionists, Watkins's outsider status was more complicated. A free black woman from the South forced to live outside her home state, Watkins was technically free. But she was an exile from her Maryland home and was treated by most white Americans with contempt and as an inferior. Her eloquence combined with her liminal status—as free but not free—helped her achieve success as a public speaker. Historian Julie Roy Jeffrey suggests that her speeches about the horrors of slavery "became more powerful and real because her color encouraged imaginative connections with her subject" on the part of her white audiences.[17]

Frances Watkins accomplished something that Sarah Grimké was unable even to consider a viable possibility: she earned enough money from her publications and lecture fees to be able to support herself. According to William Still, by 1872 "fifty thousand copies at least of her four small books have been sold to those who have listened to her eloquent lectures." From the mid-1850s on, Watkins's writings regularly appeared in newspapers such as the *National Anti-Slavery Standard, The Liberator,* the *Anglo-African Magazine,* the *Christian Recorder,* and *Frederick Douglass' Paper.* In addition to publishing in newspapers, Watkins sold her poems, fiction, and essays in books and pamphlets that went through multiple editions and reached many thousands of readers. A Christian abolitionist lecturer and writer, Watkins intended her sentimental poetry and fiction as a form of moral suasion that would raise public opposition to slavery. Her popular writings developed arguments in favor of federal legislative reforms that would protect fugitive slaves as well as the legal rights of free blacks.[18]

She knew that she could be forced into slavery if she returned to Maryland, and part of Watkins's antislavery activism was both direct and practical. A poet who believed in the power of moral suasion to achieve her reform goals, Watkins was also an activist who practiced civil disobedience. Earlier, in the 1840s, free black and white Garrisonian abolitionists in Massachusetts had initiated boycotts, lawsuits, and "ride ins" that successfully desegregated the railroad cars. Historian James Stewart suggests that abolitionists believed these "acts of civil disobedience were integral to pursuing their elusive goal of a moral revolution, for widespread public appeals . . . challenged the whole North to face its deep-rooted complacency and racism."

Frances Watkins similarly advocated purposeful and righteous civil disobedience. She engaged in direct defiance of federal law by financially assisting fugitives on the Underground Railroad. William and Letitia Still's home in Philadelphia was a stop on the Underground Railroad, and living there enabled her to meet and aid fugitive slaves. Harper gave liberally of the money she earned as a lecturer and writer in order to feed and shelter the fugitives on their journey north. Believing in direct action and personal sacrifice to end slavery, she wrote to Still, "This is a common cause; and if there is any burden to be borne in the Anti-Slavery cause—anything to be done to weaken our hateful chains or assert our manhood and womanhood, I have a right to do my share of the work."[19]

Like so many other antebellum reformers, Watkins drew on the symbolism of the American Revolution as championing the liberty of the people from oppression and domination. Hypocritical white Americans, she pointed out, lauded their nation as a land of freedom but then refused to uphold these ideals for black Americans. Upon visiting Canada in 1856, as the United States was embroiled in the question of extending slavery to the territories and the enforcement of the Fugitive Slave Act, she wrote, "Oh! it was a glorious sight to gaze for the first time on a land where a poor slave, flying from our glorious land of liberty (!), would in a moment find his fetters broken, his shackles loosed, and whatever he was in the land of Washington, beneath the shadow of Bunker Hill Monument, or even Plymouth Rock, *here,* he becomes 'a man and a brother.'"[20] Sacred monuments and symbols of the American Revolution should have promised liberty to fugitive slaves but did not.

The U.S. government's collaboration with the "Slave Power" influenced Watkins's reform perspective.[21] During her 1854 speaking tour in Maine, Watkins found herself positively impressed by the partisan, politically involved abolitionist sentiments prevalent there. The "Maine ladies," she reported, supported the Free Soil Party. In spite of their earlier critique of abolitionists who had chosen to form the Liberty Party to fight for abolition within the political system, Garrisonians did not entirely condemn the Free Soil Party when it formed in 1848. Instead, they saw it as a sign that many moderates, including non-abolitionists, had been influenced by their moral suasion. Garrisonians claimed that their more extreme antislavery disunionist arguments had led some moderates to reject the major parties and create a new party that supported the nonextension of slavery into new states and territories. Watkins saw abolitionist women's political involvement as a positive development. Watkins described the situation in Maine: "They are for putting men of Anti-Slavery principles in office, . . . to cleanse the corrupt fountains of our government by sending men to Congress who will plead for our down-trodden and oppressed brethren, our crushed and helpless sisters, whose tears and blood bedew our soil."[22] If political parties could not or did not change the system, however, Watkins believed that more dramatic steps, such as disunion between the North and the South, could certainly do so.

Watkins's criticisms of the U.S. government and its sinful laws made her sympathetic to the radical Garrisonian philosophy of no-human-government, which called on abolitionists to reject immoral laws and governments through peaceful civil disobedience. Actively disobeying the Fugitive Slave Act and speaking positively of "disunion" just before the Civil War, Watkins joined Garrisonians in renouncing the U.S. government for maintaining a union between free states and slave states. Addressing free blacks in 1859, Watkins praised Moses as "the first disunionist . . . in the Jewish Scriptures," who "would have no union with the slave power of Egypt." Asking free blacks to stop trying to get ahead financially and socially within a corrupt America, she suggested instead that they put their talent and money into fighting the U.S. government and slavery. Proclaiming that "it is no honor to shake hands politically with men who whip women and steal babies," she asked them to recognize the harsh reality that "this government has no call for our services, no aim for your children," and so should be rejected. A revolutionary change would only come to the nation, Watkins predicted, "when we have a race of men whom this blood stained government cannot tempt or flatter, who would sternly refuse every office in the nation's gift, from a president down to a tide-waiter, until she shook her hands from complicity in the guilt of cradle plundering and man stealing, then for us the foundations of an historic character will have been laid." If free blacks and whites refused to participate economically and politically in the corrupt U.S. government, they could force fundamental changes in its structure.[23]

Frances Watkins concurred with those Garrisonian abolitionists who regarded human-made laws as flawed.[24] In a speech to the twenty-fourth anniversary conference of the American Anti-Slavery Society, recorded in the *National Anti-Slavery Standard* in May 1857, Watkins privileged the fundamental moral laws of Christianity: "The law of liberty is the law of God, and is antecedent to all human legislation." The U.S. Constitution (and, by extension, the U.S. government) was so corrupted and distorted by its acceptance of slavery that it could not yet be the embodiment of justice and democracy that so many white Americans imagined it to be. Accordingly, Watkins concluded, the U.S. government was currently more unjust than either western governments, such as England and France, or "Mohammedan" governments in northern Africa.[25]

Frances Watkins roused her 1857 Anti-Slavery Society convention audience to recognize that a hostile Supreme Court and the U.S. Constitution served as obstacles to real justice by dehumanizing and sanctioning repressive actions against black Americans. At the convention Watkins joined speakers such as Robert Purvis, Wendell Phillips, and William Wells Brown in condemning the U.S. judicial system, in general, and the Supreme Court, specifically, for its *Dred Scott* (1857) decision.[26] She rejected Chief Justice Roger Taney's conclusion that no blacks, slave or free, were citizens of the United States. Receiving outbursts of applause from the audience for her critique of the Court's recent decision, Watkins exclaimed, "I stand at the threshold of the Supreme Court and ask for justice, simple justice. Upon my tortured heart is thrown the mocking words, 'You are a negro; you have no rights which white men are bound to respect!'(long and loud applause). . . .When I come here [U.S. Supreme Court] to ask justice, men tell me, 'We have no higher law than the Constitution.'" Although the U.S. judicial system and the Constitution were biased and unfair toward black Americans, Watkins insisted on the possibility that the federal government could do right. Feeling empowered as an American citizen, she challenged the government to offer "simple justice" to all. As a Christian, moreover, she believed that "any cause that has God on its side . . . is sure to triumph."[27]

The Fugitive Slave Act, Watkins charged, exposed the role of Congress in upholding the sinful institution of slavery. The act favored Southern slave owners, who could use affidavits from biased and corrupt Southern law enforcement officials and their own relatives to "prove" that virtually any African American was a fugitive slave. This act compromised Watkins's own safety as a free black woman, she reminded her audience. "Slavery is mean because it tramples on the feeble and weak. A man comes with his affidavits from the South and hurries me before a commissioner; upon that evidence *ex parte* and alone he hitches me to the car of slavery and trails my womanhood in the dust." The Fugitive Slave Act encouraged the entrapment and enslavement of free blacks as well as the re-enslavement of fugitives; it was antithetical to true womanhood and manhood, making virtue and citizenship unrealizable for all black Americans.[28]

By the late 1850s abolitionists had successfully gained more support for fugitive slaves in the North. Some Northern states tried to protect the rights of accused fugitives by enacting "personal liberty laws." Many whites also stopped enforcing the Fugitive Slave Act, thereby indirectly helping slaves to escape from bondage.[29] Watkins praised those who purposefully defied the act by attempting to rescue fugitives such as Moses Horner (who had escaped from slavery, was living in Pennsylvania, but was forcibly returned by a judge to Virginia). Writing to a free black audience in the *Weekly Anglo-African* in 1860, Watkins asked for donations for a defense fund for Horner's would-be rescuers. She praised them as having thrown "themselves across the track of the general government." Ten rescuers were jailed, "crushed by that mo[n]strous Juggernaut of organized villainy, the Fugitive Slave Law."[30] Condemning the sham "trials" that upheld the law she wrote, "Did you see the account of a last minute arrest of a man to whom about 15 minutes' trial was given? Fifteen minutes to bid adieu to freedom, and then to be cast into the gaping jaws of American despotism!" Watkins could not support this federal law and urged civil disobedience against it.[31]

Like the Grimkés before her, Watkins condemned the allowances that the founders of the United States had made for the perpetuation of slavery. The Constitution, in particular, was severely (possibly irreparably) compromised by these "fatal concessions" to the institution of slavery. Garrisonians who condemned the Constitution as a proslavery document were in conflict with Liberty Party supporters such as Samuel Chase, who claimed that the Constitution was, in fact, an antislavery document. In an 1859 issue of the *National Anti-Slavery Standard,* Frances Watkins revealed her thoughts upon reading Wendell Phillips's *The Constitution as a Pro-Slavery Compact, or Extracts from the Madison Papers*.[32] Pointing to the clause of the Constitution that allowed the importation of slaves to the United States until 1808 and to the clause promising the return of fugitives to the individual states, Watkins critiqued the framers of the Constitution—"our nefarious government"—for betraying the ideals of the American Revolution by compromising with slave interests:

> I never saw so clearly the nature and intent of the Constitution before. Oh, was it not strangely inconsistent that men fresh, so fresh, from the baptism of Revolution should make such concessions to the foul spirit of Despotism! that, when fresh from gaining their own liberty, they could permit the African slave trade. . . . And then the dark intent of the fugitive clause veiled under words so specious that a stranger unacquainted with our nefarious government would not know that such a thing was meant by it. Alas for these fatal concessions.

Anticipating the coming Civil War, Watkins predicted the end of this era in which "the wicked are in power. . . . [A]s nations and individuals, God will do right by us," Watkins predicted, and "in the freedom of man's will," a better nation would be formed.[33]

In a short story from 1860, as the nation was on the verge of war, Watkins blended her critique with some hope for the future. The allegorical goddess of Slavery was confronted by Agitation, or moral public opinion, which pointed to the government's responsibility for the sin of slavery: "The blood-stained goddess [Slavery] felt it [Agitation] shaking her throne . . . and she said to her worshipers: 'Hide me beneath your constitutions and laws—shield me beneath your parchments and opinions.' And it was done; but the restless eye of Agitation pierced through all of them."[34] Federal laws still protected the system of slavery, but Northern public opinion was beginning to see slavery as a sin. Agitation and Freedom would eventually prevail; in the meantime, the federal government acted as an obstructive, violent force against positive social change and would continue to do so until its laws were changed.

Watkins insisted on the right of slaves and abolitionist sympathizers to use force to end slavery. Thus, John Brown's 1859 attempt to create a slave rebellion inspired her; she could not be a pacifist nonresistant. Free blacks like Watkins were among Brown's first supporters after he was captured. Watkins sympathized with Brown and his family, reaching out directly to his bereaved wife, Mary Day Brown, with moral and financial support.[35] Another group of black women wrote to Mary Brown as "our beloved sister" and promised to raise funds to help sustain her family.[36] Watkins spent the two weeks leading up to John Brown's execution at William Still's house in Philadelphia with Mary Brown. The Brown family already knew of and appreciated Watkins's poetry. Before the raid, Oliver Brown, their son, carried Watkins's poem "Bury Me in a Free Land" with him and transcribed it for others.[37] Responding to John Brown's execution, Watkins portrayed the U.S. government as the villain in an 1860 story about Brown entitled "The Triumph of Freedom—A Dream." She wrote, "Then I saw an aged man [John Brown] standing before her [Slavery's] altars. . . . It seemed to me as if his very gaze would have almost annihilated her; but just then I saw, bristling with bayonets, a blood-stained ruffian, named the General Government, and he caught the hands of the aged man and fettered them, and he was then led to prison." Caricaturing the federal government as "a blood-stained ruffian" who acted outside of true justice through the coercive force of his bayonets, Watkins made clear that this was not a government that black Americans could trust.[38]

In 1860 Frances Ellen Watkins married Fenton Harper, a widower with three children, in Cincinnati, Ohio. She used her own money to purchase a farm for them where she worked as a farmwife, step-mother, and mother to her baby daughter, Mary, who was born in 1862. Harper continued to publish articles and poems when she could, yet lectured less frequently until her husband died unexpectedly in 1864. At that point, she returned to the lecture circuit to support herself and her daughter.[39]

Looking back, in an 1871 poem, Harper denied that rebellion had been a realistic option for slaves. Responding to a news report of a Union officer who criticized slaves for not having risen up in rebellion against their slave owners before the Civil War, Harper charged that if slaves had in fact attempted "to murder helpless babes and wife / . . . Were you not ready to impale / Our hearts upon your Northern steel?"[40] Northern whites would have defended Southern whites and repressed rebellion, she insisted. With the federal government committed to forcibly suppressing all rebellions, slaves would have had no chance of success.

Since slave rebellions would be crushed, only a Civil War could free the slaves. Thus, when it came, Harper embraced it. In an 1861 poem subtitled "An Appeal from One of the Fugitive's Own Race," she offered her own Old Testament vision of a world cleansed of sin by violent upheaval:

> And your guilty, sin-cursed Union
> Shall be shaken to its base,
> Till ye learn that simple justice
> Is the right of every race.[41]

Simple justice would be the hallmark of a new era, marked by a Christian government on earth.

"A GOVERNMENT STRONG ENOUGH"—HARPER'S CIVIL WAR AND RECONSTRUCTION ERA POLITICS

Harper's positive assessment of the reformative and protective powers of the federal government increased during the Civil War and Reconstruction, as she celebrated the possibility that the federal government might finally help her oppressed people. President Abraham Lincoln's 1863 Emancipation Proclamation highlighted the potentially positive role that the chief executive could play in reform. Lincoln's was the first action by a U.S. president that truly encouraged Harper's faith in the federal government by demonstrating the power of the president to end slavery and improve the nation. Abolitionists and slaves alike were thrilled by the president's proclamation because it made the abolition of slavery an important war aim.[42] Celebrating the Emancipation Proclamation, Harper commented, "Oh, it would have been so sad . . . had the arm of Executive power failed us in the nation's fearful crisis!" Furthermore, she called on the central government to take a strong stance against Southern states' abridgments of the civil rights of African Americans. Observing that "the slave . . . has become a useful ally to the American government," Harper suggested that the "shadow of the American army becomes a covert for the slave, and beneath the American eagle he grasps the key of knowledge and is lifted to a higher destiny."[43] Black American men participated in the war as soldiers in the Union Army, thereby claiming full citizenship based on their military service and sacrifices. By expressing their patriotism and hope for the future through their participation in the military, black men became representatives rather than the victims of federal power.[44]

The 1865 assassination of President Lincoln moved Harper to write of "our honored and loved chieftain," hoping that his violent demise could help the Union stay focused on the most important goals of

Reconstruction: "Well, it may be in the providence of God this blow was needed to intensify the nation's hatred of slavery, to show the utter fallacy of basing national reconstruction upon the votes of returned rebels, and rejecting loyal black men; making (after all the blood poured out like water, and wealth scattered like chaff) a return to the old idea that a white rebel is better or of more account in the body politic than a loyal black man."[45] Harper was clearly concerned that needs and rights of white rebel soldiers, including voting rights and property claims, would be answered before those of black men who had fought so loyally for the U.S. government.

Overall, Harper saw true promise in a strong central government. Literary biographer Melba Boyd describes Harper as "ever suspicious of government," yet Harper usually wanted its power to increase. Arguably, more than "ever suspicious" of it, Harper was disappointed about the disjuncture between the government's rhetoric of democracy and freedom and its practice and enforcement of these rights.[46] She was most suspicious in the antebellum period, when she criticized the federal government for its constitutional and legal support for the institution of slavery, and again in the 1890s, when the Supreme Court sanctioned Jim Crow segregation in *Plessy v. Ferguson* (1896) and lynchings were at their peak in the U.S. South. Yet, even during the 1890s, when Harper found more to criticize than to praise in the role of the federal government in reform, she continued to press it to do more.

The durability or strength of the state, in Harper's view, was dependent upon citizen support. Writing to William Still from the South during Andrew Johnson's presidency, she expressed her commitment to working with sympathetic whites to strengthen the federal government: "I hold that between the white people and the colored there is a community of interests, and the sooner they find it out, the better it will be for both parties; but that community of interests does not consist in increasing the privileges of one class and curtailing the rights of the other, but in getting every citizen interested in the welfare, progress, and durability of the state."[47] Harper embraced the opportunity for blacks to participate as full citizens in American society and politics.

Radical Republicans' championship of the Reconstruction amendments, and especially of black men's voting rights, inspired hope and enthusiasm in most black Americans. Harper similarly viewed increased federal power as directly improving black Americans' civil

rights. Supportive of the Thirteenth, Fourteenth, and Fifteenth Amendments to the Constitution, she praised the U.S. Congress for offering a
promising model of the federal government's necessary involvement
in reconstructing the Southern states. Republican Reconstruction,
theoretically at least, guaranteed political equality for black Americans. Ideally, a strong federal government would include blacks as full
citizens and protect their bodies and their rights against limitations
imposed by the states. Harper's criticisms of the government did not
preclude these hopes. Lamenting the continued pervasiveness of racial
prejudice, Harper saw the vote as a possible solution and criticized the
federal government for not doing enough to protect Southern blacks.
In an 1867 letter, she commented, "I am glad the colored man gets his
freedom and suffrage together; that he is not forced to go through the
same condition of things here [in the South], that has inclined him
so much to apathy, isolation, and indifference, in the North." Focusing on what white reformers would not, she called attention to the
unequal condition of free blacks in the North, who were often denied
the right to vote, both before and after the Civil War.[48]

Harper's Reconstruction era fiction articulated her view of the
necessary role of the central state in guaranteeing African Americans'
safety and civil rights. Carla Peterson describes Harper's Reconstruction era fiction as insisting that "the practice of self-government must
apply not only to individuals but to communities and *nation* as well.
This disciplinary ideology reinforced African-American antebellum
concepts of self-control as a strategy of resistance and survival." In
Harper's short novel *Minnie's Sacrifice* (1869), serialized in the African
Methodist Episcopal church's *Christian Recorder,* her fictional heroine,
Minnie, argued that "basing our rights on the ground of common
humanity is the only true foundation for national peace and durability. If you would have the government strong and enduring you should
entrench it in the hearts of both men and women of the land." African
Americans would strengthen the nation, Harper predicted, if they
were invested in its health and longevity, and especially if they felt the
sense of ownership, patriotism, and responsibility that accompanied
the acquisition of voting rights. Full citizenship for black Americans
was essential to the health of the central government, Harper insisted,
and could be ignored only at its peril.[49]

In *Minnie's Sacrifice*, Harper described her vision of the promise and
weakness of Republican Reconstruction: "For awhile the aspect of

things looked hopeful. The Reconstruction Act, by placing the vote in the hands of the colored man, had given him a new position. There was a lull in Southern violence. It was a great change from the fetters on his wrist to the ballot in his right hand, and the uniform testimony of the colored people was, 'We are treated better than we were before.'" Progress was blocked by Southern whites, however, who responded to black males' enfranchisement by trying to deceive them and take away their rights, sometimes through false claims of a history of friendship between the races; "they tried flattery and cajolery. . . . 'We are the best friends of the colored people.' . . . [but] when the colored people were not to be caught by such chaff, some were trying to force them into submission by intimidation and starvation.'"[50] Violence and economic sanctions, she correctly feared, kept blacks from using the ballot effectively as a tool to stop white oppression and discrimination.

Black men's political support of the Radical Republicans so enraged and scared white Southern Democrats that they were now determined to limit black men's voting rights. "Some of the rebels indulged in the hope that their former slaves would vote for them," Harper explained, "but they were learning the power of combination, and having no political past, they were radical by position, and when Southern State after State rolled up its majorities on the radical side, then the vials of wrath were poured upon the heads of the colored people."[51] When it appeared that blacks would vote for their own interests and reject the Democratic Party, Southern whites viciously persecuted them.

Thus, although Harper hoped for a strong central government, she found it lacking. Decrying the federal government's inaction in face of attempts by Southern whites to buy black men's votes or keep them from voting altogether through intimidation and violence, Harper's Reconstruction era writings and speeches were designed to build public pressure for increased federal intervention and enforcement. In *Minnie's Sacrifice* her husband, Louis, expressed his fears and dissatisfactions with life for blacks during Reconstruction:

> The question that presses upon us with the most fearful distinctness is how can we make life secure in the South. I sometimes feel as if the very air was busting with bayonets. There is no law here but the revolver. There must be a screw loose somewhere, and this government that taxes its men in peace and drafts them in war, ought to be wise enough to know its citizens and strong enough to protect them.

In light of their role as taxpayers and soldiers, Louis insisted that the federal government must use its powers to recognize and protect its best Southern citizens—African American men. In this instance, Harper rejects and reverses the developing ideology of protection that was based on a caricature of black men as dangerous "brutes." Once white Southerners created the myth that all black men were violent, they claimed that Southern white women were the only ones who deserved protection from their "saviors"—Southern white men. In this racist myth, there was no room for protection of black men and their rights from dangerous, violent whites.[52]

Harper warned about the imminent demise of Reconstruction: "Oh, when will we have a government *strong enough* to make human life safe?" Lecturing in the North in 1875, she condemned the federal government for its passivity: "I do not believe there is another civilized nation under Heaven where there are half so many people who have been brutally and shamefully murdered, with or without impunity, as in this republic within the last ten years. . . . But let there be a supposed or real invasion of Southern rights by our [federal] soldiers, and our great commercial emporium will rally its forces . . . in protesting against military interference."[53]

Capitalist business interests would protect whites' rights but not those of blacks, she charged. While the federal government ignored the illegal murders and lynchings of Southern blacks, it was too responsive to any potential infringement of the rights of Southern whites. By the mid-1870s, Harper correctly perceived that Congress's priority had shifted toward achieving a national reconciliation among white Americans. Through neglect and racist intent, Northern white Republicans directly contributed to the failure of Reconstruction.[54]

"JUSTICE IS NOT FULFILLED SO LONG AS WOMAN IS UNEQUAL BEFORE THE LAW"—WOMEN AND RECONSTRUCTION

Throughout her reform career Harper's primary focus was on improving the plight of all black Americans, regardless of gender. Yet even before her own marriage in 1860, she was aware of the inequalities facing all married women, white and black. Not only could good husbands die, but bad husbands could tyrannize and torment their wives with legal impunity. "The Two Offers," a short story that appeared in the *Anglo-African Magazine* in 1859, highlighted problems with married women's legal and economic dependence.[55] Critiquing men's unrestrained power within marriage, her story warned of drunken and spendthrift husbands. The fictional character who chose not to marry was ultimately the "wiser woman" because she dedicated her life instead to a righteous but "unpopular cause" (abolition). "The Two Offers" articulated a notion of "redemptive womanhood" instead of the conventional ideal of women as weak or dependent:

> You may paint her [woman] in poetry or fiction, as a frail vine, clinging to her brother man for support, and dying when deprived of it; and all this may sound well enough to please the imaginations of school-girls, or love-lorn maidens. But woman—the true woman—if you would render her happy, needs more than the mere development of her affectional nature. Her conscience should be enlightened, her faith in the true and right established, and scope given to her Heaven-endowed and God-given faculties. The true aim of female education should be, not a development of one or two, but all of the faculties of the human soul, because no perfect womanhood is developed by imperfect culture.

Explicitly rejecting the white middle-class version of the "true woman" that focused only on her emotional development and her sheltered space within the domestic sphere, Harper insisted that the real "true woman" should be strong, educated, and given adequate "scope" for full development. Historian Shirley Yee observes that the "strength and complexity of negative sexual imagery about black women, however sexist, gave the idea of 'true womanhood' deep significance, racial as well as sexual, for free blacks." By claiming true womanhood for themselves, black women tried to gain respectability, claim purity, and fashion a more positive public image for themselves. Women of any color, Harper suggested, could be true women who could then unite to work for reforms that affected them all.[56]

Frances Harper's epiphany regarding the need for black and white women to organize for women's rights came when she was widowed in 1864. At that point she recognized the fundamental legal discrimination faced by all married women:

> My husband had died suddenly, leaving me a widow, with four children, one my own, and the others step-children. I tried to keep my children

together. But my husband died in debt; and before he had been in his grave three months, the administrator had swept the very milk-crocks and wash tubs from my hands. I was a farmer's wife and made butter for the Columbus market; but what could I do when they had swept all away? . . . Had I died instead of my husband, how different would have been the result! By this time he would have another wife, it is likely; and no administrator would have gone into his house, broken up his home, and sold his bed, and taken away his means of support. . . . I say, then, that *justice is not fulfilled so long as woman is unequal before the law.*

Harper's own savings from royalties and lecture fees had paid for the farm, but this investment was legally her husband's, not hers. She had already advocated for women's economic and political equality in her antebellum era writings, but her convictions were clearly strengthened by this traumatic event, which proved to her that as a married woman (and a widow) she was powerless before the law. Forced to leave her stepchildren with her husband's relations, she took her daughter and resumed public speaking and writing as a way to support them both.[57]

Clearly, a growing awareness of women's legal subordination and dependency in marriage led Harper into women's rights activism at the end of the Civil War.[58] In one of her most powerful recorded speeches, Harper addressed the Eleventh National Woman's Rights Convention, held in New York City in May of 1866. At this convention, Susan B. Anthony proposed turning the convention into a new organization, the American Equal Rights Association, in recognition of the fact that black women, black men, and white women were all seeking a "Human Rights platform" based on "universal suffrage." Some former antislavery activists, including prominent men such as Wendell Phillips, opposed introducing the "new" and controversial issue of woman suffrage into the constitutional debates over the Fourteenth and, then, the Fifteenth Amendment, yet a variety of other black and white abolitionists supported this move. Valuing its goal of universal suffrage, Harper joined the new Equal Rights Association (ERA).[59]

At this, her first woman's rights convention, Harper's speech set out many of the priorities of her post–Civil War reform career. She began by noting her outsider status at this mostly white women's convention, explaining, "I feel I am something of a novice upon this platform. Born of a race whose inheritance has been outrage and wrong, most of my life had been spent in battling against those wrongs. But I did not feel as keenly as others, that I had these rights, in common with other women, which are now demanded." In the antebellum era the collective concerns of black men and women had taken precedence. Her sudden widowhood, Harper explained, changed her understanding of the need for women's legal equality.[60]

Drawing on her positive experiences of working in the antebellum interracial antislavery movement, Harper favored interracial collaboration based on women's common humanity. She believed that, strategically, white and black women's collective protest would gain more attention from the white politicians who ran the federal government than could black women's separate protests. Harper committed herself to collaborating with white women, but only if they were willing to work with black women on an equal footing. Accusing white women reformers of being directly complicit in the oppression of blacks, Harper challenged them to take responsibility for the unequal position of blacks in America and to rid themselves of their own prejudices:

> We are all bound up together in one great bundle of humanity, and society cannot trample on the weakest and feeblest of its members without receiving the curse in its own soul. *You* tried that in the case of the negro. You pressed him down for two centuries; and in so doing you crippled the moral strength and paralyzed the spiritual energies of the white men of the country. When the hands of the black were fettered, white men were deprived of the liberty of speech and the freedom of the press.

Oppression denigrates the oppressors as well as the oppressed, Harper noted. She reminded her audience that the antebellum "gag rule" in Congress had tabled antislavery petitions and limited all reformers' First Amendment rights to protest against policies and laws they objected to.[61]

Harper insisted that white women were as guilty as white men in perpetuating prejudice and hate. She rejected the idealized notions of womanhood so prevalent in the dominant culture. Speaking with honesty (and some apt sarcasm), she explained to the predominantly white audience that:

> I do not believe that giving the woman the ballot is immediately going to cure all the ills of life. I do not believe that white women are dew drops

just exhaled from the skies. I think that like men they may be divided into three classes, the good, the bad, and the indifferent. The good would vote according to their convictions and principles; the bad, as dictated by preju[d]ice or malice; and the indifferent will vote on the strongest side of the question, with the winning party.

Wary of claims of white women's purity, claims that were implicitly based on black women's contrasting impurity, Harper insisted that white women were fallible and certainly not pure "dew drops." In this context, she rejected a view that she herself sometimes espoused—that women would vote differently than men did, because their interests were inherently moral and pure. Instead, when thinking about white women, Harper voiced the pragmatic (and ultimately accurate) view that women would vote according to their class, regional, and racial prejudices and interests, as well as sometimes from their sense of the common good.[62]

To further highlight for her audience the discrepancies between her experience as a black woman and theirs as white women, Harper noted the double burdens of racism and sexism for black women: "You white women here speak of rights. I speak of wrongs. I, as a colored woman, have had in this country an education which has made me feel as if I were in the situation of Ishmael, my hand against every man, and every man's hand against me." In order to form a true alliance, she explained, white women must understand the nature of black women's oppression and agree to their equal inclusion in reform organizations and goals.[63] Offering her audience an example of black women's constant experience of prejudice, even in the North, Harper described their unequal position:

> Going from Washington to Baltimore this Spring, they put me in the smoking car. (Loud Voices—"Shame") Aye, in the capital of the nation, where the black man consecrated himself to the nation's defense, faithful when the white man was faithless. . . . They did it once; but the next time they tried it, they failed; for I would not go in. I felt the fight in me; but I don't want to have to fight all the time.[64]

Smoking cars were filled with men of all classes; women usually sat in the "ladies' car," which only allowed respectable male escorts (not men traveling alone). Even in the antebellum era black women's place in the railroad cars was a source of contention. Both before and after the war, respectable, educated, middle-class black women insisted on being recognized and treated like the ladies they were, regardless of their race. This right was increasingly disputed by whites, especially in the South, after the Civil War. Black women did not relinquish their seats willingly, as their lawsuits and multiple court cases at the local and state levels show.[65] Responding to Harper's account of her mistreatment, the white women at the New York City convention exclaimed aloud, "They will not do that here" and "Shame" when they heard of Harper's trials on the railroad. Yet Harper challenged each of them to take responsibility for this state of affairs: "Have women nothing to do with this? Not long since, a colored woman took her seat in an Eleventh Street car in Philadelphia, and the conductor stopped the car, and told the rest of the passengers to get out, and left the car with her in it alone, when they took it back to the station. . . . Are there not wrongs to be righted?"[66] Northern white women, like those who left the black woman alone in the streetcar, shared responsibility for the terrible treatment of black women in the United States. Tellingly, Anthony and Stanton chose not to transcribe Harper's speech in their 1881 record of the convention proceedings. Nell Painter suggests that Harper's willingness to hold white women responsible for their role in racism made these leading white suffragists uncomfortable: "This kind of talk was too strong" for them to immortalize in their *History of Woman Suffrage*.[67]

During its short three-year existence, the Equal Rights Association was beset by disagreements. ERA members argued first about whether to support the Fourteenth Amendment or to oppose it, because it added the word "male" to the U.S. Constitution for the first time. The real breaking point came in 1869, when Congress proposed a Fifteenth Amendment that officially endorsed male suffrage, thereby allowing black men—before black and white women—to get the right to vote.[68] Frances Harper was present at the May 1869 ERA meeting that led to its dissolution. This meeting helped clarify her support for black male and female suffrage. Painter argues that in the strategic moment when the Fifteenth Amendment was being debated, Harper concluded "that she must now choose between her identity as a woman and her identity as a Negro." Painter claims that "she abandoned black women and rallied to the side of black men." More specifically, Harper viewed the passage of the Fifteenth Amendment, which guaranteed black male enfranchisement, as offering the prospect of real improvement in the civil rights of black men, and by extension of her entire race. At the ERA convention, Harper heard the increasingly racist rhetoric of Stanton, in particular, who negatively compared the rights of "Sambo" to those of white women. In that context, Harper rose to speak, noting that in Boston, sixty white women had recently walked off their jobs in protest of the hiring of one black woman who simply wanted "to gain a livelihood in their midst." She charged that white women had not united with black women, not even on the most fundamental issues of economic equality and self-support. Thus, she joined Frederick Douglass in supporting the Fifteenth Amendment (ratified in 1870), which guaranteed black male suffrage, saying, "If the nation could only handle one question, she would not have the black women put a single straw in the way, if only the men of the race could obtain what they wanted."[69]

Harper accepted the Fifteenth Amendment's enfranchisement of black males and supported the launching of an immediate campaign for woman suffrage. Her support of black men's right to vote should not be mistaken as a lack of support for woman suffrage or vice versa. As historian Rosalyn Terborg-Penn describes it, "African American woman suffrage strategies combined demands for Black women's right to vote and civil rights for all Black people."[70] Harper explored these issues in her serialized novel, *Minnie's Sacrifice,* that she was contracted to write for the *Christian Recorder* between March 20 and September 25 of 1869. Tellingly, even in segments of the novel written and published after the convention, Harper emphasized women's "common humanity" with men as the main reason for giving them the right to vote.[71] The main character, Minnie, declared:

> "I think the nation makes one great mistake in settling this question of suffrage. . . . When they are reconstructing the government why not lay the whole foundation anew, and base the right of suffrage not on the claims of service or sex, but on the broader basis of our common humanity."
>
> "Because, Minnie, we are not prepared for it. This hour belongs to the negro."
>
> "But, Louis, is it not the negro woman's hour also? Has she not as many rights and claims as the negro man?"[72]

In this way, Harper's fiction diverged from her own public stance at the ERA convention. Minnie rejected the assertion of Radical Republicans and most male abolitionists, including Frederick Douglass, that this was the "negro's hour," insisting, "'I cannot recognize that the negro man is the only one who has pressing claims at this hour."[73]

When thinking of the difference that black women voters could make, Harper's fictional heroine believed that they would vote as a bloc for issues that concerned them. Minnie argued, "To-day our government needs woman's conscience as well as man's judgment. And while I would not throw a straw in the way of the colored man, *even though I know that he would vote against me as soon as he gets his vote,* yet I do think that woman should have some power to defend herself from oppression, and equal laws as if she were a man." In this case, Harper's heroine perceived men and women as having fundamentally different—even opposing—interests, implying that women needed the vote for self-defense. Believing men to be more likely to vote against the prohibition of alcohol, she emphasized women's greater commitment to temperance legislation and moral reform: "'When I see intemperance send its floods of ruin and shame to the homes of men,' Minnie said, 'I long for the hour when woman's vote will be leveled against these charnel houses; and have, I hope, the power to close them throughout the length and breadth of the land.'"[74] Women would vote for prohibition legislation in order to stop the destruction of their homes and families that occurred because of men's drinking. Morally superior women voters would pass temperance legislation that was stalled under men's control. Here, Harper linked home protection, suffrage, and temperance several years before Frances Willard coined the powerful phrase the "Home Protection Ballot" to explain why women needed the right to vote.

The dissolution of the ERA created two rival groups, which both supported woman suffrage but differed over whether to endorse or fight against the proposed Fifteenth Amendment. Stanton and Anthony formed the National Woman Suffrage Association (NWSA), which prioritized the fight for a federal constitutional amendment for woman suffrage and opposed the Fifteenth Amendment as blatantly discriminating against women. Harper could not join with Anthony and Stanton in the NWSA because their stance jeopardized black men's voting rights. On the issue of federal versus state-level legislative reforms, Harper's preference for federal reform might otherwise have led her to support the NWSA over the other new group, the American Woman Suffrage Association (AWSA), which adopted a state-by-state approach to gaining woman suffrage. But AWSA members, led by Lucy Stone, Henry Blackwell, and Julia Ward Howe, accepted the need for black male suffrage to come first, accepting the argument that adding women to the Fifteenth Amendment might lead to its defeat. Determined to achieve full equality for all Americans, Harper joined in the AWSA's endorsement of the Fifteenth Amendment that enfranchised black men first and then began working to gain woman suffrage in the states. When Harper gave the closing speech of the AWSA convention in 1873, Terborg-Penn points out, she presented woman suffrage as a "nationalist position, a Black survival issue," by claiming that "much as white women need the ballot, colored women need it more." In her speech, Harper also insisted on black women's need for equal education and equal rights.[75]

Frances Harper's Reconstruction era poetry and fiction celebrated black women's resistance to attempts by whites to dismantle Radical Reconstruction, including their efforts to keep black men from voting.[76] Black women, Harper asserted, were morally strong pillars of their community. Politically active and astute, they demanded that the federal government uphold its commitment to African Americans' civil rights. Black women were also political partisans who favored the Republicans and were directly involved in their husbands' voting decisions. If the federal government would not safeguard black men, Harper suggested, black women should try. Although they could not vote, they played a crucial role in strengthening their husbands' determination to resist white pressure. Historian Elsa Barkley Brown convincingly points to black women's participation in partisan political campaigns, constitutional conventions, and political meetings to prove that "African American women and men understood the vote as a collective possession, not an individual one. . . . African American women, unable to cast a separate vote, viewed African American men's vote as equally theirs." Vigilance on the part of Southern black women was crucial, Harper asserted, if African Americans were to gain political equality.[77]

Harper's 1872 collection of poems, entitled *Sketches of Southern Life,* is replete with poems in which black women insist their men must resist efforts to buy their votes. "The Deliverance" provides a long catalog of the ways that African American men were bribed into selling their votes to white Southern Democrats. In each case the man is chastised by his wife; Harper's message is that black women can influence the outcome of elections even without the right to vote:

> But when John Thomas Reeder brought
> His wife some flour and meat,
> And told her he had sold his vote
> For something good to eat,
> You ought to seen Aunt Kitty raise,
> And hear her blaze away;
> She gave the meat and flour a toss,
> And said they should not stay.
> And I should think he felt quite cheap
> For voting the wrong side.[78]

The economic difficulties facing former slaves left them particularly vulnerable to bribery. In "The Deliverance," each man sold his vote for food for his hungry family, but each wife refused it, insisting that political freedom and moral integrity were worth more than ill-gained food. Barkley Brown confirms that women tried to enforce political loyalty to the Republican Party: "Black Democrats were subject to the severest exclusion . . . mobs jeered, jostled, and sometimes beat black Democrats. . . . Women were often reported to be in the forefront of this activity."[79]

Harper's poetry depicted African American women as political activists who were the moral and political saviors of their community:

> I think that [Confederate] Curnel Johnson said
> His side had won the day,
> Had not we women radicals
> Just got right in the way.[80]

Many brave black women maintained a high standard of vigilance on election day, enabling the Republicans to stay in power a bit longer.

Harper's characters explicitly demanded women's political equality and real power for women—power that could not be realized if women remained disenfranchised. In her short novel *Sowing and Reaping* (1877), a "pleasant and wealthy spinster," Miss Tabitha Jones, argued in favor of woman suffrage: "We single women who are constantly taxed without being represented, know what it is to see ignorance and corruption striking hands together and voting away our money for whatever purposes they choose." Women's tax money would be better spent if they could have some say in helping to choose government laws and programs. Through her fictional heroine, Harper rejected as inadequate women's conventional claims to being satisfied with an indirect influence over male voters. Tellingly, she again connected woman suffrage and temperance:

> With all our influence we never could have the same sense of responsibility which flows from the possession of power. I want women to possess power as well as influence, I want every Christian woman as she passes by a grog-shop or liquor saloon, to feel that she has on her heart a burden of responsibility for its existence, I hold my dear that . . . a nation as well as an individual should have a conscience, and on this liquor question there is room for woman's conscience not merely as a persuasive influence but as an enlightened and aggressive power.[81]

Dismissing "persuasive influence" (the moral suasion the Grimkés had held so dear) as weak and ineffective, Harper asserted unapologetically that women wanted and needed something more: an "aggressive power" to close the saloons that destroyed women's families. Congress needed to give women the power to make positive change by passing a suffrage amendment to the Constitution.

"ON STATUTE BOOKS SHE LAID HER HAND"—HARPER AND THE WCTU'S PROGRAM OF FEDERAL REFORM

At the end of Reconstruction, Harper returned from her lecture tours and work with freed people in the South, settled in Philadelphia, and began alliance-building with white women in order to promote temperance. While working briefly as assistant superintendent of the YMCA, she continued writing poetry and fiction. An intellectually curious and voracious reader, Harper prepared for her continuing career as published author and lecturer by reading a wide range of European and American writers. In 1872 William Still described her determination to continue her education: "Mrs. Harper reads the best magazines and ablest weeklies, as well as more elaborate works, not excepting such authors as De Tocqueville, Mill, Ruskin, Buckle, Guizot, etc. In espousing the cause of the oppressed as a poet and lecturer, had she neglected to fortify her mind in the manner she did, she would have been weighed and found wanting long since."[82] Harper read European thinkers, including historians such as François Guizot and Henry Thomas Buckle, in order to gain insight into their interpretations of the history of Western civilization. Furthermore, she wanted to be judged as a writer and lecturer according to the same standards these prominent writers were judged by.

In spite of the obvious problems involved in any collaboration of white and black women (problems that Harper herself first addressed publicly in her 1866 speech to the women's rights convention), she deemed it necessary to try to forge that alliance to gain prohibition, suffrage, and equal rights. Harper's continued commitment to interracial activism was fostered by her observations that white women's organizations had comparatively greater power and influence and that black women needed to build stronger coalitions with them, and by her optimistic assessment of the power of education. White women, she believed, could be educated to understand black women's plight and then to work for improved conditions.

Determined to gain the power needed to effect political change, Harper joined the largest women's organization of the nineteenth century, the Woman's Christian Temperance Union. This part of Harper's reform career has been comparatively neglected by scholars, who have focused on her antebellum and Reconstruction era work, and especially her literary career. Harper's antebellum era anti-alcohol poems as well as her pro-temperance and pro-suffrage positions of the 1860s and 1870s demonstrate her deep sympathy with the goals of the WCTU.[83] The WCTU's Department of Work Among Colored People, with Harper as its national superintendent, deserves greater attention as part of the story of black women's championing of federal legislative reforms in the last decades of the 1800s.[84] Like many WCTU members, Harper argued that women's special conscience and morality made it necessary for them to promote legislative reforms. The WCTU appealed to black women reformers such as Harper because it had a large and influential membership base, a focus on Christian reform, and a commitment to protecting children.

Black WCTU members supported federal reforms such as woman suffrage, the prohibition of alcohol, federal funding for education, and civil rights protections for black Americans. No other major national women's organization of the late nineteenth century gave black women the option of joining as full members. Historian Glenda Gilmore explains, "black women saw in the WCTU a chance to build a Christian community that could serve as a model of interracial cooperation on other fronts."[85] Black women hoped that if they joined white women in the WCTU because of their mutual support for federal reforms such as temperance and suffrage, perhaps they could convince whites to unite with them in support of laws that promoted civil rights. Black women's pro-statist approach derived from their view of the central government as a potentially emancipatory force for their race.

As the national superintendent of the WCTU's Department of Work Among Colored People, Harper traveled extensively throughout the country, founding local unions and recruiting many black members to the group in both the North and the South. Black women appreciated her efforts and sometimes named their local unions after her, such as the "Frances E. W. Harper W.C.T.U." of St. Paul, Minnesota.[86] Black WCTU members supported a wide range of federal legislative reforms, from constitutional amendments for woman suffrage and the prohibition of alcohol to national censorship laws, funding for education, and anti-lynching legislation. Harper and other black women activists committed themselves to an interracial alliance in the WCTU in which they worked for federal solutions to moral and social problems in the United States.

Reviewing her own history with the WCTU, Harper's article in the *African Methodist Episcopal Church Review*, "The Woman's Christian Temperance Union and the Colored Woman" (1888), discussed the group's potential as a site for interracial activism. She explained to her black readership her decision to focus on temperance after Reconstruction:

> Victor Hugo has spoken of the nineteenth century as being woman's era, and among the most noticeable epochs in this era is the uprising of women against the twin evils of slavery and intemperance. . . . In the great anti-slavery conflict, women had borne a part, but after the storm cloud of battle had rolled away, it was found that an enemy . . . to all races [alcohol] . . . had entrenched itself . . . and was upheld by fashion, custom and legislation. To dislodge this enemy, to put prohibition not simply on the statute book, but in the heart and conscience of a nation, embracing within itself such heterogenous masses, is no child's play.[87]

Just as white and black women had worked together as abolitionists, they now confronted a second evil—intemperance. This time,
however, Harper pointed out that the two races were on a more equal
footing since they were fighting a problem that could affect black
and white families alike. Problems such as slavery and intemperance
needed more than political or legislative solutions, she claimed,
since they were also products of custom as well as moral, cultural,
and class differences. Harper was well aware that this same insidious
combination of "fashion, custom and legislation" reinforced and
sanctioned the racial discrimination that defined the black experience in American society.[88]

Characterizing the temperance movement as another struggle for
the conscience of the nation, Harper emphasized the commonalities
among women of both races who desired to protect children. To her,
the answer was clear:

> God gave the word, and woman heard, . . .
> She organized the grand crusade . . .
> For God, and home, and native land . . .
> *On statute books she laid her hand,*
> To save the children of the land.[89]

Harper found compelling the organization's politicized Christian
motherhood, especially its focus on legislative reform such as the
prohibition of alcohol. Prohibition would be difficult to achieve,
she predicted, because all women lacked the right to vote and so
had inadequate political power. Because only men voted, they had
to be convinced to pass appropriate reform legislation and to fully
uphold existing laws. Black and white women also had to fight
for their own right to vote. In her 1888 article in the *AME Church
Review,* Harper outlined the history of her deepening involvement
with the WCTU:

> For years I knew very little of its proceedings, and was not sure that col-
> ored comradeship was very desirable, but having attended a local Union
> in Philadelphia, I was asked to join and acceded to the request, and was
> made city and afterwards State Superintendent of work among colored
> people. Since then, for several years I have held the position of National
> Superintendent of work among the colored people of the North.[90]

Harper was asked by the white WCTU members to join, and she agreed; her concern about whether she would be accepted as a black woman had initially inhibited her. Harper seems to have begun her affiliation with the Philadelphia WCTU in the late 1870s.[91] In 1883, she was appointed national superintendent for "Work Among the Colored People of the North."[92]

Frances Willard, WCTU president, wrote of this appointment in the group's main organ, the *Union Signal*. She described Harper as "probably the most gifted and cultured woman of her race in the United States. She has a fervid and eloquent tongue and desires no better portion than to work among 'her very own.' Mrs. Harper's daughter is a gifted young woman and recites with great acceptability in her mother's meetings." Willard did not directly mention Harper's literary accomplishments and focused instead on her public speaking and status as a mother with a pro-temperance daughter (at that point, a young adult). Willard circumscribed her praise of Harper as "the most gifted" by comparing her accomplishments only to others in "her race." Perhaps attempting to reassure members who might be uncomfortable with an interracial WCTU, Willard also emphasized Harper's willingness to stay within racial boundaries—she would work among "her very own." Willard continued, "Write to her, dear sisters, and see if she can come and help influence your colored population for the right. And when she comes, remember, as you have always done, so far as my experience goes, 'The laborer is worthy of his hire.'" This last comment alluded to the problem of racial discrimination and asked that WCTU members rise above prejudice to work in Christian communion with Harper. From the outset, both Harper and Willard recognized the challenges of trying to incorporate black women into this predominantly white organization.[93]

Harper employed a range of strategies—at times invoking sympathy and charity, then increasingly demanding equal partnership based on Christian values and a shared set of reform goals—to win the support of white, often racist, WCTU women. Historian Kevin Gaines argues that Harper adopted the Christian missionaries' notion of "uplift as an evangelical mission of mercy" that "was the antithesis of Anglo-Saxon dominance and brutality. Indeed, in Harper's view, . . . a divine teleology of uplift would supplant conquest." In each annual report, Harper quoted extensively from the reports submitted to her by the state superintendents of colored work. Harper also described her own extensive travels and speeches (all conducted without any funding from the national WCTU) as she organized local and state departments of colored work.[94]

Recognizing persistent white prejudice within the WCTU as well as blacks' suspicions of the organization, Harper welcomed the organization's support for the National Education Bill (also called the Blair Education Bill after its sponsor, Republican senator Henry W. Blair of New Hampshire). When the national WCTU began, in 1887, to gather petitions in favor of the bill, Harper was optimistic. Senator Blair, the chair of the Senate Education and Labor Committee from 1881 to 1891, proposed to use federal taxes to help fund public schools in those states that had the highest levels of illiteracy. Since the South had high rates of illiteracy, millions of dollars would be distributed over a ten-year period to (segregated) black and white schools in the South. The proposed legislation would benefit Southern blacks who were severely disadvantaged financially, who had poor facilities and a lack of books because of unequal funding from their state education systems. Harper hoped that the WCTU's national campaign would increase the credibility of the group in the eyes of black male voters (who resented the way that they were negatively caricatured by its members as corrupt and easily manipulated anti-temperance voters) and of black women who might then join the WCTU.[95]

Thus, it must have disturbed Harper to hear the debate over the WCTU's support of the bill during its 1887 annual convention in Nashville, Tennessee. Thinking about white reconciliation across regional lines, some white members took a states' rights stance. They began to question the WCTU's official endorsement of and lobbying for the bill, now wondering if it inappropriately "put federal control over the local schools." Resisting this line of thinking, a Mrs. Snell reminded the majority of the (Northern) delegates of their earlier antislavery sympathies: "When I look into your faces I know that I am looking into the faces of women who were abolitionists, in favor of the freedom of the slave. You have not finished your work. The colored people of the South to-day are in slavery, the slavery of ignorance."[96] Frances Harper then rose in agreement to support this federal law, asking that the organization's commitment to national white reconciliation not leave blacks behind. Referring to the symbolic significance of holding their convention in a Southern state, she declared:

> In this meeting you have been clasping hands over the bloody chasm, but when Mrs. Snell gets up here and asks for education in the South, I can reach out my hands and clasp hands with Mrs. Snell. I belong to a race having suffered ages of oppression, you belong to a race having ages of education, domination, civilization, and I simply ask this body to really indorse the aims of this educational bill for the people of my race.

After listening to the debate for some time, WCTU president Frances Willard intervened and reminded the delegates why they were already petitioning for the bill. She persuaded them to approve a resolution reaffirming the organization's support of the bill, arguing that "I shall go home with my head bowed if a society which has repeatedly indorsed the Blair bill now say they never understood it. . . . I should think, what an aspersion on our intelligence! . . . [L]et us show to our Southern allies we want to help them educate that vote [the black vote] up beyond the being bought." Willard's defense problematically characterized black men as uneducated and easily manipulated into voting against temperance. Although the WCTU did go on record as reaffirming its support of the bill, Harper had reason to be concerned about the depth of its members' commitment to working for issues of concern to black Americans.[97]

To her *AME Church Review* readers Harper condemned those white women who maintained their racism, thereby denying the reality of the Reconstruction era's progress in terms of civil rights laws:

> Once between them and the Negro were vast disparities, which have been melting and disappearing. The war obliterated the disparity between freedom and slavery. The civil law blotted out the difference between disfranchisement and manhood suffrage. . . . With these old landmarks going and gone, one relic remains from the dead past, "Our social customs." In clinging to them let them [white women] remember that the most ignorant, vicious and degraded voter outranks, politically, the purest, best and most cultured woman in the South, and learn to look at the question of Christian affiliation on this subject. . . . Though scorn may curl her haughty lip, and fashion gather up her dainty robes from social contact, if your [black women's] lives are in harmony with God and Christly sympathy with man, you belong to the highest nobility in God's universe.

In this context Harper raised the specter of "ignorant" male voters who had more political power than elite and educated woman precisely because they had the right to vote; she did so to emphasize that pro-temperance women of both races and all classes must unite.[98] Harper lamented that political and legal improvements in the status of African Americans did not translate into comparable social changes or what she called "social contact." Invoking the Reconstruction era amendments to the constitution, she affirmed that blacks were citizens whose rights were legally protected. White women's insistence on enforcing racist "social customs" contributed to the undermining of the legal advancements that African Americans had made during Reconstruction.

Frances Harper filed her last annual report as national superintendent in 1890. By this time she was fed up with the recalcitrance and racism she faced from many white WCTU members. Harper consistently refused to mince words with her white allies. Historian Bettye Collier-Thomas suggests that, by the 1890s, some younger black women activists had moved beyond the strategies and approach of Frances Harper because they "favored a more direct frontal attack on racism in the woman's movement." In fact, Harper had launched "direct frontal" attacks on white women's racism ever since the 1860s, consistently trying to spark in them a sense of conscience and change. Harper concluded her 1890 annual report with the following:

> In closing this which may be my last report, permit me to thank the sisters who have helped in this department and sent me words of hope and cheer. To this nation God has given the talent of glorious opportunity. May it never be said to any of us: "I was afraid and hid thy talent in the earth." Afraid of the world's "dread laugh," afraid of Christless prejudices and hid thy talent in the dust of selfishness and worldly prudence.

"Christless prejudices" had kept the majority of the white membership and leadership of the WCTU from giving her and the black WCTU members the support, time, and respect they deserved.[99]

By 1890 Harper was in direct conflict with the organization's white leadership over the issue of whether the WCTU might try to gain white Southern support for suffrage by lobbying for a constitutional amendment for woman suffrage with restrictions attached. Harper knew that literacy requirements, in particular, could disproportionately limit poor Southern black women's access to the polls. The willingness of Willard and WCTU members' to entertain the possibility of supporting a restricted amendment for woman suffrage (this was never officially endorsed by the national organization) was a blow to Harper and her fight for universal suffrage. Such a move would disfranchise precisely those poor, uneducated black women whom Harper believed needed a full voice in their government. Collier-Thomas concludes, "It appeared to Harper that for the sake of expediency the WCTU was capitulating to southern racism. After 1890 her role in the WCTU was effectively diminished through a series of reorganizations that removed Harper from the Executive Committee and the Board of Superintendents."[100] As she clashed with the white leadership over the WCTU's Southern strategy, Harper's department was (not coincidentally) reorganized. This resulted in her being forced out of her national leadership positions.[101]

"A GREAT AND GLORIOUS FIRST PARTY"—BLACK POLITICS AND CIVIL RIGHTS IN THE 1890S

Like most black leaders, Frances Harper had to reconstruct her own politics by the end of the century. Her demotion within the WCTU in 1890, when she lost her position on its board of superintendents, was part of a wider trend of worsening race relations in the 1890s, as lynchings reached their peak and Jim Crow segregation laws were given official federal sanction by the U.S. Supreme Court in *Plessy v. Ferguson* (1896).[102] Black reformers such as Harper found themselves pursuing progressive politics in a conservative age.

In an 1891 symposium on "Temperance" in the *AME Church Review* Harper urged her readership to "[c]onsecrate, educate, agitate and legislate." Under the category "agitate," remembering her own recent experiences in the WCTU, Harper suggested to black women a path similar to her own—one that led to her recent departure from her WCTU leadership roles: "If you meet in any part of the country, women lacking breadth of soul, so that they wish to draw the color-line, when they draw the line at color, draw your line at self-respect and fight without them." Asking black women and men to "agitate" in order to "legislate," Harper prioritized a Christian politics: "Wherever your political influence is needed to vote against the liquor traffic,

This photograph of Frances Harper, from the 1890s, shows her in her seventies, with her hand resting on a table with three books, highlighting her self-presentation and identification as a successful author. This image of Harper appeared in a book by H. F. Kletzing entitled *Progress of a Race; or, The Remarkable Advancement of the American Negro from the bondage of slavery, ignorance, and poverty to the freedom of citizenship, intelligence, affluence, honor, and trust.*

let me simply say, vote as a Christian. . . . Is there another branch of the human race on this Western Hemisphere, which has more need of a righteous and just government than we colored people?" A government based more explicitly upon Christian precepts might better protect the rights of black Americans. Harper's essay also included a message to black men:

Men of my race, do not think when colored men are still murdered, lynched, and even burned for real or supposed crimes that our work is done, and that there is no need for us except as appendages to some political party or faction. With clear brains and earnest hearts strive not to patch up old parties, but to help to create, not a third party, but a great and glorious first party, first in numerical strength, first in moral power, first in spiritual influence, a party wearing sobriety as a crown, and righteousness as the girdle of its loins.

Loyalty to the Republican Party had not brought African Americans tangible results; Harper correctly suggested that the Republican Party had abandoned black voters and the cause of protecting blacks' civil rights. Given that black voters were being variously disenfranchised, manipulated, or taken for granted by the existing political parties, she bluntly suggested they could do more than be "the appendages of any political party." Harper's language seems to reject the Prohibition Party as merely a "third party" that could not represent them. Therefore, blacks should not work to "patch up" and repair it but should start anew with a completely different political party. This radical idea did not gain a significant amount of attention from African Americans, who generally decided to continue working from within the Republican Party for as long as possible. It shows, however, that Harper was still committed to legislation and partisan politics—to engaging and transforming the federal government, but now under a new "first party."[103]

Harper insisted that the overall condition of African Americans as citizens of the United States would not truly improve unless the central state served as their ally. Thus she never backed away from her conviction that a strong federal government could best support blacks' rights, even though she recognized it was unwilling to do so at that point. That same year (1891), Harper gave an important speech before the new National Council of Women, organized by Susan B. Anthony, May Wright Sewell, and Frances Willard. In her speech she raised her favored themes of patriotism, the proper role of the federal government in reform, and the evils of lynching. Although the council patronizingly chose her topic ("Duty to Dependent Races"), Harper reframed the issue for her predominantly white audience. At the start of her talk she asserted she would be discussing "the negro not as a mere dependent" but as "a member of the body politic who has a claim upon the nation for justice, simple justice, which is the right of every race, upon the government for protection, which is the rightful claim of every citizen." Insisting that blacks were good patriots who had fought in the American Revolution and all subsequent wars for the United States, she demanded that whites fully recognize and accept their legitimate claims to citizenship. Harper drew a clear distinction between the necessary role of the national government in contrast to that of state governments: "When parents are too poor or selfish to spare the labor of their children from the factories, and the State too indifferent or short-sighted to enforce their education by law, then let the Government save its future citizens from the results of cupidity in the parents or short-sightedness in the State." To Harper, a focus on states' rights was dangerous because, without federal regulation or enforcement, states would try to control black Americans within their borders. She knew that blacks had more to lose if states alone controlled access to rights and protections. Supporting national child labor laws, anti-lynching legislation, and the Blair Education Bill (none of which passed), Harper persisted in her view of the federal government as the most important site and agent for significant social change.[104]

"INTO THE NEW COMMONWEALTH OF FREEDOM"— HARPER'S IOLA LEROY AND RACIAL UPLIFT

Just after Harper's departure from her leadership positions in the WCTU, she published *Iola Leroy, or Shadows Uplifted* (1892), her first full-length novel. Harper wrote fiction and poetry to reach a broader audience of people who might not be as interested in a nonfiction article or book, and *Iola Leroy* is a piece of fiction intended to motivate readers to change their real world. As Melba Boyd points out, "the appeal at the end of *Iola Leroy* is a calling to black people to commit themselves to the struggle of institution building and racial uplift in the face of white supremacist terrorism at the turn of the nineteenth century." Abolitionist William Still wrote the introduction to the novel's second edition, in which he predicted that Harper's novel would attract a substantial audience of black and white readers. White temperance women and their families who knew Harper from her leadership role in the WCTU might read it as well as African Americans in the North. He also suggested that "the thousands of colored Sunday-schools in the South, in casting about for an interesting, moral story-book, full of practical lessons, will not be content to be without 'IOLA LEROY, OR SHADOWS UPLIFTED.'"[105] By the 1890s Harper was a popular poet and fiction writer who had developed a significant following. Throughout her life, she supported herself by selling her books; we do not know how many copies of *Iola Leroy* were published, but we know at least that it "was reprinted four times in four years."[106] Harper saw her fiction as an integral part of her political activism, not as a diversion from it.

The main character, Iola, is a light-skinned black woman who serves as a role model for Harper's readers. Significantly, Iola commits herself to the improvement of her race and refuses to reject her friends and relatives by marrying a white man (a marriage that would have required her to pass as white and live a life of lies in the North). She declares to her white suitor, "I intend . . . to cast my lot with the freed people as a helper, teacher, and friend." Harper's *Iola Leroy* raises the question as to who gets to determine their own racial identity and how much the government or other outside forces can make that decision for a person. In the novel the characters' (mixed) racial identities are not fixed but are determined by parents, laws, judges, customs, and the characters themselves. Giulia Fabi argues that Iola's "choice in favor of the African American community turns blackness from a mark of inferiority into the emblem of heroism." Harper's novel lauds light-skinned individuals who chose to be identified as black, arguing that their choice was heroic precisely because it was dangerous and difficult to live as a black person in the United States. When Dr. Frank Latimer, also a light-skinned African American, asks Iola to marry him and move back to the South to help the recently freed slaves, Iola responds positively. Together, "they esteemed it a blessed privilege to stand on the threshold of a new era and labor for those who had passed from the old oligarchy of slavery into the new commonwealth of freedom."[107] Iola, her new husband, and her brother risk their safety by choosing to become black political activists and social reformers in the Reconstruction South. Harper valorizes their choice to prioritize conscience, social responsibility, and racial uplift over selfishness or fear.[108]

UNITY—HARPER AND THE NATIONAL ASSOCIATION OF COLORED WOMEN

Frances Harper's last significant group affiliation after the WCTU was her participation in the formation of the National Association of Colored Women (NACW) in 1896. At age seventy-one, she was made a vice president of the NACW; Mary Church Terrell, representing a younger generation that came of age after the Civil War, became its first president. Harper's 1896 talk at the NACW convention, entitled "The Ideal Home," reflected the self-help approach outlined in her 1891 "Temperance" article. In addition to being a positive force for affirmation and activism, the NACW represented black women's collective sense that a separate national organization was necessary. The creation of the NACW was a coming of age for well-established, ambitious black women's groups. It was also a direct response to the increasingly hostile racial climate in the last decade of the nineteenth century. Supporting black women's role as economic providers and political activists while also embracing the notion of women's difference, Harper's deepest convictions about human equality *and* difference motivated her ideas about how to achieve reform.[109]

Fifty-five black women's clubs joined together as dues-paying members of the NACW in 1896. Throughout the decade Frances Harper's name and reform legacy remained strong. Out of the fifty-five clubs that formed the NACW, nine were explicitly pro-temperance or WCTU local unions, of which four were named after Harper.[110] In its annual report to the NACW, a Pennsylvania black women's group named after Harper wrote of her glowingly as an activist and a writer: "We have no need to explain the meaning of this name, for the person who does not know of the grand and noble woman who has done so much for the good cause of Temperance and who has contributed so largely to the literature of the race, must indeed be obscure." The NACW adopted pro-temperance resolutions and officially recognized the influence of the WCTU in black women's organized reform work. Frances Harper, Lucy Thurman, and the other black women who were still WCTU members were now also in the NACW. They successfully encouraged the organization to pass the following resolution: "Resolved, That we do heartily endorse the W.C.T.U. as an absolute necessity to the best and spiritual uplifting of all people." By 1899 Harper was no longer listed as a vice president of NACW, yet she was a featured speaker at that year's national convention, with a talk on "Racial Literature."[111]

$\mathcal{F}$rances Harper's political thought illustrates the ways in which race affected the possibility of black women's political activism and participation in reform. During and after the Civil War, black Americans had placed high hopes in a strong federal government, which they hoped could protect and empower them by guaranteeing their full rights as citizens and political actors with valuable contributions to offer their country. When the federal government offered the most hope in terms of political and military protection for African Americans during the Civil War and Reconstruction, Harper was optimistic and asked for more. As the white supremacist "Redeemers" reclaimed the South and actively suppressed blacks' hopes for political, economic, and social equality and respect, however, Harper became concerned that the federal government would not live up to its responsibilities. By the 1890s blacks faced heightened doubts as to whether their expectations of the federal government were realistic. Harper's own strenuous efforts to work within the largest women's organization of the nineteenth century were based in large part on her faith in federal solutions to moral problems. Her hopes for an interracial alliance faltered as it became clear that white women's national reform agenda did not include federal anti-lynching laws or other laws aimed at securing blacks' civil rights. Harper and the other black women who created and joined the NACW did so with a clear sense that they had fewer options for interracial political and reform efforts in the 1890s, but they did so also with the persistent conviction that they must organize on their own for improved legal, political, and social conditions for all black Americans.

Frances Willard

FEDERAL REGULATIONS FOR THE COMMON GOOD

As president of the Woman's Christian Temperance Union, the largest women's organization in the nineteenth-century United States, Frances Elizabeth Willard (1839–1898) helped shape the political, reform, and legislative goals of a generation of middle- and upper-class white women. Willard's strength as WCTU leader came from her brilliant melding of an insistent demand for women's direct participation in politics and power with the Victorian rhetoric of true womanhood. Noting that women made up approximately two-thirds of most Christian congregations, Willard suggested that they were generally more religious, moral, and pious than men. She identified her priorities as "influencing legislation so that what is physically wrong and morally wrong shall not, on the statute books of a Christian land, be set down as legally right;—and to this end putting the ballot in woman's hands for the protection of her little ones and of her home." Rather than act as a barrier, women's greater purity and religiosity warranted their full participation in politics and public life. As Willard put it: "Half of the world's wisdom, more than half its purity, and nearly all its gentleness, are to-day to be set down on woman's credit side."[1]

Willard wanted women to help create a stronger nation that would enforce religious and moral precepts through its laws. Christianity would legitimize the increased power of the central state and allow

Frances Willard served as dean of the Women's College at Northwestern University in the early 1870s, just a few years before she became president of the National Woman's Christian Temperance Union in 1879.

the government to regulate the lives of its citizens for their own good. Willard celebrated the notion of women's moral difference and used it to expand women's options, seeking a public role for her sex. She disagreed with those who claimed that wage work in the public sphere threatened or diminished women's moral purity: "[A] true woman is womanly in whatever she chooses to do and wherever she chooses to live. Whether she be found at the bar, in the pulpit, the Senate or bench, she may still be a woman in the highest, noblest sense." Women's exclusion from professional careers, as well as from voting and partisan politics, she believed, could only have dire consequences for the nation.[2]

Participating in an ongoing struggle in national identity formation, Willard represents a new generation of American women who accepted—even demanded—a stronger federal state after the Civil War. In their view, Congress should pass constitutional amendments for woman suffrage and for the prohibition of alcohol. Although Frances Watkins Harper similarly supported constitutional amendments for suffrage and prohibition, she often framed her arguments for more federal power around the need to protect the civil rights of individuals from violations by the states. In contrast, Willard openly called upon the federal government (and states, for that matter) to limit individuals' rights in order to protect the common good.

"BORN TO A FATE"—WILLARD'S ANTISLAVERY AND REFORM GENEALOGY

Frances Willard identified herself with the Free Soil and Republican parties and with the antebellum era abolition movement. A devout Methodist from a New England family, Frances Willard was born in western New York and then lived until she was seven in Ohio, where her father, Josiah Willard, was preparing to be a minister by attending Oberlin College (the first college in the United States to accept both blacks and women). Health concerns prompted Josiah to leave Oberlin and resume a career as a farmer, this time on the southeastern Wisconsin frontier. Both her parents were abolitionists, pro-temperance abstainers from alcohol, and Free Soilers, who later became Republican Party loyalists. Josiah Willard successfully ran for a seat in the Wisconsin legislature as a member of the Free Soil Party in 1848. The Free Soil Party, a coalition of Whigs, Democrats, and Liberty Party members, expressed the idea that the U.S. Constitution was an antislavery document that disallowed the federal government from extending or supporting slavery. Free Soilers opposed the extension of slavery, promoted free white labor in the territories, and discouraged black migration to those free territories. To build a larger coalition (including disgruntled Northern Democrats), former Liberty Party members abandoned any calls for guarantees of civil rights protections for free blacks, including voting rights, in the new party's platform. As an adult Willard made compromises similar to those of the Free Soilers who sacrificed protections of free blacks' civil rights. In her case, she abandoned the legislative and reform priorities of black WCTU members in order to build up its Southern white membership.[3]

The Willard family's strong involvement in partisan politics shaped Frances's own lifelong engagement in politics and reform. Even though her father was a legislator, Willard came to believe that her mother was the more political of her parents, but her ambitions had been thwarted by women's exclusion from partisan politics. Her mother, Mary Hill Willard, had been a teacher for eleven years before her marriage and taught their three children at home until a schoolhouse was finally built in their rural community. In Frances's 1889 autobiography she speculated, "Mother was a very motherly woman, and a tremendously potential politician, though I don't think she ever knew it, and I only discovered it within the last fourteen years. I never knew quite what was the matter with her, but in these days I believe she was born to be a Senator, and never got there." Political ambitions for women drove Willard throughout her life. In 1893, only five years before she died, for instance, she recorded in her journal, "Had vision in the night of a novel I might write in which a woman becomes Pres't of the United States after a complete Revolution which she leads!" The Willards lived on the Wisconsin frontier until 1858, when the family moved to Evanston, Illinois, so that Frances and her sister could study at the North Western Female College while her older brother prepared to become a Methodist minister at the Garrett Biblical Institute.[4]

Even as a young girl Frances Willard believed she "'was born to a fate.'" Accordingly, she never envisioned her first career, as a teacher, to be her last. She explained, "Women were allowed to do so few things then, that my ideas were quite vague as to the what and why . . . but I knew that I wanted to write, and that I would speak in public if I dared, though I didn't say this last, not even to mother." This grander vision propelled her to search for teaching jobs with more responsibility; she became preceptress of the coeducational Genesee Wesleyan Seminary in western New York and was appointed president of the newly founded Evanston College for Ladies in 1871 at age thirty-two. After the college merged with Northwestern University in 1873, she became dean of the women's college. Willard resigned the following year over disagreements with Charles Fowler, a prestigious Methodist minister and the new president of Northwestern University, about whether she could run the women's college autonomously. Unfortunately, Charles

Fowler was also Willard's former fiancé with whom she had broken off her engagement in 1862, concerned that she was not truly in love. She was ambivalent about taking on the role of wife to the exclusion of all other ambitions. Their subsequent struggle over her autonomy and power at Northwestern led her to resign and to turn away from higher education, in search of a new calling.[5]

That same year (1874), Willard joined the newly formed Woman's Christian Temperance Union, becoming its national corresponding secretary and the president of its Chicago chapter. However, she had not yet definitively chosen the WCTU as her calling; she continued to experiment with the possibility of developing a career as a public lecturer, by now a less controversial or problematic choice for women reformers than it had been for Wright and the Grimkés. An opportunity to demonstrate her skills—and save souls—occurred when she was hired by the famous evangelist Reverend Dwight L. Moody in 1877. Although she was exceptionally well received, Willard was unhappy at being confined by Moody to leading revivals in mostly sex-segregated "ladies meetings." When she resigned, she cited as a reason her discontent with the subordinate role of women in Moody's revivals and explained that she did not have the same vision as Moody. His priority was the "regeneration of men," whereas she defined her priority as creating a nation governed by Christian morals and values. Hence, legislation that contradicted God's laws would need to be rescinded and new laws put into place.[6]

Women must be at the forefront of these sweeping changes in the nature of the state as agent of reform and regulator of personal behavior. With this revelation Willard turned decisively toward work within a Christian women's organization, where she could avoid the limitations placed on her by powerful men such as Fowler and Moody. She was elected president of the WCTU in 1879 and held that position until her death in 1898. The WCTU was built on the base of the 1873–1874 Christian but nonsectarian Woman's Crusade against saloons. This movement of Christian women, who prayed in front of saloons demanding they be shut down, spread throughout the American Midwest and some parts of the Northeast. Willard celebrated the WCTU's origins in this spontaneous crusade, describing it as "that wonderful Crusade" that "broke down sectarian barriers." By appealing to all Protestant denominations and even by reaching out to and including as members some Catholics and Jews, the WCTU

distinguished itself from most other faith-based organizations, with
Methodist, Baptist, Episcopalian, Catholic, and Presbyterian women
overcoming their doctrinal differences to achieve morals-based legislation and other shared reform goals. As its president Willard proudly
encouraged the group's nondenominational philosophy of Christian
reform. Her emphasis on nonsectarian religious inclusiveness helped
build a broad movement of women who could insist on their right to
full participation in their nation's politics and laws.[7]

INCREASING WOMEN'S POWER—THE HOME PROTECTION BALLOT

The first WCTU president, Annie Wittenmyer, had been an ardent
anti-suffragist who, like the anti-feminist reformer Catharine Beecher
before her, believed that women must use indirect influence (moral
suasion) alone rather than sully themselves with corrupt partisan
politics. In 1876 Willard gave her first speech at a WCTU convention
in support of woman suffrage. She began by acknowledging the basic
logic and fairness of a rights-based Lockean argument of government
by consent of the people. Willard agreed with other women's rights
activists such as Stanton and Anthony who echoed American Revolutionary doctrine by insisting on taxation only with representation.
As a single woman and the daughter of a widow, Willard explained,
"I thought that women ought to have the ballot as I paid the hard-
earned taxes upon my mother's cottage home." Although she agreed
that governments could exist only with the consent of the people (as
Locke put it: "Politick Societies all began from a voluntary, and the
mutual agreement of Men"), she declined to draw on these arguments
as the basis for her support of woman suffrage. Willard pragmatically
determined that most women—especially married women who did
not pay direct taxes—might not find taxation without representation
a compelling or personally relevant cause. As for her own rights as a
taxpayer, she confessed, "—but I never said as much—somehow the
motive did not command my heart. For my own sake, I had not the
courage, but I have for thy sake, dear native land."[8]

Thus, whereas activists such as Stanton and Anthony extended
Locke's argument that government must have the consent of its male
citizens and made claims for the necessity of *female* citizens' full participation in their government, Willard highlighted instead what she

termed the "magnificent burdens" of being a republican citizen. Only for the good of the nation, out of a sense of moral duty, would she and other Christian women demand the vote. Willard claimed a place for women in the republic by conceiving of their citizenship as vital to the nation. She played a crucial role in popularizing woman suffrage far beyond the relatively small number who demanded the right to vote based on women's natural rights and equality. As WCTU president, Willard understood that women were more likely to demand the vote as a means to protect their homes and families, cities and towns: "Not rights, but duties; not her need alone, but that of her children and her country; not the 'woman' but the 'human' question is stirring women's hearts." Reconceptualizing citizenship around the obligation to vote and to reform American politics and society, she strategically merged the more radical demand for suffrage with religiosity and conventional conceptions of womanhood.[9]

In this 1876 speech to the WCTU delegates, Willard challenged president Wittenmyer's anti-suffrage policies by promoting what she brilliantly termed the "Home Protection Ballot." Willard chose a rhetoric of Christian duty and obligation as most effective for mobilizing masses of women to activism. The familiar language of evangelical Christianity helped make her message more palatable. Willard shared her "conversion" narrative with WCTU members, explaining how her support of woman suffrage came from divine inspiration. She had prayed to God and received a vision of herself leading the organization to support the "home protection ballot" for women. By strategically adopting this phrase, as rhetorician Carol Mattingly suggests, "Willard recognized the enculturating effect of words, hoping to change their customary use in order to alter modes of thinking." Framing women's access to the vote in terms highlighting their role as mothers and wives made the idea seem considerably less threatening. She explained that women's sense of duty to God and nation, not to self, "made them willing to take up for their homes and country's sake the burdens of that citizenship they would never have sought for their own." Citizenship would place "burdens" on women; only duty made them reluctantly accept these burdens.[10]

By using the metaphor of housekeeping, Willard domesticated and tamed women's otherwise bold, threatening demands for suffrage and full involvement in national partisan politics.[11] Responding to those who claimed that women were too pure to enter the corrupt world of politics, Willard declared, "My friend, we don't expect to leave political affairs as we find them; not at all." As she later explained in a speech before the International Council of Women in 1888, "I want to say to my brothers, that we are coming in . . . just as we should go into a bachelor's hall. We should take along broom and dust-brushes and dust-pans, open the windows and ventilate the place. . . . [I]f ever a place needed 'clarin' out we think it is the kitchen of Uncle Sam." Ideally, homes were safe, clean, protected spaces run by women; by extension, cities and government would be safer and do more to cure societal ills if women helped run them. Willard expanded this vision to the entire world, stating, "Indeed, if I were asked the mission of the ideal woman, I would reply: IT IS TO MAKE THE WHOLE WORLD HOMELIKE."[12]

This language of domesticating the world was not merely metaphorical. It reflected Willard's missionary ambitions abroad. Indeed, the Christian evangelical members of the WCTU acted on this missionizing impulse by founding the World's Woman's Christian Temperance Union in 1884 in order to spread "modern" women's progressive and civilizing ideas across the less civilized world. With a program focused on spreading American women's values abroad—especially evangelical Christianity, anti-alcohol ideology, and women's rights—the World's WCTU established affiliates in more than forty countries, with about one million members by the 1920s. As historian Louise Newman points out, like "so many others in the woman's movement, [Willard's] advocacy of Christian, Anglo-Saxon civilization prevented her from altering her presumptions regarding the higher status of [white] women in 'civilized,' as opposed to 'primitive,' societies."[13]

Willard's belief in women's difference from men made their participation crucial as "joint rulers" of the nation. Like Sarah Grimké before her, Willard thought in terms of "co-equality," defining this as a "joint-partnership" between males and females in all realms of life. Again, co-equality did not mean sameness but allowed for a recognition of women's moral difference and biological and social role as mothers. Co-equality also gave Willard a rationale for women's participation in politics not only as voters but as legislators. She advocated "the co-equal power of the co-partners, man and woman, in working out the problem of human destiny." Insisting that civil society should be founded on consent, in this context she argued that neither men nor women should have to live under or obey laws they did not help to create.[14]

"AT THE CAPITOL"—WCTU WOMEN LEARN TO LOBBY AT THE STATE AND NATIONAL LEVELS

Under Willard's expert guidance, the national WCTU by 1881 had officially endorsed woman suffrage, and by 1885 it was campaigning for federal, state, and local laws and had even endorsed a partisan political party—the Prohibition, or "Home Protection Prohibition" Party. Willard's approach for the first time recruited large numbers of women to the suffrage cause. The strategic value of her approach is revealed in the numbers: in the mid-1890s, the newly combined National American Woman Suffrage Association (NAWSA) had only 13,000 members whereas Willard's WCTU had well over 150,000 members. Janet Giele claims that the WCTU's "organization and membership in many places kept suffrage sentiment alive when the official suffrage associations were tiny or nonexistent."[15]

How did the WCTU organize to fight for suffrage? Ever the diplomat, Willard took her job as president of all WCTU members very seriously. She began by reassuring the more conservative members that local unions could interpret the national organization's support for woman suffrage in a variety of ways. First, no one had to work for suffrage. Second, as we will see, she bowed to racism by allowing Southern white WCTU members to attempt to add educational requirements to any expansion of the ballot, thereby sacrificing the citizenship rights of black women in order to gain more white members nationally. Third, each local and state union could decide to fight for the more limited women's *temperance* ballot—state or local laws that allowed women to vote in elections only when temperance-related issues such as "local option" (a town or county could vote to be dry) liquor licenses or Sunday blue laws, which restricted all sale of alcohol on Sundays, were on the ballot. Willard supported WCTU members who adopted this narrow interpretation of "home protection," but she always repeated her message that women needed full enfranchisement at the national level in order truly to protect their homes and families from social problems ranging from intemperance and immorality to low wages for wage-earning mothers. Willard rightly predicted that WCTU members' support for full suffrage at the national level would solidify as they experienced the difficult realities of trying to gain or defeat legislation (through lobbying) without the right to vote.[16]

When WCTU members resolved to gain the passage of legislation at the state or national level, they put into place a sophisticated, coordinated grassroots lobbying campaign modeled on one that Willard had organized in Illinois before she became the group's national president in 1879. First, WCTU members had to find men in the state legislature (or, for national legislation, in the U.S. Congress) who would be willing to sponsor their bill. Second, they initiated a large petition drive, with signatures from both men and women, to send to the legislature. As with the earlier abolitionist campaigns, the WCTU's petition drives involved middle-class white women (who may not have ever broached political topics outside of their own homes) in politicking door-to-door. In a more positive assessment of door-to-door campaigning than Sarah Grimké gave, Willard argued that if WCTU members were allowed into other women's homes long enough to present their pro-temperance and pro-suffrage positions, they could motivate these apolitical, isolated women into action: "The quiet house-to-house canvass of an army of women who could not speak in public has brought home to the fireside and wife and mother, with little time to read, reasons enforced by practical illustrations taken from every-day life; and thus hosts of friends for woman's temperance ballot have been raised up where all were passive and inert before." The results were not just in the moral suasion of women by women. Willard presented statistics to show that WCTU members had made a difference in (men's) voting results as well: "Of the 832 towns that voted on the question of license while our campaign was in progress, 645 declared for no license—a much larger number than ever before; and experienced men say it was largely due to the Home Protection Petition work of the W.C.T Unions." Third, WCTU women visited the legislators' local offices and brought with them prominent community members who favored the bill, proving to legislators that the proposed law had widespread support beyond the nonvoting female members of the WCTU. Finally, as the legislature convened, WCTU lobbyists gathered at the Capitol from around the state (or nation) for a final push.[17]

Although Stanton and Anthony's National Woman Suffrage Association (NWSA) met regularly in Washington, D.C., between 1869 and 1890 in order to lobby Congress, Willard's WCTU was the first women's organization successfully to use grassroots methods to build real support on a range of issues at the local, state, and national levels. The WCTU's strategies, identified by Nancy Cott as "modern methods of pressure-group politics," were adopted by a host of other new black and white women's groups in the 1890s and early part of the twentieth century, such as the General Federation of Women's Clubs, the National Consumers' League, the National Association of Colored Women, and the National American Woman Suffrage Association.[18]

"NO SEX IN CITIZENSHIP"—WOMEN'S CITIZENSHIP OBLIGATIONS IN A CHRISTIAN NATION

Willard devoted significant attention to defining citizenship. In an 1888 speech to the International Council of Women, she declared she must continue her own activism until "a young woman shall be able to say *to the state,* 'I am a part of you, just as much as anything that breathes.'" Identifying women as integral parts of the state, as full citizens (just as men were), Willard argued that their incorporation into every aspect of government and society was crucial. Her goal of a real unity between women and their nations meant that she carefully construed women's lack of voting rights as damaging to the nation rather than to individual women. Willard mourned what she termed "the state's irreparable loss" when women, who were, in her judgment, more caring and compassionate than men, could not act as full citizens, directly making the laws, voting, or sitting on juries.[19]

Women citizens, Willard stated, must help the United States become a nation whose fundamental Christianity was reflected in its laws and social order. They "*ought* to—ask for power to help forward the coming of their Lord in government." Like Christian fundamentalists today, or civil rights activists of the 1950s and 1960s, or perfectionist abolitionists of the antebellum era, Willard envisioned Christian moral values embodied in secular laws. To persuade the WCTU's middle-class white members of their duties as citizens, Willard argued that they must participate in national affairs because each piece of legislation alternatively reflected or rejected good morals and biblical teachings. Rejecting the conventional view of citizens as exclusively male, she predicted that "civilization, in proportion as it becomes Christianized, will make increasing demands upon creation's gentler half; that the Ten Commandments and the Sermon on the Mount are voted up or voted down upon election day; and that a military exigency requires the army of the Prince of Peace to call out its reserves." Willard desired a nonsectarian Christian nation, believing that women would guide it to its highest level of civilization.[20]

For women to be able to create this ideal Christian state, they must be full citizens. Willard could not accept the U.S. Supreme Court's ruling in *Minor v. Happersett* of 1875, just a year after the WCTU was formed, that women were indeed citizens but did not automatically have the right to vote. The plaintiffs—a husband and wife team, both of whom were lawyers—had argued that women's inclusion as citizens in the Fourteenth Amendment assured their right to vote. But the Court ruled that each state could decide the issue (just as each state could impose its own limitations on male voters). Willard rejected the Court's assertion that disfranchised adult women really could be full citizens. Describing a Prohibition Party convention, she noted that "above the platform . . . the loyal white ribboners [WCTU members] . . . had flung their pennon forth, '*No sex in citizenship.*' They know the Supreme Court had said there was none, but they knew also that those cannot really be citizens who have no voice in making the laws they must obey." Citizenship would be wrongly sexed, or gendered, until all men and women (or, at least, all whites) could vote.[21]

Making suffrage an integral part of women's obligations of full citizenship became an increasingly urgent priority for Willard during her WCTU presidency. In an article published in 1898, just before she died, Willard argued that one of "the strongest points in favor of woman suffrage" was "that it is not right to . . . inflict penalties upon a class that had no hand in determining what those penalties should be, to govern one-half of the human race by the other half." The Supreme Court's unfair and illogical 1875 ruling would remain the final word on the subject, Willard knew, until it could be overturned by a constitutional amendment for woman suffrage.[22]

As part of her plan to redefine citizenship, Willard realized that full citizenship must be separated from men's military service. Instead, she highlighted women's positive intellectual contributions as writers and speakers for reform. Recognizing that reformative words must become as important as or more important than men's physical strength or military service, Willard argued that Americans must "perceive brain, and not bulk, to be the rational basis of citizenship." Since many individual men never served in the military but were still eligible to vote, she pointed out that military service could not be a determining criterion for any particular citizen's right to vote. She challenged politicians: "Pray tell us when the law was promulgated that we must analyze the vote at an election, and throw out the ballots of all men aged and decrepit, halt and blind?"

She further claimed that women voters would be incorruptible because they possessed pacifist "mother hearts," which would enable them to calmly state, for instance, "'I will not give my sons to be butchered in great battles,' and 'we would have international arbitration'" rather than war. By the end of the century, at least, those women reformers who espoused pacifism and attempted to decouple military service from male citizenship were on the defensive, as the country prepared itself for its first major imperialist ventures abroad.[23]

Even as she dismissed this classic theory of citizenship based on military service, Willard recognized the appeal of military language and its links to patriotic citizenship. She therefore mobilized military metaphors throughout her writings. By calling on women to use their "great guns of influence" at election time, for instance, she identified voting itself as an equivalent to military service that could be performed by women. Women's service would be inherent in their moral votes; these "guns" would not harm people but improve society. Willard implored, "Only give us the opportunity to turn [women's public sentiment] to account where in the least time it can achieve the most! Let the *great guns of influence,* now pointing into vacancy, *be swung to the level of benignant use* and pointed on election day straight into the faces of the foe!" Willard's ironic fondness for military metaphors (given her repeated assertion that women were inherently "gentler") reflects her recognition of their rhetorical power and her frustration that women were kept from the "battle" or the fray of politics. Alluding to Julia Ward Howe's *Battle Hymn of the Republic,* she reconfigured women as Christian soldiers who had the power (the "great guns of influence"), but as yet these guns were unloaded and not aimed at the enemies of their homes such as saloon keepers, drunkards, and corrupt politicians. Using this metaphor of crusading soldiers, Willard insisted that the United States could become a Christian nation only with women's participation in partisan politics.[24]

"WE SHALL INTERFERE WITH YOUR PERSONAL LIBERTY"— WILLARD'S PRO-REGULATORY STANCE

Willard developed a political theory in favor of a strong federal government whose laws could restrain individuals' behavior. To justify and explain the WCTU's pro-regulatory work, she provided a theory of reform based in large part on her understanding of Edmund Burke's opposition to unrestrained natural rights. Although not recognized as a serious political thinker, Willard explicitly engaged the ideas of eighteenth-century British politicians and thinkers such as Burke and Locke. (Fanny Wright is most similar in that she was deeply influenced by the Scottish common sense philosophers and by her contemporary discussions with philosopher Jeremy Bentham, utopian socialist Robert Owen, and republican Thomas Jefferson.) Willard drew on Burke in demanding that the state legally impose moral standards such as temperance on all its citizens. She echoed his emphasis on duty and order over liberty and similarly prioritized the needs of the collective civil society over the rights of individuals.[25]

Willard suggested that membership in a civil society implies an acceptance of burdens (including restrictions on alcohol consumption) for the greater good of that society: "I felt, girl as I was, that *the loss was not a small one to the country I loved, when she lost my vote.* The Republic profited but half, when it might have registered the full force of our home teaching; it needed mother and all 'the women folks' to offset the self-indulgent vote that sheltered the liquor traffic and other crimes under the aegis of law." Here, Willard transformed her girlhood sorrow of learning that she would not be able to vote into altruistic sorrow for her country. Her comment about men's "self-indulgent vote" drew on the ideas of Edmund Burke, who stated, "Every kind of government . . . required that a man should surrender part of his natural rights to obtain those that belong to society; in a word, that he should forego part of his liberty for the security of the remainder." Viewing individual freedoms as potential dangers, Willard joined Burke in condemning "the lawless days of the French Revolution." She celebrated, for instance, "that noblest of patriots and martyrs," Madame Roland, who "said as her last words, 'O, Liberty! what crimes are committed in thy sacred name.'"[26]

Willard's political theory explicitly addressed the necessity of passing laws to protect people by regulating and limiting their individual liberties. Historian Jean Baker mistakenly claims that "Willard never addressed the issue of infringing on the personal liberties of citizens to engage in what for most was merely a recreation, not an addiction." In fact, as a moralist and a prohibitionist, Willard openly advocated legislation that was explicitly restrictive. To objections that the legal prohibition of alcohol unfairly restricted individuals' free will, Willard had a sophisticated response. She selectively drew upon and quoted the politicians Edmund Burke and William Gladstone to justify legal restrictions of all sorts. Willard accepted John Locke's (and Burke's) notion that the state was originally a compact voluntarily made by the people, but she also agreed with Burke that the compact should not later be dissolved. Burke wanted to uphold traditional ways and customs whenever possible but was not opposed to reform. As he put it, "A state without the means of some change is without the means of its conservation."[27] The strength of the British constitution, he argued, was its amendability, which allowed for non-revolutionary change, thereby ensuring the safety and integrity of the nation. The United States, too, could be improved by carefully and gradually amending its constitution. Willard argued, "the people being sovereign, being themselves the original source of power, may put into their constitution whatsoever they please." Willard's vision represented a more democratic process of constitutional change but was also devoted to maintaining the nation-state at the expense of individual rights.[28]

Burke's insistence on the necessity of restrictive laws helped Willard justify legal prohibitions on alcohol. Advocating restrictions on individual liberty in order to protect the state and its citizens from those who might act irresponsibly, Burke wrote in his 1791 *Letter to a Member of the [French] National Assembly,* "Men are qualified for civil liberty in exact proportion to their disposition to put moral chains upon their own appetites; in proportion as their love of justice is above their rapacity. . . . Society cannot exist unless a controlling power upon will and appetite be placed somewhere. . . . [M]en of intemperate minds cannot be free. Their passions forge their fetters."[29] Burke's logic worked well for the prohibitionist Willard, who saw intemperance as a threat to civil society and the prohibition of alcohol as a reasonable regulation to help control those who could not control themselves—all in the interest of the collective well-being of the state and its citizens.

Willard made a comprehensive case against individual liberty and for the common good in her 1883 book, *Woman and Temperance.* She articulated these ideas early on and remained true to them over the course of her almost two-decade tenure as president of the WCTU. Willard explained that she supported legal regulations "so that we can dwell together in this good and pleasant estate of brotherly kindness, and mould our laws so that they shall illustrate Gladstone's motto, 'The state should make it as easy as possible for everybody to do right.'" Like Sarah Grimké, Willard feared that individuals could not fully control their own passions; the state would make it easy for people to do right by passing laws condoning—or forbidding and punishing—certain behaviors. Legal regulations, to Willard, were a natural result of the progress of civilization. Demonstrating an easy familiarity with Burke, she pointed out, "Edmund Burke says that when man enters the civil out of the solitary state, he relinquishes the very first of personal liberties upon the threshold. What is that? The liberty to defend himself—he must resign his case to judge and jury." Once an individual becomes part of civil society, he or she has to live by its rules; in this case, an impartial judicial system must replace violence as the way to defend oneself—in Burke's words, "Government is a contrivance of human wisdom to provide for human *wants*. . . . Among these wants is to be reckoned the want . . . of a sufficient restraint upon their passions. Society requires not only that the passions of individuals should be subjected, but that even in the mass . . . the inclinations of men should frequently be thwarted, their will controlled, and their passions brought into subjection." For Willard, a stronger state, with the power of coercion to enforce its values through its laws, was a marker of a "civilized" society. Willard's talk of advancing civilization fit with her view that the entire (less civilized) world would benefit from the types of legal changes that WCTU members were seeking in the United States, ranging from prohibition to the right to vote for women.[30]

Imbued with late eighteenth-century Burkean thought, Frances Willard challenged a developing post–Civil War legal culture that championed individual rights. In their battle for the prohibition of alcohol, "radical drys" such as Willard espoused an Anglo-American legal culture based on the idea of the convergence of law and morality. "Radical prohibitionists" would not accept any regulation of alcohol such as licensing and taxing, but only its prohibition. Laws should not be the result of corrupt political compromises, Willard believed, but must embody moral truths and strict prohibitions, as in the biblical tradition of Mosaic law. Historian Richard Hamm argues that, after the Civil War, this legal tradition lost ground as lawyers began to promote individual rights and liberties in order to protect against possible "governmental tyranny." Yet, in the decades after the Civil War, many reformers (if not lawyers) promoted the passage of laws to regulate behavior and create an increasingly moral society, ranging from the Comstock Acts of 1873 to age-of-consent laws at the turn of the twentieth century.[31]

Whereas woman's rights activists such as suffragist Elizabeth Cady Stanton and free love advocate Victoria Woodhull embraced a Lockean championing of natural rights and individual liberty, prohibitionists such as Frances Willard prioritized regulation and order. Viewing individualism as a sign of backwardness, ignorance, and even lawlessness, Willard believed that citizens would accept restrictive laws if parents, educators, and ministers took responsibility for inculcating in all children the value and good sense of a well-regulated civil society. Edmund Burke argued that "the *restraints* on men, as well as their liberties, are to be reckoned among their *rights.*" Similarly, Willard insisted that those who accepted "the clear-cut theory of a restricted liberty" as the "benignant basis" of civilized life would not miss their unrestricted "personal liberty." Only those who failed to heed the "good opinion of the law" would be so reckless as to, in Willard's words, "project their ignorant and lawless individuality across the wide sweep of its sharp, relentless circle, to their wounding and their hurt." Reckless freedom would hurt the individual and the state and, certainly, did not warrant protection from the state.[32]

The pro-regulatory positions of WCTU members and of those in the turn-of-the-century Social Gospel movement exemplify the persistence of this Anglo-American legal tradition, which supported Mosaic morality over base individualism. Radical drys used positive law—both statutory and constitutional—as a means to achieve prohibition. They avoided relying on English common law, which seemed to them (as it had to Fanny Wright and Sarah Grimké) more muddled, less direct, and symbolically less powerful than amending a state or federal constitution. Many Progressive Era reformers similarly favored expanded governmental regulation. From the 1880s through the first decades of the twentieth century, for instance, progressive reformers fought for protective labor laws for women and children, factory safety inspections, and a pure food and drug division of the federal government.[33]

Embracing the inherently restrictive nature of laws, Willard warned people to heed "the sharp circle of the law," which justly proscribed individual behavior and even speech. Taking a narrow view of the protections offered by the First Amendment, she retorted, "Nay, friend, you cannot speak what you please." The WCTU's "Do Everything" policy encouraged members to engage in a wide variety of reform efforts from the 1880s through the 1930s, including campaigns for social purity laws (including age-of-consent laws, prohibitions on "white slavery," and the abolition of prostitution) and the censorship of "impurity" in literature, art, and movies. Until the 1930s the U.S. Supreme Court supported censorship by broadly defining a whole range of literary and artistic "speech" as commercial, and thus censorable. The courts did not define free speech as a truly First Amendment right until the mid-twentieth century. Willard reminded critics that the government could rightly pass restrictive laws on a whole variety of subjects: "You may not even build a house of such material as you happen to prefer. We legislate on all these matters in the interest of the majority." Referring to a person's "right" to sell alcohol or "vile literature," Willard exclaimed, "O, no you won't; we shall interfere with your personal liberty just at that point in the sacred interest of childhood and of home." Similarly, Burke had celebrated the fact that, under the British constitution, "I am free, and I am *not* free dangerously to myself or to others." Willard's insistence upon the need for and validity of coercive laws reflects her belief that regulations were the most effective way to achieve social change and also social order.[34]

Willard sometimes linked individual liberties and the need for regulation to an explicitly racist critique of those who were ostensibly at a lower level of civilization. This could include peoples of other nations, but in an 1890 interview with the *New York Voice*, she caricatured African American men in the South as "unreasonable" libertines who valued their right to drink over the common good:

> The Anglo-Saxon race will never submit to be dominated by the Negro so long as his altitude reaches no higher than the personal liberty of the saloon and the power of appreciating the amount of liquor that a dollar will buy. . . . "Better whisky and more of it" has been the rallying cry of great dark-faced mobs in the Southern localities where local option was snowed under by the colored vote. Temperance has no enemy like that, for it is unreasoning and unreasonable.

Here, Willard vilified black men as "unreasoning" creatures who were clearly not full citizens and perhaps not even fully human. In her mind, they had thus far failed to "progress"—to make the shift described by Burke as moving from a "state of nature" to being members of a civilized society who are willing to be governed by law rather than reveling in absolute freedom. As national superintendent of the Department of Work Among Colored People, Frances Watkins Harper frequently found herself fighting these stereotypes and disputing the contentions of Willard and other WCTU members that black male voters were irrationally and selfishly against prohibition. Although Willard assumed that black men routinely voted to protect their "personal liberty" to drink, in cities such as Atlanta, Georgia, their votes in fact helped pass prohibitory laws.[35]

The pro-regulatory stance of temperance reformers reflects a political theory of reformism that prioritized a well-functioning civil state over personal liberty—and, especially, over selfish individualism. In a marked shift from the values espoused by abolitionists, including the Grimkés, historian Catherine Murdock argues, "In contrast with the earlier enthusiasm for moral suasion, these temperance activists now supported involuntary abstinence." Restrictive laws—justified because they ostensibly signified the collective will of the people—could force people to do what was right, no matter whether they had come to this realization themselves. Murdock suggests that "the WCTU became so dogmatic" in its support for prohibitory laws for a somewhat unexpected reason—in order to shift attention away from punishing the drinker and toward regulating the drink. The WCTU certainly avoided becoming a virulently nativist, anti-immigrant organization in part because its members sometimes perceived male drinkers as being pawns or victims of the liquor industry and saloon keepers. Furthermore, those members who worked in the WCTU's departments of Work Among Miners and Work Among Lumberjacks found that the men's terrible working conditions drove many of them to drink. These WCTU activists did not advocate punishment of alcoholics and instead supported laws for safer working conditions and higher wages as a way to increase workers' temperance. Overall, however, the WCTU's stance toward a constitutional amendment for prohibition was not driven by an emotional desire to protect male drinkers but, rather, to promote a well-ordered civil society. Radical prohibitionists placed their faith in the power of the central government, favoring increased governmental regulations on a number of reform issues.[36]

Frances Willard and other post–Civil War prohibitionists contended that the majority of women were already morally and intellectually convinced of the need for constitutional amendments for woman suffrage and prohibition as well as for national laws to curb child labor, among other reform priorities. All they needed was to practice politics and vote in elections. Moral suasion was thus a comparatively small component of the prohibitionists' political strategy. In contrast, Fanny Wright's Nashoba experiment had relied on the power of example to influence the antislavery debate. In the antebellum era, abolitionists such as the Grimké sisters had also focused upon achieving moral suasion—on convincing as many Americans as possible of the rightness of their cause—in order to win the passage of various antislavery laws. Willard disagreed with those who persisted in stating that "women should content themselves with educating public sentiment." To her, this implied that women could have only indirect influence over politics by convincing their fathers, brothers, and husbands to vote for reform. Most women had already been persuaded that a pro-regulatory stance was the correct one, Willard declared. They needed the right to participate fully in politics in order to make the necessary reforms: "we have the sentiment all educated and stored away, ready for use." Having made her case for women's voting rights and full citizenship, Willard then undertook the difficult task of moving the WCTU into partisan party politics in the 1880s and 1890s.[37]

THE "PROHIBITION HOME PROTECTION PARTY"—WOMEN AND PARTISAN POLITICS

Once Willard had convinced WCTU members they needed the vote, she strove to convince them to abandon their non-partisanship and to participate actively in party politics in order to pass their legislative agenda more successfully. If politicians were elected with WCTU support, she reasoned, they should be more willing to sponsor and vote for women's legislative reform goals. The nineteenth century's cult of domesticity idealized women as being separate from the corrupt world of male politics, yet a conception of female civic duty had simultaneously existed since at least the American Revolution. As a way to maintain their status as respectable ladies, even those antebellum women reformers who broke gender barriers by lecturing in public usually rejected any overt involvement in *partisan* politics. In the 1820s, only freethinking women radicals such as Fanny Wright were willing to defy convention by actively endorsing and campaigning for the Working Men's Party and later the Democratic Party. A mainstream political party, the Whig Party, had finally taken the radical new step of encouraging women's partisanship in the 1840s. The Whigs broke with tradition by inviting women to political rallies and soliciting their help with legislative petitions, as well as by asking them to write letters, essays, and pamphlets in support of Whig candidates and positions. Historian Elizabeth Varon points out that, even as some women accepted partisanship, many of them, especially white Southern women, "did not lay claim to the male prerogatives of voting, office-holding, and public speaking."[38]

During and after the Civil War, most African American women and men endorsed the Republican Party. After all, President Lincoln had passed the Emancipation Proclamation, and the Radical Republicans in Congress had passed federal laws guaranteeing black Americans their rights of citizenship, including voting rights. Activist women at the national and local levels, including Frances Harper, endorsed the Reconstruction Amendments, encouraged African American men to vote for the Republican Party, and urged them to resist terrorist threats from groups such as the Ku Klux Klan. Especially when it came to be linked with pro-Union sentiment and nationalism, white and black women's partisanship became comparatively more acceptable during and after the Civil War.[39]

The WCTU, Willard believed, had the strength, as a huge and well-organized lobbying group, to pressure at least one of the major parties to adopt prohibition platforms and laws. Rejecting some men's criticism that women, as she put it, "have not the ballot yet, and must not expect recognition from a party," she countered by recording many successful WCTU campaigns for reform legislation, including local option, closings of saloons, and the passing of scientific temperance instruction laws for public schools. "Be it well understood," Willard insisted, "we do not come [to political parties] as empty-handed supplicants, but as victorious allies."[40] Women had proved themselves to be significant political players in lobbying for reform bills even without the constitutional right to vote and so, she argued, should be welcomed and even courted by the political parties.

Convincing most WCTU members to abandon the organization's (and women's) traditional non-partisanship proved far more difficult and divisive than convincing them to endorse woman suffrage, however. WCTU members' resistance was due in part to Willard's decision to back the Prohibition Party rather than the Republican Party. When she assessed which party to endorse, Willard moved away from Northern reformers' traditional alliance with the Republican Party (this includes her own family's strong Free Soil and Republican connections). Many

white and black WCTU members and their families had been abolitionists and Republican Party loyalists since before the Civil War. They were
particularly reluctant to abandon women's traditional non-partisanship
if it meant supporting an arguably more marginal third party.[41] Recognizing this partisan loyalty, Frances Willard made a last-ditch attempt
to gain Republican support for the WCTU's legislative goals. She spoke
before the Republican National Convention in 1884, imploring it to
include national prohibition and woman suffrage in its platform. She
explained that the WCTU "stands not only for total abstinence and prohibition, but for no sectarianism in religion, no sectionalism in politics,
no sex in citizenship." When the Republican Party declined to endorse
either suffrage or temperance, she concluded that "'the party of moral
ideas' has ceased to have a distinctive policy," as it had when it was
associated with antislavery ideas.[42]

   Willard had other reasons to support a third party. She feared that
the Democratic and Republican parties were each overly identified
with only one side of the sectional dispute that had culminated in
the Civil War and Reconstruction. Traveling extensively throughout
the South in the early 1880s, Willard had successfully expanded the
WCTU into a truly national organization. Knowing that the Republican
Party would not be fully accepted by Southern whites, she predicted
that a third party might be more effective in uniting Northerners and
Southerners: "But this new party cannot bear the name of Republican
or Democrat. Neither victor nor vanquished would accept the old war-
cry of a section."[43]

   Thus, when Willard spoke of "no sectionalism in politics," she
referred to her desire to help heal the divide between North and South.
This vision of reunification sometimes included white and black voters:
"my heart has glowed with the hope of a real 'home government' for
the South, and a 'color line' broken, not by bayonets nor repudia-
tionists, but by ballots from white hands and black, for prohibitory
law." Here, black men had a right to vote—as long as they proved their
worth by voting for prohibitory legislation. Yet Willard's vision usually
excluded black Americans altogether. She hoped that prohibition, as
a moral issue that crossed regional boundaries, could be the basis of
a new political party that would "weld the Anglo-Saxons of the New
World into one royal family, and give us a really re-United States." In
this striking sentence, Willard crowned the white population of the
"New World" into a European-style royalty that would be hierarchi-

cally above other inhabitants, such as Native American Indians and African Americans.[44] Black women reformers seemingly had little role in Willard's vision of a third party, except perhaps to ensure that black men voted for prohibition.

Willard did not just endorse the Prohibition Party from the sidelines. She became a full member of the party in 1881 and was appointed to its central committee a year later. In a clear attempt to win organized women's support, delegates at the Prohibition Party's 1882 convention voted to become the "Prohibition Home Protection" Party. By adopting Willard's "Home Protection Ballot" motto as part of its official name, the party signaled that it took women's political power and reform goals seriously. Its platform supporting woman suffrage represents the official acceptance by many pro-temperance men of the idea that women should vote, and that when they did, they would vote for moral reform and prohibition.[45]

Leveraging quite a bit of her own political capital with WCTU members, by 1885 Willard had finally managed to get the national organization to pass a resolution explicitly endorsing the Prohibition Party. As early as 1884, many WCTU branches had entered political campaigns for the Prohibition Party in state and national elections. Then, Republican Party loyalists lashed out against the WCTU's partisanship in these elections. Willard observed that "A party [Republican] long accustomed to success is in defeat. . . . The W.C.T.U. is termed 'a political party,' and subjected to the sharpest criticism by men who found no fault with our societies in Iowa, Kansas, and other states where they 'lent their influence' to the Republicans." As WCTU members and others campaigned for prohibition amendments to twenty state constitutions (they won in eight states), the Prohibition Party grew. It reached its peak membership level in 1886 and received its record number of votes—over 250,000—in 1892. The WCTU's official endorsement of the Prohibition Party, although it entailed a fight, strengthened both the women's group and the party. In addition to lobbying Congress through its Office of National Legislation located in Washington, D.C., the WCTU helped popularize and publicize the Prohibition Party and its various goals through its paper, the *Union Signal*.[46]

The WCTU based its support of the Prohibition Party on the party's willingness to endorse a series of reforms that would strengthen the central government's power to enforce morality on its citizens. Willard and the WCTU influenced the Prohibition Party, ostensibly a single-issue party, to become more broadly reform-oriented. As WCTU members declared in an 1888 convention resolution, *"Resolved,* That we re-affirm our allegiance to that party which makes its dominant issue the suppression of the liquor traffic, declares its belief in Almighty God as the source of all power in Government, defends the sanctity of the Christian Sabbath, recognizes equal suffrage and equal wages for women, demands the abolition of polygamy and uniform laws governing marriage and divorce."[47]

As WCTU president, Frances Willard led more white women into partisan party politics than ever before in American history. Over the next two decades, women's partisan political work became more accepted in the two dominant parties, Republican and Democratic. Most African Americans were committed to the party of Lincoln and worked from within it to achieve their legislative priorities. Mary Church Terrell, for instance, was deeply involved in Republican Party state and national campaigns through the first three decades of the twentieth century. Historian Melanie Gustafson argues that, "By the turn of the century, women worked [routinely] on behalf of the . . . political parties, but continued to present themselves and be perceived as principled political actors in an unprincipled political world." Women did not abandon their claims to greater moral purity even as they immersed themselves in partisan politics; Willard's articulation of the "Home Protection Ballot" helped make this possible.[48]

"GOD'S OWN FREE WOMAN"—MARRIAGE, RAPE, AND WHITE WOMEN'S LEGAL STATUS

Willard's view of (white) women as morally and sexually pure informed her articulations of their right to control their own bodies and to demand legal protections. Joining women's rights advocates such as Fanny Wright, Sarah Grimké, Frances Harper, and Elizabeth Cady Stanton, Willard sharply critiqued marriage laws in the United States. In a fascinating section of her autobiography, *Glimpses of Fifty Years* (1889), entitled "Is Marriage a Failure?" Willard outlined what she perceived to be the problems with marriage. First, to deflect criticism and make her subsequent critique appear less radical, the unmarried Willard firmly declared that she viewed "the present marriage system to be the greatest triumph of Christianity." Marriage, she exclaimed,

By the mid-1880s, Frances
E. Willard's vision for her
organization expanded to
include the rest of the world.
With the help of WCTU
missionaries, she founded the
World's Woman's Christian
Temperance Union, which
established unions throughout the British empire as well
as in Japan, Denmark, China,
and Mexico, among other
countries.

"alone renders possible a pure society and a permanent state." After
issuing this ringing endorsement of Christian marriage as the basis of a
stable nation-state, she turned to the harsh realities of marriage under
English common law. In particular, she wholly rejected the idea that
"Husband and wife are one, and that one is the husband." Coverture
and common law were wrongly based on "a warlike age" where men
used "fist and spear" to defend their homes and the state.[49]

Denying states' rights and supporting federal marriage laws, Willard argued that women could not hold equal power and rights until
marriage law was the same in each state in the union and fair to both
sexes. "I believe in uniform national marriage laws," she declared. In
this new "age of peace," uncivilized, outdated laws—based on women
being, as Willard put it, "the booty chiefly sought in war"—must be
eliminated and replaced with better ones. Willard listed many of the
outdated laws that must be changed:

It will not do to give the husband of the modern woman power to whip his wife, provided that the stick he uses must not be larger than his finger; to give him the right to will away her unborn child; to have control over her property; and, in the state, to make all the laws under which she is to live, adjudicate all her penalties, try her before juries of men, conduct her to prison under the care of men, cast the ballot for her, and in general hold her in the estate of a perpetual minor. It will not do to let the modern man determine the "age of consent," settle the penalties that men shall suffer whose indignities and outrages toward women are worse to their victims than death, and by his exclusive power to make all the laws and choose all officers, judicial and executive, to have his own case wholly in his own hands.

Women must be able to participate in politics and the government in order to pass new laws, for instance, that disallowed and severely punished wife beating and rape. Women also needed laws allowing them to vote, to control their property, wages, and children, and to have access to equal education. Willard concluded, "Last of all and chiefest, the *magnum opus* of Christianity, and Science, which is its handmaid, the wife will have undoubted custody of herself, and, as in all the lower ranges of the animal creation, she will determine the frequency of the investiture of life with form and of love with immortality."[50] The term "custody of herself" meant that women must control their own bodies and reproduction, through voluntary motherhood. To illustrate the lack of married women's legal rights, Willard used the metaphor of slavery to describe the plight of all married women. Marriage laws must recognize the wife as "God's own free woman, not coerced into marriage for the sake of a support, nor a bond-slave after she is married." Willard imagined a future when "the wife shall surrender at marriage no right not equally surrendered by the husband—not even her own name."[51]

In addition to arguing for federal protections for married women, Willard also raised the controversial issue of passing new laws to protect women from sexual violence such as rape and the entrapment of girls and young white women into prostitution, sometimes referred to as "white slavery." The impetus for the WCTU's open critiques of rape and the double standard of sexuality for men and women was an exposé that appeared in the British *Pall Mall Gazette* (1885) entitled "The Maiden Tribute of Modern Babylon," written by journalist William T. Stead. His series helped generate a social purity movement in

England that had forced Parliament to raise age-of-consent laws to sixteen by the end of that year. Impressed by the movement's rapid success in England, Willard decided that the WCTU should confront the reality of women's legal and sexual vulnerability in the United States. The WCTU investigated the laws in the United States and found that "the age of consent was ten in most states."[52]

"Respectable" white women were generally discouraged from discussing sexual violence on the grounds that even by talking about it they could sully their own purity, yet Willard argued that women could not expect legislative reform if they refused to name the problem publicly and demand a solution. Arguing that they must no longer be "the victims of conventional cowardice," Willard insisted they must take up this fight even if it meant openly talking about taboo topics such as prostitution and rape. She bluntly declared, "men alone will never gain the courage to legislate against other men." Accordingly, Willard condemned the weak punishments meted out to white slavers, for example: "in Massachusetts and Vermont it is a greater crime to steal a cow than to abduct and ruin a girl." Legal scholar Jane Larson argues that WCTU members "questioned the state's conferral of privilege in law of male sexual interests to the detriment of women and girls; they thus exposed the state's complicity in what otherwise appeared to be wholly private acts of sexual oppression."[53]

In 1886 the WCTU's Department for the Promotion of Social Purity began a national petition campaign asking the U.S. Congress to raise the age of consent and to institute "extreme penalties" at the federal level for rape and for luring women into prostitution. Willard described the campaign as "a great petition to Congress, asking for better protection of women and girls through severer penalties for assaults upon them, and that the age of protection might be raised to eighteen years."[54] Instead of organizing expensive and time-consuming campaigns in each state, the WCTU hoped to make one uniform federal law. To make her point that the safety of young girls was at stake, Willard renamed "age of consent" laws, calling them "age of protection" laws instead.

Knowing that working men could help advance their cause among the representatives and senators in Congress, Willard personally solicited and received the endorsement of Terrence Powderly, head of the Knights of Labor. Powderly distributed ninety-two thousand copies of the WCTU's national petition to the local assemblies for signatures. (Dedicated to building mutually beneficial coalitions and in a reciprocal show of support for male and female workers, Willard's WCTU joined with the Knights of Labor in advocating the eight-hour day as a matter of workers' safety and expanded family time.) The WCTU-led social purity coalition produced results. In 1889 Congress raised the age of consent to sixteen in the District of Columbia, "spearheading a movement that eventually changed the law in every state." Larson argues that "Credit for this sweeping and successful legal reform belongs to the Woman's Christian Temperance Union."[55]

However, the WCTU's age-of-consent campaign did not reach out to or include those women who were arguably most vulnerable to rape—black women. Violation of slave women (and their resistance to it) had been a cornerstone of antislavery discourse. During Reconstruction and beyond, black women viewed suffrage, rape, and lynching as entirely intertwined.[56] Nannie Helen Burroughs, founder of the National Training School for Girls, for instance, noted that black women could not win legal challenges against white male rapists: "She needs the ballot, to reckon with men who place no value upon her virtue, and to mould healthy sentiment in favor of her own protection." The right to vote was the solution to black women's vulnerability to rape, not age-of-consent laws. Larson notes that "Black clubwomen proved reluctant to enter into the age-of-consent reform campaign, partly because of their harsh experiences as women of color with discriminatory law enforcement, especially with respect to rape law." Black women feared that the age-of-consent laws might be unevenly enforced, ignoring the vulnerability of black girls to sexual violence at the hands of white men. As historian Mary Odem points out, they feared "that the law would be used to target black men" and perpetuate "the racist stereotype of them as dangerous rapists." Given that most white women envisioned all rape victims as white, black women were not welcomed into age-of-consent campaigns as virtuous equals whose purity also deserved protection. Black women anti-lynching activists strongly critiqued white society's stereotypes of black women as sexually loose and immoral—stereotypes that served virtually to sanction or deny the rape of black women.[57]

FEDERAL ANTI-LYNCHING LEGISLATION AND WILLARD'S WCTU

Just as the WCTU's age-of-consent campaign ignored the perspective and needs of black women, Frances Willard was ultimately willing to sacrifice black women—both as WCTU members and as full citizens—in order to turn the WCTU into a truly national organization that permanently moved white women (both North and South) into the realm of politics. Beginning in 1881, Willard made several extended lecture and recruiting tours in the South, with her last trip occurring in 1896, just two years before she died. During her Southern trips, Willard's approach to interracial work depended upon her audience. When speaking to black women, she encouraged them to form black unions of the Woman's Christian Temperance Union, aiming in part to have them influence their male relatives to vote for antialcohol dry laws. When courting Southern white women, however, she talked favorably of attaching literacy tests to woman suffrage bills and condoned their strict segregationist practices, such as isolating black women in separate local WCTU unions and appointing white women to be state-level superintendents of Work Among the Colored People. Thus, although Willard encouraged black women to join the WCTU, she prioritized her goal of recruiting Southern white women and positioned black women outside her notion of an expanded citizenship for (white) women. Once Willard achieved her goal of significant white WCTU membership gains across the South, she became less responsive to black women's attempts to influence the WCTU's reform agenda to include their demands for a federal law to protect blacks against lynch mobs.[58]

The WCTU's record on race in the 1880s was mixed at best. During Frances Watkins Harper's tenure as the WCTU's national superintendent of "Colored Work," she frequently found herself marginalized and without significant support from the national organization. She was never given a budget and had to push hard to get herself and three other black women onto the executive committee and the board of superintendents. In 1890, the same year that the national WCTU temporarily disbanded its Department of Colored Work and permanently eliminated Harper as national superintendent, Willard gave an interview with the pro-temperance paper the *New York Voice* in which she revealed her fundamental racism. In the interview, she sympathized with Southern whites who had been "wronged" by federal Reconstruction and by the unrestricted granting of the vote to black men. Willard rejected the proposed Force Act of 1890, a bill that would have provided federal supervision of national elections to protect black men's voting rights against attempts by Southern states to deny them (the bill passed in the House, but not the Senate). Instead, she advocated "an educational test" as a way to protect implicitly superior native-born whites from the ignorant votes of those she termed "alien illiterates" in the North and the "plantation Negro" in the South.[59]

Accepting the white South's cries that it had suffered under a brutal Republican Reconstruction, Willard applied a states' rights lesson from what she perceived to be the "failure" of Reconstruction to her approach to winning woman suffrage in the South. Whereas during Reconstruction, "Negro suffrage at the South was forced upon wide areas occupied by a voting population bitterly hostile to the innovation," Willard reassured white male Southerners that woman suffrage would not be forcibly imposed upon the states: "woman's vote must first be granted by free consent of a majority of the representatives chosen directly by those who are already citizens; and by operating over the small area of a single state at a time it would arouse no violent upheaval of the opposition." This states' rights approach to gaining the vote meant that Willard was willing to sacrifice black women's voting rights for the gains of white women. In most other instances, of course, Willard fought *for* an expansion of federal power and authority, particularly when she endorsed constitutional amendments for woman suffrage and prohibition. When not pandering to her white Southern constituents, she generally did not favor states' rights. Yet, in this instance, she implied that she and the white women she represented in the WCTU would turn a blind eye to Southern states' restrictions on black voting rights. Black women might join black men as a newly enfranchised group, but they would be almost immediately disenfranchised, for they would not be able to vote in the face of a "bitterly hostile" white population.[60] Just as Anthony and Stanton had done before her, Willard tried to make woman suffrage appealing to conservatives by endorsing an educational test that would allow middle- and upper-class white women to be added to the voter rolls without including uneducated, working-class white and black women.[61] Although I have not discovered an explicit record of Harper's dissatisfaction with Willard's position on the Force Act, it was probably another factor that led to Harper's departure as national superintendent.

When Harper's department was replaced in 1891 by a new "Department of Home and Foreign Missionary Work to Colored People," the new emphasis on African Americans' otherness—their status as lesser beings (colonial others) in need of missionary work by white

Christian evangelical women—indicated a rejection of black women as equal members within the WCTU. Blacks were now explicit objects of white women's missionary work. The implications of this change were twofold. The National WCTU now admitted that "work among colored people" was not a priority for the organization and did not deserve separate departmental status. It was also a way to fulfill a different WCTU goal of recruiting African American Christian women to proselytize in Africa as part of its worldwide program of missionary work. Yet these changes did not signal the end of Frances Harper's or other black women's involvement with the WCTU. Many black women still saw the union as one of the most important sites available for interracial organized reform work. Consequently, at the group's annual convention held during the Chicago World's Fair in 1893, the black activist and clubwoman Lucy Simpson Thurman successfully convinced the national WCTU to reinstate the Department of Colored Work and to appoint her as its new national superintendent.[62] Born in Ottowa, Canada, Thurman taught school in Maryland during Reconstruction, organized colored women's clubs in Michigan, and began her temperance work in 1875.[63] A WCTU lecturer who was popular with white audiences throughout the Midwest, Thurman was well-known to white and black WCTU members, and she continued Harper's calls for federal laws against lynching and other federal protections of the rights of African Americans. Yet working from within the WCTU became even more challenging when anti-lynching crusader Ida B. Wells launched a campaign exposing the WCTU's refusal to promote the one piece of federal legislation that African Americans wanted most—a federal anti-lynching bill.

FEDERAL PROTECTIONS AGAINST LYNCHING?
IDA B. WELLS AND THE WCTU

In the early 1890s, during the period of transition and instability for the Department of Colored Work and for black members of the WCTU, Ida B. Wells began a national and international anti-lynching campaign. As historians such as Patricia Schechter have established, Wells believed that Willard and the WCTU must bring their considerable moral authority to bear against lynching. She aimed her critique at the WCTU precisely because it was a powerful Christian organization that consistently promoted federal legislation as a solution for many moral problems in American society, accepted black members, and had given some black women, including Frances Harper and Lucy Thurman, a forum for leadership.[64]

The public controversy began in 1893 when Ida B. Wells took her campaign to England, and international attention put pressure on the WCTU, as the largest American women's reform group, to respond. Harper, Thurman, and other black WCTU members supported Wells and tried to push the organization from within to adopt a strong anti-lynching stance. Feeling the pressure, Willard called for and achieved a resolution against lynching at the WCTU's 1893 national convention. Yet she then drained the resolution of its import by stating in her presidential address of the same year, "Our duty to the colored people have [sic] never impressed me so solemnly as this year when the antagonism between them and the white race have [sic] seemed to be more vivid than at any previous time, and lurid vengeance has devoured the devourers of women and children." As historian Ruth Bordin points out, "She condemned lynching but took as fact the assertion that lynching resulted from the rape of white women by blacks. She was responding to liberal northern civil rights champions and her southern white colleagues at the same time." Willard tried to play to both sides of the lynching debate, but Ida B. Wells made it more difficult for her to do so by exposing her hypocrisy and racism.[65]

On Wells's second anti-lynching tour of England in 1894, she responded to critics who were reluctant to believe what she was saying about the disinterestedness of American Protestants in the anti-lynching campaign. Wells called attention to the interview Willard had given to the *New York Voice* back in 1890. Characterizing African American voters as "great dark-faced mobs," Willard had expressed "pity" for Southern whites who faced the "problem" that "the colored race multiplies like the locusts of Egypt." Combining an almost visceral level of disgust toward African Americans with a condoning of white-on-black violence, Willard had declared:

> Half-drunken white roughs murder them at the polls, or intimidate them so that they do not vote. But the better class of people must not be blamed for this, and a more thoroughly American population than the Christian population of the South does not exist. They have the traditions, the kindness, the probity, the courage of our forefathers. The problem on their hands is immeasurable. . . . The safety of woman, of childhood, of

the home, is menaced in a thousand localities at this moment, so that the men dare not go beyond the sight of their own roof-tree.[66]

Characterizing Southern blacks as less than citizens, as being outside of civilized society, Willard suggested they were an unchristian and uncontrollable menace. This re-published interview damaged Willard's reputation as an egalitarian and set the stage for what proved to be a difficult 1894 annual convention in Cleveland, Ohio, on the WCTU's twentieth anniversary.

Ida B. Wells attended the WCTU's 1894 convention as the "fraternal delegate from the Woman's Mite Missionary Society of the A.M.E. [African Methodist Episcopal] Church at Cleveland," and she issued a challenge to the WCTU delegates to adopt a strong anti-lynching resolution. In response Willard gave a speech personally attacking Wells for having defamed white women by suggesting that they sometimes willingly had sex with black men (in other words, for suggesting that not all rape charges were true). Patricia Schechter argues that "Frances Willard rejected the idea that white women acted on desire for black men; even the mere *suggestion* of such sexual initiative defamed every white woman in America ('half the white race'). Willard's racial chauvinism and her investment in the notion of the inherent sexual passivity of white women allowed her to define any such sexual contact as rape." Wells denied that Southern white women needed protection, and especially not the extralegal protection of their "virtue" by white lynch mobs. She focused instead on the need for federal laws to protect black men unfairly accused of rape. Wells also noted sarcastically that the WCTU, usually willing to take a stance on almost any issue, had decided to remain silent on the subject of lynching, although "that great Christian body . . . in its resolutions had expressed itself in opposition to the social amusement of card playing, athletic sports and promiscuous dancing; had protested against the licensing of saloons, inveighed against tobacco, pledged its allegiance to the Prohibition party, and thanked the Populist party in Kansas, the Republican party in California and the Democratic party in the South." Clearly, the WCTU "wholly ignored the seven millions of colored people of this country whose plea was for a word of sympathy and support for the movement in their behalf."[67]

Frances Watkins Harper stood with Ida B. Wells throughout the controversy, endorsing a strong federal government that could protect all its citizens. The same year as the convention-floor debate regarding the WCTU's stance on lynching, Harper wrote a powerful article in the *Women's Era*, a journal published by the black clubwoman and suffragist Josephine St. Pierre Ruffin, entitled "How to Stop Lynching." In this article, Harper insisted that white men must pay for their crimes. Since murder is a crime, "Why not hang the murderers?" she asked. Decades after she first began fighting for social justice, Harper concluded:

> No, the truth is this, nothing is to be expected from the South. The colored people must look to the general government. It had a right to their services and lives in time of war. They have a right to its protection certainly in time of peace. It is idle to say that it must leave to state governments the protection of the lives of its citizens. Why not leave to state governments the punishment of counterfeiters? If the United States government can protect money . . . it can protect . . . against loss of life at the hands of the murderer.

Supporting Wells's anti-lynching crusade, Harper insisted on the absolute necessity that the federal government protect its black citizens. Her article was a political statement against states' rights and for federal protection. She pointedly listed all the responsibilities that the federal government willingly shouldered, including punishment of counterfeiters and moonshiners, prohibition of the sale of tobacco without a revenue tax, and war abroad to protect Americans. Given its broad claims to authority, Harper argued that it was inconceivable that the government "cannot spend a cent to protect a loyal, native-born colored American murdered without provocation by native or alien in Alabama." The refusal of the federal government to stop lynchings inspired her to exclaim, "Shame on such a government!" Just as Harper had earlier asserted that white Northerners and the federal government bore responsibility for perpetuating the institution of slavery, she now targeted President Grover Cleveland's Democratic administration. Harper concluded her editorial with the indictment: "The administration in power is *particeps criminis* with the murders. It can stop lynching, and until it does, it has on its hands the innocent blood of its murdered citizens." If only white Americans, including her colleagues in the WCTU, would fully support the passage of a federal anti-lynching law, the government would use its strength to protect black Americans from extralegal violence.[68]

A WCTU anti-lynching resolution recorded in the December 1894 issue of the organization's official organ, the *Union Signal,* presumed that white women really were being raped by black men—disallowing the fact that black men were often lynched on false charges and for a variety of other perceived "crimes," such as stepping out of rigid racial boundaries by being politically active or economically successful:

> Resolved, That the National W.C.T.U., which has for years counted among its departments that of peace and arbitration, is utterly opposed to all lawless acts . . . praying that the time may speedily come when no human being shall be condemned without due process of law; and when the unspeakable outrages which have so often provoked such lawlessness shall be banished from the world, and childhood, maidenhood and womanhood shall no more be the victims of atrocities worse than death.

Although mentioning its members' pacifism and the need for due process, the WCTU's resolution virtually condoned lynching as a justified response to the horrors of rape. It also ignored the reality of black women's vulnerability to rape in the homes of white families where they worked as domestic servants.[69]

Lynchings, as an extralegal form of violence, were based on the premise that African Americans were not full citizens and were therefore undeserving of both the penalties and the protections that the formal legal system ostensibly offered to all American citizens. The WCTU resolution characterized white women and girls as the "victims of atrocities." Its focus on alleged white female victims blatantly ignored the fact that many innocent black men were lynched. Despite their efforts to build an interracial organization, Willard and the WCTU ignored the devastating effect of lynching on black women who were themselves sometimes lynched. Many more were emotionally scarred, and all were politically and socially circumscribed by the practice of terrorizing blacks through lynchings. The WCTU's continued weak stance on lynching hurt its credibility among black women and men in the United States but kept its Southern white members loyal to the organization.[70]

Although the Wells-Willard controversy eventually faded from national and international news, black women such as Lucy Thurman, the WCTU's national superintendent of Colored Work from 1893 to 1908, continued to push for a federal anti-lynching law. Like Harper before her, Thurman found it difficult to develop a good working relationship with Willard. She did not receive the level of institutional support she needed as she recruited more black members, and she failed to convince Willard and the national WCTU to work for federal anti-lynching laws. In a revealing diary entry from 1896, Willard noted, "Mrs. Thurman and Preston of our colored work came for a re-hearing— discontent &c—I said they'd better stay but whatever happened—we should go on with our work for their race just the same. O the 'scenes & unseens'! Wrote [national WCTU treasurer] H.M. Barker gave Lucy T. 50 dols." Lacking in sympathy for them or their cause, Willard clearly found this encounter to be an ordeal. She asked them not to leave the WCTU but gave them no grounds for hope that the WCTU could be the site of a real interracial alliance to promote civil rights. Historian Carolyn Gifford suggests that Thurman and her WCTU co-worker Frances Preston were dissatisfied with the WCTU's lack of financial support for their organizing efforts and speaking tours (a problem that Harper had also faced) as well as with the WCTU's weak stance on lynching and the convict lease labor system, which forced black male and female prisoners throughout the South into hard labor as punishment for minor and often false charges.[71] In spite of these difficulties, Thurman remained the national superintendent of Colored Work until she became president of the NACW in 1908.

Lucy Thurman joined Frances Watkins Harper and Mary Church Terrell as an early member of the NACW. Like Harper, she served as a liaison or "diplomat" between that organization and the WCTU.[72] In its 1897 annual report, the NACW voted to send Thurman to the World's WCTU meeting being held in Toronto, Canada, that year: "Mrs. Thurman said that if the pamphlets on the Convict Lease System were printed and sent to her in time, she would see that they were distributed. Accepted." As a member of both organizations, Thurman represented the NACW as it kept up the pressure on Willard and the WCTU, demanding that the latter campaign against lynching and against the convict lease system.[73]

Another prominent NACW member, Margaret (Mrs. Booker T.) Washington, attempted to influence the WCTU's position on lynching through careful diplomacy and open communication. In 1897 Washington was elected to be the NACW "Fraternal Delegate" to the WCTU's annual convention in Buffalo, New York. In this position she served as a liaison between the two groups concerning the WCTU's stance on lynching. At the NACW convention, which was held just prior to the WCTU's annual convention, "Mrs. Washington read a letter from Miss Frances E. Willard . . . concerning the attitude of that body against lynching, and then made a motion which was carried that the Secretary be instructed to communicate with Miss Willard and inform her of the appreciation of this body for the stand taken by the Woman's Christian Temperance Union."[74] Washington focused on winning over Willard and her organization by complimenting its more strongly worded anti-lynching resolutions—and by downplaying the fact that its members still took no action to campaign for a federal law.

Even after they founded the NACW, black women clearly valued their interracial pro-temperance and pro-suffrage work in the WCTU for it provided them with a forum from which to advocate their civil rights legislative agenda to an audience of reform-oriented whites. Through their WCTU club work, moreover, women such as Harper and Thurman gained national recognition and a network of connections with other black women within which they became leaders in their own organizations. Thus, in spite of the WCTU's troubled record on race, black women did not completely abandon the organization. Even Ida B. Wells did not give up on white women and their powerful organizations. Instead, she characterized them as a necessary part of the solution. Addressing black women, she suggested, "You can be instrumental in having churches, missionary societies, Y.M.C.A.'s, W.C.T.U.'s and all Christian and moral forces in connection with your religious and social life, pass resolutions of condemnation and protest every time a lynching takes place; and see that they are sent to the place where these outrages occur." Change could happen only if whites and blacks protested loudly (nationally and locally) with a unified voice each and every time a lynching occurred. Although they met with considerable resistance, black women responded positively and persistently to the challenge of promoting their reform agenda in the racist climate that pervaded turn-of-the-century politics.[75]

When black women supported the WCTU's reform priorities of suffrage and temperance, president Frances Willard could see them as important allies. But when they raised difficult issues that threatened to create rifts among the group's white members, then she perceived them as liabilities. Ida B. Wells's anti-lynching campaign and the issues it raised about race, sexuality, and violence were not accepted by Willard or the WCTU's white members. Willard could not conceive of black women's concerns as anything other than those of a marginalized, strategically less important part of the organization she was trying to build. Her privileging of an expanded white WCTU membership in the South meant that her vision of the common good did not include advocating legal rights and protections for African Americans. Whereas Willard's goal of full citizenship for women did not include a demand for black women's equal status as full citizens, these two goals were inextricably linked for black women activists.

$\mathscr{O}$verall, it was critical to Frances Willard's political agenda that white women claim the rights and serious obligations of citizenship. Rights talk appealed to Willard and is evident in her commitment to (white) woman suffrage, yet she recognized that arguments for woman suffrage based on equal rights had not worked to create a mass movement. Willard's political theory drew upon the ideas of Edmund Burke, whose writings provided her with a rationale for accepting national governmental regulation at a point, in the late 1800s, when some were interpreting Locke's natural rights arguments as rejecting positive law as coercive. In contrast to those who emphasized Locke's libertarian strain and therefore prioritized liberty and individualism above all else, Willard and her supporters saw federal regulation based on the restraint of liberty as the best solution to intractable problems such as child labor, urban poverty, and alcoholism. A pragmatic political strategist, she provided an alternative rationale for woman suffrage and women's citizenship by focusing on the *needs* of civil society. Because of their difference from men, women must participate in reform work, legislative campaigns, and party politics; they would add moral purity to the nation. Willard's goal was to create a better, stronger nation, and she included a whole new class of citizens in this nation, white women (whom Burke had never thought of including). Unable to overcome her own prejudices, Willard rarely included black women in her vision of politically active full citizens, often sacrificing their interests in legislation that would protect and advance liberty to her goal of national white reconciliation through the Woman's Christian Temperance Union. To Willard, white women must enter into partisan politics to protect and expand the interests of, as a popular WCTU motto put it, "God, Home, and Native Land."

Mary Church Terrell

CRITIQUES OF "WHITE LAWLESSNESS"

With an impressively long career in public service, Mary ("Mollie") Eliza Church Terrell (1863–1954) helped found several important reform organizations, including the National Association of Colored Women (NACW) in 1896, the National Association for the Advancement of Colored People (NAACP) in 1909, and the Coordinating Committee for the Enforcement of the D.C. Anti-Discrimination Laws in the early 1950s. Her leadership positions and reputation for eloquence as a public speaker secured her invitations to speak before many different audiences. In 1915 Terrell was invited to give a talk at the Woman's Congress of Missions in San Francisco, California, which was held at the same time as the Panama-Pacific Exposition and which attracted two thousand delegates, including missionaries from two dozen denominations serving in the United States and around the world.[1]

Terrell was used to being the only black woman at national and even international women's conventions, so she accepted the invitation "to represent colored women" at this congress. Once there, however, Terrell had an unnerving experience: "For the first time in my life I was referred to as an 'alien' by the chairman who introduced me at the San Francisco meeting. I had never thought of myself as an 'alien' and I was greatly shocked and pained. As I arose to speak, I remarked that even if I were technically an alien in the United States, I certainly did not feel like one.

Mary Church Terrell's formal half-length portrait shows off her beautiful gown, with its finely crafted design of beads and sequins on a satin dress. Terrell believed that her elegant self-presentation could disarm critics, give her access to more varied audiences, and help elevate the status of all African Americans.

It occurred to me afterwards that everybody in this country is an alien except the Indians." Pondering her status as a U.S. citizen, Terrell tried to make sense of the comment and imagined that the chairman referred to the fact that, because some of her ancestors were from Africa, she was "technically" an alien. Historian Mae Ngai points out that white Americans created the concept of "alien citizens" to describe "persons who are American citizens by virtue of their birth in the United States but who are presumed to be foreign by the mainstream of American culture and, at times, by the state."[2] In this instance, Terrell found herself and all African Americans categorized by white missionary women as foreigners—as "alien" citizens. Only after the convention, when she had time to think about this comment, did it occur to her that "technically," whites were also "aliens" who had originally come to America as immigrants from other lands. According to this logic, she realized, only Indians could qualify as real Americans.[3] Terrell hoped that white Americans would abandon this line of argument once they realized that it put their own citizenship status into question, too. This incident was one of many that forced Terrell to confront the meaning of citizenship in the United States and to explore the relationship of black Americans to the nation-state.

In her autobiography, *A Colored Woman in a White World,* Terrell described white Americans' racism as a form of "assault and battery committed on a human being's soul."[4] As "a colored woman in a white world," Terrell worked to understand who she was, in terms of her color, class, sex, and citizenship. Although she found the incident at the Woman's Congress of Missions to be disturbing, Terrell's own crisis of alienation and questioning as to whether she belonged to the nation had come earlier, when she was studying in Europe in the late 1880s. She considered the possibility of living abroad permanently but determined that she had a legitimate claim to citizenship in the United States: "My African ancestors helped to build and enrich it with their unrequited labor and soul in the most cruel bondage the world has ever seen. My African ancestors suffered and died for it as soldiers in every war which it has waged. It has been cruel to us in the past and it is often unjust to us now, but it is my country after all . . . and with all its faults I still love it." Africans and their descendants had contributed economically and militarily to enrich America. Terrell refused to be literally and figuratively alienated from her country; nor would she be defeated by the racial prejudice she fought against throughout her life. Determined to improve her nation, Terrell returned to the United States as a civil rights activist—pursuing full citizenship for black Americans from the late 1880s until her death in 1954, just before her ninety-first birthday.[5]

"MY CONNECTION WITH SLAVERY"—MOLLIE CHURCH'S RACE AWARENESS

Like virtually all Southern blacks after the Civil War, Mollie Church and her family experienced racism and alienation, yet their relationship with whites was also mediated by their high-class status and fair skin. Born in Memphis, Tennessee, in 1863, Mollie was so light-skinned she often found herself poised on the threshold between black and white worlds. Her earliest childhood experiences made her aware of the arbitrary nature—indeed, the social construction—of categories of racial difference. Although her grandfather and father looked "exactly alike," her "black" father, Robert Reed Church, was the son and former slave of his "white" father, the Tennessee slave owner Captain C. B. Church. Captain Church trained his enslaved son to be a steward on his boats. After the Civil War they maintained a relationship; Mollie's father brought her to visit with her grandfather (whom she "simply adored") at his home every Sunday morning. Mollie was aware from age five, at least, that her family members lived on both sides of America's racial divide.[6]

The daughter of light-skinned former slaves, Mollie had more advantages than most freed slaves and their descendants. Her family's wealth came first from her mother's beauty parlor and then from her father's saloon and investments in Memphis real estate. Unlike Frances Willard's alcohol-abstaining parents, Mollie recounted that when she was a child her saloon-owning father gave her a hot toddy every morning for her health. As an adult she sometimes became self-conscious when she spoke at purity congresses or mothers' meetings, for she worried that her father's ownership of most of the property on notorious Beale Street in Memphis (including saloons and nightclubs) might somehow disqualify her from speaking with legitimacy on the subject of moral purity. In spite of her upbringing, as an adult she supported prohibition as an important way to protect young men from dangerous "temptations." Indeed, she sounded remarkably like Frances Willard in her use of military metaphors as she promoted woman's suffrage as a way to increase temperance: "Speaking to a women's group at Howard University in 1910," for instance, "she argued that temperance workers were 'engaged in a warfare which is as tremendous as the many battles that have been waged with gun and sword.'" She also wrote of cherishing an autographed book given to her by WCTU president Frances Willard.[7]

When studying in the North, at the Model School affiliated with Antioch College in Yellow Springs, Ohio, Mollie Church first fully understood her subordinate racial status:

> While we were reciting our history lesson one day, it suddenly occurred to me that I, myself, was descended from the very slaves whom the Emancipation Proclamation set free. I was stunned. I felt humiliated and disgraced. When I had read or heard about the Union army and the Rebel forces, I had never thought about my connection with slavery at all. But now I knew I belonged to a group of people who had been brutalized, degraded, and sold like animals. This was a rude and terrible shock indeed.

Mollie had, in fact, heard firsthand tales of slavery from her grandmother on her mother's side but had not connected these disturbing stories to her Civil War history lessons at school. According to her autobiography, from this point forth, she vowed to prove through her own achievements that African Americans could overcome this terrible history of slavery and subjection to be recognized as full citizens who had contributed positively to the development of the nation's laws and cultural and political institutions.[8]

An eager and highly intelligent student, Church identified access to higher education as a crucial step in racial uplift. She obtained a bachelor's degree in 1884 from Oberlin College, the first institution of higher education in the United States to admit blacks and women. Prior to 1884, only one or two other black women had ever received a B.A. from an American college. The newly graduated Mollie Church was a sought-after teacher, joining the faculty at Wilberforce University in Ohio and then in the Latin Department at Washington, D.C.'s M Street Colored High School. Two other black women each became an Oberlin graduate with a B.A. that year, Anna Julia Cooper and Ida Gibbs (Hunt), and both also became teachers at the M Street Colored High School; Cooper succeeded Robert Terrell as principal in 1901 and remained until 1906.[9] Having received the finest education available

to a black woman at that time, Mollie Church continued her intellectual engagement by voraciously reading histories, autobiographies,
and novels. By the 1890s she had settled in a neighborhood near
Howard University and had a wide circle of friends from the arts,
education, and the professions, including poets, university professors,
school teachers, administrators, lawyers, doctors, judges, and those
with other civil service professional jobs. As a member of the nation's
black elite, she came to know most of the other civil rights activists,
including Booker T. Washington, W. E. B. Du Bois, poet Paul Laurence
Dunbar, Alice Dunbar (a poet, teacher, and journalist), Anna Julia
Cooper, Nannie Burroughs, and many more.[10]

"IT'S MY COUNTRY"—TRANSNATIONAL EXPOSURE AND QUESTIONS OF CITIZENSHIP

In the late 1880s Mollie Church lived and studied abroad in Europe for
two years, an experience that shaped her understanding of the politics
of race and citizenship in the United States. In Europe she experienced
a comparatively unprejudiced social environment. Contrasting democratic America to an older, aristocratic Europe, she found the United
States lacking; its subordinating system of legal segregation of the races
was, in fact, anti-democratic. As a young educated American woman,
she found that most Europeans did not categorize her as "colored," nor
did they seem to care when she told them about her racial background.
Mollie, fluent in both French and German, made many friends and
learned that prejudice against skin color was not always ingrained in
whites. Although there was a long history of racism in Europe, visiting
black American elites often experienced fewer social barriers and less
hostility from Europeans. In Europe, she reported, "My nerves were not
on edge, neither was my heart in my mouth because I feared I would be
persona non grata to people I met abroad, if perchance they happened
to discover I was of African descent." In contrast, in the United States,
whites often treated her as a "persona non grata," unwelcome in her
own nation.[11]

During Church's extended stay in Europe, she wrestled with the
questions involved in identifying herself as an American citizen, as well
as with the politics of race and interracial marriage. These questions
became personal and immediate when she considered the possibility
of marrying a European white man. In Berlin, she grew very close to a

young German lawyer and baron. He surprised her by writing to her father to ask his permission to marry her, without consulting her first. Bristling a bit at his presumption, Mollie told him that in her circles in the United States, the couple would decide between themselves and only then would the woman's father be approached. She also explained, "I knew father's views on intermarriage of the races and was certain he would not consent." Although her father had maintained cordial relations with his own white father, the harsh reality was that he had been his father's slave. Robert Church rejected interracial marriage for his daughter, believing that no interracial marriage could be free of the inequalities and humiliations that derived from the institution of slavery and from legally and socially enforced racial hierarchies in the United States. As Mollie considered the proposal, she saw that if she married the German baron and lived in Europe, she could avoid calling attention to her racial background most of the time and could simply identify herself as a cultured American expatriate. In spite of her affection for the young man, Mollie Church had reservations, not just about interracial marriage but about living abroad permanently: "I had made up my mind definitely that I would not marry a white man if I lived in the United States, and I feared that I would not be happy as an exile in a foreign land."[12] Choosing not to become an "exile," Mollie rejected the German baron as well as two white American men whom she met abroad and who also proposed marriage. One suitor wanted to return to the United States and live as an interracial couple in open defiance of white Americans' racism (and laws); the other suggested that they could live in Mexico: "'You look like a Mexican,' he argued." She summarily rejected both these proposals: "I knew I would be unhappy if I were the wife of a man belonging to the group which sanctioned or condoned these injustices and perpetrated these wrongs."[13]

Recounting the crisis of identity that her stay in Europe precipitated, she minced no words about what exactly was wrong with America for people of color:

> I thought of the rights, privileges, and immunities cold-bloodedly withheld from the colored people in the United States which practically everybody else is allowed to enjoy. I thought how they are disfranchised in that section where the majority live in spite of the fourteenth and fifteenth amendments, while the whole country looks on with utter indifference at this

flagrant violation of the Constitution and thus, by reprehensible silence and connivance, actually gives its consent. . . . [But] "It's my country," I said indignantly. "I have a perfect right to love it and I will."[14]

In spite of the complexities of her status as an American citizen, the United States was the country of her birth, and she felt she had a right to it and that she belonged there. Mollie Church returned to the United States, determined to pressure the government to fully assume its responsibilities to protect and extend the rights of citizenship to all Americans. Invoking the power of the Reconstruction Era constitutional amendments, she knew that without all three branches of the federal government working to enforce the laws that gave blacks citizenship, they would continue to be denied their rights.

Resolving a moral dilemma through what Steven Belluscio terms an act of "racial allegiance," she reflected, "I knew I would be much happier trying to promote the welfare of my race in my native land, working under certain hard conditions, than I would be living in a foreign land where I could enjoy freedom from prejudice, but where I would make no effort to do the work which I then believed it was my duty to do. I doubted that I could respect myself."[15] If a more noble, activist-oriented life included facing white prejudice, Church was willing to take that path. She was realistic about what she would experience in her native land, knowing that blacks were still second-class citizens: "Life had been so pleasant and profitable abroad. . . . I knew that when I returned home I would face again the humiliations, discriminations, and hardships to which colored people are subjected all over the United States."[16] Just as she had the right to consider (and reject) marriage proposals from white European and American men, she also claimed "a perfect right to love" the United States of America. Once she claimed it as her own, she could move toward her vision of improving her nation.

Soon after her return from Europe, Mollie Church became engaged to Robert Heberton Terrell, a successful and talented light-skinned "colored" American. Robert was the first African American to receive an undergraduate degree with magna cum laude from Harvard University in 1884. Chair of the Latin Department at the M Street "Colored" High School (where Mollie had taught with him before leaving for Europe), he then became its principal. At the same time, he took night classes and graduated from Howard University's Law School in 1889. Once he was an attorney, Robert Terrell was hired in the Auditor's Office of the Treasury Department and later won a prestigious—and because of his race, controversial—appointment as justice of the peace and then as first black municipal court judge in Washington, D.C., beginning in 1901.[17] Robert and Mollie came to the marriage as educated equals—both had college degrees and a mastery of Greek and Latin. Although in college she had feared that the dire predictions of her friends might be true (that men would not want to marry an educated woman like herself), Robert Terrell was undeterred. Even before their marriage in 1891, he favored woman suffrage. Later, he supported her decisions to become the first black woman ever appointed to a school board in the United States (in 1895), to take a leadership role in the black women's club movement, and to go on the lecture circuit.[18]

"LYNCHING FROM A NEGRO'S POINT OF VIEW"— PERSONAL LOSS AND PUBLIC ACTIVISM

Once she settled in Washington, D.C., in the early 1890s, Mollie Church Terrell became involved in black literary clubs and helped found a women's club. Her first significant entry into public political activism occurred as a result of a personal tragedy. The 1892 murder of three Memphis shop owners whose businesses economically competed with (and thus threatened) local whites directly touched Terrell and Ida B. Wells, who were both close friends with one of the victims, Tom Moss. Terrell had known Moss since her childhood in Memphis, describing him as "one of my best friends. We were children together and he was always invited to the parties which my parents gave me." They remained friends, and he had attended her wedding in 1891, the year before he was murdered. For Terrell, Moss's death was "an awful tragedy" that motivated her lifelong anti-lynching activism. As she put it, "when a woman has been closely associated with the victim of the mob from childhood and knows him to be above reproach, the horror and anguish which rend her heart are indescribable." From her home base in the nation's capital, Terrell took immediate action. With her friend and respected mentor Frederick Douglass, she visited President Benjamin Harrison in the White House to implore him to use the power of his office and of the federal government to stop lynching. Although their appeal was unsuccessful, it confirmed and strengthened Terrell's determination to have black Americans recognized by the U.S. government as citizens who deserve equal protection under federal laws.[19]

Moss's lynching inspired Ida B. Wells to write *Southern Horrors: Lynch Law in All Its Phases* (1892), in order to raise public awareness about the horrors of lynching. Subsequently, Wells received invitations to speak to Northern black women's clubs, including Terrell's, which raised money to further her campaign. The two women sometimes collaborated; at a meeting of prominent black women organized by Frederick Douglass in Washington, D.C., in 1893, for example, Terrell introduced Wells as the featured speaker. Historians Darlene Hine and Kathleen Thompson note that the two "worked together in spite of their differences in viewpoint and philosophy. The NACW . . . became one of the strongest supporters of Wells-Barnett's anti-lynching campaign." Like Wells, Terrell decided to write against lynching and tried to find mainstream white newspapers or magazines that would be willing to publish her anti-lynching articles.[20]

After receiving countless rejections, Terrell attributed the 1904 publication of her "Lynching from a Negro's Point of View" to the forceful intervention of the famous author William Dean Howells. Her article in the *North American Review* implicated all whites in the crime of lynching. She asserted that black women were the victims of rape (as they had been under slavery) and that black men were lynched not because they were rapists but "due to race hatred." Arguing that "reputable, law-abiding negroes should protest against the tortures and cruelties inflicted by mobs which wreak vengeance upon the guilty and innocent . . . alike," she insisted, "It is to the credit . . . of the negro that he tries to uphold *the sacred majesty of the law,* which is often trailed in the dust and trampled under foot by white mobs." Inverting common assumptions of black lawlessness, she charged whites with disregarding the laws against murder. Terrell further argued that all American citizens accused of a crime deserved due process, including the right to a fair trial, whether they were guilty or innocent.[21]

Especially as it expanded its overseas empire, the United States presented itself abroad as a missionizing agent of democracy, Christianity, and civilization, Terrell charged that this epidemic of lynching was damaging its international standing. She described lynchings in terms calculated to make whites unable to ignore or condone them any longer. Terming them "wild and diabolical carnival[s] of blood," Terrell predicted that white Americans' lawlessness would ruin the nation's high standing in the "civilized world." She hoped that white Americans would rectify the situation by lobbying Congress to pass federal anti-lynching legislation. In 1905 Terrell attended the annual meeting of the Afro-American Council—a precursor of the NAACP, with a leadership list that included Terrell, AME Bishop Alexander Walters, W. E. B. Du Bois, Archibald Grimke, and William Monroe Trotter. At the 1905 Detroit convention, Terrell's commitment to passing a federal law against lynching led to her appointment as head of its Anti-Lynching Bureau.[22]

"LISTEN TO A PLEA FOR JUSTICE BY AN OUTSIDER"— TERRELL AND WOMAN SUFFRAGE

Like Frances Watkins Harper, Terrell supported woman suffrage but initially saw herself as an "outsider" in the white-dominated woman suffrage movement. In spite of her misgivings, she attended meetings of the newly merged National American Woman Suffrage Association (NAWSA), beginning in the early 1890s. She hoped that if black women had the vote, they could elect politicians who would pass laws to help black Americans achieve the full citizenship that had been guaranteed to them in the Fourteenth and Fifteenth Amendments.[23] Terrell's attendance at a NAWSA meeting in 1896 highlighted her outsider status. At one point during the suffrage meeting, "when the members of the Association were registering their protest against a certain injustice," Terrell relates, "I arose and said, 'As a colored woman, I hope this Association will include in the resolution the injustices of various kinds of which colored people are the victims.'" She identified lynching, segregation, and the convict lease system as the injustices she wanted this white organization to recognize and protest. Although Terrell was already a leading black clubwoman, she was not recognized by the white suffragists at NAWSA's 1896 meeting: "'Are you a member of this Association?' Miss Susan B. Anthony asked. 'No, I am not,' I replied, 'but I thought you might be willing to listen to a plea for justice by an outsider.'" Recognizing and naming herself as an "outsider" based on her race, Terrell nevertheless contested her exclusion and insisted on being heard.[24]

Although Terrrell was initially addressed as a stranger at this NAWSA convention, she found a space for herself within it. She appreciated the fact that she was treated with respect: "Then Miss Anthony invited

me to come forward, write out the resolution which I wished incorpo-
rated with the others, and hand it to the Committee on Resolutions.
And thus began a delightful, helpful friendship with Miss Anthony
which lasted till she passed away [1906]." This encounter initiated a
close personal and professional relationship between the two leaders.
Subsequently, Terrell was invited to give speeches at NAWSA conventions and even became a life member of the organization. Among her
many suffrage talks was one she gave in Rochester, New York, where
she pointedly noted that she stayed as a welcome guest in Susan B.
Anthony's home.[25]

Terrell was well aware of NAWSA's problematic and inconsistent
stance on race. Susan B. Anthony's record on race, like that of Frances
Willard's and those of many white suffragists, was flawed. To mollify
Southern white suffragists, for instance, Anthony had insisted that
Terrell's good friend Frederick Douglass not attend the 1895 NAWSA
convention held in Atlanta, Georgia. Also for fear of alienating Southern whites, Anthony refused to allow a group of African American
women to form their own branch of NAWSA.[26] Terrell deeply admired
Douglass, who died in 1895. At the 1898 NAWSA convention, she
pointedly celebrated Douglass's decision to support Elizabeth Cady
Stanton's resolution in favor of woman suffrage at the 1848 Seneca
Falls woman's rights convention and downplayed his shift to black
male enfranchisement after the war. During her eleven years as the
first black female member of the Board of Education of the District
of Columbia, Terrell created a role for herself as a promoter of universal suffrage and civil rights. She successfully instituted a "Frederick
Douglass Day" (1897) in the black schools of Washington, D.C., to
celebrate this great advocate of abolition and universal suffrage. In
1908 she was pleased to be invited by NAWSA to represent Frederick
Douglass at the sixtieth anniversary of the Seneca Falls Convention,
where she delivered two addresses, one on Douglass's legacy and one
on the "Justice of Woman Suffrage."[27]

Like Frances Harper, Terrell tried to make the most of her prominent
position in interracial organizations in order to confront white racism.
She told white suffragists that although she had experienced sexism
throughout her life, her sex had not as fully defined and circumscribed
her experiences and opportunities as had her race: "But I assure you
that nowhere in the United States have my feelings been so lacerated,
my spirit so crushed, my heart so wounded, nowhere have I been so

humiliated and handicapped on account of my sex as I have been on account of my race." Denying an easy universal sisterhood, she insisted on calling attention to the difference that race made in black women's lives. Terrell's hard-hitting statement was meant to force white suffragists to take seriously black women's unique concerns and legislative priorities.[28]

Terrell also tried to interest black men in black women's continued exclusion from full political citizenship. Prodding them to make the connection between racism and sexism, Terrell predicted that, if they did, black men would realize, "the same arguments advanced against the right of women to participate in the affairs of their government and their respective States are used by those enemies of the Colored American who have robbed him of his right of citizenship in 11 States." Because all blacks were equally vulnerable to attempts to keep them from the polls, Terrell argued that black men should be women's best allies in the fight for full citizenship at the federal and state levels. Sometimes feeling like an "outsider" among black male reformers who ignored the issue of woman suffrage, Terrell published "The Justice of Woman Suffrage" in a 1912 edition of the NAACP's official organ, *The Crisis*. Her article directly addressed the persistent problem that some black men were skeptical of or indifferent toward black women's suffrage claims. Terrell argued for federal woman suffrage as part of a broader campaign for racial justice and progress: "for an intelligent colored man to oppose woman suffrage is the most preposterous and ridiculous thing in the world. What could be more absurd than to see one group of human beings who are denied rights which they are trying to secure for themselves working to prevent another group from obtaining the same rights?" A united campaign for rights on behalf of all second-class citizens made sense as a political strategy and as a principled position.[29]

"OUR PECULIAR STATUS IN THIS COUNTRY"—FORMING THE NATIONAL ASSOCIATION OF COLORED WOMEN

Terrell's background of living and working in integrated environments, which included attending schools with whites, meant that she willingly worked within predominantly white organizations such as NAWSA and the D.C. School Board, as well as in the integrated NAACP. Terrell found her voice as an activist in the 1890s, when the

time seemed right to organize a separate national black women's organization. Frances Harper and Terrell helped found the new National
Association of Colored Women (NACW) in 1896. The formation of
the NACW had multiple sources and drew on multiple trajectories of
political momentum.[30]

For Terrell the chance to organize nationally as black women was an
opportunity not to be missed. In part she was inspired, she explained, as
she watched the growing political influence of the National American
Woman Suffrage Association in the early 1890s. NAWSA exemplified
the reasons that a powerful unified national organization for black
women would be a positive development:

> Having observed from attending the Woman Suffrage meetings how
> much may be accomplished through organization, I entered enthusiasti-
> cally into club work among the women of my own group. For many years
> colored women had been binding themselves together in the interest of
> the church and had done very effective work in many ways. But secular
> organizations among them were comparatively rare. As soon as the idea
> of uniting their forces outside the church dawned upon them, it took
> definite, tangible form quickly, and women of all classes and conditions
> seized upon it with enthusiasm.

Expanding black women's base from the churches to a secular collectivity of women's groups would bridge denominational divides and
allow them more control over the objectives of their reform work and
the funds they raised. Many black women in Christian organizations
such as the Woman's Convention Auxiliary of the National Baptist
Convention and the WCTU joined the new secular, national, black
women's association.[31]

A significant factor in the formation of NACW, according to historian Evelyn Brooks Higginbotham, was "the exclusionary policies
of white women's clubs." As we have seen, black women were not
fully accepted as equals in groups such as the WCTU. They also found
themselves excluded completely from other major organizations such
as the General Federation of Women's Clubs, as well as from special
exhibitions such as the women's building (itself a new achievement
for white women) of the 1893 World's Columbian Exposition in
Chicago. Although she did not necessarily expect them to accept her
offer, Josephine St. Pierre Ruffin, editor of the *Woman's Era,* pointedly

invited white women to join as members of black women's clubs and work together on their many common reform goals. Historian Floris Cash explains that since "[m]any African American women had experienced exclusion from white women's organizations . . . they did not intend to discriminate." Symbolically, Ruffin knew that black women must offer a clear contrast to white women's racial exclusivity by being nondiscriminatory and inclusive.[32]

By the 1890s Frances Watkins Harper, Mary Church Terrell, Josephine St. Pierre Ruffin, Nannie Helen Burroughs, and many of their fellow black clubwomen decided to organize separately. Terrell helped found the first black women's group with national ambitions, the Colored Women's League (1892), in Washington, D.C., while Ruffin soon organized the Federation of Afro-American Women in Boston. Terrell explained the rationale of the Colored Women's League as follows:

> We denominate ourselves colored, not because we are narrow, and wish to lay special emphasis on the color of the skin, for which no one is responsible, which of itself is not proof of an individual's virtue nor of his vice . . . but we refer to the fact that this is an association of colored women, because our peculiar status in this country at the present time seems to *demand* that we stand by ourselves in the special work for which we have organized.

If black women had a choice their color would not be an issue, but in the United States at the turn of the twentieth century, a "color blind" approach was not an option. Black women would continue to work together with white women for suffrage and temperance; they also intended to educate white women further on the need for expanded and enforceable civil rights laws. But black women recognized that they must organize themselves separately to begin a national discussion about their priorities: passing federal legislation to stop lynching, overturning Jim Crow segregation laws as unconstitutional (a goal made difficult by the U.S. Supreme Court's 1896 ruling in *Plessy v. Ferguson*), and defining the convict lease labor system (which functioned as a form of debt peonage in Southern prisons) as unconstitutional.[33]

Several other factors motivated African American clubwomen to organize themselves into a national organization. According to historian Dorothy Salem, black women successfully organized to promote Ida B. Wells's anti-lynching campaign, starting with a testimonial dinner held for her in New York in 1892, but they soon recognized their failure to organize an effective protest against their exclusion from the Chicago World's Columbian Exposition. In addition, in 1894, black women were informed they could send representatives to the 1895 meeting of the National Council of Women, but only if these were representatives of national organizations. Then, Josephine Ruffin circulated amongst subscribers to her *Woman's Era* copies of a hostile 1895 letter from the white male president of the Missouri Press Association to the secretary of the Anti-Lynching Society of England, ridiculing and casting doubt upon all black women's virtue. This letter helped galvanize black women to organize in their own defense. Finally, there were two different women's clubs who were both claiming to represent black women nationally, a situation that led to confusion and bad public relations.[34]

Thus, in 1896, black clubwomen united in the National Association of Colored Women, with Mary Church Terrell as president and Frances Watkins Harper as a vice president. By that time, Terrell had made a name for herself as a teacher at the M Street "Colored" High School in Washington, D.C., as a founder of the Colored Woman's League of Washington, D.C., as the first female president (1892–1893) of the prestigious Bethel Literary and Historical Association, and as the first black woman on the District of Columbia's Board of Education. Defending black womanhood, the members of NACW organized to confront and combat the combined forces of sexism and racism. Terrell incisively described her status, and the status of all black women, in these terms: "A white woman has only one handicap to overcome—that of sex. I have two—both sex and race. I belong to the only group in the country which has two such huge obstacles to surmount. Colored men have only one—that of race." Determined to change a white- and male-dominated society and its laws, Terrell endorsed self-help and local community activism on the part of organized black women while simultaneously pushing for national reforms and an expansion of federal power to protect black Americans' civil rights.[35]

Terrell and Harper advocated that the name of the new organization should be the "National Association of Colored Women" over an alternative proposal to call it the "National Association of Afro-American Women." "Colored" was more accurate, Terrell reasoned, since it recognized most African Americans' mixed heritage and was more inclusive of a variety of skin tones. The term "colored" also highlighted the history of rape and sexual domination of black women by white men, which had produced so many generations of mixed-race children. Suffering from the double burden of being female and black in the United States, black women created a national organization at a time when each of these groups was unequal and subordinate under the law.[36]

"TO THE CHILDREN OF THE RACE"—MATERNALISM AND THE NACW

During her tenure as NACW president from 1896 to 1901, Terrell set an agenda that began with mothers and children in their homes and immediately moved out into the public sphere. The agenda of the NACW is part of a long tradition of prioritizing mothering within African American history. Black women had strong traditions around motherhood and community life; black Baptist women, for instance, had already introduced mothers' training schools and social service programs. These self-help programs were modified and adopted by many of the other women's clubs affiliated with the NACW. Historian Judith Weisenfeld clarifies that, although black clubwomen "focused attention on encouraging the building of Christian homes, by no means did this serve as a call for women to remain supportive and invisible in the home to the exclusion of other activities."[37]

Terrell argued that black mothers needed help and training to raise healthy, thriving children just as much as or more than white mothers did. In part, Terrell's emphasis on women's power in the home represents a more generalized trend toward a maternalist rhetoric that informed women's activism at the turn of the century. Yet her rhetoric did more than echo white women's maternalist ethos; it also subversively upheld the virtue and purity of black women and their homes, thereby displacing white women from their solitary position on the pedestal of "true womanhood."[38] This rhetoric of purity and maternalism allowed black clubwomen to claim access to genteel white middle-class norms and ideals and provided a respectable rationale for their political activism.

Using the rhetoric of home missionary work, Terrell called on black clubwomen to work for the salvation of poorer, illiterate black women.[39] In her presidential addresses, especially her first in 1897, Terrell used language that acknowledged class differences between most NACW members and poor blacks. Connecting criminal behavior to what she termed "the miserable hovels from which these youthful criminals come," for instance, Terrell highlighted economic differences among black women. She did not, however, condemn or ignore poor black women and their families. Instead, she insisted, "It is, therefore, into the home, sisters of the Association, that we must go, filled with all the zeal and charity which such a *mission* demands. To the children of the race we owe, as women, a debt which can never be paid, until herculean efforts are made to rescue them from evil and shame for which they are in no way responsible."[40] She perceived poor black mothers and their children as being those in need of salvation—something they could only achieve, she implied, with the assistance of elite clubwomen. To some extent Terrell articulated NACW members' class status and prejudices, yet she also resisted some middle- and upper-class black women's efforts to define their clubs as elite social cliques rather than as reform-oriented groups. Demanding that clubwomen not ignore their poorer sisters, she reminded them that, because of pervasive racism, they could not retreat from those less fortunate than themselves even if they wanted to. White women reformers generally did not feel compelled to defend the purity of poor white women in order to maintain their own honor. In contrast, middle- and upper-class black women saw that racist whites systematically linked their status to that of poorer black women. Although, as an upper-class light-skinned woman, Terrell might arguably have made the choice to distance herself from poorer blacks, she realized that white society did not often bother to distinguish between black women on the basis of class, education, or skin tone. She knew that differences in black women's class and educational status were often ignored by whites who collapsed them together as racial inferiors.[41]

Racial uplift would only work, therefore, if all African Americans benefited from reform. Historian Gerda Lerner argues that "black club women frequently successfully bridged the class barrier and concerned themselves with issues of importance to poor women, working mothers, tenant farm wives."[42] Terrell's passionate advocacy for the rights, health, and safety of convict laborers in the South, her opposition to lynching, and her support for working mothers demonstrates her willingness to fight for the most unpopular causes and people. Terrell maintained this commitment for decades, in spite of being received with indifference or resistance on the part of whites who did not want to admit or to solve complex and deeply entrenched manifestations of institutionalized racism.

The NACW's focus on self-help in the home was also a strategy to defuse violence in the South in the late 1890s, at a time when white resistance was increasing against any political, economic, or social gains by black Americans. As overt political activism and attempts to pass reform legislation grew ever more difficult and dangerous, Southern black women reformers focused on children and their homes as more neutral sites of reform that might be freer from white supervision and control. In the post-Reconstruction South most black men were already disfranchised, and all blacks were subject to segregation, violence, and the threat of lynching. As a native Southerner, Terrell knew that blacks who created and supported explicitly political organizations faced potentially violent reprisals. Floris Cash observes that "African American clubwomen provided leadership during a time when voluntary action was most frequently the only solution for solving problems in African American communities" that were facing "severe oppression." Yet even mothers' training for black women was not always accepted as a neutral enterprise by whites. Evelyn Brooks Higginbotham notes that white and black reformers opened up many training schools for mothers across the South. The teachers' "dictums on housekeeping, maternal, and wifely duties carried a message of black dignity and equality that did not rest well with white supremacists," who threatened reformers and their pupils with harassment and intimidation as well as beatings and shootings.[43]

Terrell's maternalist rhetoric and agenda for the NACW had a tragic personal dimension. Beginning with her first pregnancy in 1892, when she was in her early thirties, she delivered three babies in five years, each of whom died within a few days of birth. As a pregnant woman trying to get quality health care, Terrell faced discrimination in Washington, D.C., and she attributed her infants' deaths to inadequate medical care at segregated facilities. At least one baby was hooked up to an improvised incubator because the hospital did not have a proper one. In 1896, when she was voted in as the first president of NACW, Terrell was pregnant with the last of the three babies she would lose; privately, she suffered from episodes of deep depression during these years. When Terrell became pregnant once again, she felt she had no choice but to temporarily leave her home and husband to try to give birth to a healthy child. Her only surviving child, Phyllis, was born in 1898 in New York

City, where Terrell stayed with her mother, Louisa Church, to get better treatment for her newborn in a hospital with proper equipment. After Phyllis's birth, Mollie Terrell's mother, reaching the end of her own successful business career and recognizing her daughter's unique talents, decided to move into the Terrell home to take over some housekeeping duties, freeing her daughter for public service. Mollie and Robert also adopted her young niece soon after. As her family grew, she continued her reform activism. Throughout these personal crises, Terrell persisted in her role as leader of the NACW, publicly taking on the burdens of all mothers and children as she grieved for her loss. She knew the challenges facing black women and tried to respond with concrete, positive reform proposals.[44]

As NACW president, Terrell set an ambitious maternalist self-help agenda that echoed Willard's earlier "Do Everything Policy" for the WCTU. Defining upper- and middle-class black women's "duty to the race," Terrell outlined a full program of pragmatic reforms:

> Homes for the orphaned and aged must be established; sanatoriums, hospitals, and training schools for nurses founded; unfortunate women and tempted girls encircled by the loving arms of those who would woo them back to the path of rectitude and virtue; classes formed for cultivating the mind; schools of domestic science opened in every city and village in which our women and girls may be found. All this is our *duty,* all this is an *obligation,* which we should discharge as soon as our means will permit.[45]

Over a dozen departments were formed by the NACW at the national level; local clubwomen often worked on several of these program goals over the course of any given year. Sadly, Terrell's agenda demonstrates the extra burden facing black women's clubs. The NACW had first to provide the most basic of services and programs as well as to engage in substantial efforts toward the building of hospitals, orphanages, and old age homes that local and state governments had often already provided to whites.

As their first reform goal Terrell asked NACW members to establish free kindergartens "in every city and hamlet of this broad land." White women's organizations such as the National Congress of Mothers and the WCTU had already begun setting up kindergartens but most were open only to white children. NACW leaders and members recognized that black children needed kindergartens and daycare facilities more, not less, than white children since many more black mothers had no choice but to be the primary wage earners in their families. Poor children lacked supervision and encouragement, Terrell sympathetically explained, because their mothers had to work for wages in order to try to feed, clothe, and house them. As wage earners, these mothers were eager to find good quality and affordable day care for their children. "Side by side in importance with the kindergarten," Terrell announced, "stands the day nursery. . . . Thousands of our wage-earning mothers with large families dependent upon them for support are obliged to leave their infants all day" in unsafe situations with siblings or over-burdened neighbors.[46]

By engaging in institution building, black women acted, in effect, as an arm of the state. This was a huge burden for organized black women to take on. Recognizing that kindergartens, day nurseries, and infant-care facilities were very expensive to set up and operate, Terrell anticipated concerned resistance from NACW members. She asked clubwomen not to feel overwhelmed and insisted that these goals were achievable. A kindergarten or day nursery started by clubwomen might acquire local or state funding within a few years, she reported encouragingly. Pointing to instances where cities had taken over part of the funding of successful institutions, Terrell lauded institution building as a reasonable goal: "A sanitarium with a training school for nurses has been set on such a firm foundation by the Phyllis Wheatley Club of New Orleans, Louisiana, . . . that the municipal government has voted it an annual appropriation of several hundred dollars."[47]

Institution building was just one part of NACW members' civic engagement. Since the antebellum era, black abolitionists and women's rights advocates had been interested in gaining universal suffrage for black men and women. During Reconstruction, they became involved in partisan politics, committed to supporting the Republican Party. A strong Republican Party loyalist, Terrell built on this tradition of black women's involvement in politics and reform to campaign for a constitutional amendment for woman suffrage. She helped gain organized support for a constitutional amendment for woman suffrage among rank-and-file members of the NACW. Her membership in NAWSA and her leadership of NACW enabled her to become one of the most prominent woman suffrage proponents in the black community in the late 1890s and early twentieth century. Terborg-Penn notes that, "From the onset, woman suffrage was a notable department of the NACW and continued to be for the duration of the movement."[48]

In 1908 Terrell joined other prominent members of the NACW such as Lucy Thurman and Margaret Murray Washington in petitioning for a federal woman suffrage bill that would extend the vote to women and protect the voting rights of black men. The petition resolved, in part, "That we, the members of The Equal Suffrage League, representing the National Association of Colored Women through its Suffrage Department, in the interest of Enfranchisement, Taxation with Representation, ask to have enacted such legislation as will enforce the 14th and 15th Amendments of the Constitution of our country, the United States of America, throughout all its sections." The federal government, especially Congress, was a necessary ally in their fight to enforce the Reconstruction Amendments. The signatories of this petition realized that a new woman suffrage amendment would be immediately undermined unless Congress included strong and effective enforcement provisions. Historian Beverly Guy-Sheftall argues that black clubwomen supported federal woman suffrage as a way "to assume a broader place within the public sphere, which will in turn assure her equality with men. Equally as important, granting black women the vote will also contribute to the overall emancipation of the race since black women will help black men get elected to public office." For Terrell and NACW members, women's rights were always linked to improved civil rights for all African Americans.[49]

Those women who were willing to enter into more controversial, overtly political fights were sympathetically described by Terrell as "most progressive." She encouraged black women to launch more campaigns, such as those in Louisiana and Tennessee, where "colored women have several times petitioned the legislatures of their respective states to repeal the obnoxious Jim Crow Car Laws. Against the Convict Lease System . . . colored women here and there in the South are waging a ceaseless war." As they gained experience and organizational strength, Terrell wanted and expected African American women to engage increasingly in overtly political and legislative struggles. In 1913, for example, she convinced the NACW to set up a Department for the Suppression of Lynchings, which aimed at passing a national anti-lynching bill, demanding that the federal government counter lawlessness at the state level.[50]

As its first president, Terrell helped the NACW grow into a prominent national organization. She remained popular with NACW members who appreciated her powerful speeches and ability to represent black women with grace and honor. They voted her "honorary president for life" in 1901 and for decades invited her to speak at their national, state, and local conventions.[51]

TELLING "THE DISAGREEABLE TRUTH"—TERRELL'S SPEAKING AND PUBLISHING CAREER

NACW leadership allowed Terrell to become, in Glenda Gilmore's phrase, a more effective "diplomat" to the white community by authorizing her to speak as a representative of her race. In this capacity Terrell provided her audiences with pointed and extensive critiques of the most serious problems facing black Americans: lynching, peonage, and Jim Crow segregation. Knowing that reforming black homes was only part of the solution to advancing the status and condition of African Americans, Terrell moved to the forefront of work against institutionalized racism, arguing in the early 1900s that white laws and attitudes played a more central role in stunting opportunities for black youths than did their impoverished home environments.[52]

Subversively inverting the standard rhetoric of reform and missionary work by focusing on reforming and uplifting white Americans, Terrell pointed out that their barbaric treatment of blacks marked white Americans as even more in need of salvation than black Americans, who were more often stereotyped as the needy recipients of reform benevolence. Identifying racism as the root cause of problems in the African American community, she exposed whites' lawless violence and brutal exploitation of blacks' labor and bodies. Terrell's direct attacks on white racism anticipate—"almost prophetically," in Stephanie Shaw's characterization—a strand of black women's reform activism that became especially prominent in the 1930s. Shaw argues that during the Great Depression, when organized black women "realized that community development and racial uplift would not get them where they wanted to be as long as they were uplifting only the black race, they went to work on uplifting the white race." Mollie Church Terrell and Ida B. Wells were among those black activists who adopted an earlier version of this missionary approach toward whites.[53]

By the early 1900s Terrell's outspokenness against white racism as well as her focus on federal legislative remedies to guarantee African

Americans' civil rights aligned her more closely with W. E. B Du Bois than with Booker T. Washington. In 1906, for instance, Terrell, Du Bois, and the white reformer and journalist John Milholland formed the Constitution League, a group that monitored violations of citizens' constitutional rights and called for the full enforcement of the U.S. Constitution by federal authorities, especially since state and local authorities were often less effective or interested.[54] Terrell agreed with Du Bois's more confrontational, politically engaged approach to gaining civil rights for African Americans. By 1909 she was a member of the Committee of Forty on Permanent Organization, which founded the NAACP, the interracial civil rights group.[55] When Terrell participated in its founding, she and her husband had to resist the pressures of Booker T. Washington's Tuskegee machine, especially those who "warned that this action on his wife's part would alienate Dr. Washington from him and finally lead to his political ruin."[56] She recollected that "By some I was severely criticized . . . because it [the NAACP] was supposed to have been founded to counteract the influence of Booker T. Washington and to discredit him." Terrell followed her conscience and became a member of the NAACP board of directors nonetheless. Deborah Gray White points out that the NAACP's fast growth was aided by the NACW leadership and its local black women's clubs, which set up NAACP chapters across the country.[57] Terrell traveled extensively under its auspices as a public lecturer in order to promote its antiracism campaigns, especially anti-lynching. Through her public speaking she served as a liaison who could bring "the goals of the NAACP before white organizations."[58]

Terrell was a particularly effective diplomat because she gained access to white audiences who otherwise would not necessarily have come to hear a black woman speak about the controversial topics she raised. In addition to her status as honorary NACW president for life, her white Oberlin College friends and others she met through her club, suffrage, and school-board work in Washington, D.C., provided her with important contacts as she developed what became a thirty-year career of public speaking. Terrell's close white friend from high school and college, Janet McKelvey Swift, the wife of a Congregational Church minister, helped to facilitate one of her first public lectures to a predominantly white audience, the Congregational Association of Maryland and the District of Columbia. From there she was recruited to work for the Slayton Lyceum Bureau, a circuit Chautauqua Bureau booking agency run from Steinway Hall in Chicago. Pointing to her celebratory speeches and articles concerning prominent black artists and politicians, historian Sharon Harley suggests that Terrell "naively thought that the more whites knew about black progress, the quicker they would embrace blacks as equals."[59]

In fact, Terrell knew only too well that white racism was deeply entrenched and very difficult to combat. However, she was committed to forcing white Americans to recognize the accomplishments of black Americans as well as to apply the same rules of justice to all. After a successful speech before the World's Purity Congress in Columbus, Ohio, in 1911, she wrote her husband, "I tell you white people like to hear the disagreeable truth, if one has tact and good taste enough to present it forcibly but politely. I am amazed myself at the quantity of hard pummeling they are willing to stand from me." As a featured speaker for the Chautauqua lecture series, she confronted white audiences and asked for changes in federal laws to outlaw lynching, segregation, and the convict leasing system. She did so from a lecture platform where they were just as likely to hear from popular racists. Terrell ironically noted, for example, that "on several occasions I spoke to the same audience Tom Dixon addressed—the same Tom Dixon who wrote *The Clansman* [1905], which, as a novel, a movie [*Birth of a Nation*, 1915] and a talkie, has done a great deal of harm." She saw her presence on these platforms as a way to represent the civil rights demands of black Americans to audiences who were not used to considering the consequences of racial discrimination.[60]

Trying to force whites out of their complacency, she included in her Chautauqua lectures a standard talk, "'Uncle Sam and the Sons of Ham,'" in which she "dwelt upon the Government's relation to the race" focused especially on the convict lease system, black men's disfranchisement, and the federal government's responsibility for letting these blatantly unconstitutional practices continue. Terrell declared, "Although I was warned by some of my friends not to present certain facts showing the injustice and brutality to which colored people are sometimes subjected, for fear it would militate against my success as a speaker, I felt that I could not be true to myself or to my race, if I did not touch upon this phase of the subject." In addition to her lectures on the primarily white Chautauqua circuit, Terrell was often invited to speak as a representative of the interracial NAACP to black audiences such as at the NACW state conventions or colored teachers state associations as well as at many black and white high schools, colleges, and universities.[61]

"A STRANGER IN A STRANGE LAND"—SEGREGATION AND CITIZENSHIP

As part of her attempt to spread enlightenment among Northern whites, Terrell hoped to prove that Jim Crow segregation (both de facto and de jure) jeopardized African Americans' status as full citizens. To do so, she wrote an article that incisively described the disabilities faced by black Americans in the U.S. capital. Just as her anti-lynching article had been published only because of William Dean Howell's timely intervention, her article on segregation and white racism finally gained a white readership only because she happened to submit it at a moment when race relations were being vigorously debated in the Senate. In 1907 an American journal, *The Independent,* published Terrell's searing article, "What It Means to Be Colored in the Capital of the United States." The editors prefaced her anonymously published article (she was identified as "a colored woman of much culture and recognized standing") with an explanation that it was "timely" since it coincided with a Senate debate about the 1906 dismissal without honor of African American soldiers in Texas who were falsely charged with rioting (the soldiers were finally cleared in the 1970s, after all but two were dead). Newspapers had already reported Terrell's direct involvement in calls for their exoneration; she met personally with the secretary of war, William H. Taft, and with President Theodore Roosevelt to protest their dismissals.[62]

Highlighting the outsider status and second-class citizenship of all blacks in the capital, Terrell lamented, "As a colored woman I might enter Washington any night, a stranger in a strange land, and walk miles without finding a place to lay my head." Courageously attacking the increasing segregation in the nation's capital, she emphasized that although Washington, D.C., was her home, she was alienated and separated from it, knowing that so few hotels and restaurants would serve her. Appealing to white Americans' patriotism and to their pride in the founding principles of the U.S. government, Terrell hoped to make them see that segregation was a betrayal of these fundamental principles: "And surely nowhere in the world do oppression and persecution based solely on the color of the skin appear more hateful and hideous than in the capital of the United States, because the chasm between the principles upon which the Government was founded, in which it still professes to believe, and those which are daily practiced under the protection of the flag, yawns so wide and deep." African Americans had fought for and deserved—yet had not truly secured—the full citizenship rights guaranteed to them by the Reconstruction Amendments.[63]

African Americans lost the battle against formal segregation laws in the nation's capital in 1913, when President Woodrow Wilson's administration instituted segregation in federal offices, lunchrooms, and the galleries of the Senate. She never reconciled herself to the discriminatory segregation laws in the District of Columbia, and by 1953 she had successfully helped defeat them through a series of protests, boycotts, and lawsuits—four decades later, just before her ninetieth birthday. At that point, she could finally feel a true sense of national belonging as a black American citizen.[64]

"SAVING THE WHITE SOUTH FROM ITS OWN LAWLESS-NESS"—BLACK WOMEN REFORMERS AS MISSIONARIES

With a goal of developing a sense of national identity, belonging, and purpose for African Americans, Terrell made a subversive proposal. She suggested that blacks volunteer to serve as missionaries to a "lawless" white South that was desperately in need of reform and salvation. Whereas most white American publishers refused to print her articles, black publishers regularly accepted them, including "Service Which Should Be Rendered the South," which appeared in a 1905 edition of Voice of the Negro, edited by J. Max Barber in Atlanta, Georgia. Proposing that African American reformers undertake a new missionary service in the South, Terrell again targeted Southern whites as objects of reform. Inverting the missionizing rhetoric usually aimed at poor blacks, she alerted the journal's black readership of "the need of enlightening and civilizing the thousands of ignorant, slothful, unaspiring and vicious white people of the South." Turning the tables on white racists who claimed that only blacks were in need of reform and assistance, Terrell declared that progressive blacks needed to become new modern-day missionaries: "When one thinks of the lawlessness which so generally prevails in the South today, among the educated and rich as well as among the ignorant and poor, he can have no doubt of the crying need of men and women who are willing to devote their lives to the work of creating a holy respect for law and order among all classes of white people of that section." What Southern whites needed most, she declared, was to learn a sacred respect

Mary Church Terrell, elegant and refined, sits on an ornate chair. In the backdrop, a curtain pulls back to reveal a grand staircase, suggesting a stately residence.

for the U.S. Constitution and the protections it offered all American citizens, regardless of the color of their skin.[65]

Among white publications only a British journal, *Nineteenth Century and After,* provided a forum for a revised version of her *Voice of the Negro* article. Entitled "A Plea for the White South by a Coloured Woman," this 1906 exposé focused on the white South's refusal to honor the Reconstruction Amendments to the U.S. Constitution. Participating in a transnational discussion of the need for increased civil rights protections for black American citizens, Terrell spread her message abroad, charging that the "majority of white people in the South acquiesce in the crimes committed by the lynchers, the white caps, and the Constitution-smashers who have violently snatched the right of citizenship from more than a million men." Klan members were not just renegade terrorists, she informed her British audience, but an integral and accepted part of the white community's efforts to limit black Americans' civil rights. In her autobiography Terrell regretted that, "in spite of the fourteenth and fifteenth amendments," African Americans were lynched, forced into labor, and "disfranchised in that section where the majority live." She hoped to generate international protest against white Americans' racist betrayal of black Americans. Southern whites were not the only ones who contributed to this condition of lawlessness; she pointed out that "the whole country looks on with utter indifference at this flagrant violation of the Constitution and thus, by reprehensible silence and connivance, actually gives its consent."[66]

Repeatedly emphasizing their "lawlessness," Terrell portrayed whites rather than blacks as the dangerous lawbreakers, whose anarchistic vigilante actions were destroying respect for the country's founding documents, especially the U.S. Constitution, the basis of the Republic. Warning that the condition, mind-set, and actions of most white Southerners undermined the fundamental stability of the nation as a whole, Terrell placed racism in the South in a national context and then exposed it to an international audience:

> If one section of this country is permitted to trample with impunity upon any provision of the Constitution with which it takes issue, another will surely resort to the same expedient to render null and void any section or clause to which it is opposed. It does not require a great amount of profundity or perspicacity to see that the violation of one fundamental law invariably leads to the infraction of another.[67]

By focusing on white lawlessness and by rejecting the states' rights arguments of white Southerners, Terrell hoped to make her British readers pause and reconsider whether blacks were indeed the problem as so many white Americans charged. Trying to convert the British to her point of view, she hoped to generate international pressure to improve U.S. civil rights laws and protections.

Positioning blacks as the real American citizens, whose love of the values and laws upon which the country was founded had kept the nation strong, Terrell argued that "there are no truer patriots in the United States to-day than are the 10,000,000 coloured people who know and love no fatherland but this. In every war which this country has waged in the past, coloured men have fought and died with a courage and a patriotism surpassed by none." Knowing that citizenship was often tied to men's military service, she pointed to black men's service to prove their patriotic loyalty. "[T]he intelligent coloured people in this country have learned to love liberty more than they love life," Terrell observed, by reading "the speeches of the Revolutionary fathers, which breathe forth hatred of oppression in every line." They had learned from the founders of their country to value liberty, but even after the U.S. fought the Civil War and amended the Constitution to give African Americans full citizenship, Terrell lamented, "yet they know they are not free."[68]

"CONGRESS HAS POWER"—TERRELL'S CAMPAIGN
TO END CONVICT LABOR

Southern whites' lawlessness, Terrell observed, was compounded by the willful ignorance of Northern whites. Constantly challenged by skeptical and resistant white audiences as she traveled the lecture circuit, Terrell felt compelled to provide proof of her charges of white lawlessness while acting herself as a missionary spreading enlightenment. She was particularly disturbed to find that many Northern whites categorically denied that the Reconstruction Amendments were not being enforced. They refused to admit or acknowledge that, by the end of Reconstruction, black men's voting rights had been eviscerated throughout the South. Terrell explained to her audiences that Southern white Democrats had only won seats in Congress by illegally disfranchising black men who would have voted for Republican candidates. In a typical exchange, a white Bostonian challenged her assertion that "he would need only a few thousand votes to get elected to Congress from Mississippi because colored men were disfranchised in that State." He asked:

> "What has become of the fourteenth amendment?" . . . with a fine show of indignation. When I told him that the fourteenth amendment had been null and void, not only in Mississippi, but in the other southern States for years, he replied, "Walk softly, Mrs. Terrell, walk softly, when you declare that an amendment to the Constitution is so flagrantly violated as you claim it is." Even after I gave him definite facts and figures . . . . he showed plainly that he thought I was either greatly exaggerating the facts or was not telling the truth.

Northern whites stubbornly maintained the fiction that the Reconstruction Amendments were still in force; this stance allowed them to assert that they had done their duty to freed slaves and their descendants and could do no more. Waging an informational campaign to disrupt the complacency of her white Northern audiences, Terrell had to fight continuously and assiduously for the enforcement of the Thirteenth and Fourteenth Amendments in order to protect blacks from abuses such as lynching, convict labor, and disfranchisement.[69]

Ironically, it was after talking to a group of white missionary women who professed ignorance about convict leasing that she "decided to write an article on the subject." Terrell "learned . . . during an address that I delivered before the Baptist Woman's Home Missionary Society in Beverly, Massachusetts, that even well-educated people . . . knew nothing whatever . . . about the Convict Lease System." Thus, she "went to the Congressional Library and spent six weeks looking over old files of the *Atlanta Constitution* and other newspapers published in the South." Following Ida B. Wells's lead and the Grimkés' earlier technique of collecting Southern white testimony against slavery, Terrell relied upon reports from white Southern newspapers for evidence of whites' misdeeds in order to expose the exploitative convict lease system and chain gangs. She quoted also from government documents such as state-level investigatory commission reports in order to prove to Northern whites that she was not exaggerating the problem.[70]

Hoping that her exposure of the convict leasing system in the South would lead blacks and whites to demand federal laws to end these abuses, Terrell was fighting white indifference on the one hand and

Southern black hopelessness on the other. Sympathetically describing the victims of the convict lease system as poor, exploited, Southern black men, Terrell documented how they were often charged with minor misdemeanors such as spitting on the sidewalk, only to find themselves facing long jail terms or heavy fines. If they could not pay, they were given over to the custody of white farmers, factory owners, or others, who paid off their fines but then forced them to work indefinitely at hard labor under inhumane, even deadly, conditions to pay off their debts (with interest and penalties).[71]

To educate Northern whites about this abusive system, Terrell submitted a brutally honest article, "Peonage in the United States: The Convict Lease System and the Chain Gangs," to many white publishers in America. It was uniformly rejected as being too controversial. Having successfully published her anti-lynching article in the *North American Review*, Terrell submitted her work to the editor. This time, however, when he rejected it he suggested that she send it to the British *Nineteenth Century and After*, which published it in 1907. Its publication abroad suggests that the quality of her work was not in question; white U.S. publishers were simply unwilling to publish articles that unambiguously exposed white Americans' racism. Ironically, her article gained credibility in the United States through its publication in a British journal; several New York daily newspapers subsequently excerpted portions of the article for their readers—but usually without crediting her as its author. To further publicize the convict leasing system, Terrell distributed her *Nineteenth Century and After* article to a wide variety of people, including Raymond Patterson of the *Chicago Tribune*, whom she convinced to let her "institute some investigations personally" when she was on her next lecture tour in the South.[72]

To prove the constitutionality of her case against the convict lease system, Terrell cited a 1905 U.S. Supreme Court ruling, *Clyatt v. United States*. Reminding white Americans of this Supreme Court decision whenever possible, Terrell explained that in *Clyatt*, the justices affirmed the Thirteenth Amendment's declaration that neither "slavery nor involuntary servitude" could exist in the United States or its territories. Defining involuntary servitude as peonage, compulsory service, or involuntary labor, the Court's ruling also affirmed that the Thirteenth Amendment gave Congress the right of enforcement against these illegal practices. In spite of this definitive ruling by the highest court in the land, however, various states and locales persisted in these illegal practices—primarily because so many government officials directly profited from the system through bribes from those using convict laborers. Black and white Americans, she argued, must demand that the U.S. government be strong enough to fully enforce the decisions of the judicial branch. Rejecting all states' rights arguments, Terrell denied that states or local officials had the right to circumvent the Constitution: "it was explicitly stated in the decision rendered by the Supreme Court that even though 'there might be in the language of the court either a municipal ordinance or State law sanctioning the holding of persons in involuntary servitude, Congress has power to punish those who thus violate the thirteenth amendment and the law against peonage at one and the same time.'"[73]

Without strong national and international campaigns to pressure U.S. political leaders to take action, however, Terrell feared that Congress would not be forced to uphold the Constitution and that individual states would ignore the Supreme Court's mandates at will: "in spite of the power which the Supreme Court asserts is possessed by Congress, but feeble efforts are being put forth to suppress the chain gangs and the convict lease camps of the South." She noted, too, that "the South is daily proving how resolute and unshaken it is in its purpose to defy even the Constitution of the United States, whenever it runs counter to its opinions and offends its prejudices." In spite of the obstacles, Terrell's goal was always the passage and enforcement of strong federal protections of civil rights for African Americans.[74]

As racism and segregation hardened in the 1890s and early 1900s, Terrell searched for ways to combat the worsening conditions for African Americans. As leader of the NACW, she advocated a strategy of maternalist reform focused on black women's homes and families. Like Willard's strategy for the WCTU, Terrell's inclusive approach allowed a broad spectrum of women to join this national organization. Some club members chose to work in the Suffrage Department while others focused on creating day nurseries or on mothers' training. Overall, during the 1890s, she focused more of her attention on justifying women's activism from a maternalist perspective, yet in that decade Terrell also lobbied the president of the United States and members of Congress against lynching and for the enforcement of the Reconstruction Amendments to the Constitution. After she finished her terms as

NACW president in 1901, Terrell was able to capitalize on her stature as a national reform leader to secure new venues from which to educate whites and to pursue her legislative and political reform goals. She gained new audiences in print and through public lecturing, speaking directly about the problems facing African Americans and promoting federal, legislative solutions to these problems.

Terrell consistently advocated federal anti-lynching laws, congressional enforcement of the Reconstruction Amendments to the Constitution, and a constitutional amendment for woman suffrage. The civil rights protections of the Reconstruction Amendments represented to Terrell "the sacred majesty of the law," which whites needed to respect.[75] She directly engaged the political system at the federal level, an engagement made easier by the fact that she lived in the nation's capital for over sixty years. Terrell regularly met in person with senators, representatives, cabinet members, and even some presidents in order to garner their support for or opposition to various pieces of reform legislation. Suspicious of states' rights as a tool of white supremacists, Terrell fought for a stronger federal government in all three branches.

Terrell used her popularity as a public speaker to educate white audiences, implicating them in the perpetuation of racism in the United States She inverted the standard missionary rhetoric that was conventionally aimed at reforming blacks. Instead, she applied the rhetoric of uplift to reform (and criticize) white racists. Terrell called on black Americans to become "missionaries" devoted to the service of saving the South by ridding it of racists and of racist laws. Aiming to disrupt the nation's complacency concerning race relations and the second-class status of black citizens, Terrell hoped that progressive whites and blacks would demand that Congress take action to enforce the U.S. Constitution. Her honest descriptions of the humiliations of Jim Crow segregation as well as the injustices of the convict lease system and lynching challenged the legitimacy of white Americans' claims to racial and moral supremacy. Aware that she frequently pushed the boundaries of what blacks were expected to write and speak about when addressing white audiences, Terrell dismissed criticisms that she was "bitter": "Colored people so seldom tell certain truths about conditions which confront their race that, when they do, even white people who are interested in them feel they must be 'bitter.' In this case truth is confounded with bitterness."[76] Terrell was determined to tell whites the truth, even when they resisted hearing it.

When she could, Terrell extended her conversation about the neces-sary changes in the legal and social status of African Americans to an international setting. In 1919, for instance, Terrell participated in the Women's International League for Peace and Freedom conference in Zurich, Switzerland. She wrote and presented a "resolution protesting against the discriminations, humiliations and injustices perpetrated upon Colored people in the United States," which passed without a dissenting vote. Introduced by Jane Addams, Terrell also gave a speech in flawless German, during which she linked together the plight of all people of color. Writing to her husband, she summarized part of her speech: "my white friends you are talking about permanent peace, but permanent peace is an impossibility, so long as the Colored races are the victims of injustice and prejudice. I expressed my opinion about the way two of the most christian and highly-civilized races had denied racial equality to Japan which she had a right to demand. When I said that, you could have heard a pin drop."[77] Asians as well as Africans and their descendants must be treated as equals on the world stage. From Terrell's perspective, this would result in their achievement of full citizenship in their nation-states and would help obliterate false legal, social, and political distinctions of race and sex.

Conclusion

During the nineteenth century, women's activism and reform agendas changed their roles and their views of the central state. Their politicized reform agenda helped women see themselves as full citizens, entitled to appeal to the federal government in an increasing number of ways. Engaging in an ongoing ideological struggle about national identity formation, they articulated their sense of the legitimacy of the nation and helped define where its constitutive powers should begin and end. Black women reformers demanded that the central state use its military power, for instance, to protect blacks from white Southerners' violence. Others insisted that the state restrict individuals' rights to drink alcohol. Several of the women under consideration here believed that Christian beliefs should be the basis for reform legislation and that the United States must become a Christian state. Black and white women's political thought, as well as their changing tactics and reform agendas, helped shape the emergence of a stronger federal government over the course of the nineteenth century. By placing more demands upon the state, from opposing the extension of slavery in the territories to supporting constitutional amendments for woman suffrage and prohibition of alcohol, women reformers encouraged the growth of the central state. Thus, black and white women entered the twentieth century with a broader sense of what they could, and should, accomplish as reformers and citizens. Their campaigns for federal legislation show that they—and many other Americans—had moved beyond suspicion of the federal government to calling upon it to solve seemingly intractable problems within American society. Definitions of women's proper role expanded to accommodate this new version of women's citizenship, which eventually included granting white and black women the right to vote. In the process of broadening societal expectations concerning women's roles, they also transformed politics and the state.

Each of the six women featured in this study was part of a transatlantic network of reform and exchange. Scotswoman Fanny Wright brought her continental perspectives on reform and revolution to the United

States, including a free-thought critique of the Christian church and its ministers for restricting women's equality. Christian values suffused the other women's reform politics, but Wright's views were echoed by them in a modified way. The devout Grimké sisters, for instance, refuted Congregational ministers and members of their own Orthodox faction of the Society of Friends who condemned women's public speaking in favor of abolition and women's rights. Frances Willard, too, was a devout Christian who deeply resented the strictures against women's preaching in the Methodist Church. She wrote and spoke in favor of giving women a formal role at the top of the church hierarchy. Frances Watkins Harper's reform ideas were also rooted in her Christian evangelical faith, which empowered her to call for reform. Abolitionists' voices reached Europe through a vital transatlantic exchange. Although Harper and the Grimkés never traveled abroad, their speeches, letters, and articles reached an audience in Great Britain especially, as well as in other European countries. Frances Willard and Mary Church Terrell traveled extensively in Europe, acting as missionaries, bringing their reform agenda to Europe from across the Atlantic.

In the early 1800s, women's volunteer and reform work emphasized moral suasion and local benevolent projects. Women relied more often on moral suasion as a reform strategy at a point when, with the exception of petitioning, they were not granted other citizenship rights that would enable them to make more expressly political demands upon the state. Fanny Wright approached moral suasion from a states' rights perspective. Employing a combination of moral suasion and direct action in her particular model of reform, Fanny Wright established her own antislavery experiment in the South.[1] Wright's endorsement of states' rights was grounded in the Jeffersonian view, common among white Southerners, that the U.S. Constitution limited the scope of federal powers.

Antislavery perfectionists such as the Grimké sisters believed in the power of moral suasion and began their reform careers rejecting involvement with the federal government and with political parties. Like most Garrisonian abolitionists, they read the U.S. Constitution as condoning slavery and favored instead God's higher moral laws. Yet they began calling for change at the federal level as they recognized the increased power that could come to women by supporting, for example, a constitutional amendment for woman suffrage or to abolish slavery.

Black women reformers in the antebellum era, including Frances Watkins Harper, knew that they were not considered full citizens and that the state and federal governments represented the interests of white slave owners, not those of free or enslaved blacks. Consequently, they relied on a combination of moral suasion and direct action to end slavery. Black women wrote poetry, articles, and speeches in favor of immediate abolition and against Northern white racism. They participated in civil disobedience by aiding fugitive slaves on the Underground Railroad. Since Frances Watkins identified the central government as the source of the problem (because the Constitution upheld slavery), only rarely in the antebellum era did she call for the government itself to initiate change.

As women reformers in the antislavery and temperance movements began to explore new ways to achieve social change, they found themselves confronting critics of women's participation in public debates on legislative reform and politics. To counter their critics, they formulated definitions of womanhood and women's proper sphere that allowed for their political activism while often acknowledging the central role of mothers within the home. For the Grimké sisters and Frances Willard, their co-equality arguments accepted the difference of sex—the physical differences between male and female bodies—while articulating an ideal of politicized motherhood. Co-equality gave many women a rationale for using their physical and moral differences to claim their rights as full citizens. In the decades after the Civil War, as more women joined movements working for the right to vote, for temperance, and for greater rights for married women, they asserted that it was their moral duty to participate in reform movements in order to improve the larger society. Willard justified women's political activism and full citizenship by framing political and reform issues within the construct of co-equality (by finding equality in gender difference). Feminist maternalists refused to accept restrictions on their rights to participate in politics as full citizens. The women reformers explored here were producers of ideas as well as leaders of social movements. Their definition of womanhood created real change in American society by expanding the woman's sphere, increasing the acceptability of white women's full political engagement, and calling on the federal government to commit itself to legislatively enacting women's reform agenda.

During Reconstruction, Republican politicians abandoned universal suffrage in favor of black male suffrage, thereby sacrificing black and white women's votes to ensure a solid majority of (black male) votes for the Republican Party in the South. Women reformers recognized the increased importance of gaining the right to vote but then split into two different factions regarding how to achieve that goal. Some white women, such as Elizabeth Cady Stanton and Susan B. Anthony, felt betrayed by the Republicans' refusal to pass universal suffrage and did not enthusiastically support the Reconstruction Amendments. After black men gained the right to vote, some prominent white women activists perceived the promotion of black Americans' civil rights as being in opposition to their attempts to advance their own rights. Louise Newman argues that "white activists worked . . . to establish the white woman as the primary definer and beneficiary of woman's rights at a time when the country was growing increasingly hostile toward attempts to redress the political, social, and economic injustices to which African Americans were subjected." Some white women activists' privileging of race over sex became more extreme during and after the debate over the Fourteenth Amendment. Because of their persistent racism, many white women reformers dismissed black women's civil rights concerns and adopted racist reform agendas such as the advocacy of states' rights or of literacy qualifications on the ballot. Black women's citizenship was clearly hindered by the limits placed upon them by the color of their skin as well as by their sex. Frances Watkins Harper and Mary Church Terrell insisted that black women must also work for political change at the federal level in order to protect their children and families. Their claims to piety and maternal concern for their children were often challenged or ignored by whites, who often tried to restrict this privileged motherhood—with its claims to expanded citizenship rights—to white women alone. A shared interest in promoting national legislation could not resolve the tensions between black and white women activists over their perceived abilities and their right to participate in the political process.[2]

The Republicans' plan to enfranchise black men put black women activists in an awkward position. They wanted and intended to gain the right to vote for themselves as soon as possible; however, they generally decided to support black male suffrage first. In this decision they were joined by most white female former abolitionists who feared jeopardizing Radical Reconstruction. After all, the Reconstruction Amendments represented the culmination of successful campaigns by activists who demanded an increase in the power of the federal government. The

Women's National Loyal League, for instance, had led a huge petition drive for a federal amendment to abolish slavery. Black women called for legislative change at the federal level, including the right to vote. They recognized that their families could not be adequately protected from Southern white vigilantes, from the consequences of excessive alcohol consumption, or from exploitative employers, among other dangers, without women's entry into the political and legislative arenas. They must force a strong central state to be the guarantor of progress and of civil rights rather than an impediment to both. Black women rightly saw the Thirteenth, Fourteenth, and Fifteenth Amendments as representing an important guarantee of citizenship rights for all Americans. Even though they were soon disappointed with how far the president, the Supreme Court justices, and members of Congress were willing to go to protect black Americans' new citizenship rights, from this point forth, black women held the federal government responsible for any and all failures of the constitutional amendments and federal laws to protect Americans' civil rights. They knew that the government could do more—if and when it chose.

Overall, black and white women reformers expanded their involvement in the partisan political system and organized campaigns to pass new federal laws. The promotion of national legislation became particularly attractive to women during and after the 1860s. As more women reformers began wholeheartedly to support a range of national laws, their reform agenda helped create and bolster a strong federal government by placing increasing demands upon it. Many tens of thousands of women in the Woman's Christian Temperance Union, for instance, campaigned for national woman suffrage and the prohibition of alcohol. The WCTU's campaigns insisted upon federal intervention in social problems, a stance that gained even more support among Progressive reformers in the early twentieth century.[3] Activists such as Frances Willard identified additional ways for the government to take on new regulatory functions such as legislative restrictions on alcohol, "impure" literature, or child labor, that often (ironically) removed responsibility from lay reformers and parents and gave it to the national government—all in the hopes of better regulating citizens' behavior. Like Willard, Frances Watkins Harper supported the government's increased role in restraining the behavior of citizens, not just to enforce the prohibition of alcohol but to disarm and prosecute members of the Ku Klux Klan. In addition to increased regulatory restrictions, WCTU members endorsed an expansion of the government's power in order to advance the liberty of women by granting them the right to vote. Black women's reform agenda prominently featured calls for federal legislation in support of an expansive set of reform goals, which included federal funding for impoverished schools, anti-lynching laws, and anti–convict labor laws as well as constitutional amendments for woman suffrage and prohibition. In these ways, they prioritized the federal government's emancipatory role as a guarantor and protector of African Americans' liberties and rights as citizens.

Even during the nadir of race relations in the 1890s, black women reformers such as Mary Church Terrell and Frances Watkins Harper believed in the central government's necessary role as an agent of change. They continued to push for federal legislation to achieve reforms, especially anti-lynching and national education. Harper and Terrell engaged in political activism at the federal level, worked in inter-racial organizations throughout their reform careers, and also created a separate black women's national organization. They consistently advo-cated expanded rights for all Americans and pushed against the legal and social manifestations of white prejudice that kept African Americans from attaining the status they deserved as full citizens. Privileging what Stephanie Shaw terms "an ethic of socially responsible individualism," they envisioned the National Association of Colored Women, founded in 1896, as a national group that would enable them to coordinate and encourage black women's reform efforts.[4] The problems of interracial activism and the insistence of white racists that black women had no legitimate claim to a political voice in the South further inspired black women reformers to organize the NACW. This organization, like the General Federation of Women's Clubs and the Woman's Christian Temperance Union, demanded federal legislative change and promoted local initiatives for self-help.

The political thought of these six women, along with that of other nineteenth-century women activists, helped lay the groundwork for Progressive women reformers and their domestic, maternalist feminism in the early decades of the twentieth century. These earlier arguments made women's "civic housekeeping" of the Progressive era seem like a natural extension of their domestic role. Their willingness to combine arguments about women's difference with arguments about rights and equality helped women reformers in the Progressive era rhetorically to accommodate the prevailing gender prescriptions with demands for political equality in order to gain power and influence in the government. Women's increasing demands on the state help explain how and why the government was able to claim more power and move into a wide range of new regulatory areas, from censorship and food and drug oversight to prohibition and woman suffrage. Women reformers' articulation of a new vision of women's citizenship encouraged an expanded role for the state in reform.

ABBREVIATIONS USED IN THE NOTES

AEG   Angelina E. Grimké

AEGW   Angelina E. Grimké Weld

BCD   Frances Smith Foster, ed.,
           A Brighter Coming Day: A Frances Ellen Watkins Harper Reader

FWH   Frances Watkins Harper

MCT   Mary Church Terrell

NHG   New Harmony Gazette

RHT   Robert H. Terrell

SMG   Sarah M. Grimké

TDW   Theodore Dwight Weld

WG Papers Weld-Grimké Papers, William L. Clements Library,
           University of Michigan, Ann Arbor

INTRODUCTION

1. Ian Haney Lopez, *White by Law: The Legal Construction of Race,* rev. ed. (New York: New York University Press, 2006); Michael Omi and Howard Winant, *Racial Formation in the United States,* 2nd ed. (New York: Routledge, 1994); David R. Roediger, *The Wages of Whiteness: Race and the Making of the American Working Class,* rev. ed. (1991; New York: Verso Press, 1999).

2. See Lizabeth Cohen, *A Consumers' Republic: The Politics of Mass Consumption in Postwar America* (New York: Alfred A. Knopf, 2003); Kristin L. Hoganson, *Fighting for American Manhood: How Gender Politics Provoked the Spanish-American and Philippine-American Wars* (New Haven, Conn.: Yale University Press, 1998); Linda K. Kerber, "A Constitutional Right to Be Treated like American Ladies: Women and the Obligations of Citizenship," in *U.S. History as Women's History: New Feminist Essays,* ed. Linda K. Kerber, Alice Kessler-Harris, and Kathryn Kish Sklar (Chapel Hill: University of North Carolina Press, 1995); Linda K. Kerber, "The Meanings of Citizenship," *Journal of American History* (December 1997); Alice Kessler-Harris, "In the Nation's Image: The Gendered Limits of Social Citizenship in the Depression Era," *Journal of American History* (December 1999). For discussions of citizenship in American and transnational contexts, see Candice Lewis Bredbenner, *A Nationality of Her Own: Women, Marriage, and the Law of Citizenship* (Berkeley and Los Angeles: University of California Press, 1998); Laura Briggs, *Reproducing Empire: Race, Sex, Science, and U.S. Imperialism in Puerto Rico* (Berkeley and Los Angeles: University of California Press, 2002); Catherine Ceniza Choy, *Empire of Care: Nursing and Migration in Filipino American History* (Durham: Duke University Press, 2003); Ann Laura Stoler, ed., *Haunted by Empire: Geographies of Intimacy in North American History* (Durham: Duke University Press, 2006).

3. Jean Baker, ed., *Votes for Women: The Struggle for Suffrage Revisited* (New York: Oxford University Press, 2002); Eleanor Flexner and Ellen Fitzpatrick, *Century of Struggle: The Woman's Rights Movement in the United States*, exp. ed. (Cambridge, Mass.: Belknap Press of Harvard University Press, 1996); Sarah Hunter Graham, *Woman Suffrage and the New Democracy* (New Haven, Conn.: Yale University Press, 1996); Rosalyn Terborg-Penn, *African American Women in the Struggle for the Vote, 1850–1920* (Bloomington: University of Indiana Press, 1998); Marjorie Spruill Wheeler, ed., *One Woman, One Vote: Rediscovering the Woman Suffrage Movement* (Troutdale, Ore.: New Sage Press, 1995).

4. William Novak, *The People's Welfare: Law and Regulation in Nineteenth-Century America* (Chapel Hill: University of North Carolina Press, 1996), introduction.

5. See Peter B. Evans, Dietrich Rueschemeyer, and Theda Skocpol, "On the Road toward a more Adequate Understanding of the State," in Peter B. Evans, Dietrich Rueschemeyer, and Theda Skocpol, eds., *Bringing the State Back In* (New York: Cambridge University Press, 1985); Stephen Skowronek, *Building a New American State: The Expansion of National Administrative Capacities, 1877–1920* (New York: Cambridge University Press, 1982); John M. Murrin, "A Roof without Walls: The Dilemma of American National Identity," in *Beyond Confederation: Origins of the Constitution and American National Identity*, ed. Richard Beeman, Stephen Botein, and Edward C. Carter II (Chapel Hill: University of North Carolina Press, 1987); Richard F. Bensel, *Yankee Leviathan: The Origins of Central State Authority in America, 1859–1877* (New York: Cambridge University Press, 1990); Charles C. Bright, "The State in the United States during the Nineteenth Century," in *Statemaking and Social Movements: Essays in History and Theory*, ed. Charles Bright and Susan Harding (Ann Arbor: University of Michigan Press, 1984).

For the role of women reformers, see Linda Gordon, "The New Feminist Scholarship on the Welfare State," and Paula Baker, "The Domestication of Politics: Women and American Political Society, 1780–1920," in Linda Gordon, ed., *Women, the State, and Welfare* (Madison: University of Wisconsin Press, 1990); also Libby Schweber, "Progressive Reformer, Unemployment, and the Transformation of Social Inquiry in Britain and the United States, 1880–1920s," in Dietrich Rueschemeyer and Theda Skocpol, eds., *States, Social Knowledge, and the Origins of Modern Social Policies* (Princeton, N.J.: Princeton University Press, 1996), 163–200; Allison Sneider, "Woman Suffrage in Congress: American Expansion and the Politics of Federalism, 1870–1890," in Baker, *Votes for Women*, 77–89.

6. Key examples of this approach include Anne M. Boylan, *The Origins of Women's Activism: New York and Boston, 1797–1840* (Chapel Hill: University of North Carolina Press, 2002); Laura F. Edwards, *Gendered Strife and Confusion: The Political Culture of Reconstruction* (Urbana: University of Illinois Press, 1997); Glenda Elizabeth Gilmore, *Gender and Jim Crow: Women and the Politics of White Supremacy in North Carolina, 1896–1920* (Chapel Hill: University of North Carolina Press, 1996); Louise M. Newman, *White Women's Rights: The Racial Origins of Feminism in the United States* (New York: Oxford University Press, 1999); Patricia A. Schechter, *Ida B. Wells-Barnett and American Reform, 1880–1930* (Chapel Hill: University of North Carolina Press, 2001); Terborg-Penn, *Struggle for the Vote*; Jean Fagan Yellin, *Harriet Jacobs, a Life: The Remarkable Adventures of the Woman Who Wrote* Incidents in the Life of a Slave Girl (New York: Basic Civitas Books, 2004).

7. For the making of the white middle class in the early national period, see Mary P. Ryan, *Cradle of the Middle Class: The Family in Oneida County, New York, 1790–1865* (New York: Cambridge University Press, 1981); Nancy F. Cott, *The Bonds of Womanhood: "Woman's Sphere" in New England, 1780–1835* (New Haven, Conn.:

Yale University Press, 1977), ch. 5. For black women, reform, and respectability, see Darlene Clark Hine, "'We Specialize in the Wholly Impossible': The Philanthropic Work of Black Women," in *Lady Bountiful Revisited: Women, Philanthropy, and Power*, ed. Kathleen D. McCarthy (New Brunswick, N.J.: Rutgers University Press, 1990), 70–93; Anne Meis Knupfer, *Toward a Tenderer Humanity and a Nobler Womanhood: African-American Women's Clubs in Turn-of-the-Century Chicago* (New York: New York University Press, 1996); Dorothy Salem, *To Better Our World: Black Women in Organized Reform, 1890–1920* (Brooklyn, N.Y.: Carlson, 1990); Stephanie J. Shaw, *What a Woman Ought to Be and to Do: Black Professional Women Workers during the Jim Crow Era* (Chicago, Ill.: University of Chicago Press, 1996); Deborah Gray White, *Too Heavy a Load: Black Women in Defense of Themselves, 1894–1994* (New York: W. W. Norton, 1999).

8. Jacqueline Jones, *Labor of Love, Labor of Sorrow: Black Women, Work, and the Family from Slavery to the Present* (New York: Vintage Books, 1985); Tera W. Hunter, *To "Joy My Freedom": Southern Black Women's Lives and Labors after the Civil War* (Cambridge, Mass.: Harvard University Press, 1997), ch. 2.

9. Kathleen Barry, *Susan B. Anthony: A Biography of a Singular Feminist* (New York: New York University Press, 1988); Brenda Stakup, *Susan B. Anthony* (San Diego, Calif.: Greenhaven Press, 2002); Elisabeth Griffith, *In Her Own Right: The Life of Elizabeth Cady Stanton* (New York: Oxford University Press, 1984); Lois W. Banner, *Elizabeth Cady Stanton: A Radical for Woman's Rights* (Boston: Little, Brown, 1980); Vivian Gornick, *The Solitude of Self: Thinking about Elizabeth Cady Stanton* (New York: Farrar, Straus and Giroux, 2005); Kathi Kern, *Mrs. Stanton's Bible* (Ithaca, N.Y.: Cornell University Press, 2001); Andrea Moore Kerr, *Lucy Stone: Speaking Out for Equality* (New Brunswick, N.J.: Rutgers University Press, 1992); Joelle Million, *Woman's Voice, Woman's Place: Lucy Stone and the Birth of the Woman's Rights Movement* (Westport, Conn.: Praeger, 2003); Linda McMurry Edwards, *To Keep the Waters Troubled: The Life of Ida B. Wells* (New York: Oxford University Press, 1998); Schechter, *Ida B. Wells-Barnett*; Mildred I. Thompson, *Ida B. Wells-Barnett: An Exploratory Study of an American Black Woman, 1892–1930* (Brooklyn, N.Y.: Carlson, 1990); Lois Beachy Underhill, *The Woman Who Ran for President: The Many Lives of Victoria Woodhull* (Bridgehampton, N.Y.: Bridge Work Publishers, 1995).

10. The exception to this would be Gerda Lerner, *The Feminist Thought of Sarah Grimké* (New York: Oxford University Press, 1998). My book is organized like Whitney Walton's book, *Eve's Proud Descendants: Four Women Writers and Republican Politics in Nineteenth-Century France* (Palo Alto, Calif.: Stanford University Press, 2000), which looks at the political thought of four French women after the French Revolution. Hilda Smith's edited volume *Women Writers and the Early Modern British Political Tradition* (New York: Cambridge University Press, 1998) similarly places women's ideas within British political thought.

11. Lori Ginzberg, *Untidy Origins: A Story of Woman's Rights in Antebellum New York* (Chapel Hill: University of North Carolina Press, 2005).

12. Elizabeth Cady Stanton, Susan B. Anthony, and Matilda Joslyn Gage, eds., *History of Woman Suffrage*, 2 vols. (New York: Fowler and Wells, 1881; repr., Arno Press and the *New York Times*, 1969).

13. Ernestine L. Rose, "Letters to the Editor: Lecture Tour of 'The West' and the Legacy of Frances Wright, November 20, 1855," in the *Boston Investigator*, cited in *Mistress of Herself: Speeches and Letters of Ernestine L. Rose: Early Women's Rights Leader*, ed. Paula Doress-Worters (New York: Feminist Press at the City University of New York, 2008), 195. See also Ellen Carol DuBois, "Ernestine Rose's Jewish Origins and the Varieties of Euro-American Emancipation in 1848," in Kathryn Kish Sklar and

James Brewer Stewart, eds., *Women's Rights and Transatlantic Antislavery in the Era of Emancipation* (New Haven, Conn.: Yale University Press, 2007), 279–98.

14. Jefferson to Lafayette, Monticello, November 4, 1823, in Paul Leicester Ford, ed., *The Writings of Thomas Jefferson*, vol. 10, *1816–1826* (New York: G. P. Putnam's Sons, 1899), 281–82.

15. There is a large literature on women in nineteenth-century utopian communities, including Wendy E. Chmielewski, Louis J. Kern, and Marlyn Klee-Hartzell, eds., *Women in Spiritual and Communitarian Societies in the United States* (Syracuse, N.Y.: Syracuse University Press, 1993); Carol Kolmerten, *Women in Utopia: The Ideology of Gender in the American Owenite Communities* (Bloomington: Indiana University Press, 1990); Louis J. Kern, *An Ordered Love: Sex Roles and Sexuality in Victorian Utopias—the Shakers, the Mormons, and the Oneida Community* (Chapel Hill: University of North Carolina Press, 1981); Lawrence Foster, *Women, Family, and Utopia: Communal Experiments of the Shakers, the Oneida Community, and the Mormons* (Syracuse, N.Y.: Syracuse University Press, 1991).

16. Ryan P. Jordan, *Slavery and the Meetinghouse: The Quakers and the Abolitionist Dilemma, 1820–1865* (Bloomington: Indiana University Press, 2007), introduction; Jonathan H. Earle, *Jacksonian Antislavery and the Politics of Free Soil, 1824–1854* (Chapel Hill: University of North Carolina Press, 2004), 40; Alisse Portnoy, *Their Right to Speak: Women's Activism in the Indian and Slave Debates* (Cambridge, Mass.: Harvard University Press, 2005). For a perspective on the South, see John P. Daly, *When Slavery Was Called Freedom: Evangelicalism, Proslavery, and the Causes of the Civil War* (Lexington: University Press of Kentucky, 2002).

17. Robert J. Connors, "Frances Wright: First Female Civic Rhetor in America," *College English* 62, no. 1 (September 1999): 42–43, 52.

18. Carol Mattingly, "Friendly Dress: A Disciplined Use," *Rhetorical Society Quarterly* 29, no. 2 (Summer 1999): 31.

19. Nancy Isenberg, "'Pillars in the Same Temple and Priests of the Same Worship': Woman's Rights and the Politics of Church and State in Antebellum America," *Journal of American History* (June 1998): 98–128; Nancy Isenberg, *Sex and Citizenship in Antebellum America* (Chapel Hill: University of North Carolina Press, 1998), ch. 4.

20. Stanton, Anthony, and Gage, *History of Woman Suffrage*, vol. 1.

21. For a discussion of women as public lecturers, see Barbara Cutter, *Domestic Devils, Battlefield Angels: The Radicalism of American Womanhood, 1830–1865* (DeKalb: Northern Illinois University Press, 2003), ch. 4. For a state-level response to the Grimké sisters' speeches, see Deborah Bingham Van Broekhoven, *The Devotion of These Women: Rhode Island in the Antislavery Network* (Amherst: University of Massachusetts Press, 2002), 25–31.

22. Lydia Maria Child, born in 1802, supported immediate abolition, was a leader in the American Anti-Slavery Society, helped Harriet Jacobs edit *Incidents in the Life of a Slave Girl*, advocated federal support for Native Americans in the 1860s, and was a founder of the Massachusetts Woman Suffrage Association. Child conceded that black men must gain the vote first but argued that a woman suffrage amendment to the U.S. Constitution was the next reform priority. The Grimké sisters and Frances Watkins Harper held many of the same reform positions. Carolyn L. Karcher, *The First Woman of the Republic: A Cultural Biography of Lydia Maria Child* (Durham, N.C.: Duke University Press, 1994); and Deborah Pickman Clifford, *Crusader for Freedom: A Life of Lydia Maria Child* (Boston: Beacon Press, 1992).

23. Mark Perry, *Lift Up Thy Voice: The Grimké Family's Journey from Slaveholders to Civil Rights Leaders* (New York: Penguin Books, 2001).

24. For discussions of women's proper sphere, see Cott, *Bonds of Womanhood*;

Martha Saxon, *Being Good: Women's Moral Values in Early America* (New York: Hill and Wang, 2003), ch. 18. Women's contested place in public life is examined in Boylan, *Origins of Women's Activism.*

25. Lois W. Banner, "The Protestant Crusade: Religious Missions, Benevolence, and Reform in the United States, 1790–1840" (Ph.D. dissertation, Columbia University, 1970, University Microfilms), ch. 6; Boylan, *Origins of Women's Activism,* ch. 4; Cott, *Bonds of Womanhood,* conclusion; Ann Douglass, *The Feminization of American Culture* (1977; repr., New York: Anchor Press/Doubleday, 1988), 97–103; Lori D. Ginzberg, *Women and the Work of Benevolence: Morality, Politics and Class in the Nineteenth-Century United States* (New Haven, Conn.: Yale University Press, 1990); Nancy A. Hewitt, *Women's Activism and Social Change: Rochester, New York, 1822–1872* (Ithaca, N.Y.: Cornell University Press, 1984), introduction; Ryan, *Cradle of the Middle Class,* ch. 3; Saxon, *Being Good,* 11–12, 254–63.

26. Janet Zollinger Giele, *Two Paths to Women's Equality: Temperance, Suffrage, and the Origins of Modern Feminism* (New York: Twayne, 1995), 45, 64–65. See also Jed Dannenbaum, *Drink and Disorder: Temperance Reform in Cincinnati from the Washingtonian Revival to the WCTU* (Urbana: University of Illinois Press, 1984), ch. 6; John W. Frick, *Theatre, Culture and Temperance Reform in Nineteenth-Century America* (New York: Cambridge University Press, 2003), ch. 1; Mark E. Lender and James K. Martin, *Drinking in America* (New York: Free Press 1987); Thomas R. Pegram, *Battling Demon Rum: The Struggle for a Dry America: 1800–1933* (Chicago, Ill.: Ivan R. Dee, 1998); Ian R. Tyrrell, *Sobering Up: From Temperance to Prohibition in Antebellum America, 1800–1860* (Westport, Conn.: Greenwood Press, 1979), introduction.

27. Lewis Perry and Michael Fellman, eds., *Antislavery Reconsidered: New Perspectives on the Abolitionists* (Baton Rouge: Louisiana State University Press, 1979); Lewis Perry, *Radical Abolitionism: Anarchy and the Government of God in Anti-slavery Thought* (Ithaca, N.Y.: Cornell University Press, 1973), ch. 8.

28. Linda K. Kerber, *No Constitutional Right to Be Ladies: Women and the Obligations of Citizenship* (New York: Hill and Wang, 1998), ch. 5.

29. Carla L. Peterson, *"Doers of the Word": African-American Women Speakers and Writers in the North, 1830–1880* (New York: Oxford University Press, 1995); Julie Winch, "Sarah Forten's Anti-slavery Networks," in Sklar and Stewart, *Transatlantic Antislavery,* 143–57; Charlotte Grimké, *The Journals of Charlotte Forten Grimké,* ed. Brenda E. Stevenson (New York: Oxford University Press, 1988).

30. Carla L. Peterson, "Literary Transnationalism and Diasporic History: Frances Watkins Harper's 'Fancy Sketches,' 1859–1860," in Sklar and Stewart, *Transatlantic Antislavery,* 189–210.

31. Ginzberg, *Work of Benevolence,* ch. 4; Stanton, Anthony, and Gage, *History of Woman Suffrage,* 2:50–86.

32. See Edwards, *Gendered Strife and Confusion,* ch. 5; Carol Faulkner, *Women's Radical Reconstruction: The Freedmen's Aid Movement* (Philadelphia: University of Pennsylvania Press, 2004), ch. 4; Eric Foner, *Forever Free: The Story of Emancipation and Reconstruction* (New York: Alfred A. Knopf, 2006), ch. 5; Hunter, *To "Joy My Freedom,"* 30–35; Elsa Barkley Brown, "Negotiating and Transforming the Public Sphere: African American Political Life in the Transition from Slavery to Freedom," in *Women Transforming Politics: An Alternative Reader,* ed. Cathy J. Cohen, Kathleen B. Jones, and Joan C. Tronto (New York: New York University Press, 1997), 346–47; Eileen Boris, "The Power of Motherhood: Black and White Activist Women Redefine the 'Political,'" in *Mothers of a New World: Maternalist Politics and the Origins of Welfare States,* ed. Seth Koven and Sonya Michel (New York: Routledge, 1993), 232.

33. Amy Dru Stanley, *From Bondage to Contract: Wage Labor, Marriage, and the*

Market in the Age of Slave Emancipation (New York: Cambridge University Press, 1998), 56–57; David E. Bernstein, *Only One Place of Redress: African Americans, Labor Regulations, and the Courts from Reconstruction to the New Deal* (Durham: Duke University Press, 2001), 1; Heather Cox Richardson, *The Death of Reconstruction: Race, Labor, and Politics in the Post–Civil War North, 1865–1901* (Cambridge, Mass.: Harvard University Press, 2001), 43, and ch. 4.

34. Cynthia Neverdon-Morton, *Afro-American Women of the South and the Advancement of the Race, 1895–1925* (Knoxville: University of Tennessee Press, 1989), 202.

35. Frances Elizabeth Willard, *Glimpses of Fifty Years: The Autobiography of an American Woman* (1889; repr., New York: Source Book Press, 1970), 7–8.

36. Frances Elizabeth Willard, diary entry December 2, 1859, in *Writing Out My Heart: Selections from the Journal of Frances E. Willard, 1855–1896*, ed. Carolyn DeSwarte Gifford (Urbana: University of Illinois Press, 1995), 51–52.

37. Ian Tyrrell, *Woman's World, Woman's Empire: The Woman's Christian Temperance Union in International Perspective, 1880–1930* (Chapel Hill: University of North Carolina Press, 1991), 62–72.

38. Ellen Carol DuBois, "Taking the Law into Our Own Hands: *Bradwell, Minor,* and Suffrage Militance in the 1870s," in *Visible Women: New Essays on American Activism*, ed. Nancy A. Hewitt and Suzanne Lebsock (Urbana: University of Illinois Press, 1993), 26–27; Barbara Goldsmith, *Other Powers: The Age of Suffrage, Spiritualism, and the Scandalous Victoria Woodhull* (New York: A. A. Knopf, 1998); Underhill, *The Woman Who Ran for President*; Mary Gabriel, *Notorious Victoria: The Life of Victoria Woodhull, Uncensored* (Chapel Hill, N.C.: Algonquin Books of Chapel Hill, 1998).

39. Frances E. Willard, *Woman and Temperance or, The Work and Workers of the Woman's Christian Temperance Union* (1883; repr., New York: Arno Press, 1972), 492–93.

40. Jane E. Larson, "'Even a Worm Will Turn at Last': Rape Reform in Late Nineteenth-Century America," *Yale Journal of Law and the Humanities* 9, no. 1 (1997): n99. See Alison M. Parker, *Purifying America: Women, Cultural Reform, and Pro-Censorship Activism, 1873–1933* (Urbana: University of Illinois Press, 1997). Also see Aileen S. Kraditor, *The Ideas of the Woman Suffrage Movement* (1965; repr., New York: Norton Press, 1981); Thomas A. Krainz, *Delivering Aid: Implementing Progressive Era Welfare in the American West* (Albuquerque: University of New Mexico Press, 2005); S. J. Kleinberg, *Widows and Orphans First: The Family Economy and Social Welfare Policy, 1880–1939* (Urbana: University of Illinois Press, 2006).

For discussions of women and gender in the development of the welfare state, see Linda Gordon, *Pitied but not Entitled: Single Mothers and the History of Welfare* (New York: Free Press, 1994); Alice Kessler-Harris, *In Pursuit of Equity: Women, Men, and the Quest for Economic Citizenship in Twentieth-Century America* (New York: Oxford University Press, 2001); Molly Ladd-Taylor, *Mother-Work: Women, Child Welfare, and the State, 1890–1930* (Urbana: University of Illinois Press, 1994); Suzanne Mettler, *Dividing Citizens: Gender and Federalism in New Deal Public Policy* (Ithaca, N.Y.: Cornell University Press, 1998); Gwendolyn Mink, *The Wages of Motherhood: Inequality in the Welfare State, 1917–1942* (Ithaca, N.Y.: Cornell University Press, 1990); Robyn Muncy, *Creating a Female Dominion in American Reform, 1890–1935* (New York: Oxford University Press, 1991); Charles Noble, *Welfare as We Knew It: A Political History of the American Welfare State* (New York: Oxford University Press, 1997); Theda Skocpol, *Protecting Mothers and Soldiers: The Political Origins of Social Policy in the United States* (Cambridge, Mass.: Belknap Press of Harvard University Press, 1992); Susan Ware, *Beyond Suffrage: Women in the New Deal* (Cambridge, Mass.: Harvard University Press, 1981).

41. Gaines M. Foster, *Moral Reconstruction: Christian Lobbyists and the Federal Legislation of Morality, 1865–1920* (Chapel Hill: University of North Carolina Press, 2002), ch. 1.

42. Quoted in Ruth Bordin, *Frances Willard: A Biography* (Chapel Hill: University of North Carolina Press, 1986), 216.

43. Willie Coleman, "'Like Hot Lead to Pour on the Americans . . .': Sarah Parker Remond—From Salem, Mass., to the British Isles," in Sklar and Stewart, *Transatlantic Antislavery*, 173–88; Peterson, *"Doers of the Word,"* 145, 198, 231.

44. Lisa Gail Materson, "Respectable Partisans: African American Women in Electoral Politics, 1877–1936" (Ph.D. dissertation, University of California, Los Angeles, 2000); Lisa G. Materson, *For the Freedom of Her Race: Black Women and Electoral Politics in Illinois, 1872–1932* (Chapel Hill: University of North Carolina Press, 2009). In 1920 Terrell was appointed by the Republican National Committee to be the director of the Committee for Eastern District Work among Colored Women. Terborg-Penn, *Struggle for the Vote*; Evelyn Brooks Higginbotham, *Righteous Discontent: The Women's Movement in the Black Baptist Church, 1880–1920* (Cambridge, Mass.: Harvard University Press, 1993), 227.

45. Higginbotham, *Righteous Discontent*, 221; Christopher Waldrep, ed., *Lynching in America: A History in Documents* (New York: New York University Press, 2006); Philip Dray, *At the Hands of Persons Unknown: The Lynching of Black America* (New York: Random House, 2002); Michael J. Pfeifer, *Rough Justice: Lynching and American Society, 1874–1947* (Urbana: University of Illinois Press, 2004); also Edwards, *Gendered Strife and Confusion*, 1–23.

CHAPTER 1—FRANCES WRIGHT

1. I would like to thank Stephanie Cole, Lori Ginzberg, Sarah Barringer Gordon, and Kathleen Underwood for their critiques of earlier versions of this chapter. Orphaned at two, Fanny Wright was separated from her older brother and baby sister and sent from Dundee, Scotland, to live with her Tory grandfather and teenaged aunt in London. At age eleven, she was reunited with her sister, Camilla, when their aunt moved the three of them to a country estate in Devonshire. Accusing her aunt of being harsh and unloving, Fanny insisted at the age of eighteen that she and Camilla be allowed to move to Glasgow to live with their uncle, James Mylne, a professor of moral philosophy. He welcomed them into his family's home, where Fanny was introduced to Scottish common sense philosophy and British Jacobinism. From her uncle's friends and his library, Wright also fed her passion for the new United States, viewing it as an ideal nation that was formed by the people. The two young Wright sisters, breaking with conventional behavior, traveled unaccompanied from Glasgow to New York. Fanny had rejected her uncle's suggestion of a more respectable tour of European cities, where British young ladies frequently traveled to see the art and architecture and to acquire an air of cultured refinement. Celia Morris, *Fanny Wright: Rebel in America* (1984; repr., Urbana: University of Illinois Press, 1992), 1–13.

2. Frances Wright, *Altorf: A Tragedy . . . First Represented in the Theatre of New York, Feb. 19, 1819* (Philadelphia: M. Carey and Son, 1819; microfilm, New Haven, Conn.: Research Publications, History of Women, reel 114, no. 749). Also see "Altorf, by Frances Wright," in *Plays by Early American Women, 1775–1850*, ed. Amelia Howe Kritzer (Ann Arbor: University of Michigan Press, 1995), 217–78.

3. Thomas Jefferson to Frances Wright, Monticello, May 22, 1820, and Wright to Jefferson, Whitburn, Sunderland, July 27, 1820, in *Thomas Jefferson Correspondence:*

Printed from the Originals in the Collections of William K. Bixby, ed. Worthington Chauncey Ford (Boston: Plimpton Press, 1916), 254, 256.

4. Richard B. Morris, *The Forging of the Union, 1781–1789* (New York: Harper and Row, 1987); David Szatmary, *Shay's Rebellion: The Making of an Agrarian Insurrection* (Amherst: University of Massachusetts Press, 1980); Skowronek, *New American State,* 19; Bensel, *Yankee Leviathan,* 17; Novak, *People's Welfare,* 24.

5. Robert Abzug, *Cosmos Crumbling: American Reform and Religious Imagination* (New York: Oxford University Press, 1994), 189, 204–5, 228; Lori D. Ginzberg, "'The Hearts of Your Readers Will Shudder': Fanny Wright, Infidelity, and American Freethought," *American Quarterly* 46, no. 2 (June 1994): 196, 202; Richard L. McCormick, *The Party Period and Public Policy: American Politics from the Age of Jackson to the Progressive Era* (New York: Oxford University Press, 1986).

6. Paul A. Baker, ed., *Frances Wright, Views of Society and Manners in America* (1821; repr., Cambridge, Mass.: Belknap Press of Harvard University Press, 1963), 173. Also see Frances Wright, *Views of Society and Manners in America; in A Series of Letters from that Country to a Friend in England, During the Years 1818, 1819, and 1820, by AN ENGLISHWOMAN* (London: Longman, Hurst, Pubs., 1821).

7. Wright, *Views of Society,* 175, 359.

8. Bright, "State in the United States," 123, 138; Bensel, *Yankee Leviathan,* 2. Also see Murrin, "Roof without Walls," 333–48.

9. Bensel, *Yankee Leviathan,* 192; Novak, *People's Welfare,* 17, 24, 248. See also Skowronek, *New American State,* 19; Bensel, *Yankee Leviathan,* 17. Some historians see more significant changes occurring during and after the Civil War. George Fredrickson, *The Inner Civil War: Northern Intellectuals and the Crisis of the Union* (New York: Harper and Row, 1965); Daniel Feller, *The Jacksonian Promise: America, 1815–1840* (Baltimore: Johns Hopkins University Press, 1995), 195–98.

10. Harry L. Watson, *Liberty and Power: The Politics of Jacksonian America* (New York: Hill and Wang, 1990), 13–14; Morris, *Fanny Wright,* 3–4, 174, 180, 282–83; William Randall Waterman, *Frances Wright, 1795–1852* (New York: AMS Press, 1967), 222, 255–56; Helen Heineman, *Restless Angels: The Friendship of Six Victorian Women, Frances Wright, Camilla Wright, Harriet Garnett, Frances Garnett, Julia Garnett Perz, Frances Trollope* (Athens: Ohio University Press, 1994), 26, 59; Ginzberg, "The Hearts of Your Readers Will Shudder," 196, 200; Susan Kissel, *In Common Cause: The "Conservative" Frances Trollope and the "Radical" Frances Wright* (Bowling Green, Ohio: Bowling Green State University Popular Press, 1993), 94, 145.

11. Stanton, Anthony, and Gage, *History of Woman Suffrage,* 1:35.

12. Frances Wright, speech "Delivered in the Walnut Street Theater, Philadelphia, on the Fourth of July, 1829," in *Course of Popular Lectures, Historical and Political, as delivered by Frances Wright D'Arusmont, in various cities, towns and counties of the United States Being Introductory to a Course on the Nation and Object of America's Political Institutions,* vol. 2 (Philadelphia: Published by the Author, 1836; folder 44, Celia Morris Eckhardt Papers at the New Harmony Workingmen's Institute and Library, New Harmony, Indiana; repr., New York: Arno Press, 1972), 133. Unless otherwise noted, all emphasis in quotations is original.

13. Wright, *Views of Society,* 364; Murrin, "Roof without Walls," 333 (quote). See also Charles Bright, "State in the United States during the Nineteenth Century," in *Statemaking and Social Movements: Essays in History and Theory,* ed. Charles Bright and Susan Harding (Ann Arbor: University of Michigan Press, 1984), 125–26; Theda Skocpol, "Bringing the State Back In: Strategies of Analysis in Current Research," in Evans, Rueschemeyer, and Skocpol, *Bringing the State Back In,* 22.

14. Wright, *Views of Society,* 316.

15. Wright, "Geographical, Political, and Historical Sketch of the American United States" (Lecture 1, 1836), in *Course of Popular Lectures*, 36–37.

16. Wright, *Views of Society*, 365.

17. Wright, *Views of Society*, 328; see also 326, 429, for her use of Edmund Burke.

18. Wright, "Letter XX," in *Views of Society*, 362. See also Novak, *People's Welfare*, 1; Wright, "Delivered in the New Harmony Hall, on the Fourth of July, 1828," in *Course of Popular Lectures*, 119–20.

19. Wright, *Views of Society*, 417, 421–25.

20. Ibid., 67, 64–65.

21. Peter Kolchin, *American Slavery, 1619–1877* (New York: Hill and Wang, 1993), 49–50, 139; Gail Bederman, "Revisiting Nashoba: Slavery, Utopia, and Frances Wright in America, 1818–1826," *American Literary History* (2005): 438.

22. Wright, *Views of Society*, 67, 69, 269.

23. Baker, *Frances Wright, Views of Society and Manners*, xii–xiii; Bederman, "Revisiting Nashoba," 444.

24. Wright, *Views of Society*, 367.

25. Bentham quoted from the Marquis de Lafayette to Thomas Jefferson, La Grange, June 1, 1822, in Gilbert Chinard, ed., *The Letters of Lafayette and Jefferson* (Baltimore: Johns Hopkins University Press, 1929), 412–13; acknowledgments page of Frances Wright, *A Few Days in Athens; Being the Translation of a Greek Manuscript Discovered in Herculaneum* (1822; repr., New York: Arno Press, 1972).

26. Lafayette to Jefferson, La Grange, June 1, 1822, in Chinard, *Lafayette and Jefferson*, 412–13; Wright, *A Few Days in Athens*, 189, 199, 212–13; Lafayette to Jefferson, La Grange, June 1, 1822, Jefferson to Lafayette, Monticello, November 4, 1823, Lafayette to Jefferson, La Grange, December 20, 1823, Lafayette to Jefferson, Philadelphia, October 1, 1824. In Chinard, *Lafayette and Jefferson*, 412–13, 416, 419, 422–23.

27. Jefferson to Lafayette, Monticello, October 28, 1822, in Ford, *Writings of Thomas Jefferson*, 233–34. The political parties were in flux in the 1820s, as Jefferson's tentative and inconsistent use of terms such as "old federalists," "republicans," "tories," and "whigs" suggests. Jefferson to Lafayette, Monticello, November 4, 1823, ibid., 281–82.

28. Jefferson to Lafayette, Monticello, December 26, 1820, ibid., 180–81; Lafayette to Jefferson, La Grange, July 1, 1821, and June 1, 1822, in Chinard, *Letters of Lafayette and Jefferson*, 407, 409.

29. A. J. G. Perkins and Theresa Wolfson, *Frances Wright, Free Enquirer: The Study of a Temperament* (New York: Harper and Brothers, 1939), 54–60; Morris, *Fanny Wright*, 47–53, 83–88.

30. Chinard, *Letters of Lafayette and Jefferson*, 359. For more on Jefferson's pro-colonization views, see Eric Burin, *Slavery and the Peculiar Solution: A History of the American Colonization Society* (Gainesville: University Press of Florida, 2005), 9–10; P. J. Staudenraus, *The African Colonization Movement, 1816–1865* (New York: Columbia University Press, 1961), 1–4.

31. Wright, "On Existing Evils and their Remedy, as delivered in Philadelphia, on June 2, 1829," in *Course of Popular Lectures*, 104; Isenberg, "Pillars in the Same Temple."

32. Bederman, "Revisiting Nashoba," 449–50. For more on Jackson, see H. W. Brands, *Andrew Jackson: His Life and Times* (New York: Doubleday, 2005), 92–94, 231–35, 315–20, 383–85; Sean Wilentz, *Andrew Jackson* (New York: Times Books, 2005), 42–49; Robert Vincent Remini, *Andrew Jackson and the Course of American Freedom*,

1822–1832 (New York: Harper and Row, 1981), 82–96; Ronald N. Satz, *American Indian Policy in the Jacksonian Era* (Lincoln: University of Nebraska Press, 1995), 9–11; Anthony F. C. Wallace, *The Long, Bitter Trail: Andrew Jackson and the Indians* (New York: Hill and Wang, 1993), 4–6, 50–53.

33. George M. Fredrickson, *The Black Image in the White Mind: The Debate on Afro-American Character and Destiny, 1817–1914* (New York: Harper and Row, 1971), 7–13, 25; Staudenraus, *African Colonization Movement*, 104–7; Janet Sharp Hermann, *Joseph E. Davis: Pioneer Patriarch* (Jackson: University Press of Mississippi, 1990), 38–45; Janet Sharp Hermann, *Pursuit of a Dream* (New York: Oxford University Press, 1981), 8–12; Earle, *Jacksonian Antislavery*, 5, 14–15.

34. Frances Wright, "On the Sectional Question—Southern Slavery" (Lecture 3, 1836), in *Course of Popular Lectures*, 78.

35. Frances Wright, "Biography and Notes of Frances Wright D. Arusmont" (1844), reprinted in Frances Wright, *Life, Letters and Lectures* (New York: Arno Press, 1972), 24–25.

36. Wright wrote her "Explanatory Notes" in December 1827 and published them in the *Memphis Advocate*. She subsequently published them in the January and February 1828 issues of the *New Harmony Gazette* (hereafter cited as *NHG*). Frances Wright, "Nashoba: Explanatory Notes, respecting the Nature and Objects of the Institution of Nashoba, and of the Principles upon which it is founded. Addressed to the Friends of Human Improvement, in all Countries and of all Nations," *NHG*, February 6, 1828, 133 (emphasis added).

37. Frances Wright, "Origin and History of the Federal Party; With a General View of the Hamilton Financial Scheme," Lecture 2, in *Course of Popular Lectures*, 53.

38. For this reason, Wright later rejected the abolition movement of the 1830s onward.

39. Wright, "Of Southern Slavery," in *Course of Popular Lectures*, 74–75; Wright, "Origin and History of the Federal Party," 53.

40. Wright, "Nashoba: Explanatory Notes," *NHG*, January 30, 1828, 124–25.

41. For discussions of utopian communitarianism, see Priscilla J. Brewer, *Shaker Communities, Shaker Lives* (Hanover: University Press of New England, 1986), 203; Philip N. Dare, ed., *American Communes to 1860: A Bibliography* (New York: Garland, 1990); Robert S. Fogarty, *Dictionary of American Communal and Utopian History* (Westport, Conn.: Greenwood, 1980); Lawrence Foster, *Religion and Sexuality: The Shakers, the Mormons, and the Oneida Community* (1981; repr., Urbana: University of Illinois Press, 1984); Carl Guarneri, *The Utopian Alternative: Fourierism in Nineteenth-Century America* (Ithaca, N.Y.: Cornell University Press, 1991); Gairdner B. Moment and Otto F. Kraushaar, eds., *Utopias: The American Experience* (Metuchen, N.J.: Scarecrow Press, 1980); Donald E. Pitzer, ed., *America's Communal Utopias* (Chapel Hill: University of North Carolina Press, 1997); Robert P. Sutton, *Communal Utopias and the American Experience: Religious Communities, 1732–2000* (Westport, Conn.: Praeger, 2003); Robert P. Sutton, *Communal Utopias and the American Experience: Secular Communities, 1824–2000* (Westport, Conn.: Praeger, 2004).

42. Morris, *Fanny Wright*, 100–104. On Jefferson and American racism, see James Oakes, *Slavery and Freedom: An Interpretation of the Old South* (New York: Vintage Books, 1990), 29–30; A. Leon Higginbotham, Jr., *In the Matter of Color: Race and the American Legal Process: The Colonial Period* (New York: Oxford University Press, 1978), 10–11.

43. Wright, "Biography and Notes," 24–25, 28–30. She did break taboos, however, by openly advocating miscegenation as a way to erase racial differences. Ibid., 28–30. Robert V. Remini, *Andrew Jackson and His Indian Wars* (New York: Viking, 2001),

116, 178–82. For discussions of racism and racial hierarchies, see David Brion Davis, *Inhuman Bondage: The Rise and Fall of Slavery in the New World* (New York: Oxford University Press, 2006), 62–63; James Oakes, *The Ruling Race: A History of American Slaveholders* (New York: Alfred A. Knopf, 1982), 3–9; Derrick Bell, *Race, Racism, and American Law*, 4th ed. (New York: Aspen Law and Business, 2000), 10–11; William L. Van Deburg, *Slavery and Race in American Popular Culture* (Madison: University of Wisconsin Press, 1984), 25–26; Fredrickson, *The Black Image in the White Mind*, 1–2.

44. Wright, "Explanatory Notes," *NHG*, January 30, 1828, 133. See also Roediger, *Wages of Whiteness*, 80–87; Richard H. Sewell, "Slavery, Race, and the Free Soil Party, 1848–1854," in Alan M. Kraut, ed., *Crusaders and Compromisers: Essays on the Relationship of the Antislavery Struggle to the Antebellum Party System* (Westport, Conn.: Greenwood Press, 1983), 104.

45. Jefferson to Wright, Monticello, August 7, 1825, in Ford, *Writings of Thomas Jefferson*, 343, 344–45.

46. Ibid., 344–45, 345.

47. Lafayette to Jefferson, Paris, February 25, 1826, in Chinard, *Letters of Lafayette and Jefferson*, 437–38.

48. Perkins and Wolfson, *Frances Wright, Free Enquirer*, 172–74, 182–207; Wright, "Nashoba: Explanatory Notes," *NHG*, January 30, 1828, 124. Also see Morris, *Fanny Wright*, ch. 6.

49. Wright, "Nashoba: Explanatory Notes," *NHG*, January 30, 1828, 1125, and February 6, 1828, 133.

50. James Richardson, "Frances Wright's Establishment," *The Genius of Universal Emancipation*, July 28, 1827 (ODY Periodicals, APS II, year 35, microfilm 134.2, reel 1272–73, 1–16; 1826–1839), 29–30.

51. Wright, "Nashoba: Explanatory Notes," *NHG*, January 30, 1828, 125; Richardson, "Frances Wright's Establishment," 30 (1827 journal entry); Wright, "Nashoba: Explanatory Notes," *NHG*, February 13, 1828, 140 (emphasis added). See discussions of Native American boarding schools by Michael C. Coleman, *American Indian Children at School, 1850–1930* (Jackson: University Press of Mississippi, 1993); David Wallace Adams, *Education for Extinction: American Indians and the Boarding School Experience* (Lawrence: University Press of Kansas, 1995).

52. Richardson, "Frances Wright's Establishment," 30 (emphasis added); trustees' log quoted in Perkins and Wolfson, *Frances Wright, Free Enquirer*, 167.

53. Wright, "Nashoba: Explanatory Notes," *NHG*, February 6, 1828, 132.

54. Elizabeth Ann Bartlett, *Liberty, Equality, Sorority: The Origins and Interpretations of American Feminist Thought: Frances Wright, Sarah Grimké, and Margaret Fuller* (Brooklyn, N.Y.: Carlson Publishing, 1994), 15–16; Wright, *A Few Days in Athens*, excerpted in *NHG*, April 11, 1827, 220.

55. Wright, "Nashoba: Explanatory Notes," *NHG*, February 6, 1828, 132. Wright also referred to "generous attachments" as a good alternative to legal marriages. Wright, *Free Enquirer* (formerly *New Harmony Gazette*), series 2, vol. 4, no. 207 (Ann Arbor, Michigan: University Microfilm), 407.

56. Lewis Perry argues that more women reformers made this connection in the 1850s. Perry, *Radical Abolitionism*, 214, 228. An early and strong proponent of the notion that marriage was a form of coercive bondage for women, Wright admired the feminist writings of Mary Wollstonecraft and supported equal education for girls and women. In the *New Harmony Gazette* (later called the *Free Enquirer*), she reprinted in serial form Mary Wollstonecraft's *A Vindication of the Rights of Woman with Strictures on Political and Moral Subjects* (1967; repr., New York: Norton Press, 1972).

57. Stanley, *From Bondage to Contract*, 177; Bartlett, *Liberty, Equality, Sorority*, 41;

Kathleen S. Sullivan, *Constitutional Context: Women and Rights Discourse in Nineteenth-Century America* (Baltimore: Johns Hopkins University Press, 2007), 25–30; Peggy A. Rabkin, *Fathers to Daughters: The Legal Foundations of Female Emancipation* (Westport, Conn.: Greenwood Press, 1980), 52–60; G. J. Postema, "The Expositor, the Censor, and the Common Law," in *Jeremy Bentham: Critical Assessments*, ed. Bhikhu Parekh (New York: Routledge, 1993), 232–33.

58. Foster, *Religion and Sexuality*, ch. 2; Wright, "Nashoba: Explanatory Notes," *NHG*, February 6, 1828, 132–33.

59. Wright, "Nashoba: Explanatory Notes," *NHG*, February 6, 1828, 133, 132. See also Joanne E. Passet, *Sex Radicals and the Quest for Women's Equality* (Urbana: University of Illinois Press, 2003), 147–51. Ironically, most whites refused to acknowledge that black women could have chaste standards when it came to sexuality. Harriet A. Jacobs, *Incidents in the Life of a Slave Girl: Written by Herself*, ed. Jean Fagan Yellin (1861; repr., Cambridge, Mass.: Harvard University Press, 1987, 2000).

60. Richardson, "Frances Wright's Establishment," 30.

61. Wright, "Nashoba: Explanatory Notes," *NHG*, February 6, 1828, 132.

62. Richardson, "Frances Wright's Establishment," 30.

63. Ibid.; letter from Mentor, Philadelphia, August 8, 1827, in *The Genius of Universal Emancipation*, ed. Benjamin Lundy (ODY Periodicals Microfilm 134.2); Richardson quoted in Perkins and Wolfson, *Frances Wright, Free Enquirer*, 171.

64. Wright, "Nashoba: Explanatory Notes," *NHG*, February 6, 1828, 133.

65. In contrast, Jefferson supported European amalgamation with Native Americans. Thomas Jefferson, *Notes on the State of Virginia* (1785), in *Documents of American Prejudice: An Anthology of Writings on Race from Thomas Jefferson to David Duke*, ed. S. T. Joshi (New York: Basic Books, 1999), 9.

66. Annette Gordon-Reed, *Thomas Jefferson and Sally Hemings: An American Controversy* (Charlottesville: University Press of Virginia, 1997), 158–209.

67. Wright, "Nashoba: Explanatory Notes," *NHG*, February 6, 1828, 133. For discussions of feminism and utopian ideas in the nineteenth century, see Barbara Taylor, *Eve and the New Jerusalem: Socialism and Feminism in the Nineteenth Century* (Cambridge, Mass.: Harvard University Press, 1993); William Leach, *True Love and Perfect Union: The Feminist Reform of Sex and Society* (1980; repr., Middletown, Conn.: Wesleyan University Press, 1989); Dolores Hayden, *The Grand Domestic Revolution: A History of Feminist Designs for American Homes, Neighborhoods, and Cities* (1981; repr., Cambridge, Mass.: MIT Press, 1995).

68. Leslie M. Harris, "From Abolitionist Amalgamators to 'Rulers of the Five Points': The Discourse of Interracial Sex and Reform in Antebellum New York City," in Martha Hodes, ed., *Sex, Love, Race: Crossing Boundaries in North American History* (New York: New York University Press, 1999), 191–212.

69. On white Americans' obsession with maintaining racial difference, see Roediger, *Wages of Whiteness*; Suzanne Lebsock, *The Free Women of Petersburg: Status and Culture in a Southern Town, 1784–1860* (New York: W. W. Norton, 1984), ch. 4. See Martha Hodes, *White Women, Black Men: Illicit Sex in the Nineteenth-Century South* (New Haven, Conn.: Yale University Press, 1997), introduction.

70. Wright, "Nashoba: Explanatory Notes," *NHG*, February 6, 1828, 133. Robert Dale Owen also endorsed miscegenation in "Address to the Inhabitants of New Orleans," *NHG*, April 9, 1828, 186–87.

71. Wright, "Nashoba: Explanatory Notes," *NHG*, February 6, 1828, 133.

72. Ibid., 132. See also Cott, *Bonds of Womanhood*; Martha Saxton, *Being Good: Women's Moral Values in Early America* (New York: Hill and Wang, 2003), 299–301. For excellent discussions of illegitimacy and unmarried women, see Regina G. Kunzel,

Fallen Women, Problem Girls: Unmarried Mothers and the Professionalization of Social Work, 1890–1945 (New Haven, Conn.: Yale University Press, 1993); Mary E. Odem, *Delinquent Daughters: Protecting and Policing Adolescent Female Sexuality in the United States, 1885–1920* (Chapel Hill: University of North Carolina Press, 1995).

73. Hendrik Hartog, *Man and Wife in America: A History* (Cambridge, Mass.: Harvard University Press, 2000), 90, 118; Morris, *Fanny Wright*, ch. 8.

74. Wright, "Nashoba: Explanatory Notes," *NHG*, February 6, 1828, 132. See also Norma Basch, *In the Eyes of the Law: Women, Marriage, and Property in Nineteenth-Century New York* (Ithaca, N.Y.: Cornell University Press, 1982), 164, 180; Michael Grossberg, *Governing the Hearth: Law and the Family in Nineteenth-Century America* (Chapel Hill: University of North Carolina Press, 1985). For a perspective on "husbands' rights," see Hendrik Hartog, "Lawyering, Husbands' Rights, and 'the Unwritten Law' in Nineteenth-Century America," *Journal of American History* (June 1997): 67–95.

75. Wright, "Address," *NHG*, October 31, 1829, 1; Wright, "Nashoba: Explanatory Notes," *NHG* , January 30, 1828, 124.

76. See Foster, *Religion and Sexuality*; Perry, *Radical Abolitionism*, 150, 212; Morris, *Fanny Wright*, 141–45, 167.

77. Wright, "On the Sectional Question—Southern Slavery" (Lecture 3, 1836), in *Course of Popular Lectures*, 77–78.

78. Robert Dale Owen and Frances Wright, "Prospectus of the New-Harmony and Nashoba Gazette, in Continuation of the New-Harmony Gazette," *NHG*, July 30, 1828, 318. Colonization became a part of her program for the Working Men's Party. See also Charles Sellers, *The Market Revolution: Jacksonian America, 1815–1846* (New York: Oxford University Press, 1991); Watson, *Liberty and Power*, 4–8; Michael Feldberg, *The Turbulent Era: Riot and Disorder in Jacksonian America* (New York: Oxford University Press, 1980), 90–91, 96.

79. Maria Stewart, a free black woman, first spoke publicly in 1831. Connors, "Frances Wright," 31–32; Barbara Bardes and Suzanne Gossett, *Declarations of Independence: Women and Political Power in Nineteenth-Century American Fiction* (New Brunswick, N.J.: Rutgers University Press, 1990), 47–48; Marilyn Richardson, ed., *Maria W. Stewart, America's First Black Woman Political Writer: Essays and Speeches* (Bloomington: University of Indiana Press, 1987).

80. Sean Wilentz, *Chants Democratic: New York City and the Rise of the American Working Class, 1788–1850* (New York: Oxford University Press, 1984), 176.

81. Wright, *Views of Society* (London, 1821), 63; Morris, *Fanny Wright*, 185, 195.

82. Jules Witcover, *Party of the People: A History of the Democrats* (New York: Random House, 2003), 138–39; Feller, *Jacksonian Promise*, 129–34; Wilentz, *Chants Democratic*, 182, 200; Wright, "Editorial: Jefferson Institute," *NHG*, April 8, 1829, 190. For a discussion of labor's suspicion of lawyers, see Skowronek, *New American State*, 33. For her appeal to (and among) the working classes, see Wright, "To the Intelligent among the Working Classes; and Generally to All Honest Reformers," *NHG*, December 5, 1829, 46–47.

83. Gerda Lerner, *The Grimké Sisters from South Carolina: Pioneers for Women's Rights and Abolition* (1967; rev. ed., Chapel Hill: University of North Carolina Press, 2004), 4–5, 173–75; Cutter, *Domestic Devils*, 113–17.

84. Morris, *Fanny Wright*, 171, 197. For an interesting discussion of how eighteenth-century Americans embraced the principles of the American Revolution, see Andrew Burstein, *Sentimental Democracy: The Evolution of America's Romantic Self-Image* (New York: Hill and Wang, 1999). The tensions Wright saw between states' rights and the central government and between liberty and coercion were not fully

resolved by the Constitution. Murrin, "Roof without Walls," 346.

85. Frances Wright, "State of the Public Mind" (1829), in *Supplement Course of Lectures, Containing the Last Four Lectures Delivered in the United States* (London, 1834), 178. See also Wilentz, *Chants Democratic*, 176–212; Skocpol, "Bringing the State Back In," 26.

86. Wright, "Address, Containing a Review of the Times" (1830), in *Life, Letters and Lectures*, 196; Wright, "Wealth and Money, No. 5," *NHG*, October 16, 1830, 405; Wright, "Parting Address" (1830), in *Life, Letters and Lectures*, 216.

87. Wright, "To the Intelligent among the Working Classes; and Generally to All Honest Reformers," *NHG*, December 5, 1829, 46–47; Wright, "State of the Public Mind," in *Supplement Course of Lectures*, 179.

88. Wright, "On Existing Evils and their Remedy, as Delivered in Philadelphia, on June 2, 1829" (Lecture 7, 1829), in *Life, Letters and Lectures*, 114. See also Wright, "Review of the Times" (1830), in *Supplement Course of Lectures*, 196.

89. Wright, "On Existing Evils and their Remedy," 109–10. See also Wright, "Plan of National Education," reprinted in Frances Wright and Robert Dale Owen, *Tracts on Republican Government and National Education: Addressed to the inhabitants of the United States of America* (London: James Watson/Holyoake and Company, 1857), 15.

90. Wright, "On Existing Evils and their Remedy," 114–15.

91. Morris, *Fanny Wright*, 41–42.

92. Wright, "On Existing Evils and their Remedy," 114; Wilentz, *Chants Democratic*, 180. See also Lewis Corey, "Outline of Last 12 Chapters" and "Chapter 11. Education for the People" (unpublished manuscript on Frances Wright, ca. 1950), 7, in box 5, Lewis Corey Papers, Columbia University Rare Books and Manuscripts Library. Wright, "State of the Public Mind," in *Supplement Course of Lectures*, 178–81.

93. Wright, "The Nature of True Civilization: The Third and Best Age of Man," *NHG*, October 30, 1830, 7; Wright, "Address: Containing a Review of the Times," *NHG*, August 14, 1830, 329–30. See also Wright, "Parting Address," in *Life, Letters and Lectures*, 218; Wright, "Nashoba: Explanatory Notes," *NHG*, January 30, 1828, 124; Wright, "Wealth and Money, No. 5," *NHG*, October 16, 1830, 405.

94. Wright, "Nashoba: Explanatory Notes," *NHG*, February 6, 1828, 133; Morris, *Fanny Wright*, 207–8.

95. Morris, *Fanny Wright*, 223.

96. Wright, "Geographical, Political, and Historical Sketch," 39–40; Witcover, *Party of the People*, 146–47; Sean Wilentz, *The Rise of American Democracy: Jefferson to Lincoln* (New York: W. W. Norton, 2005), 361–67, 524. Quotes from Wright, "Origin and History of the Federal Party," 62, 70.

97. Murrin, "Roof without Walls," 346; Michael F. Holt, *The Rise and Fall of the American Whig Party: Jacksonian Politics and the Onset of the Civil War* (New York: Oxford University Press, 1999), 2, 7, 43–44.

98. Wright, "Origin and History of the Federal Party," 65, 68; Jefferson to Lafayette, Monticello, November 4, 1823, in Chinard, *Writings of Thomas Jefferson*, 281–82. See also Witcover, *Party of the People*, 149–51; Edward Pessen, *Jacksonian America: Society, Personality, and Politics* (Homewood, Ill.: Dorsey, 1969), 211–19.

99. Portnoy, *Their Right to Speak*, 230; William Lloyd Garrison, *Thoughts on African Colonization, or an Impartial Exhibition of the Doctrines, Principles, and Purposes of the American Colonization Society*, Elibron Classics Replica Edition (Boston: Garrison and Knapp, 1832; repr., Adamant Media Corporation, 2003); Susan M. Ryan, "Errand into Africa: Colonization and Nation Building in Sarah J. Hale's Liberia," in *New England Quarterly* 68, no. 4 (December 1995), 558–59; Ralph D. Carter, "Black American or African: The Response of New York City Blacks to African Colonization,

1817–1841" (Ph.D. dissertation, Clark University, 1974), 115.

100. Wright, "On the Sectional Question," 80, 88; Wright, "Biography and Notes," 30.

101. See Ginzberg, "The Hearts of Your Readers Will Shudder," 196, 200; Morris, *Fanny Wright*, 3–4, 174, 180, 282–83; Waterman, *Frances Wright*, 222, 255–56; Heineman, *Restless Angels*, 26, 59; Kissel, *In Common Cause*, 94, 145.

102. Dubois, "Ernestine Rose's Jewish Origins," 281–83.

103. Wright held contradictory notions regarding the primacy of personal action on the one hand and the necessity for achieving the collective good on the other. See Bartlett, *Liberty, Equality, Sorority*, 36–37; Murrin, "Roof without Walls," 346–47.

104. Wright, "State of the Public Mind," in *Supplement Course of Lectures*, 179.

CHAPTER 2—SARAH AND ANGELINA GRIMKÉ

1. Sarah M. Grimké (hereafter SMG) and Angelina E. Grimké Weld (hereafter AEGW) to Sarah M. Douglass, September 8, 1839, Weld-Grimké Papers, William L. Clements Library, University of Michigan, Ann Arbor (hereafter WG Papers). At the Institute for Colored Youth, Sarah Mapps Douglass "ran the Institute's Preparatory Department from 1852 to 1877." Donna McDaniel and Vanessa Julye, *Fit for Freedom, not for Friendship: Quakers, African Americans, and the Myth of Racial Justice* (Philadelphia: Quaker Press, 2009), 75, 127; Marie J. Lindhorst, "Sarah Mapps Douglass: The Emergence of an African American Educator/Activist in Nineteenth-Century Philadelphia" (Ph.D. dissertation, Pennsylvania State University, 1995), 139–40.

2. For discussion of the racialized nature of U.S. citizenship, see Leonard Dinnerstein, Roger L. Nichols, and David M. Reamers, *Natives and Strangers: Blacks, Indians, and Immigrants in America* (New York: Oxford University Press, 1990); Gary Gerstle, "Liberty, Coercion, and the Making of Americans," in *Journal of American History* (September 1997): 524–58; Reginald Horsman, *Race and Manifest Destiny: The Origins of American Racial Anglo-Saxonism* (Cambridge, Mass.: Harvard University Press, 1981); Kerber, "Meanings of Citizenship"; Roediger, *Wages of Whiteness*.

3. Jean R. Soderlund, "Priorities and Power: The Philadelphia Anti-slavery Society," in Jean Fagan Yellin and John C. Van Horne, eds., *The Abolitionist Sisterhood: Women's Political Culture in Antebellum America* (Ithaca, N.Y.: Cornell University Press, 1994), 68–71; Julie Winch, "'You Have Talents—Only Cultivate Them': Philadelphia's Black Female Literary Societies and the Abolitionist Crusade," ibid., 105, 115.

4. SMG to Sarah M. Douglass, November 23, 1837, WG Papers.

5. Kristin Hoganson, "Garrisonian Abolitionists and the Rhetoric of Gender, 1850–1860," *American Quarterly* 45, no. 4 (December 1993): 558–95.

6. The sisters were officially disowned in 1838 over their participation in Angelina's non-Quaker wedding ceremony. See letters from Mary Horner and Edith Kite to SMG and AEGW, July 1838, in Gilbert H. Barnes and Dwight L. Dumond, eds., *Letters of Theodore Dwight Weld, Angelina Grimké Weld, and Sarah Grimké, 1822–1844* (Gloucester, Mass.: Peter Smith, 1965; hereafter cited as *Letters of TDW*), 683–702; also Dorothy Sterling, *Ahead of Her Time: Abby Kelley and the Politics of Antislavery* (New York: W. W. Norton, 1991), 122–24; Blanche Glassman Hersh, *The Slavery of Sex: Feminist-Abolitionists in America* (Urbana: University of Illinois Press, 1978), 6–38; Jordan, *Slavery and the Meetinghouse*, ch. 1.

7. Henry Mayer, *All On Fire: William Lloyd Garrison and the Abolition of Slavery* (New York: St. Martin's Press, 1998), 232. For detailed biographies of the sisters, see

the outstanding book by Lerner, *The Grimké Sisters*; also Catherine H. Birney, *The Grimké Sisters: Sarah and Angelina Grimké, the First American Women Advocates of Abolition and Woman's Rights* (1885; repr., New York: Haskell House, 1970).

8. Kathryn Kish Sklar, "'The Throne of My Heart': Religion, Oratory, and Transatlantic Community in Angelina Grimké's Launching of Women's Rights, 1828–1838," in Sklar and Stewart, *Transatlantic Antislavery*, 218. See also Bruce Dorsey, "Friends Becoming Enemies: Philadelphia Benevolence and the Neglected Era of American Quaker History," *Journal of the Early Republic* 18 (Fall 1998): 406, 425. For a helpful chapter on Quakerism and woman's rights, see Judith Wellman, *The Road to Seneca Falls: Elizabeth Cady Stanton and the First Woman's Rights Convention* (Urbana: University of Illinois Press, 2004), 91–120.

9. Lerner, *The Grimké Sisters*, 91–92; Angelina Grimké, *Walking by Faith: The Diary of Angelina Grimké, 1828–1835*, ed. Charles Wilbanks (Columbia: University of South Carolina Press, 2003), 211–13; Mayer, *All On Fire*, 230–34; Richard S. Newman, *The Transformation of American Abolitionism, 1780s–1830s: Fighting Slavery in the Early Republic* (Chapel Hill: University of North Carolina Press, 2002).

10. Gilbert Hobbs Barnes, *The Anti-slavery Impulse, 1830–1844* (1933; repr., New York: Harcourt, Brace and World, 1964), chs. 2, 3; Laurence Veysey, ed., *The Perfectionists: Radical Social Thought in the North, 1815–1860* (New York: John Wiley and Sons, 1973), 10.

11. Catherine A. Brekus, *Strangers and Pilgrims: Female Preaching in America* (Chapel Hill: University of North Carolina Press, 1998), 29–30; Boylan, *Origins of Women's Activism*, 46; Richardson, *Maria W. Stewart*. Beecher quoted from Morris, *Fanny Wright*, 249–50.

12. Angelina E. Grimké (hereafter AEG) to Theodore Dwight Weld (hereafter TDW) and John Greenleaf Whittier, August 20, 1837, in Larry Ceplair, ed., *The Public Years of Sarah and Angelina Grimké: Selected Writings, 1835–1839* (New York: Columbia University Press, 1989), 283 (hereafter cited in notes as Ceplair). See Cutter, *Domestic Devils*, 114–15; Katherine Henry, "Angelina Grimké's Rhetoric of Exposure," *American Quarterly* 49, no. 2 (June 1997): 328–55; Sandra F. Van Burkleo, *"Belonging to the World": Women's Rights and American Constitutional Culture* (New York: Oxford University Press, 2001), ch. 5.

13. For discussions of women's proper sphere, see Barbara Welter, "The Cult of True Womanhood, 1820–1860," in *American Quarterly* 18, no. 2, pt. 1 (Summer 1966): 151–74; Ryan, *Cradle of the Middle Class*; Linda K. Kerber, "Separate Spheres, Female Worlds, Woman's Place: The Rhetoric of Women's History," *Journal of American History* 75, no. 1 (June 1988): 9–39; also Dana D. Nelson, *National Manhood: Capitalist Citizenship and the Imagined Fraternity of White Men* (Durham: Duke University Press, 1998), ch. 1. For discussions of the Congregational clergy's attack on women's public speaking, see Mayer, *All On Fire*, 235–38; Isenberg, *Sex and Citizenship*, 46; Clifford, *Crusader for Freedom*, 135–37.

14. AEG to TDW, August 12, 1837, in Ceplair, 277; Robert Abzug, *Passionate Liberator: Theodore Dwight Weld and the Dilemma of Reform* (New York: Oxford University Press, 1980), 178; Amy Swerdlow, "Abolition's Conservative Sisters: The Ladies' New York City Anti-slavery Societies, 1834–1840," in Yellin and Van Horne, *Abolitionist Sisterhood*, 43.

15. Abzug, *Passionate Liberator*, 263–67; Lerner, *The Grimké Sisters*, chs. 15, 16; Ceplair, *Public Years*, xv–xviii; Hewitt, *Women's Activism and Social Change*, 170.

16. Joanne Pope Melish, *Disowning Slavery: Gradual Emancipation and "Race" in New England, 1780–1860* (Ithaca, N.Y.: Cornell University Press, 1998), 265. For a discussion of how most antebellum Americans critiqued aspects of the Constitution

while accepting it as a whole, see Michael Vorenberg, *Final Freedom: The Civil War, the Abolition of Slavery, and the Thirteenth Amendment* (New York: Cambridge University Press, 2001), 8–34. Philip S. Foner, ed., *Frederick Douglass: Selected Speeches and Writings*, abridged and adapted by Yuval Taylor (Chicago: Lawrence Hill Books, 1999), 127–29, 188–205, 379–89.

17. SMG and AEG to Queen Victoria, October 26, 1837, in Lerner, *Sarah Grimké*, 51; also AEG to TDW, April 7, 1838, *Letters of TDW*, 627; Philadelphia Female Anti-Slavery Society from Swerdlow, "Abolition's Conservative Sisters," 37. See also Julie Roy Jeffrey, "'No Occurrence in Human History Is More Deserving of Commemoration Than This': Abolitionist Celebrations of Freedom," in Timothy Patrick McCarthy and John Stauffer, eds., *Prophets of Protest: Reconsidering the History of American Abolitionism* (New York: New Press, 2006), 200–219.

18. "Clarkson," letter to New Haven *Religious Intelligencer*, February 11, 1837; SMG and AEG to "Clarkson," *Friend of Man*, March 1837, in Ceplair, 119; John Stauffer, *The Black Hearts of Men: Radical Abolitionists and the Transformation of Race* (Cambridge, Mass.: Harvard University Press, 2002), 22.

19. SMG and AEG to "Clarkson," *Friend of Man*, March 1837, in Ceplair, 123.

20. Lerner, *The Grimké Sisters*, 33, 351–52; Wendy Hammand Venet, *Neither Ballots nor Bullets: Women Abolitionists and the Civil War* (Charlottesville: University of Virginia Press, 1991), ch. 5; Wendy F. Hammand, "The Woman's National Loyal League: Feminist Abolitionists and the Civil War," in *Civil War History* 35, no. 1 (1989): 39–58; AEGW, "Remonstrance of the Citizens of Belleville, N.J. To the Honorable Court of Quarter Sessions for Essex County Now in Session in the City of Newark," 1842, in *Letters of TDW*, 917–18.

21. Susan Zaeske, *Signatures of Citizenship: Petitioning, Antislavery, and Women's Political Identity* (Chapel Hill: University of North Carolina Press, 2003); Shirley J. Yee, *Black Women Abolitionists: A Study in Activism, 1828–1860* (Knoxville: University of Tennessee Press, 1992), 130; Richard H. Sewell, *Ballots for Freedom: Antislavery Politics in the United States, 1837–1860* (New York: Oxford University Press, 1976), 8. For discussions of abolition's appeal to evangelical women already active in reform, see Sterling, *Ahead of Her Time*, 38, 105; Stanton, Anthony, and Gage, *History of Woman Suffrage*, 1:52–53; Ellen Carol DuBois, *Feminism and Suffrage: The Emergence of an Independent Women's Movement in America, 1848–1869* (Ithaca, N.Y.: Cornell University Press, 1978); Ellen Carol DuBois, *Woman Suffrage and Women's Rights* (New York: New York University Press, 1998).

22. AEG, *Letters to Catherine [sic] E. Beecher, in reply to An Essay on Slavery and Abolitionism, addressed to A.E. Grimké*, 1837, in Ceplair, 193; Julie R. Jeffrey, *The Great Silent Army of Abolitionism: Ordinary Women in the Antislavery Movement* (Chapel Hill: University of North Carolina Press, 1998), 87; Zaeske, *Signatures of Citizenship*, 2. See also Deborah Bingham Van Brockhoven, "'Let Your Names Be Enrolled': Method and Ideology in Women's Antislavery Petitioning," in Yellin and Van Horne, *Abolitionist Sisterhood*, 184; SMG and AEG, "Letter to Queen Victoria," October 26, 1837, in Lerner, *Sarah Grimké*, 52; AEGW, speech at Pennsylvania Hall, May 16, 1838, in Ceplair, 323.

23. SMG, *Letters on the Equality of the Sexes and the Condition of Woman, Addressed to Mary S. Parker, President of the Boston Female Anti-Slavery Society*, first published in the *New England Spectator* in 1837, in Ceplair, 231, 262–63.

24. William Lee Miller, *Arguing about Slavery: The Great Battle in the United States Congress* (New York: Alfred A. Knopf, 1996); James Brewer Stewart, "Reconsidering the Abolitionists in an Age of Fundamentalist Politics," *Journal of the Early Republic* 26 (Spring 2006): 1–23.

25. For ministers' reaction, see the "Pastoral Letter: The General Association of Massachusetts to the Churches Under Their Care," July 12, 1837, in Ceplair, 211–12; Jacqueline Bacon, *The Humblest May Stand Forth: Rhetoric, Empowerment, and Abolition* (Columbia: University of South Carolina Press, 2002); Barbara A. White, *The Beecher Sisters* (New Haven, Conn.: Yale University Press, 2003), 16. Sarah Grimké responded to the Pastoral Letter in the next installment of her series of *Letters on the Equality of the Sexes*, in Ceplair, 215.

26. Zaeske, *Signatures of Citizenship*, 27; Kathryn Kish Sklar, *Catharine Beecher: A Study in American Domesticity* (New York: W. W. Norton, 1976), 132–37; Joan D. Hedrick, *Harriet Beecher Stowe: A Life* (New York: Oxford University Press, 1994), 58–59.

27. *Massachusetts Abolitionist*, July 4, 1839, quoted in Sewell, *Ballots for Freedom*, 11; Veysey, *The Perfectionists*, 5.

28. SMG to Sarah M. Douglass, January 27, 1845, WG Papers.

29. SMG, *An Epistle to the Clergy of the Southern States*, 1836, in Ceplair, 94–96.

30. SMG to TDW, December 9, 1836, in *Letters of TDW*, 348–49; SMG, *Epistle to the Clergy*, 111.

31. SMG, *Equality of the Sexes*, 223.

32. For her extended critique of Blackstone, see SMG, *Equality of the Sexes*, 231–37. Beginning in the mid-1830s, white women reformers began campaigning for married women's legal equality. Ernestine Rose, Lucy Stone, Elizabeth Cady Stanton, and Paulina Wright, for instance, launched state-level campaigns to gain legal rights for married women. Initially, activists focused on property rights but then included women's rights to their own wages and to joint or sole custody of their children after divorce. See Wellman, *Road to Seneca Falls*, 145–49; Miriam Gurko, *The Ladies of Seneca Falls: The Birth of the Woman's Rights Movement* (New York: Schocken Books, 1974), 86–90; Hersh, *The Slavery of Sex*, 54; Ryan, *Cradle of the Middle Class*, 227; Jean V. Matthews, *Women's Struggle for Equality: The First Phase, 1828–1876* (Chicago: Ivan R. Dee, 1997); Flexner and Fitzpatrick, *Century of Struggle*; Van Burkleo, *"Belonging to the World."*

33. SMG, *Equality of the Sexes*, 233, 231. For other discussions of married women's status, see Norma Basch, "Equity vs. Equality: Emerging Concepts of Women's Political Status in the Age of Jackson," *Journal of the Early Republic* 3 (Fall 1983): 297–318; Basch, *In the Eyes of the Law*; Nancy F. Cott, *Public Vows: A History of Marriage and the Nation* (Cambridge, Mass.: Harvard University Press, 2000); Marylynn Salmon, *Women and the Law of Property in Early America* (Chapel Hill: University of North Carolina Press, 1986); SMG, *Equality of the Sexes*, 231. Stanley, *From Bondage to Contract*, 11.

34. SMG, *Equality of the Sexes*, 232.

35. AEG, *An Appeal to the Women of the Nominally Free States, Issued by an Anti-Slavery Convention of American Women*, 1837, in Ceplair, 131–32; "Motion of AEG," from the *Proceedings of the Anti-Slavery Convention of American Women*, 1837, ibid., 130.

36. SMG, *Equality of the Sexes*, 232–33; also Lori D. Ginzberg, *Women in Antebellum Reform* (Wheeling, Ill.: Harlan Davidson, 2000).

37. Lawrence J. Friedman, *Gregarious Saints: Self and Community in American Abolitionism, 1830–1870* (New York: Cambridge University Press, 1982), 200.

38. Sewell, *Ballots for Freedom*, 95, 94, 50–51. By 1839, Stewart advocated the creation of a political party devoted to antislavery, a move that neither Grimké explicitly endorsed. Lysander Spooner's 1845 argument, *The Unconstitutionality of Slavery*, pointed to the same sections as proof that "the Constitution was in fact

an anti-slavery document." For Lysander Spooner, see Mason I. Lowance, Jr., ed., *A House Divided: The Antebellum Slavery Debates in America, 1776–1865* (Princeton, N.J.: Princeton University Press, 2003), 447–49. For Henry C. Wright and William Lloyd Garrison, see Perry, *Radical Abolitionism*, 58, 76–80; Jordan, *Slavery and the Meetinghouse*, 47.

39. The sisters already advocated pacifism, civil disobedience, and a higher Christian moral law—all ideas that found some sanction in Quaker ideology. Thomas D. Hamm, *The Quakers in America* (New York: Columbia University Press, 2003), 44–45; H. Larry Ingle, *Quakers in Conflict: The Hicksite Reformation* (Knoxville: University of Tennessee Press, 1986).

40. Lewis Perry, *Radical Abolition: Anarchy and the Government of God in Antislavery Thought* (Ithaca: Cornell University Press, 1973), 189; Ronald G. Walters, *The Antislavery Appeal: American Abolitionism after 1830* (Baltimore: Johns Hopkins University Press, 1976), 8.

41. SMG to TDW, September 20, 1837, in Ceplair, 290. See also SMG to Sarah Douglass, November 23, 1837, in Ceplair, 297; SMG to TDW, November 30, 1837, in *Letters of TDW*, 486.

42. TDW to SMG and AEG, January 5, 1838, in *Letters of TDW*, 512–15; AEG to TDW, January 21, 1838, in Ceplair, 304–6.

43. AEG to Jane Smith, May 29, 1837, in Ceplair, 141; AEG, *Letters to Catherine E. Beecher*, ibid., 197.

44. SMG, *Equality of the Sexes*, 235; Ginzberg, *Work of Benevolence*, 79; Van Burkleo, *"Belonging to the World,"* 123.

45. Perry, *Lift Up Thy Voice*, 190–91, 56; AEG, *An Appeal to the Women of the Nominally Free States, Issued by an Anti-Slavery Convention of American Women*, 1837, in Ceplair, 132; AEG, *Letters to Catherine E. Beecher*, 1837, in Ceplair, 150. Later, the sisters rejected Wendell Phillips's pointedly entitled *The Constitution, a Pro-Slavery Compact* (1844) and William Lloyd Garrison's defiant burning of a copy of the Constitution at an 1854 Fourth of July protest to express his alienation from the slavery-sanctioning federal government. Even free thinker Fanny Wright never abandoned her respect for the U.S. Constitution. For Wendell Phillips, see Lowance, *A House Divided*, 441–46. See William E. Cain, "Introduction," in William Cain, ed., *William Lloyd Garrison and the Fight against Slavery: Selections from* The Liberator (Boston: Bedford/St. Martin's Press, 1995), 35–36; Mayer, *All On Fire*, 443–45; Walters, *The Antislavery Appeal*, 8, 130. AEGW to Anne Warren Weston, October 14, 1838, in Ceplair, 329–30.

46. AEG, *Letters to Catherine E. Beecher*, in Ceplair, 185; Ginzberg, *Work of Benevolence*, 97; SMG to Henry C. Wright, November 19, 1838, in Ceplair, 330–31.

47. Friedman, *Gregarious Saints*, 196–222; SMG to Augustus and Susan Wattles, April 2, 1854, in Lerner, *Sarah Grimké*, 69–72; Jordan, *Slavery and the Meetinghouse*, ch. 5. For the situation in Kansas at that time, see Nicole Etcheson, *Bleeding Kansas: Contested Liberty in the Civil War Era* (Lawrence: University Press of Kansas, 2004), ch. 5; Thomas Goodrich, *War to the Knife: Bleeding Kansas, 1854–1861* (Mechanicsburg, Penn.: Stackpole Books, 1998); James A. Rawley, *Race and Politics: "Bleeding Kansas" and the Coming Civil War* (Philadelphia: Lippincott, 1969); Michael F. Holt, *The Fate of Their Country: Politicians, Slavery Extension, and the Coming of the Civil War* (New York: Hill and Wang, 2004), 112–27.

48. Lerner, *The Grimké Sisters*, 243; Abzug, *Passionate Liberator*, 273; William Lloyd Garrison, "John Brown and the Principle of Nonresistance," December 16, 1859, in Cain, *William Lloyd Garrison and the Fight against Slavery*, 156–59. For Harper, see William Still, *The Underground Railroad: A Record of Facts* . . . (1872; repr.,

New York: Arno Press, 1968), 762; Benjamin Quarles, *Allies for Freedom: Blacks and John Brown* (New York: Oxford University Press, 1974), 128, 145.

49. Birney, *The Grimké Sisters*, 184–85.

50. Abzug, *Passionate Liberator*, 204; Lerner, *The Grimké Sisters*, 155; Robert K. Nelson, "'The Forgetfulness of Sex': Devotion and Desire in the Courtship Letters of Angelina Grimké and Theodore Dwight Weld," *Journal of Social History* (Spring 2004): 663–79.

51. List of persons invited to the wedding of Theodore D. Weld and Angelina Grimké, May 1838, WG Papers. See also Margaret Hope Bacon, "By Moral Force Alone: The Antislavery Women and Nonresistance," in Yellin and Van Horne, *Abolitionist Sisterhood*, 286; Angelina Grimké Weld, "Speech at Pennsylvania Hall," May 16, 1838, in Kathryn Kish Sklar, *Women's Rights Emerges within the Antislavery Movement, 1830–1870: A Brief History with Documents* (Boston: Bedford/St. Martin's Press, 2000), 153–56.

52. SMG to Elizabeth Pease, May 1838, in Ceplair, 317.

53. Theodore Dwight Weld, *American Slavery As It Is: Testimony of a Thousand Witnesses* (1839; repr., New York, Arno Press, 1968); Lerner, *The Grimké Sisters*, 266; AEGW to Sarah Douglass, March 21, 1839, in Ceplair, 331. Also see Elizabeth B. Clark, "'The Sacred Rights of the Weak': Pain, Sympathy, and the Culture of Individual Rights in Antebellum America," *Journal of American History* (September 1995): 467.

54. SMG, "Narrative and Testimony of Sarah M. Grimké," in TDW, ed., *American Slavery As It Is*, 22–24.

55. Lerner, *Sarah Grimké*, 51, 37, 41; Stanley, *From Bondage to Contract*, 27; SMG, *Equality of the Sexes*, 223.

56. SMG, *Equality of the Sexes*, 223; Annette Gordon-Reed, "Celia's Case, 1857," in Annette Gordon-Reed, ed., *Race on Trial: Law and Justice in American History* (New York: Oxford University Press, 2002), 48–60; Yellin, *Harriet Jacobs*, ch. 3.

57. SMG, *Equality of the Sexes*, 224.

58. This is a quote from S. A. Forrall, ibid.

59. Ibid., 224–25; Salmon, *Law of Property*, 79; Elizabeth Fox-Genovese, *Within the Plantation Household: Black and White Women of the Old South* (Chapel Hill: University of North Carolina Press, 1988); Marli F. Weiner, *Mistresses and Slaves: Plantation Women in South Carolina, 1830–1880* (Urbana: University of Illinois Press, 1998).

60. SMG, *Equality of the Sexes*, 225.

61. Bertrand Wyatt-Brown, *Lewis Tappan and the Evangelical War against Slavery* (1969; repr., Baton Rouge: Louisiana State University Press, 1997); AEGW to Lewis Tappan, August 1842, in *Letters of TDW*, 872–74.

62. AEGW to Anne Warren Weston, October 13, 1838, in Ceplair, 329–30.

63. Whitney R. Cross, *The Burned-Over District: The Social and Intellectual History of Enthusiastic Religion in Western New York, 1800–1850* (Ithaca, N.Y.: Cornell University Press, 1950); Paul E. Johnson, *A Shopkeeper's Millennium: Society and Revivals in Rochester, New York, 1815–1837* (New York: Hill and Wang, 1978); Timothy L. Smith, *Revivalism and Social Reform: American Protestantism on the Eve of the Civil War* (New York: Harper and Row, 1957).

64. SMG, *The Education of Women*, ca. 1852–1857, in Lerner, *Sarah Grimké*, 86; SMG to Pease, February 11, 1842, in *Letters of TDW*, 921 (emphasis added), 920.

65. Ginzberg, *Work of Benevolence*, 62–66; Cutter, *Domestic Devils*, 122; Friedman, *Gregarious Saints*, 140–51; SMG to Pease, February 11, 1842, in *Letters of TDW*, 920 (emphasis added). See Kathryn Kish Sklar, "'Women Who Speak for an Entire Nation': American and British Women at the World Anti-slavery Convention, London, 1840," in Yellin and Van Horne, *Abolitionist Sisterhood*, 301–33.

66. Margaret H. McFadden, *Golden Cables of Sympathy: The Transatlantic Sources of Nineteenth-Century Feminism* (Lexington: University Press of Kentucky, 1999), 52–53; Karen Offen, *European Feminism, 1700–1950: A Political History* (Stanford, Calif.: Stanford University Press, 2000), 102; Bonnie S. Anderson, *Joyous Greetings: The First International Women's Movement, 1830–1860* (New York: Oxford University Press, 2000), 2–3; Isenberg, *Sex and Citizenship*, xviii, 71. Sarah Grimké first used the word "co-equal" in 1842 but articulated the concept as early as her 1837 *Letters on the Equality of the Sexes* when she explained that men and women were "created in perfect equality" and "were expected to exercise the *viceregency* intrusted to them by their Maker, in harmony and love" (emphasis added); SMG, *Equality of the Sexes*, 205. See also SMG to Pease, February 11, 1842, in *Letters of TDW*, 920; AEG to Jane Smith, July 10, 1837, in Ceplair, 276; SMG to *The Lily*, April 12, 1852, in Lerner, *Sarah Grimké*, 62–64.

67. Sklar, "Women Who Speak for an Entire Nation"; Clare Midgley, "British Abolition and Feminism in Transatlantic Perspective," in Sklar and Stewart, *Transatlantic Antislavery*, 121–36; SMG, *Education of Women*, 88 (emphasis added).

68. Lynn Sherr, *Failure Is Impossible: Susan B. Anthony in Her Own Words* (New York: Random House, 1995), 110–18; Van Burkleo, *"Belonging to the World,"* 150–55; DuBois, "Taking the Law into Our Own Hands," 19–40. For an excerpt from Susan B. Anthony's 1873 trial, see *On Trial: American History through Court Proceedings and Hearings*, vol. 2, ed. Robert D. Marcus (St. James, N.Y.: Brandywine Press, 1998), 14–27.

69. Lerner, *The Grimké Sisters*, 33, 351–52; Venet, *Neither Ballots nor Bullets*, ch. 5; Hammand, "Woman's National Loyal League," 39–58; Flexner and Fitzpatrick, *Century of Struggle*; AEGW, "Remonstrance of the Citizens of Belleville, N.J. To the Honorable Court of Quarter Sessions for Essex County Now in Session in the City of Newark," 1842, in *Letters of TDW*, 917–18.

70. SMG to Pease, February 11, 1842, in *Letters of TDW*, 921; also Sarah M. Douglass to AEGW, March 18, 1874, and SMG and AEG to Sarah Douglass, April 3, 1873, WG Papers; Carolyn Williams, "The Female Antislavery Movement: Fighting against Racial Prejudice and Promoting Women's Rights in Antebellum America," in Yellin and Van Horne, *Abolitionist Sisterhood*, 164, 168–69.

71. SMG to Sarah Douglass, September 8, 1839, and Grace Douglass to Charles Stuart Faucheraud Weld, September 28, 1840, WG Papers.

72. SMG to Sarah M. Douglass, January 27, 1845, and Sarah M. Douglass to SMG, May 28, 1873, WG Papers.

73. See, for instance, Sarah M. Douglass to Charles Stuart Faucheraud Weld, May 1, 1874 (a letter of condolence for the loss of his aunt Sarah), and June 1, 1876 (encouraging him to work with "Mr. Garrison," probably Francis Jackson Garrison, William's son, on a memoir of the Grimké sisters); to Theodore Dwight Weld, October 30, 1879 (consoling Theodore after Angelina's death), and June 11, 1880 (hoping that Lydia Maria Child would "write a memoir of the precious sisters," and predicting her own imminent death, which occurred in 1882), all in WG Papers.

74. Perry, *Lift Up Thy Voice*, 227–30; Christine Stansell, "Missed Connections: Abolitionist Feminism in the Nineteenth Century," in Ellen Carol DuBois and Richard Candida Smith, eds., *Elizabeth Cady Stanton, Feminist as Thinker: A Reader in Documents and Essays* (New York: New York University Press, 2007), 32–49.

75. SMG to Sarah Mapps Douglass, January 14, 1839, and to Pease, April 10, 1839, which includes a copy of a letter from Sarah Mapps Douglass to SMG of April 13, 1837, WG Papers. In Douglass's 1837 letter, she writes to Grimké, "you ask me for some account of my beloved brother and of his trials." Jordan, *Slavery and the Meetinghouse*, 67–80.

76. Sarah Mapps Douglass, "Letter to the Editor," *The Friend* (September 1840), and letter regarding the treatment of African Americans at Friends meetings, April 2, 1844, WG Papers.

77. SMG, *Sisters of Charity*, ca. 1852–1857, in Lerner, *The Grimké Sisters*, 292–93. For a history of marriage laws in the U.S., see Hartog, *Man and Wife in America*.

78. SMG, *Sisters of Charity*, in Lerner, *Sarah Grimké*, 142–43. Also see SMG, *Condition of Women*, ca. mid-1850s, in Elizabeth Ann Bartlett, ed., *Sarah Grimké: Letters on the Equality of the Sexes and Other Essays* (New Haven: Yale University Press, 1988), 127–33. For a discussion of the fight for married women's legal rights, see Isenberg, *Sex and Citizenship*, 156–57.

79. SMG, *Marriage*, mid to late 1850s, in Lerner, *The Grimké Sisters*, 303.

80. SMG to Jeanne Deroin, May 21, 1856, in Lerner, *Sarah Grimké*, 119.

81. Grimké rejected the double standard of morality precisely because it gave men more sexual latitude without having to pay a legal or social price, in terms of their reputations. Antebellum female moral reformers argued, as Helen Horowitz puts it, that "Women should demand of unmarried men the same moral purity—i.e., virginity—that men demand of unmarried women." Elizabeth Cady Stanton pushed the woman's movement to include a strong critique of marriage. Horowitz, *Rereading Sex*, 151. See Ellen Carol DuBois, "'The Pivot of the Marriage Relation': Stanton's Analysis of Women's Subordination in Marriage," in Dubois and Smith, *Stanton, Feminist as Thinker*, 82–92.

82. SMG, *Marriage*, 306. See also SMG, *Equality of the Sexes*, 209; SMG, *Sisters of Charity*, in Lerner, *The Grimké Sisters*, 290.

83. In the 1850s Sarah also subscribed and wrote letters to the feminist temperance paper *The Lily*. Abzug, *Passionate Liberator*, 297; Lerner, *The Grimké Sisters*, 111, 240. AEGW, "Remonstrance of the Citizens of Belleville, N.J. to the Honorable the Court of Quarter Sessions for Essex County Now in Session in the City of Newark," 1842, in *Letters of TDW*, 917–18.

84. Lerner, *Sarah Grimké*, 136; SMG, *Sisters of Charity*, in ibid., 145; Stephanie Coontz, *Marriage, a History: From Obedience to Intimacy or How Love Conquered Marriage* (New York: Viking Press, 2005), 187.

85. SMG, *Education of Women*, 81. See also SMG, *Marriage*, 113; Lyndall Gordon, *Vindication: A Life of Mary Wollstonecraft* (New York: Harper Collins Publishers, 2005), 145–55; Stanley, *From Bondage to Contract*, 260 (quote).

86. See Lerner's "Introduction," *Sarah Grimké*, 3–41; SMG to Jeanne Deroin, May 21, 1856, in ibid., 116–22; SMG, *Equality of the Sexes*, 235; Harriot H. Robinson, *Massachusetts in the Woman Suffrage Movement* (Boston: Roberts Brothers, 1883), 214–16. See Kerber, *No Constitutional Right*. On Harriot Hunt, see Stanton, Anthony, and Gage, *History of Woman Suffrage*, 1:226; Barbara M. Solomon, *In the Company of Educated Women: A History of Women and Higher Education in America* (New Haven: Yale University Press, 1985); Lynn D. Gordon, *Gender and Higher Education in the Progressive Era* (New Haven: Yale University Press, 1990); Lynn D. Gordon, "Education and the Professions," in *A Companion to American Women's History*, ed. Nancy A. Hewitt (Malden, Mass.: Blackwell, 2002), 227–28.

87. Grimké finished and published her translation of Alphonse de Lamartine's *Joan of Arc* from French into English in 1867. Lerner, *The Grimké Sisters*, 255–57. SMG, letter draft to George Sand, undated, ca. 1866 or 1867 (?), SMG to Jeanne Deroin, May 21, 1856, in Lerner, *Sarah Grimké*, 149, 120.

88. SMG, *Education of Women*, 85. See also Birney, *The Grimké Sisters*, 297–99; Sherr, *Failure Is Impossible*, 107.

89. SMG, *Sisters of Charity*, in Lerner, *The Grimké Sisters*, 295–96; SMG, *Educa-*

NOTES TO PAGES 91–99   241

tion of Women, 81, 87; also Charles Capper, *Margaret Fuller: An American Romantic Life: The Private Years* (New York: Oxford University Press, 1992), 294–96.

90. SMG, *Education of Women*, 80, 84–85. See also Michael Goldberg, "Breaking New Ground, 1800–1848," in Nancy F. Cott, ed., *No Small Courage: A History of Women in the United States* (New York: Oxford University Press, 2000), 197–99.

91. SMG, *Education of Women*, 85. See SMG to *The Lily*, April 12, 1852, in Lerner, *Sarah Grimké*, 62; Charles W. Akers, *Abigail Adams: An American Woman* (New York: Longman Press, 2000), 48.

92. SMG, *Education of Women*, 88.

93. Solomon, *Company of Educated Women*, 43–47; SMG, *Education of Women*, 80, 88.

94. SMG to *The Lily*, April 12, 1852, in Lerner, *Sarah Grimké*, 61–63; SMG to Sarah M. Douglass, August 1, 1853, WG Papers; also Lerner, *The Grimké Sisters*, 221–25; Lerner, *Sarah Grimké*, 30–31.

95. Soderlund, "Priorities and Power," in Yellin and Van Horne, *Abolitionist Sisterhood*, 76–77; SMG to Sarah M. Douglass, February 22, 1837, and January 27, 1859, WG Papers.

96. See "A Tribute of Respect to the Veteran Teacher, Mrs. Sarah M. Douglass," undated, soliciting friends of Douglass to establish an annuity for her support after fifty years of teaching; Sarah M. Douglass to SMG, May 28, 1873, WG Papers. For more on Douglass, see Lindhorst, "Sarah Mapps Douglass"; Winch, "You Have Talents—Only Cultivate Them," 101–18; Emma Jones Lapansky, "The World the Agitators Made: The Counterculture of Agitation in Urban Philadelphia," in Yellin and Van Horne, *Abolitionist Sisterhood*, 97.

97. SMG to Sarah M. Douglass, September 15, October 18, 1863, WG Papers.

98. Elizabth Grosz, *Volatile Bodies: Toward a Corporeal Feminism* (Bloomington: Indiana University Press, 1994), 15–17; Carol Gilligan, *In a Different Voice: Psychological Theory and Women's Development* (Cambridge, Mass.: Harvard University Press, 1982).

99. SMG, *Condition of Women*, 128 (emphasis added); also Michele Mitchell, "'Lower Orders,' Racial Hierarchies, and Rights Rhetoric: Evolutionary Echoes in Elizabeth Cady Stanton's Thought during the Late 1860s," and Ann D. Gordon, "Stanton and the Right to Vote: On Account of Race or Sex," in Dubois and Smith, *Stanton, Feminist as Thinker*, 111–27, 128–54. Also see Newman, *White Women's Rights*; Kern, *Mrs. Stanton's Bible*.

100. SMG, *Sisters of Charity*, in Lerner, *The Grimké Sisters*, 292.

101. SMG, *Condition of Women*, 130 (emphasis added); SMG to *The Lily*, April 12, 1852, in Lerner, *Sarah Grimké*, 63; Basch, "Equity vs. Equality," 300.

102. SMG to Sarah Wattles, December 27, 1858, in Lerner, *Sarah Grimké*, 153–54; SMG, *Condition of Women*, 128–29 (emphasis added).

103. Abzug, *Cosmos Crumbling*, 219, 228.

CHAPTER 3—FRANCES WATKINS HARPER

1. Frances Ellen Watkins to William Still, ca. 1852–1853, in Still, *The Underground Railroad*, 757. Sherita L. Johnson, "In the Sunny South: Reconstructing Frances Harper as Southern," *Southern Quarterly* 45, no. 3 (2008): 77; Mae M. Ngai, *Impossible Subjects: Illegal Aliens and the Making of Modern America* (Princeton, N.J.: Princeton University Press, 2004), 4.

2. Watkins to Still, ca.1853, in Still, *Underground Railroad*, 758. Still described Watkins as "a homeless maiden (an exile by law)," ibid.

3. The literary critic Carla L. Peterson has done the best job of analyzing Harper's thought, in a series of articles and in *"Doers of the Word,"* but there are other studies of her work as well. See, for example, Dickson D. Bruce, Jr., "Print Culture and the Antislavery Community: The Poetry of Abolitionism, 1831–1860," in McCarthy and Stauffer, *Prophets of Protest*, 220–34; Hazel V. Carby, *Reconstructing Womanhood: The Emergence of the Afro-American Woman Novelist* (New York: Oxford University Press, 1987); Barbara Christian, *Black Women Novelists: The Development of a Tradition, 1892–1976* (Westport, Conn.: Greenwood, 1980); Maryemma Graham, "Frances Ellen Watkins Harper," in *Afro-American Writers before the Harlem Renaissance*, ed. Trudier Harris and Thadious M. Davis (Detroit: Gale, 1986), 164–73; Ruth Bordin, *Woman and Temperance: The Quest for Power and Liberty, 1873–1900* (Philadelphia: Temple University Press, 1981), 82–83.

4. Jane Dailey, *Before Jim Crow: The Politics of Race in Postemancipation Virginia* (Chapel Hill: University of North Carolina Press, 2000), 3–4, 47. The NAWSA had 13,000 members in the mid-1890s whereas the WCTU had over 150,000 members by that time. See Bordin, *Woman and Temperance*, 3; Joseph Gusfield, *Symbolic Crusade: Status, Politics, and the American Temperance Movement* (Urbana: University of Illinois Press, 1963), 162; Carol Mattingly, *Well-Tempered Women: Nineteenth-Century Temperance Rhetoric* (Carbondale: Southern Illinois University Press, 1998), 176, 188.

5. Still, *Underground Railroad*, 755–56; "Introduction," in Frances Smith Foster, ed., *A Brighter Coming Day: A Frances Ellen Watkins Harper Reader* (New York: Feminist Press at the City University of New York, 1990; hereafter cited as Foster, *BCD*), 6.

6. For more information about William Watkins, see Bettye Jane Gardner, *Free Blacks in Baltimore, 1800–1860*, 2 vols. (Ph.D. dissertation, George Washington University, 1974), 1:122–23, 209–18. For his articles and information about his life, see C. Peter Ripley, ed., *The Black Abolitionist Papers*, vol. 3, *The United States, 1830–1846* (Chapel Hill: University of North Carolina Press, 1991), 92–100, and David S. Reynolds, *John Brown, Abolitionist: The Man Who Killed Slavery, Sparked the Civil War, and Seeded Civil Rights* (New York: Alfred A. Knopf, 2005), 116–17. Melba Boyd connects Harper's thought with the revolutionary David Walker's by noting similarities in her poetry and ideas to his; William Lloyd Garrison reprinted David Walker's *An Appeal to the Coloured Citizens of the World* in 1830, and Frances's uncle William Watkins distributed it. See Melba Joyce Boyd, *Discarded Legacy: Politics and Poetics in the Life of Frances E. W. Harper, 1825–1911* (Detroit: Wayne State University Press, 1994), 81.

7. There is no extant copy of this volume. Still, *Underground Railroad*, 755–56; Bettye Collier-Thomas, "Frances Ellen Watkins Harper: Abolitionist and Feminist Reformer, 1825–1911," in Ann D. Gordon with Bettye Collier-Thomas, eds., *African American Women and the Vote, 1837–1965* (Amherst: University of Massachusetts Press, 1997), 44–45; Erica Armstrong Dunbar, "Writing for True Womanhood: African-American Women's Writings and the Antislavery Struggle," in Sklar and Stewart, *Transatlantic Antislavery*, 310; Margaret Hope Bacon, "'One Great Bundle of Humanity': Frances Ellen Watkins Harper (1825–1911)," in *Pennsylvania Magazine of History and Biography* 113, no. 1 (January 1989): 22–23.

8. Willard, *Glimpses of Fifty Years*, 133.

9. Peterson, *"Doers of the Word,"* 125; Still, *Underground Railroad*, 758–59; Frances Ellen Watkins Harper, *Poems on Miscellaneous Subjects* (Philadelphia: Merrihew & Thompson, 1857; repr., Library of American Civilization microfiche collection, LAC 40118, poetry).

10. The Anti-Slavery Office was located on the ground floor and the Stills lived in an apartment above it. Still, *Underground Railroad*, 758.

11. Ibid., 757–59; Harriet Beecher Stowe, *Uncle Tom's Cabin, Or, Life Among the*

Lowly (Boston, Mass.: John P. Jewett, 1852); Solomon Northrup, *Twelve Years a Slave: Narrative of Solomon Northup, a Citizen of New-York, Kidnapped in Washington City in 1841, and Rescued in 1853* (Auburn, N.Y.: Derby and Miller, 1853.

12. The Reverend William Watkins allied himself with Garrison and joined the American Moral Reform Society. See Ripley, *Black Abolitionist Papers*, 3:92–101, 189–200, 232–34, 278–83. His son William Watkins became an associate editor of *Frederick Douglass' Paper*. Peterson, *"Doers of the Word,"* 120–21; Mayer, *All On Fire*, 71–82, 115; James Brewer Stewart, *William Lloyd Garrison and the Challenge of Emancipation* (Arlington Heights, Ill.: Harlan Davidson, 1992), 43.

13. William Lloyd Garrison, "Preface," Boston, August 15, 1854, in Watkins, *Miscellaneous Subjects*.

14. Still, *Underground Railroad*, 758.

15. Peterson, *"Doers of the Word,"* 120–21; Yee, *Black Women Abolitionists*, 27; Rosalyn Terborg-Penn, "Black Male Perspectives on the Nineteenth-Century Woman," in Sharon Harley and Rosalyn Terborg-Penn, eds., *The Afro-American Woman: Struggles and Images* (Port Washington, N.Y.: Kennikat Press, 1978), 35.

16. After a fierce battle and a bitter split in 1840, the American Anti-Slavery Society definitively sanctioned an equal role for women in abolition. Peterson, *"Doers of the Word,"* 122.

17. Jeffrey, *Great Silent Army*, 207.

18. Still, *Underground Railroad*, 779. The first extant book by Watkins is her 1854 *Poems on Miscellaneous Subjects*, in Foster, *BCD*, 55. Carolyn Sorisio, "The Spectacle of the Body: Torture in the Antislavery Writing of Lydia Maria Child and Frances E. Harper," *Modern Language Studies* 30, no. 1, pt. 1 (2000): 63.

19. Stewart, *William Lloyd Garrison*, 143; Still, *Underground Railroad*, 758–61.

20. Frances Ellen Watkins, "Breathing the Air of Freedom," Niagara Falls, New York, September 12, 1856, in Watkins, *Miscellaneous Subjects*, 47–48.

21. Mayer, *All On Fire*, 381–82; Stewart, *William Lloyd Garrison*, 156.

22. Frances Ellen Watkins, "Letter from Buckstown Centre, Maine," September 28, 1854, in Still, *Underground Railroad*, 759.

23. Yee, *Black Women Abolitionists*, 130. Garrison first espoused disunionism in 1844; see Mayer, *All On Fire*, 328. Frances Ellen Watkins, "Our Greatest Want," *Anglo-African Magazine* 1, no. 5 (May 1859), in *Anglo-African Magazine, Volume I—1859* (1859; repr., New York: Arno Press and the *New York Times*, 1968), 160. See also Midgley, "British Abolition and Feminism," 128.

24. John Mayfield, *Rehearsal for Republicanism: Free Soil and the Politics of Antislavery* (Port Washington, N.Y.: Kennikat Press, 1980), 61.

25. "Speech of Miss Watkins," delivered during the twenty-fourth anniversary meeting of the American Anti-Slavery Society, May 13, 1857, published in *National Anti-Slavery Standard* 18, no. 1 (May 23, 1857). All citations of this paper are from the microfilm collection of the *National Anti-Slavery Standard* (American Anti-Slavery Society, New York, 30 v.: ill; 60cm).

26. Charles C. Burleigh "Speech of Mr. Burleigh," ibid.

27. "Speech of Miss Watkins," ibid.

28. Ibid. Two other women speakers were recorded as speaking at the twenty-fourth anniversary meeting of the American Anti-Slavery Society. Lucy Stone spoke of her concern that all the talk of the duties of men meant that "all the women in the audience will be likely to . . . fail to feel what needs, on their part, to be done." Ernestine Rose defended William Wells Brown's promotion of slave insurrection. Like Stone, Rose reminded her audience "that woman is disfranchised as well as the slave." *National Anti-Slavery Standard*, May 23, 1857.

29. Hannah Geffert, "Regional Black Involvement in John Brown's Raid on Harpers Ferry," in McCarthy and Stauffer, *Prophets of Protest*, 169; also Julie Roy Jeffrey, "'No Occurrence in Human History Is More Deserving of Commemoration Than This': Abolitionist Celebrations of Freedom," ibid., 213–16; Stanley W. Campbell, *The Slave Catchers: Enforcement of the Fugitive Slave Law* (Chapel Hill: University of North Carolina Press, 1968), 170–73.

30. Frances Ellen Watkins, "To John Brown," Kendalville, Indiana, November 25, 1859, in Foster, *BCD*, 49; Frances Watkins Harper, *Minnie's Sacrifice* (1869), in Frances Smith Foster, ed., *Minnie's Sacrifice, Sowing and Reaping, Trial and Triumph: Three Rediscovered Novels by Frances E. W. Harper* (Boston: Beacon Press, 1994), 39–40; Frances Ellen Watkins, "An Appeal for the Philadelphia Rescuers," *Weekly Anglo-African*, June 23, 1860, in Foster, *BCD*, 52; Peterson, "Literary Transnationalism," 191.

31. "A Word from Miss Watkins," *National Anti-Slavery Standard* 20, no. 35, January 14, 1860.

32. Eric Foner, *Free Soil, Free Labor, Free Men: The Ideology of the Republican Party before the Civil War* (New York: Oxford University Press, 1970), 85–86. Watkins's letter to the *National Anti-Slavery Standard* shared space in this issue with "Our Foreign Correspondent," H.M. (presumably Harriet Martineau), as well as with an excerpt from Harriet Beecher Stowe's newest serialized novel from the *Atlantic Monthly*, "The Minister's Wooing"; *National Anti-Slavery Standard* 19, no. 47, April 9, 1859.

33. Frances Ellen Watkins, "Miss Watkins and the Constitution," ibid.

34. Frances Ellen Watkins, "The Triumph of Freedom—A Dream," *Anglo-African Magazine* 2 (1860), in Foster, *BCD*, 116–17.

35. Bacon, "By Moral Force Alone," 294–95; Reynolds, *John Brown*, 365–68; Louis A. DeCaro, Jr., *"Fire from the Midst of You": A Religious Life of John Brown* (New York: New York University Press, 2002), 279–84; Frances Ellen Watkins, "Letter to John Brown's Wife," 1860 (?), in Still, *Underground Railroad*, 762.

36. Reynolds, *John Brown*, 488–89; "Letter to the Wife of John Brown," November 23, 1859, in Benjamin Quarles, ed., *Blacks on John Brown* (Urbana: University of Illinois Press, 1972), 16–19.

37. Frances Ellen Watkins, "To Mary Brown," November 14, 1859, in Foster, *BCD*, 48–49; also Quarles, *Allies for Freedom*, 142–43; Peggy A. Russo and Paul Finkelman, eds., *Terrible Swift Sword: The Legacy of John Brown* (Athens: Ohio University Press, 2005), 47; Collier-Thomas, "Frances Ellen Watkins Harper," 47. Her cousin, William J. Watkins, was "said to have been informed beforehand of Brown's intentions." See Collier-Thomas, "Frances Ellen Watkins Harper," in *African American Women and the Vote*, 47. For the writings of Harper's cousin William J. Watkins, see C. Peter Ripley, ed., *The Black Abolitionist Papers*, vol. 4, *The United States, 1847–1858* (Chapel Hill: University of North Carolina Press, 1991), 207–9, 212–13, 227–29, 256–58.

38. Frances Ellen Watkins, "The Triumph of Freedom—A Dream," *Anglo-African Magazine* 2 (1860), in Foster, *BCD*, 116–17.

39. Her stepchildren stayed with members of her husband's family since she could not support them. Still, *Underground Railroad*, 764.

40. Frances Watkins Harper (hereafter FWH), "Lines to Miles O'Reiley," 1867, in Foster, *BCD*, 192–93.

41. FWH, "To the Cleveland Union-Savers: An Appeal from One of the Fugitive's Own Race," *Anti-Slavery Bugle*, February 23, 1861, ibid., 93–94.

42. Allen C. Guelzo, *Lincoln's Emancipation Proclamation: The End of Slavery in America* (New York: Simon and Schuster, 2004), 157–58.

43. FWH to William Still from Grove City, Ohio, undated (1863?), in Still, *Underground Railroad*, 766.

44. At the end of the war, some of Harper's poetry and prose were selected by Lydia Maria Child to be included in a volume called *The Freedmen's Book* (1865), which was designed to provide lessons in citizenship and pride in their history. Other authors included in the volume, distributed to freedmen's schools throughout the South, were Charlotte Forten, John Greenleaf Whittier, William Lloyd Garrison, and Harriet Beecher Stowe. Lyde Cullen Sizer, *The Political Work of Northern Women Writers and the Civil War, 1850–1872* (Chapel Hill: University of North Carolina Press, 2000), ch. 7.

45. FWH, Letter "dated Boston, April 19th, [1865?] on the Assassination of the President," in Still, *Underground Railroad*, 767.

46. Boyd, *Discarded Legacy*, 29.

47. FWH to Still, possibly 1867, in Still, *Underground Railroad*, 770.

48. FWH, "Fifteenth Amendment," ibid., 769; FWH, "A Private Meeting With the Women," Greenville, Georgia, March 29, 1870, in Foster, *BCD*, 127–28; FWH, "I Am in the Sunny South," Darlington, South Carolina, May 13, 1867, in Foster, *BCD*, 122–23. For Harper in the Reconstruction South, see Faulkner, *Women's Radical Reconstruction*, 70.

49. Carla L. Peterson, "Reconstructing the Nation: Frances Harper, Charlotte Forten, and the Racial Politics of Periodical Publication," *American Antiquarian Society* (1989): 304, 307 (emphasis added); FWH, *Minnie's Sacrifice* (1869), 78–79.

50. FWH, *Minnie's Sacrifice* (1869), 74–76.

51. Ibid., 74–75.

52. Ibid., 80–81, 85–86; Hodes, *White Women, Black Men*, 201; Grace Elizabeth Hale, *Making Whiteness: The Culture of Segregation in the South, 1890–1940* (New York: Vintage Books, 1998), 231, 237.

53. FWH, "What a Field there is Here," Demopolis, Alabama, March 1 (?), 1871, in Foster, *BCD*, 131–32 (emphasis added); FWH, "The Great Problem to Be Solved," delivered at the Centennial Anniversary of the Pennsylvania Society for Promoting the Abolition of Slavery, Philadelphia, April 14, 1875, in Foster, *BCD*, 220–21; also FWH, *Iola Leroy, or Shadows Uplifted*, 2nd ed. (1892; repr., College Park, Md.: McGrath, 1969), 224–25.

54. Faulkner, *Women's Radical Reconstruction*, 76.

55. Frances Ellen Watkins, "The Two Offers," *Anglo-African Magazine* 1, nos. 9, 10 (September 1859): 288–91, 311–13.

56. Ibid., no. 9, 291; Yee, *Black Women Abolitionists*, 44; Cutter, *Domestic Devils*, 14–16, 67.

57. FWH, "We Are All Bound Up Together," *Proceedings of the Eleventh Woman's Rights Convention*, New York, May 1866, in Foster, *BCD*, 217–19 (emphasis added); Still, *Underground Railroad*, 764. As historian Amy Stanley puts it, "For Harper, the husband's claim to property in his wife violated inalienable rights much as did the slave master's claim to his chattel property." Stanley, *From Bondage to Contract*, 31.

58. FWH to Still, from Montgomery, Alabama, 1870, in Still, *Underground Railroad*, 773.

59. Stanton, Anthony, and Gage, *History of Woman Suffrage*, 2:171, 152–53, 172; Hope, "One Great Bundle of Humanity," 34.

60. Terborg-Penn, *Struggle for the Vote*, 33, 48; FWH, "We Are All Bound Up Together," 217–219.

61. FWH, "We Are All Bound Up Together" (emphasis added); Miller, *Arguing about Slavery*, 209–16; Beth A. Salerno, *Sister Societies: Women's Antislavery Organizations in Antebellum America* (DeKalb: Northern Illinois University Press, 2005), 63–66.

62. Quoted from Stanton, Anthony, and Gage, *History of Woman Suffrage*,

2:174, 182. See also Judith E. Harper, *Susan B. Anthony: A Biographical Companion* (Santa Barbara, Calif.: ABC-CLIO, 1998), 238; Sarah Jane Deutsch, "From Ballots to Breadlines, 1920–1940," in Cott, *No Small Courage*, 419–20; Nancy F. Cott, *The Grounding of Modern Feminism* (New Haven, Conn.: Yale University Press, 1987), 101–5.

63. FWH, "We Are All Bound Up Together"; also Rosalyn Terborg-Penn, *Struggle for the Vote*, 18.

64. FWH, "We Are All Bound Up Together."

65. Barbara Welke, "When All the Women Were White, and All the Blacks Were Men: Gender, Class, Race, and the Road to *Plessy*, 1855–1914," *Law and History Review* 13, no. 2 (Fall 1995): 261–316.

66. Estelle B. Freedman, "Race and the Politics of Identity in U.S. Feminism," in Vicki Ruiz and Ellen Carol DuBois, eds., *Unequal Sisters: An Inclusive Reader in U.S. Women's History*, 4th ed. (New York: Routledge, 2008), 1; FWH, "We Are All Bound Up Together." See Yee, *Black Women Abolitionists*, 133–34; Bacon, "One Great Bundle," 33.

67. Boyd, *Discarded Legacy*, 117; Stanton, Anthony, and Gage, *History of Woman Suffrage*, 2:171; Nell Irvin Painter, *Sojourner Truth: A Life, a Symbol* (New York: W. W. Norton, 1996), 224–25.

68. Ellen Carol DuBois, "Outgrowing the Compact of the Fathers: Equal Rights, Woman Suffrage, and the United States Constitution, 1820–1878," in Dubois, *Woman Suffrage and Women's Rights*, 93–94; Jean M. Humez, *Harriet Tubman: The Life and the Life Stories* (Madison: University of Wisconsin Press, 2003), 75–76.

69. Nell Irvin Painter, "Voices of Suffrage: Sojourner Truth, Frances Watkins Harper, and the Struggle for Woman Suffrage," in Baker, *Votes for Women*, 51; "Fifteenth Amendment," in Still, *Underground Railroad*, 769; FWH, "I Am in the Sunny South," Darlington, South Carolina, May 13, 1867, in Foster, *BCD*, 122–23. For a discussion of the split and of Stanton's racist language, see DuBois, *Feminism and Suffrage*, 186–89. Stanton, Anthony, and Gage, *History of Woman Suffrage*, 2:353, 391–92.

70. Yee, *Black Women Abolitionists*, 149; Dorothy Sterling, ed., *We Are Your Sisters: Black Women in the Nineteenth Century* (New York: W. W. Norton, 1984), 416; Terborg-Penn, *Struggle for the Vote*, 36; Peterson, "Literary Transnationalism," 205.

71. The ERA Convention occurred in May 1869, in the middle of the series. Peterson, "Reconstructing the Nation," 310.

72. FWH, "Minnie's Sacrifice," in *Christian Recorder*, n.s. no. 13, September 4, 1869 (in *Christian Recorder* microfilm, reel 1, July 1865–4 March 1871, by Scholarly Resources, Inc.).

73. FWH, *Minnie's Sacrifice* (1869), 78–79. Harper had not written this section earlier, because each serialized edition was newly written. The *Christian Recorder* announced: "MINNIE'S SACRIFICE is the title of a serial story to be contributed by Mrs. F. E. W. Harper. We congratulate our readers on making this announcement. As a writer, whether of prose or poetry, Mrs. Harper stands foremost of all the colored women of our day; while as a speaker, she has been by many favorably compared to Annie Dickinson." See *Christian Recorder* 9, no. 9, whole no. 411 (March 13, 1869): 34 (in *Christian Recorder* microfilm, reel 1, July 1865–4 March 1871, by Scholarly Resources, Inc.). As proof that Harper was writing the story as the months proceeded, see the notice in *Christian Recorder* 9, no. 15 (May 8, 1869) that "An unavoidable detention of manuscript prevents the publication this week of Mrs. Harper's popular story, *Minnie's Sacrifice*. We ask the indulgence of our patrons, hoping to resume the publication in our next issue."

74. FWH, *Minnie's Sacrifice* (1869), 78–79 (emphasis added); also FWH, "John and Jacob—A Dialogue on Woman's Rights," *New York Freeman*, November 28, 1885, in Foster, *BCD*, 240–42.

75. Terborg-Penn, *Struggle for the Vote*, 42–49; DuBois, *Feminism and Suffrage*, 69, 195–200. Sojourner Truth tried to avoid choosing sides but ultimately joined the AWSA. See Painter, *Sojourner Truth*, 231–32.

76. FWH, "Fancy Sketches," *Christian Recorder*, January 15, 1874, in Foster, *BCD*, 229–30. See Willie Coleman, "Architects of a Vision: Black Women and Their Antebellum Quest for Political and Social Equality," in Gordon and Collier-Thomas, *African American Women and the Vote*, 29.

77. Elsa Barkley Brown, "To Catch the Vision of Freedom: Reconstructing Southern Black Women's Political History, 1865–1880," in Vicki L. Ruiz and Ellen DuBois, eds., *Unequal Sisters: A Multicultural Reader in U.S. Women's History*, 3rd ed. (New York: Routledge, 2000), 135; Rosalyn Terborg-Penn, "African American Women and the Woman Suffrage Movement," in Wheeler, *One Woman, One Vote*, 135–56.

78. Collier-Thomas, "Frances Ellen Watkins Harper," 49; FWH, "The Deliverance," *Sketches of Southern Life*, 1872, in Foster, *BCD*, 203.

79. Brown, "Negotiating and Transforming the Public Sphere," 354.

80. FWH, "The Deliverance," *Sketches of Southern Life*, 1872, in Foster, *BCD*, 204.

81. FWH, *Sowing and Reaping* (1876), 163, 160–61.

82. Still, *Underground Railroad*, 778.

83. See, for instance, her poem "The Revel," reprinted in Maryemma Graham, ed., *Complete Poems of Frances E. W. Harper* (New York: Oxford University Press, 1988), 11, and "The Drunkard's Child," *Miscellaneous Subjects (1854)*, 13–14.

84. Bordin, *Woman and Temperance*, 82–83.

85. Graham, *Woman Suffrage and the New Democracy*, 24–26; Gilmore, *Gender and Jim Crow*, 49.

86. "Report of the Frances Harper W.C.T.U. of St. Paul, Minn.," 1896, *Annual Report of the Second National Conference of the Colored Women of America*, in the Records of the National Association of Color Women's Clubs, 1895–1992, University Publications of America microform, 94–95.

87. FWH, "The Woman's Christian Temperance Union and the Colored Woman," *African Methodist Episcopal Church Review* 4 (1888), in Foster, *BCD*, 281–82.

88. Whereas other reformers railed against the "twin relics of barbarism," slavery and polygamy, Harper's two evils were slavery and intemperance. Sarah Barringer Gordon, *The Mormon Question: Polygamy and Constitutional Conflict in Nineteenth-Century America* (Chapel Hill: University of North Carolina Press, 2002).

89. FWH, "Woman's Work," *Christian Recorder*, February 7, 1889, in Foster, *BCD*, 260–61 (emphasis added).

90. "Speech of Miss Watkins," *National Anti-Slavery Standard*, May 23, 1857; FWH, "The Woman's Christian Temperance Union and the Colored Woman," *AME Church Review* 4 (1888), in Foster, *BCD*, 281–82.

91. Harper scholars do not agree upon the dates of her affiliation with the local WCTU and do not provide citations for their claims. For a date of 1875 see James William Clark, Jr., "Frances Ellen Watkins Harper, 1825–1911: A Literary Biography" (master's thesis, Duke University, 1967), 107. Collier-Thomas, in "Frances Ellen Watkins Harper," 55, suggests that her affiliation began in the early 1880s. Also see Theodora Williams Daniel, "The Poems of Frances E. W. Harper" (master's thesis, Howard University, 1937), 32.

92. "Report of NWCTU Annual Convention," *Union Signal*, November 8, 1883, 12. Melba Boyd (*Discarded Legacy*, 134) mistakenly suggests that Harper was

appointed to head the Department of Colored Work of the WCTU in 1869, before the WCTU even existed as an organization. Terborg-Penn (*Struggle for the Vote*, 85–86) mistakenly dates her appointment as superintendent to 1887. Some historians of Harper place her superintendency in 1888. See Bacon, "One Great Bundle," 40.

93. Frances E. Willard, "Work Among Colored People of the North," *Union Signal*, June 5, 1884; "Pen Pictures of Prominent White Ribboners: Mrs. Frances E. Harper," *Union Signal*, November 21, 1887 (Woman's Temperance Publication Association microform), 6; Bacon, "One Great Bundle," 38; Willard, "Work Among Colored People of the North," *Union Signal*, June 5, 1884.

94. Kevin Gaines, "Black Americans' Racial Uplift Ideology as 'Civilizing Mission': Pauline E. Hopkins on Race and Imperialism," in Amy Kaplan and Donald E. Pease, eds., *Cultures of United States Imperialism* (Durham, N.C.: Duke University Press, 1993), 438. For annual reports of Harper's extensive multi-state tours (at least ten states are mentioned in the first two reports), see FWH, "Work Among Colored People," 1884, *Minutes of the National Woman's Christian Temperance Union at the Eleventh Annual Meeting in St. Louis, Missouri, October 22–25, 1884* (NWCTU section of the Temperance and Prohibition Papers Microfilm Collection), lxxviii–lxxxiii; FWH, "Work Among Colored People," *Minutes of the National Woman's Christian Temperance Union at the Twelfth Annual Meeting in Philadelphia, PA, October 30th, 31st, and November 2nd and 3rd, 1885*, ibid., cx–cxv.

95. Daniel W. Crofts, "The Black Response to the Blair Education Bill," *Journal of Southern History* 37 (February 1971), 41–65, 43; FWH, "News From the Field: Words of Encouragement from Mrs. Harper," *Union Signal*, January 13, 1887, 10.

96. "Report of the Annual Meeting of the N.W.C.T.U.," *Union Signal*, November 21, 1887, 3–4; Elna C. Green, *Southern Strategies: Southern Women and the Woman Suffrage Question* (Chapel Hill: University of North Carolina Press, 1997), 20–23.

97. "Report of the Annual Meeting of the N.W.C.T.U.," *Union Signal*, November 21, 1887, 3–4. The WCTU's first national convention in the South was held in Louisville, Kentucky, in 1882 and in Nashville, Tennessee, in 1887. See also Daniel W. Crofts, "The Black Response to the Blair Education Bill," *Journal of Southern History* 37 (February 1971), 55–59. The bill was finally defeated in the Senate in 1890. Richardson, *Death of Reconstruction*, 207–9.

98. FWH, "The Woman's Christian Temperance Union and the Colored Woman," *AME Church Review* 4 (1888), in Foster, *BCD*, 282–85.

99. Collier-Thomas, "Frances Ellen Watkins Harper," 54, 60; FWH, "Work Among Colored People," 1890, *Minutes of the NWCTU at the Seventeenth Annual Meeting, Atlanta, Georgia, November 14–18, 1890*, 221.

100. Green, *Southern Strategies*, 10–11; Ann D. Gordon, "Woman Suffrage (Not Universal Suffrage) by Federal Amendment," and Marjorie Spruill Wheeler, "The Woman Suffrage Movement in the Inhospitable South," in Marjorie Spruill Wheeler, ed., *Votes for Women! The Woman Suffrage Movement in Tennessee, the South, and the Nation* (Knoxville: University of Tennessee Press, 1995), 3–52; Collier-Thomas, "Frances Ellen Watkins Harper," 58–59; Carby, *Reconstructing Womanhood*, 3–4.

101. See chapter 4 for more on this. Mrs. J. E. Ray, "Home and Foreign Missionary Work to Colored People," National Committee, Asheville, N.C., 1891, *Minutes of the NWCTU at the Eighteenth Annual Meeting, Boston, Mass., November 13–18, 1891*, 555; Collier-Thomas, "Frances Ellen Watkins Harper," 57–59.

102. For discussions of the turn of the century as being the peak in lynchings in the United States, see Stewart E. Tolnay and E. M. Beck, *A Festival of Violence: An Analysis of Southern Lynchings, 1892–1930* (Urbana: University of Illinois Press, 1995), 38; W. Fitzhugh Brundage, ed., *Under Sentence of Death: Lynching in the South* (Chapel

Hill: University of North Carolina Press, 1997), 4; William D. Carrigan and Clive Webb, *"Muerto por Unos Desconocidos* (Killed by Persons Unknown): Mob Violence against Blacks and Mexicans," in Stephanie Cole and Alison M. Parker, eds., *Beyond Black and White: Race, Ethnicity, and Gender in the U.S. South and Southwest* (College Station: Texas A&M Press, 2004), 35–74. For discussions of *Plessy v. Ferguson*, see Charles Lofgren, *The Plessy Case: A Legal-Historical Interpretation* (New York: Oxford University Press, 1987), and Thomas J. Davis, "Race, Identity, and the Law: *Plessy v. Ferguson* (1896)," in Gordon-Reed, *Race on Trial*, 61–76. Jane Dailey, "The Limits of Liberalism in the New South: The Politics of Race, Sex, and Patronage in Virginia, 1879–1883," in Jane Dailey, Glenda Elizabeth Gilmore, and Bryant Simon, eds., *Jumpin' Jim Crow: Southern Politics from Civil War to Civil Rights* (Princeton, N.J.: Princeton University Press, 2000), 88–114.

103. Ida B. Wells, "Temperance," *AME Church Review* 7, no. 4, whole no. 28 (April 1891): 379–81, 374, 375 (*AME Church Review*, reel 2, microfilm, Collections in the Schomburg Center for Research in Black Culture at the New York Public Library). Most African Americans during the Great Depression switched their allegiance to the Democratic Party of Franklin Delano Roosevelt in support of the New Deal. Lizabeth Cohen, *Making a New Deal: Industrial Workers in Chicago, 1919–1939* (New York: Cambridge University Press, 1990), 260–61; Evelyn Brooks Higginbotham, "In Politics to Stay: Black Women Leaders and Party Politics in the 1920s," in Ruiz and DuBois, *Unequal Sisters* (4th ed.), 289–302.

104. FWH, "Duty to Dependent Races," *Transactions from the National Council of Women in the United States*, 1891, reprinted in Bert Loewenberg and Ruth Bogin, eds., *Black Women in Nineteenth-Century American Life: Their Words, Their Thoughts, Their Feelings* (University Park: Pennsylvania University Press, 1976), 247, 250. A discussion of Harper's campaign for anti-lynching legislation can be found in chapter 4.

105. Boyd, *Discarded Legacy*, 16; William Still, "Introduction," to FWH, *Iola Leroy*, 3. *Iola Leroy* is one of the first novels published by an African American author. The first is thought to be *Clotel; or, The President's Daughter*, by William Wells Brown (1853). The first novel by an African American woman is thought to be Harriet Wilson, *Our Nig; or Sketches from the Life of a Free Black* (1859).

106. Frances Foster, "Introduction," in Foster, *BCD*, 26. In the antebellum era, for instance, "her first two volumes reportedly sold over 50,000 copies." Ibid.

107. FWH, *Iola Leroy*, 114. M. Giulia Fabi, *Passing and the Rise of the African American Novel* (Urbana: University of Illinois Press, 2001), 48, 58, 60; "The Mulatto as Race Leader," ch. 8, in Judith R. Berzon, *Neither White nor Black: The Mulatto Character in American Fiction* (New York: New York University Press, 1978), 193–96; FWH, *Iola Leroy*, 271.

108. FWH, *Minnie's Sacrifice*, September 25, 1869, n.s. no. 16, in the *Christian Recorder* microfilm series, reel 1, July 1865–March 1871.

109. Theda Skocpol, Ariane Liazos, Marshall Ganz, *What a Mighty Power We Can Be: African American Fraternal Groups and the Struggle for Racial Equality* (Princeton, N.J.: Princeton University Press, 2006), 222; "Evening Session," *First Annual Report of the National Conference of the Colored Women of America (National Association of Colored Women)*, 1896, 46; Cutter, *Domestic Devils*, 15.

110. Several local black WCTU's and black women's clubs throughout the country were named after her. Among those sending in reports (and possibly delegates) was the "Harper WCTU, St. Louis, Mo.," in "Treasurer's Report: Receipts," *First Annual Report of the National Conference of the Colored Women of America (National Association of Colored Women)*, 1896, 58–59, and "Report of the Frances Harper W.C.T.U. of St. Paul, Minn.," 1896, in *Annual Report of the Second National Conference*

of the Colored Women of America, 94–95. See also Darlene Clark Hine and Kathleen Thompson, *A Shining Thread of Hope: The History of Black Women in America* (New York: Broadway Books, 1998), illustration 5 caption.

111. Mrs. R. Aldridge, Pres., Mrs. Gertrude Brooks, Sec'y. "The Frances E.W. Harper League of Pittsburg and Allegheny," 1896, and "Evening Session," 1896, *Annual Report of the Second National Conference of the Colored Women of America*, 104–5, 46–47; *Annual Report of the National Conference of the Colored Women of America*, 1899.

4—FRANCES WILLARD

1. Willard, *Glimpses of Fifty Years*, 359–60; Frances Elizabeth Willard, *How to Win: A Book for Girls* (New York: Funk & Wagnalls, 1886), 49–50. Willard was WCTU president from 1879 to 1898. For recent biographies of Willard, see Bordin, *Frances Willard*; and a short entry by Ian Tyrrell, "Frances Willard and Temperance," in *Against the Tide: Women Reformers in American Society*, ed. Paul A. Cimbala and Randall M. Miller (Westport, Conn.: Praeger, 1997), 73–83. See also Barbara Leslie Epstein, *The Politics of Domesticity: Women, Evangelism, and Temperance in Nineteenth-Century America* (Middletown, Conn.: Wesleyan University Press, 1981), ch. 5.

2. Willard, assisted by Helen M. Winslow and Sallie Joy White, *Occupations for Women: A Book of Practical Suggestions for the Material Advancement, the Mental and Physical Development, and the Moral and Spiritual Uplift of Women* (New York: Success Company, 1897), 238. Willard wanted both women and men to adopt the best characteristics of the other, just as Margaret Fuller had advocated in *Woman in the Nineteenth Century: An Authoritative Text, Background, Criticism*, ed. Larry J. Reynolds (New York: W. W. Norton, 1997). See also Willard, *Glimpses of Fifty Years*, 69–70; Willard, *Writing Out My Heart*, 191n3; Parker, *Purifying America*, 171–73; Jeffrey Steele, "Introduction," in *The Essential Margaret Fuller*, ed. Jeffrey Steele (New Brunswick, N.J.: Rutgers University Press, 1992), xii; Kern, *Mrs. Stanton's Bible*, 96; Willard, *Woman in the Pulpit* (Chicago: Woman's Temperance Publication Association, 1889); Bordin, *Frances Willard*, 117.

3. Bordin, *Frances Willard*, 15; Mayfield, *Rehearsal for Republicanism*, 113–17; Douglas M. Strong, *Perfectionist Politics: Abolitionism and the Religious Tensions of American Democracy* (Syracuse, N.Y.: Syracuse University Press, 1999), 146–49; Foner, *Free Soil*, 83–87, 124.

4. Willard, *Glimpses of Fifty Years*, 593; Willard, July 21, 1893, in *Writing Out My Heart*, 375.

5. Willard, *Glimpses of Fifty Years*, 80; Carolyn De Swarte Gifford, "General Introduction," in Willard, *Writing Out My Heart*, 1–18; Bordin, *Frances Willard*, 43–44, 64. Willard had a series of intense love relationships with women and recognized her feelings toward women as being stronger than those toward her male suitors such as Charles Fowler. De Swarte Gifford, "General Introduction," in Willard, *Writing Out My Heart*, 14.

6. Willard, *Glimpses of Fifty Years*, 359–60; Greg Forster, *John Locke's Politics of Moral Consensus* (New York: Cambridge University Press, 2005), 11.

7. Bordin, *Frances Willard*, 87–89; Willard, "Introduction," to Annie Wittenmyer, *History of the Woman's Temperance Crusade* (Philadelphia: Office of the Christian Woman, 1878), 21; Willard, *Home Protection Manual: Containing an Argument for the Temperance Ballot for Woman, and How to Obtain it, as a Means of Home Protection; Also Constitution and Plan of Work for State and Local W. C. T. Unions* (New York: The Independent, 1879), 26.

8. As Richard Ashcraft summarizes, for Locke, "political authority must be

linked with the consent given by persons who are equal and independent. Hence, there is a moral autonomy to the realm of politics." Richard Ashcraft, "Locke's Political Philosophy," in *The Cambridge Companion to Locke*, ed. Vere Chappell (New York: Cambridge University Press, 1994), 242; John Locke's *Two Treatises of Government* (T II. viii.102:353), quoted in ibid., 229; Sklar, *Catharine Beecher*; Willard, *Woman and Temperance*, 458–59 (quote).

9. Kerber, *No Constitutional Right*; Kerber, "To Be Treated like American Ladies," 17, 24; Willard, *Glimpses of Fifty Years*, 594; Harper, *Susan B. Anthony*, 239–40; Gerda Lerner, "Foreword," in *Elizabeth Cady Stanton, Susan B. Anthony: Correspondence, Writings, Speeches*, ed. Ellen Carol DuBois (New York: Schocken Books, 1981), ix–x; Willard, *Home Protection Manual*, 10 (quote); John J. Jenkins, *Understanding Locke: An Introduction to Philosophy through John Locke's Essay* (Edinburgh: Edinburgh University Press, 1983), 150–53.

10. Willard, *Glimpses of Fifty Years*, 401; Martha Watson, *Lives of Their Own: Rhetorical Dimensions in Autobiographies of Women Activists* (Columbia: University of South Carolina Press, 1999), 52; Mattingly, *Well-Tempered Women*, 165; Willard, "Introduction," to Wittenmyer, *Woman's Temperance Crusade*, 21.

11. Settlement house leader Jane Addams later took a similar approach when she described women's demand for the vote as "civic housekeeping." Addams was not a committed suffragist as late as 1893, according to Louise W. Knight, *Citizen: Jane Addams and the Struggle for Democracy* (Chicago: University of Chicago Press, 2005), 263–64. See also Victoria Bissell Brown, *The Education of Jane Addams* (Philadelphia: University of Pennsylvania Press, 2004); Robin Berson, *Jane Addams: A Biography* (Westport, Conn.: Greenwood Press, 2004).

12. Willard, *Glimpses of Fifty Years*, 594; Willard, *How to Win*, 54. In fact, Willard initiated the World's Woman's Christian Temperance Union in 1883 to bring domestic feminism to the world. See Christine Bolt, *Sisterhood Questioned? Race, Class and Internationalism in the American and British Women's Movements, c. 1880s–1970s* (London: Routledge, 2004), 12–16.

13. Tyrrell, *Woman's World, Woman's Empire*, 1–3; Newman, *White Women's Rights*, 151. Newman is referring to Charlotte Perkins Gilman as well as to Frances Willard, Elizabeth Cady Stanton, Alice Cunningham Fletcher, and Mary Putnam Jacobi.

14. Isenberg, *Sex and Citizenship*; Willard, *Woman in the Pulpit* (1889), facsimile of original in *The Defense of Women's Rights to Ordination in the Methodist Episcopal Church*, ed. Carolyn De Swarte Gifford (New York: Garland Publishing, 1987), 61; Willard, *How to Win: A Book for Girls* (1886), facsimile of original in *The Ideal of "The New Woman" According to the Woman's Christian Temperance Union*, ed. Carolyn De Swarte Gifford (New York: Garland Publishing, Inc., 1988), 49–50 (a multivolume reprint facsimile collection).

15. Willard, *Woman and Temperance*, 455. Bordin (*Woman and Temperance*, 3–4) counts membership in the youth affiliates to get to over 200,000 members by 1892. The WCTU had about 344,000 members by 1921. See Gusfield, *Symbolic Crusade*, 162; Mattingly, *Well-Tempered Women*, 176, 188; Giele, *Two Paths to Women's Equality*, 107.

16. Willard, *Home Protection Manual*, 5–14; Willard, *Woman and Temperance*, 31–34; Willard, *Glimpses of Fifty Years*, 364–67.

17. Willard, *Home Protection Manual*, 11, quotes from 5, 13–14; also Zaeske, *Signatures of Citizenship*.

18. Cott, *Grounding of Modern Feminism*, 97. For the AWSA, see Andrea Moore Kerr, "White Women's Rights, Black Men's Wrongs: Free Love, Blackmail, and the Formation of the American Woman Suffrage Association," in Wheeler, *One Woman, One Vote*, 61–80; for the NWSA, see Sneider, "Woman Suffrage in Congress."

19. Willard, *Glimpses of Fifty Years*, 427 (emphasis added), 692.

20. Willard, *Woman and Temperance*, 45–46; Willard, *Home Protection Manual*, 10. See also Foster, *Moral Reconstruction*; R. R. Fennessy, *Burke, Paine, and the Rights of Man: A Difference of Political Opinion* (The Hague: Martinus Nijhoff, 1963), 150.

21. DuBois, "Taking the Law into Our Own Hands," 19–39; Willard, *Glimpses of Fifty Years*, 445. The convention was in 1888.

22. Willard, "The Ballot for the Home," *Woman's Journal* 7, no. 2 (March 1898): 1–2; Willard, *Glimpses of Fifty Years*, 611–12.

23. Willard, *Home Protection Manual*, 10; Willard, *Glimpses of Fifty Years*, 426. See also Elizabeth D. Samet, *Willing Obedience: Citizens, Soldiers, and the Progress of Consent in America, 1776–1898* (Stanford, Calif.: Stanford University Press, 2004), 141; Hoganson, *Fighting for American Manhood*; Allison L. Sneider, *Suffragists in an Imperial Age: U.S. Expansion and the Woman Question, 1870–1929* (New York: Oxford University Press, 2008); Mary A. Renda, *Taking Haiti: Military Occupation and the Culture of U.S. Imperialism, 1915–1940* (Chapel Hill: University of North Carolina Press, 2001); Briggs, *Reproducing Empire*.

24. Willard, *Home Protection Manual*, 9 (emphasis added); Willard, *Glimpses of Fifty Years*, 595.

25. For collections of Burke's works, see Ian Harris, ed., *Edmund Burke: Prerevolutionary Writings* (London: Cambridge University Press, 1993); Louis I. Bredvold and Ralph G. Ross, eds., *The Philosophy of Edmund Burke: A Selection from His Speeches and Writings* (Ann Arbor: University of Michigan Press, 1960). For a discussion of Burke as a writer, see Christopher Reid, *Edmund Burke and the Practice of Political Writing* (Dublin, Ireland: Gill and MacMillan, 1985).

26. Willard, *How to Win*, 61 (emphasis added); Edmund Burke, from Frederick A. Dreyer, *Burke's Politics: A Study in Whig Orthodoxy* (Waterloo, Ont.: Wilfrid Laurier University Press, 1979), 17; Willard, *Woman and Temperance*, 495.

27. Jean H. Baker, *Sisters: The Lives of America's Suffragists* (New York: Hill and Wang, 2005), 181; Edmund Burke, "On the Genius and Character of the French Revolution as it Regards Other Nations," in Edmund Burke, *The Works of the Right Honorable Edmund Burke*, rev. ed. (Boston: Little, Brown, and Co., 1866), 5:361, 374. See also Walter D. Love, "'Meaning' in the History of Conflicting Interpretations of Burke," in *Edmund Burke: The Enlightenment and the Modern World*, ed. Peter J. Stanlis (Detroit: University of Detroit Press, 1967), 117; Dreyer, *Burke's Politics*, 80.

28. Nevil Johnson, *Reshaping the British Constitution: The Passing of the Old Order* (Basingstoke, England: Palgrave, 2002); Jeffrey L. Jowell and Dawn Oliver, eds., *The Changing Constitution* (New York: Oxford University Press, 2004); Anthony Stephen King, *The British Constitution* (New York: Oxford University Press, 2007); Willard, *Woman and Temperance*, 496.

29. Edmund Burke from Michael Freeman, *Edmund Burke and the Critique of Political Radicalism* (Chicago: University of Chicago Press, 1980), 138. See also Bruce Frohnen, *Virtue and the Promise of Conservatism: The Legacy of Burke and Tocqueville* (Lawrence: University Press of Kansas, 1983), 44–48.

30. Willard, *Woman and Temperance*, 492, 494; Edmund Burke, "Thoughts and Details on Scarcity," in *The Works*, 166, as quoted in George Fasel, *Edmund Burke* (Boston: Twayne Publishers, 1983), 86. See also Richard Hamm, *Shaping the Eighteenth Amendment: Temperance Reform, Legal Culture, and the Polity, 1880–1920* (Chapel Hill: University of North Carolina Press, 1995), 43; Tyrrell, *Woman's World, Woman's Empire*, ch. 5; Newman, *White Women's Rights*, 52–53.

31. Hamm, *Shaping the Eighteenth Amendment*, 34–35, 42; Foster, *Moral Reconstruction*.

32. Edmund Burke, as quoted in T. E. Utley, *Edmund Burke* (London: Longmans, Green, 1957), 27 (emphasis added); Willard, *Woman and Temperance*, 492–93.

33. Wendy J. Deichmann Edwards and Carolyn De Swarte Gifford, eds., *Gender and the Social Gospel* (Urbana: University of Illinois Press, 2003); Donald K. Gorrell, *The Age of Social Responsibility: The Social Gospel in the Progressive Era, 1900–1920* (Macon, Ga.: Mercer University Press, 1988); Ronald C. White, *The Social Gospel: Religion and Reform in Changing America* (Philadelphia: Temple University Press, 1976); Hamm, *Shaping the Eighteenth Amendment*, 39, 43.

34. Willard, *Woman and Temperance*, 492–93; Parker, introduction, *Purifying America*, 1–19; Willard, *Woman and Temperance*, 494–95; J. Harvey and L. Bather, *The British Constitution* (London: Macmillan Education, 1977), 532–37; Burke from Freeman, *Edmund Burke*, 142–43 (emphasis added).

35. Willard interview, 1890, quoted in Ida B. Wells, *A Red Record: Tabulated Statistics and Alleged Causes of Lynchings in the United States, 1892–1893–1894* (Chicago, 1895), in Jacqueline Jones Royster, ed., *Southern Horrors and Other Writings: The Antilynching Campaign of Ida B. Wells, 1892–1900* (Boston: Bedford Books, 1997), 142; Jack S. Blocker, *American Temperance Movements: Cycles of Reform* (Boston: Twayne Publishers, 1989), 90; Gilmore, *Gender and Jim Crow*, 46, 250n75.

36. Catherine Gilbert Murdock, *Domesticating Drink: Women, Men, and Alcohol in America, 1870–1940* (Baltimore: Johns Hopkins University Press, 1998), 23–24; Blocker, *American Temperance Movements*, 81–94.

37. Hamm, *Shaping the Eighteenth Amendment*, 34; Willard, *Home Protection Manual*, 9.

38. Linda K. Kerber, *Women of the Republic: Intellect and Ideology in Revolutionary America* (Chapel Hill: University of North Carolina Press, 1980); Ginzberg, *Work of Benevolence*; Elizabeth R. Varon, *We Mean to Be Counted: White Women and Politics in Antebellum Virginia* (Chapel Hill: University of North Carolina Press, 1998), 1.

39. Rebecca Edwards, *Angels in the Machinery: Gender in American Party Politics from the Civil War to the Progressive Era* (New York: Oxford University Press, 1997); Melanie Susan Gustafson, *Women and the Republican Party, 1854–1924* (Urbana: University of Illinois Press, 2001).

40. Willard, *Glimpses of Fifty Years*, 387.

41. Southern white women were loyal Democrats. Edwards, *Angels in the Machinery*, 47.

42. Willard, *Glimpses of Fifty Years*, 395, 378; James Oakes, *The Radical and the Republican: Frederick Douglass, Abraham Lincoln, and the Triumph of Antislavery Politics* (New York: W. W. Norton, 2007).

43. Willard, *Glimpses of Fifty Years*, 378.

44. Ibid.; Willard, *Home Protection Manual*, 12. See also Portnoy, *Their Right to Speak*, ch. 3.

45. Blocker, *American Temperance Movements*, 73, 101; Gustafson, *Women and the Republican Party*, 65; Bordin, *Frances Willard*, 136; Edwards, *Angels in the Machinery*, 98, 150.

46. Willard, *Woman and Temperance*, 445; Willard, *Glimpses of Fifty Years*, 407; Blocker, *American Temperance Movements*, 91–93; Hamm, *Shaping the Eighteenth Amendment*, 23–24, 25, 76. Historian Jack Blocker notes that "the WCTU doubled its membership during the 1880s, and the Prohibition party vote climbed rapidly from 10,000 for its presidential candidate, Neal Dow, in 1880 to 150,000 four years later." Blocker, *American Temperance Movements*, 85.

47. Willard, *Glimpses of Fifty Years*, 459–60. Stanton, in a letter to the WCTU's *Union Signal* in 1888, broke with Anthony and endorsed the Prohibition Party as

offering the most to women in terms of its support of suffrage and temperance. Edwards, *Angels in the Machinery*, 55.

48. Edwards, *Angels in the Machinery*, 84; Willard, *Glimpses of Fifty Years*, 382, 438–39; Materson, "Respectable Partisans"; Materson, *For the Freedom of Her Race*; Richard B. Sherman, *The Republican Party and Black America: From McKinley to Hoover, 1896–1933* (Charlottesville: University Press of Virginia, 1973); Cohen, *Making a New Deal*; Frances Watkins Harper, "Temperance," *AME Church Review* 7 (1891); Melanie Gustafson, "Partisan Women in the Progressive Era: The Struggle for Inclusion in American Political Parties," in Ruiz and DuBois, *Unequal Sisters* (3rd ed.), 245 (quote); also Gustafson, *Women and the Republican Party*, 61.

49. Willard, *Glimpses of Fifty Years*, 611.

50. Ibid., 610–14.

51. Linda Gordon, "Voluntary Motherhood: The Beginnings of Feminist Birth Control Ideas in the United States," in *Mothers and Motherhood: Readings in American History*, ed. Rima Apple and Janet Golden (Columbus: Ohio State University Press, 1997), 423–43; Willard, *Glimpses of Fifty Years*, 613.

52. Brian Donovan, *White Slave Crusades: Race, Gender, and Anti-vice Activism, 1887–1917* (Urbana: University of Illinois Press, 2006), 38–39. For a discussion of the English social purity movement, see Judith R. Walkowitz, *City of Dreadful Delight: Narratives of Sexual Danger in Late-Victorian London* (Chicago: University of Chicago Press, 1992), ch. 3. For a full discussion of the age-of-consent campaign, see Odem, *Delinquent Daughters*, ch. 1.

53. Willard, *Glimpses of Fifty Years*, 420–21; Larson, "Even a Worm Will Turn at Last," 3.

54. Willard, *Glimpses of Fifty Years*, 422.

55. Larson, "Even a Worm Will Turn at Last," 69, 1. See also Stanley, *From Bondage to Contract*. Suffragists from both the NWSA and AWSA supported raising the age of consent. Odem, *Delinquent Daughters*, 16; Willard, *Glimpses of Fifty Years*, 422–24.

56. Bettina Aptheker, *Woman's Legacy: Essays on Race, Sex, and Class in American History* (Amherst: University of Massachusetts Press, 1982), 53–76. Discussions of the sexual exploitation of black women can be found in a large number of histories, including Fox-Genovese, *Within the Plantation Household*, 294, 325–26; Hunter, *To "Joy My Freedom,"* 11, 34, 106; Jones, *Labor of Love*, 150, 157; Leslie A. Schwalm, *A Hard Fight for We: Women's Transition from Slavery to Freedom in South Carolina* (Urbana: University of Illinois, 1997), 37, 248; Weiner, *Mistresses and Slaves*, 134–37.

57. Burroughs from Paula Giddings, *When and Where I Enter: The Impact of Black Women on Race and Sex in America* (1984; repr., New York: Amistad/Harper Collins, 2006), 121; Larson, "Even a Worm Will Turn at Last," 70–71; Odem, *Delinquent Daughters*, 28–29; Jacquelyn Dowd Hall, *Revolt against Chivalry: Jessie Daniel Ames and the Women's Campaign against Lynching* (New York: Columbia University Press, 1979).

58. Newman, *White Women's Rights*, 67–68; Roediger, *Wages of Whiteness*; Green, *Southern Strategies*, 20–23; Gilmore, *Gender and Jim Crow*, 50–51; Glenda Elizabeth Gilmore, "'A Melting Time': Black Women, White Women, and the WCTU in North Carolina, 1880–1900," in *Hidden Histories of Women in the New South*, ed. Virginia Bernhard, Betty Brandon, et al. (Columbia: University of Missouri Press, 1994), 153–72; Anne Firor Scott, *Natural Allies: Women's Associations in American History* (Urbana: University of Illinois Press, 1991). Willard died of pernicious anemia, a now treatable disease. Gifford, in Willard, *Writing Out My Heart*, 361.

59. Willard quoted by Ida B. Wells, in Royster, *Southern Horrors*, 141–42; Pauline Schloesser, *The Fair Sex: White Women and Racial Patriarchy in the Early American*

Republic (New York: New York University Press, 2002), 188; Barbara Hilkert Andolsen, *"Daughters of Jefferson, Daughters of Bootblacks": Racism and American Feminism* (Macon, Ga.: Mercer University Press, 1986), xi.

60. Willard, *Home Protection Manual*, 12.

61. See Marjorie Julian Spruill, "Race, Reform, and Reaction at the Turn of the Century: Southern Suffragists, the NAWSA, and the 'Southern Strategy' in Context," in Baker, *Votes for Women*; Marjorie Spruill Wheeler, "A Short History of the Woman Suffrage Movement in America," in Wheeler, *One Woman, One Vote*, 9–20; Gornick, *Solitude of Self*, 83.

62. Bordin, *Woman and Temperance*, 84. For black clubwomen's continued support of the WCTU, see *First Annual Report of the National Conference of the Colored Women of America (National Association of Colored Women)*, 1896, in Records of the National Association of Colored Women's Clubs, 1895–1992 (University Publications of America microform), 58–59. See Hallie Quinn Brown, *Homespun Heroines and Other Women of Distinction* (Xenia, Ohio: Aldine, 1926; repr., Chapel Hill: University of North Carolina Press, 2000), online version UNC-"Documenting the American South" section.

63. Lucy Thurman was in the WCTU and the NACW. "Minutes," 1897, *Annual Report of the National Association of Colored Women*, 12–13.

64. During the WCTU's campaign to reform rape laws, its black and white members acknowledged the extra burdens black women faced from sexual assaults by white men. Leslie Dunlap argues that white WCTU members lost whatever sympathy or interest they had in protecting black women by the twentieth century. Schechter, *Ida B. Wells-Barnett*; Leslie K. Dunlap, "The Reform of Rape Law and the Problem of White Men: Age-of-Consent Campaigns in the South, 1885–1910," in Hodes, *Sex, Love, Race*, 352–72.

65. Schechter, *Ida B. Wells-Barnett*, 94–95; Salem, *To Better Our World*, 36–37; Willard from Bordin, *Frances Willard*, 216; Hall, *Revolt against Chivalry*, 99–100, 201–2; Bordin, *Frances Willard*, 216.

66. Willard quoted by Ida B. Wells, in Royster, *Southern Horrors*, 142.

67. Wells, *Red Record*, in ibid., 146, 147. See also Schechter, *Ida B. Wells-Barnett*, 110–11.

68. FWH, "How to Stop Lynching," *Women's Era* 1, no. 2 (1894): 8–9. Also see Harper's poem addressed to white American women, "An Appeal to My Countrywomen," 1896, in *Witnessing Lynching: American Writers Respond*, ed. Anne P. Rice (New Brunswick, N.J.: Rutgers University Press, 2003), 43–45; Frances Watkins Harper, "Temperance," *AME Church Review* 7 (1891); Jacqueline Jones Royster, "Introduction," to *Southern Horrors and Other Writings*, 16; Schechter, *Ida B. Wells-Barnett*, 84.

69. In her second major anti-lynching manifesto, *A Red Record*, Ida B. Wells increased the pressure by including a chapter called "Miss Willard's Attitude." See Royster, *Southern Horrors*, 147, 146; Jacobs, *Incidents in the Life of a Slave Girl*; Anne Moody, *Coming of Age in Mississippi* (1968; repr., New York: Dell, 1992).

70. Hale, *Making Whiteness*, ch. 5; Royster, *Southern Horrors*, 38, 144–47; Schechter, *Ida B. Wells-Barnett*, 100, 110, 283n201; Bordin, *Frances Willard*, 221–22.

71. Willard, 11 February 1896, in *Writing Out My Heart*, 396.

72. Gilmore, *Gender and Jim Crow*, ch. 6. The first NACW annual report of 1896 used significantly different wording to describe Thurman's title, calling her "National Superintendent of the W.C.T.U. work among *Afro-Americans.*" *First Annual Report of the National Conference of the Colored Women of America (National Association of Colored Women)*, 1896, 58–59.

73. See chapter 3 on forced labor in Elliot Jaspin, *Buried in the Bitter Waters: The Hidden History of Racial Cleansing in America* (New York: Basic Books, 2007), 59–60.

"Minutes," 1897, *Annual Report of the National Association of Colored Women*, 12–13.

74. "Minutes," 1897, *Annual Report of the National Association of Colored Women*, 12–13; also Collier-Thomas, "Frances Ellen Watkins Harper," 60.

75. Salem, *To Better Our World*, 37; Schechter, *Ida B. Wells-Barnett*, 111–12; Wells, *Red Record*, in Royster, *Southern Horrors*, 154.

CHAPTER 5—MARY CHURCH TERRELL

1. Mrs. George W. Coleman, Boston President of the Council of Women for Home Missions, "The Women's Congress of Missions," in *Missionary Review of the World* (August 1915): 586–88; Patricia Ruth Hill, *The World Their Household: The American Women's Foreign Mission Movement and Cultural Transformation, 1870–1920* (Ann Arbor: University of Michigan Press, 1985); Tyrrell, *Woman's World, Woman's Empire*. For discussions of missionary work among Asian immigrants in California, see Judy Tzu-Chun Wu, "'Ministering Angel of Chinatown': Missionary Uplift, Modern Medicine, and Asian American Women's Strategies of Liminality," in *Asian/ Pacific Islander American Women: A Historical Anthology*, ed. Shirley Hune and Gail M. Nomura (New York: New York University Press, 2003); Peggy Pascoe, *Relations of Rescue: The Search for Female Moral Authority in the American West, 1874–1939* (New York: Oxford University Press, 1990).

2. Mary Church Terrell (hereafter MCT), *A Colored Woman in a White World* (1940; repr., Washington, D.C.: National Association of Colored Women's Clubs, 1968), 185; Ngai, *Impossible Subjects*, 2. See also Walter L. Williams, *Black Americans and the Evangelization of Africa, 1877–1900* (Madison: University of Wisconsin Press, 1982); Andrew Gyory, *Closing the Gate: Race, Politics, and the Chinese Exclusion Act* (Chapel Hill: University of North Carolina Press, 1998); Judy Yung, *Unbound Feet: A Social History of Chinese Women in San Francisco* (Berkeley and Los Angeles: University of California Press, 1995); Nayan Shah, *Contagious Divides: Epidemics and Race in San Francisco's Chinatown* (Berkeley and Los Angeles: University of California Press, 2001).

3. Priscilla Wald, "Terms of Assimilation: Legislating Subjectivity in the Emerging Nation," in Kaplan and Pease, *United States Imperialism*, 59–83; Jill E. Martin, "'Neither Fish, Flesh, Fowl, nor Good Red Herring': The Citizenship Status of American Indians, 1830–1924," in *American Indians and U.S. Politics: A Companion Reader*, ed. John M. Meyer (Westport, Conn.: Praeger, 2002), 51–72.

4. MCT, *A Colored Woman*, 423. Terrell began writing her autobiography in the 1910s but did not manage to get it published until 1940. See, for example, Robert H. Terrell (hereafter cited as RHT) to MCT, February 11, 1915, MCT Collection Addition, Moorland-Spingarn Research Center, Howard University, Washington, D.C. (hereafter cited in notes as MCT Addition); Beverly Washington Jones, *Quest for Equality: The Life and Writings of Mary Eliza Church Terrell, 1863–1954* (Brooklyn, N.Y.: Carlson Publishing, 1990), 63 (hereafter cited in the notes as *Quest*).

5. MCT, *A Colored Woman*, 99. See also ibid., 407; Watson, *Lives of Their Own*, 84.

6. Lopez, *White by Law*; Peggy Pascoe, "Miscegenation Law, Court Cases, and Ideologies of 'Race' in Twentieth-Century America," in Ruiz and DuBois, *Unequal Sisters* (3rd ed.), 161–82; MCT, *A Colored Woman*, 1–7. For a brief summary of Terrell's life, see Lynne Olson, "Mary Church Terrell," in *Black Women Activists: Profiles in History*, ed. Karin S. Coddon (San Diego: Greenhaven Press, 2004), 123–30.

7. Margaret McKee and Fred Chisenhall, *Beale Black and Blue: Life and Music on Black America's Main Street* (Baton Rouge: Louisiana State University Press, 1981); Terborg-Penn, *Struggle for the Vote*, 86 (quote). See also MCT, *A Colored Woman*, 24, 245. For Robert Terrell's attempts to allay his wife's concerns about her participation in a social

purity conference, see RHT to MCT, November 16, 1913, MCT Collection Addition.
    8. MCT, *A Colored Woman*, 18, 20. See also Sarah E. Torian, "Writing One's Self in Black and White: Racial Identity Construction in the Autobiographies of James Weldon Johnson, Jean Toomer, Mary Church Terrell, and Walter White" (master's thesis, University of Mississippi, 1997), 90–91.
    9. MCT, *A Colored Woman*, 60. See RHT to MCT, from September to December 1913, MCT Addition.
    10. MCT diary entries, June 18–20, July 5–8, 1905, MCT Papers, Library of Congress (hereafter cited in notes as MCT Papers), reel 1. Terrell's 1905 and 1908 diaries record that she read *The Aftermath of Slavery: A Study of the Condition and Environment of the American Negro* by William A. Sinclair (Boston: Small, Maynard, 1905); *William Lloyd Garrison, 1805–1879: The Story of His Life, Told by His Children*, vols. 1–4, by Wendell Phillips Garrison and Francis Jackson Garrison (New York: The Century Co., 1885–1889); the story of Heloïse and Abelard by John Lord, in *Lord's Lectures: Beacon Lights of History, Vol. VII, Great Women* (New York: James Clarke, 1902); "Frederick Douglass's autobiography and Elizabeth Cady Stanton's *80 Years and More*," as well as *A Little Brother of the Rich*, by Joseph Medill Patterson (New York: Grosset and Dunlap, 1908). See MCT diary entries, September 4, November 27, 1905, March 8, May 19, November 26, 1908, MCT Papers.
    11. MCT, *A Colored Woman*, 97. For books on European racism and imperialist prejudices, see Antoinette M. Burton, *Burdens of History: British Feminists, Indian Women, and Imperial Culture, 1865–1915* (Chapel Hill: University of North Carolina Press, 1994); *Cultures of Empire: Colonizers in Britain and the Empire in the Nineteenth and Twentieth Centuries: A Reader*, ed. Catherine Hall (New York: Routledge, 2000); Catherine Hall, Keith McClelland, and Jane Rendall, *Defining the Victorian Nation: Class, Race, Gender, and the British Reform Act of 1867* (New York: Cambridge University Press, 2000); Alice L. Conklin, *A Mission to Civilize: The Republican Idea of Empire in France and West Africa, 1895–1930* (Stanford, Calif.: Stanford University Press, 1997); Anne McClintock, *Imperial Leather: Race, Gender, and Sexuality in the Colonial Conquest* (New York: Routledge, 1995). For the acceptance of Josephine Baker in Europe, see the theatrical biography by Patrick O'Connor, *Josephine Baker* (Boston: Bulfinch Press Book, 1988), 79–103. For a World War I example of the better treatment of blacks in Europe, see Addie W. Hunton and Kathryn M. Johnson, *Two Colored Women with American Expeditionary Forces* (New York: Brooklyn Eagle Press, 1920).
    12. MCT to RHT, London, June 10, 1919, MCT Papers, reel 2; MCT, *A Colored Woman*, 91–92.
    13. MCT, A Colored Woman, 93. See also Peggy Pascoe, *What Comes Naturally: Miscegenation Law and the Making of Race in America* (New York: Oxford University Press, 2009); Peter W. Bardaglio, "'Shamefull Matches': The Regulation of Interracial Sex and Marriage in the South before 1900," and Barbara Bair, "Remapping the Black/White Body: Sexuality, Nationalism, and Biracial Antimiscegenation Activism in 1920s Virginia," in Hodes, *Sex, Love, Race*, 112–38, 399–419; Candice Lewis Bredbenner, *A Nationality of Her Own: Women, Marriage, and the Law of Citizenship* (Berkeley and Los Angeles: University of California Press, 1998); Ann Marie Nicolosi, "'We Do Not Want Our Girls to Marry Foreigners': Gender, Race, and American Citizenship," *NWSA Journal* 13, no. 3 (2001): 1–21.
    14. MCT, *A Colored Woman*, 98–99.
    15. Ibid., 374; Steven Belluscio, *To Be Suddenly White: Literary Realism and Racial Passing* (Columbia: University of Missouri Press, 2006), 55; Gayle Wald, *Crossing the Line: Racial Passing in Twentieth-Century U.S. Literature and Culture* (Durham, N.C.: Duke University Press, 2000), 29.

16. MCT, *A Colored Woman*, 98.

17. MCT to RHT, from Cambridge, Massachusetts, June 25, 1902, MCT Papers, reel 2; J. Clay Smith, Jr., *Emancipation: The Making of the Black Lawyer, 1844–1944* (Philadelphia: University of Pennsylvania Press, 1999), 137–39; MCT, *A Colored Woman*, 65.

18. RHT to MCT, August 15 (1919?), MCT Addition; MCT diary entry, November 27, 1908, MCT Papers, reel 1; MCT, *A Colored Woman*, 129, 141.

19. MCT, *A Colored Woman*, 105–6; Dorothy Sterling, *Black Foremothers: Three Lives* (Old Westbury, N.Y.: Feminist Press, 1979), 130–31.

20. Schechter, *Ida B. Wells-Barnett*, 75–79, 90; Salem, *To Better Our World*, 32–33; Hine and Thompson, *Shining Thread of Hope*, 198.

21. MCT, *A Colored Woman*, 225, 231; MCT, "Lynching from a Negro's Point of View," *North American Review* (June 1904), in *Quest*, 174, 171–72 (emphasis added).

22. MCT, "Lynching from a Negro's Point of View," 178; Mary Jane Brown, *Eradicating This Evil: Women in the American Anti-lynching Movement, 1892–1940* (New York: Garland Publishers, 2000), 154–55; MCT diary entry, August 30–31, 1905, MCT Papers, reel 1. The international reputation of the United States as a bastion of democracy was harmed by its race relations. For black Americans' critiques of the U.S. war in the Philippines, see *The Black Press Views American Imperialism, 1898–1900*, ed. George P. Marks (New York; Arno Press, 1971).

23. Terborg-Penn, "Woman Suffrage Movement," 145–48; MCT, "Susan B. Anthony, the Abolitionist," *Voice of the Negro* (June 1906), in *Quest*, 236. For more on the early woman's rights movement, see Wellman, *Road to Seneca Falls*; Brown, "To Catch the Vision of Freedom," 137.

24. MCT, *A Colored Woman*, 143, 145. Lucy E. Salyer, *Laws Harsh as Tigers: Chinese Immigrants and the Shaping of Modern American Immigration Law* (Chapel Hill: University of North Carolina Press, 1995), 37–68. For a broad overview of the difficulties black women faced in interracial activism, see Estelle B. Freedman, "Race and the Politics of Identity in U.S. Feminism," in Ruiz and DuBois, *Unequal Sisters* (4th ed.).

25. MCT, *A Colored Woman*, 143. See also MCT diary entry, December 6, 1905, MCT Papers, reel 1; Bolt, *Sisterhood Questioned?* 15; MCT, "Susan B. Anthony," 237.

26. Terborg-Penn, *Struggle for the Vote*, 110–11; Adele Logan Alexander, "Adella Hunt Logan, the Tuskegee Woman's Club, and African Americans in the Suffrage Movement," in Wheeler, *Votes for Women!* 78–79. For Terrell and NAWSA, see Harley, "Mary Church Terrell," 317 (from footnote 69).

27. DuBois, *Feminism and Suffrage*, 53–78. See Frederick Douglass to Josephine Sophie White Griffing, September 27, 1868, in Foner, *Frederick Douglass*, 598–600; Terborg-Penn, "Black Male Perspectives," 36; MCT, "I Remember Frederick Douglass," *Ebony* (October 1953), in *Quest*, 342. See MCT diary entries, February 22, May 20–22, 1908, MCT Papers, reel 1.

28. Terborg-Penn, *Struggle for the Vote*, 65; Terrell from Beverly Guy-Sheftall, *Daughters of Sorrow: Attitudes toward Black Women, 1880–1920* (Brooklyn, N.Y.: Carlson, 1990), 112.

29. MCT, "Susan B. Anthony," 237; MCT, "The Justice of Woman Suffrage," *The Crisis* 4 (September 1912), in *Quest*, 307. See also David R. Roediger, *Colored White: Transcending the Racial Past* (Berkeley and Los Angeles: University of California Press, 2002), ch. 7.

30. Terrell's diaries and letters reveal her frequent speeches, dinners, and social interactions with white reformers. See MCT Addition. In addition to knowing Frances Watkins Harper, Terrell was very friendly with the next WCTU superintendent

of Colored Work (and NACW president starting in 1908), Lucy Thurman. When she visited Michigan for an NACW convention, she spent several days as a guest at Thurman's farmhouse in the countryside. See MCT diary entries, August 22–27, 1905, MCT Papers, reel 1.

31. Cott, *Grounding of Modern Feminism*, 68; MCT, *A Colored Woman*, 148 (quote); Higginbotham, *Righteous Discontent*, 182–83; Evelyn Brooks Barnett (later Higginbotham), "Nannie Burrough and the Education of Black Women," in Harley and Terborg-Penn, *The Afro-American Woman*, 97–108.

32. Higginbotham, *Righteous Discontent*, 152 (quote); Rosalyn Terborg-Penn, "Discrimination against Afro-American Women in the Woman's Movement, 1830–1920," in Harley and Terborg-Penn, *Afro-American Woman*, 17–27; Terborg-Penn, *Struggle for the Vote*, 119; Floris Barnett Cash, *African American Women and Social Action: The Clubwomen and Volunteerism from Jim Crow to the New Deal, 1896–1936* (Westport, Conn.: Greenwood Press, 2001), 36–37 (quote); Sara Evans, *Personal Politics: The Roots of Women's Liberation in the Civil Rights Movement and the New Left* (New York: Vintage Books, 1979); Cynthia Griggs Fleming, "Black Women and Black Power: The Case of Ruby Doris Smith Robinson and the Student Nonviolent Coordinating Committee," in Bettye Collier-Thomas and V. P. Franklin, eds., *Sisters in the Struggle: African American Women in the Civil Rights–Black Power Movement* (New York: New York University Press, 2001), 197–213.

33. MCT, *A Colored Woman*, 148–49; MCT, "First Presidential Address to the National Association of Colored Women" (1897), in *Quest*, 134 (emphasis added). For a discussion of the dangers of a "color-blind" reading of the Constitution, see Peter Irons, *A People's History of the Supreme Court* (New York: Penguin Books, 2006), 230–31, 450–51.

34. Salem, *To Better Our World*, 7–28; Hine and Thompson, *Shining Thread of Hope*, 177–83.

35. Salem, *To Better Our World*, ch. 1; Nellie Y. McKay, "The Girls Who Became the Women: Childhood Memories in the Autobiographies of Harriet Jacobs, Mary Church Terrell, and Anne Moody," in *Tradition and the Talents of Women*, ed. Florence Howe (Urbana: University of Illinois Press, 1991), 117; MCT, *A Colored Woman*, i (quote).

36. MCT, *A Colored Woman*, 151; Cash, *Social Action*, 43.

37. Patricia Hill Collins, *Black Feminist Thought: Knowledge, Consciousness, and the Politics of Empowerment*, 2nd ed. (New York: Routledge, 2000), ch. 8; Higginbotham, *Righteous Discontent*, 17; Judith Weisenfeld, *African American Women and Christian Activism: New York's Black YWCA, 1905–1945* (Cambridge, Mass.: Harvard University Press, 1997), 23.

38. Stephanie J. Shaw, "Black Club Women and the Creation of the National Association of Colored Women," in *"We Specialize in the Wholly Impossible": A Reader in Black Women's History*, ed. Darlene Clark Hine, Wilma King, and Linda Reed (New York: Carlson, 1995), 434; Boris, "Power of Motherhood," 221. For maternalism in women's reform work, see Bordin, *Woman and Temperance*; Epstein, *Politics of Domesticity*; Parker, *Purifying America*; Ladd-Taylor, *Mother-Work*; MCT, "The Duty of the National Association of Colored Women to the Race," *AME Church Review* (January 1900), in *Quest*, 149.

39. See Willard B. Gatewood, *Aristocrats of Color: The Black Elite, 1880–1920* (Bloomington: Indiana University Press, 1990), 245; "Listening to Mary Church Terrell," *Second to None: A Documentary History of American Women*, vol. 2, ed. Ruth B. Moynihan, Cynthia Russett, and Laurie Crumpacker (Lincoln: University of Nebraska Press, 1993); Michele Mitchell, *Righteous Propagation: African Americans*

and the Politics of Racial Destiny after Reconstruction (Chapel Hill: University of North Carolina Press, 2004), 149; excerpts from "Club Work of Colored Women" and "Lynching from a Negro's Point of View," from *Major Problems in American Women's History*, 2nd ed., ed. Mary Beth Norton and Ruth M. Alexander (Lexington, Mass.: D. C. Heath, 1996), 254–57. Mary Jane Brown places Terrell's calls for domestic reform in the context of her larger anti-lynching work. See Brown, *Eradicating This Evil*, 3.

40. MCT, "First Presidential Address," 135 (emphasis added).

41. Cash, *Social Action*, 7; Amanda Frisken, *Victoria Woodhull's Sexual Revolution: Political Theater and the Popular Press in Nineteenth-Century America* (Philadelphia: University of Pennsylvania Press, 2004); Cutter, *Domestic Devils*; Passet, *Sex Radicals*; MCT, "First Presidential Address," 135; Boris, "Power of Motherhood," 220; Jones, *Labor of Love*, 4; also Jacobs, *Incidents in the Life of a Slave Girl*.

42. Gerda Lerner, "Early Community Work of Black Club Women" (originally published in *Journal of Negro History*, 1974), in *Black Women in American History: The Twentieth Century*, ed. Darlene Clark Hine, vol. 3 (Brooklyn, N.Y.: Carlson, 1990), 863.

43. Mary Kelley, *Learning to Stand and Speak: Women, Education, and Public Life in America's Republic* (Chapel Hill: University of North Carolina Press, 2006), 9; Cash, *Social Action*, 5; Higginbotham, *Righteous Discontent*, 101.

44. Around 1905 the Terrells adopted her niece Mary (her namesake), the illegitimate daughter of her brother, Thomas Church. See MCT diary entries, December 24–25, 1905, MCT Papers, reel 1; Jones, *Quest*, 55; MCT, *A Colored Woman*, 106, 126.

45. MCT, "Duty of the National Association," 144 (emphasis added); also Higginbotham, *Righteous Discontent*, 183.

46. MCT, "First Presidential Address," 135; MCT to RHT, January 1, March 24, 1919, MCT Addition; MCT, "Duty of the National Association," 141–42.

47. MCT, "What Role Is the Educated Negro Woman to Play in the Uplifting of her Race?" *Twentieth Century Negro Literature*, ed. D. W. Culp, 1902, cited in *Quest*, 152. Also see MCT, "Duty of the National Association," 140; Cynthia Neverdon-Morton, "Advancement of the Race through African American Women's Organizations in the South, 1895–1925," in Gordon and Collier-Thomas, *African American Women and the Vote*, 126; Boris, "Power of Motherhood," 215.

48. Brown, "To Catch the Vision of Freedom." Judith Ellen Foster, chair of the committee on women's work for the Republican National Committee (RNC) recommended Terrell in 1908 as a potential speaker for the Republican Party, a job Terrell was eager to take on; MCT diary entry, October 5, 1908, MCT Papers, reel 1. Guy-Sheftall, *Daughters of Sorrow*, 107; Terborg-Penn, *Struggle for the Vote*, 88 (quote).

49. Terborg-Penn, *Struggle for the Vote*, 92–96; Salem, *To Better Our World*, 104; Guy-Sheftall, *Daughters of Sorrow*, 107.

50. Welke, "When All the Women Were White"; Barbara Y. Welke, *Recasting American Liberty: Gender, Race, Law, and the Railroad Revolution, 1865–1920* (New York: Cambridge University Press, 2001); MCT, "The Progress of Colored Women," *Voice of the Negro* (July 1904), in *Quest*, 186 (quote); Brown, *Eradicating This Evil*, 95, 117.

51. Sharon Harley, "Mary Church Terrell: Genteel Militant," in *Black Leaders of the Nineteenth Century*, ed. Leon Litwack and August Meier (Urbana: University of Illinois Press, 1998), 315–16; White, *Too Heavy a Load*, 106–9; MCT, *A Colored Woman*, 155; Salem, *To Better Our World*, 32–36.

52. Gilmore, *Gender and Jim Crow*, ch. 6; Shaw, *What a Woman Ought to Be*, 210, 197.

53. Gaines, "Black Americans' Racial Uplift," 437; Shaw, *What a Woman Ought to Be*, 207.

54. Salem, *To Better Our World*, 150–51; Cynthia J. Booth, "The Herculean

Task: Anna Julia Cooper and Mary Church Terrell's Struggle to Establish the Black Woman's Voice in the American Feminist and Civil Rights Movement" (master's thesis, University of Central Oklahoma, 1997), 26, 33–34. John Milholland was a journalist and inventor, whose wealth from his invention of the pneumatic tube message system allowed him to devote himself to reform causes. His daughter was suffragist Inez Milholland.

55. Jones, *Quest*, 44; MCT, *A Colored Woman*, 191, 212; MCT diary entry, October 1, 1905, MCT Papers, reel 1; Salem, *To Better Our World*, 152, 171.

56. MCT, *A Colored Woman*, 194. See also Guy-Sheftall, *Daughters of Sorrow*, 150.

57. MCT, *A Colored Woman*, 193; White, *Too Heavy a Load*, 85.

58. Salem, *To Better Our World*, 156 (quote), 171.

59. MCT, *A Colored Woman*, 186, 157–63, 183; Harley, "Mary Church Terrell," 319.

60. MCT to RHT, from Columbus, Ohio, October 27, 1911, MCT Papers, reel 2; MCT, *A Colored Woman*, 159–60.

61. MCT, *A Colored Woman*, 162–63; also ibid., 165–72, 179–83; Salem, *To Better Our World*, 156.

62. MCT, "The Disbanding of the Colored Soldiers," *Voice of the Negro* (December 1906), in *Quest*, 275–82; MCT diary entries, January 8, 11, July 23, 1908, MCT Papers, reel 1. For accounts of Terrell's involvement, see Ann J. Lane, *The Brownsville Affair: National Crisis and Black Reaction* (Port Washington, N.Y.: Kennikat Press, 1971); John D. Weaver, *The Brownsville Raid* (College Station: Texas A&M University Press, 1996), 104–6; *Encyclopedia of American Race Riots*, ed. Walter C. Rucker and James N. Upton (Westport, Conn.: Greenwood Press, 2006), 80–81.

63. MCT, "What It Means to Be Colored in the Capital of the United States," *The Independent*, January 24, 1907, in *Quest*, 283, 291. See also MCT to RHT, undated, from Boston, MCT Addition.

64. Sherman, *Republican Party and Black America*, 113–17; Marvin Caplan, "The Lost Laws Are Found Again," in MCT, *A Colored Woman*, 434–35, 444–45.

65. MCT, "Service Which Should Be Rendered the South," *Voice of the Negro* (February 1905), in *Quest*, 206–7, 208. A different version of this article appeared as "A Plea for the White South by a Coloured Woman," in the July 1906 issue of the British journal *Nineteenth Century and After*.

66. MCT, "A Plea for the White South by a Coloured Woman," *Nineteenth Century* (July 1906), in *Quest*, 239–40; MCT, *A Colored Woman*, 99.

67. MCT, "Plea for the White South," 248–49.

68. Ibid., 250–51.

69. MCT, *A Colored Woman*, 167. For questions of U.S. imperial ambitions and race relations, see Bartholomew H. Sparrow, *The Insular Cases and the Emergence of American Empire* (Lawrence: University Press of Kansas, 2006), ch. 3; David Blight, *Race and Reunion: The Civil War in American Memory* (Cambridge, Mass.: Belknap Press of Harvard University Press, 2001).

70. MCT, *A Colored Woman*, 227.

71. MCT, "Peonage in the United States: The Convict Lease System and the Chain Gangs," *Nineteenth Century* (August 1907), in *Quest*, 262–63. See Matthew J. Mancini, *One Dies, Get Another: Convict Leasing in the American South, 1866–1928* (Columbia: University of South Carolina Press, 1996).

72. MCT, *A Colored Woman*, 227–31; MCT diary entries, March 5–6, 1908, MCT Papers, reel 1.

73. MCT, "Peonage in the United States," 257.

74. Ibid.; MCT, "Plea for the White South," 240. See also Boris, "Power of Motherhood," 215.

75. MCT, "Lynching from a Negro's Point of View," 167.
76. MCT, *A Colored Woman*, 175.
77. MCT to RHT, Zurich, May 18, 1919, MCT Papers, reel 2.

CONCLUSION

1. Wright was probably the first woman in the United States to establish a secular communitarian living experiment. Taylor, *Eve and the New Jerusalem*, 65–70; Charles Nordhoff, *The Communistic Societies of the United States: From Personal Visit and Observation* (1875; repr., New York: Dover Publications, 1966), 125–31; Priscilla J. Brewer, "The Shakers of Mother Anne Lee," in Pitzer, *America's Communal Utopias*, 42–43.

2. Newman, *White Women's Rights*, 4–5. See also Hewitt, *Women's Activism and Social Change*, 137, 143; *Throwing Off the Cloak of Privilege: White Southern Women Activists in the Civil Rights Era*, ed. Gail S. Murray (Gainesville: University Press of Florida, 2004); Linda Faye Williams, *The Constraint of Race: Legacies of White Skin Privilege in America* (University Park: Pennsylvania State University Press, 2003), introduction.

3. Bordin, *Woman and Temperance*; Ladd-Taylor, *Mother-Work*.

4. Hale, *Making Whiteness*, ch. 5; Carrigan and Webb, "*Muerto por Unos Desconocidos*," 47–48; MCT, *A Colored Woman*, 373; Kathleen Pfeiffer, *Race Passing and American Individualism* (Amherst: University of Massachusetts Press, 2003), 18–19, 34; Shaw, *What a Woman Ought to Be*, 166.

Bibliography

PRIMARY SOURCES

Published Works

Baker, Paul R., ed. *Frances Wright, Views of Society and Manners in America.* 1821Reprint, Cambridge, Mass.: Belknap Press of Harvard University Press, 1963.

Barnes, Gilbert H., and Dwight L. Dumond, eds. *Letters of Theodore Dwight Weld, Angelina Grimké Weld, and Sarah Grimké, 1822–1844.* Gloucester, Mass.: Peter Smith, 1965.

Bredvold, Louis I., and Ralph G. Ross, eds. *The Philosophy of Edmund Burke: A Selection from His Speeches and Writings.* Ann Arbor: University of Michigan Press, 1960.

Burke, Edmund. *The Works of the Right Honorable Edmund Burke.* Vol. 5. Revised ed., Boston: Little, Brown, & Co., 1866.

Cain, William E, ed. *William Lloyd Garrison and the Fight against Slavery: Selections from* The Liberator. Boston: Bedford/St. Martin's Press, 1995.

Ceplair, Larry, ed. *The Public Years of Sarah and Angelina Grimké: Selected Writings, 1835–1839.* New York: Columbia University Press, 1989.

Chinard, Gilbert, ed. *The Letters of Lafayette and Jefferson.* Baltimore: Johns Hopkins University Press, 1929.

Foner, Philip S., ed. *Frederick Douglass: Selected Speeches and Writings.* Abridged and adapted by Yuval Taylor. Chicago: Lawrence Hill Books, 1999.

Ford, Paul Leicester, ed. *The Writings of Thomas Jefferson.* Vol. 10, *1816–1826.* New York: G. P. Putnam's Sons, 1899.

Ford, Worthington Chauncey, ed. *Thomas Jefferson Correspondence: Printed from the Originals in the Collections of William K. Bixby.* Boston: Plimpton Press, 1916.

Foster, Frances Smith, ed. *A Brighter Coming Day: A Frances Ellen Watkins Harper Reader.* New York: Feminist Press at the City University of New York, 1990.

———, ed. *Minnie's Sacrifice, Sowing and Reaping, Trial and Triumph: Three Rediscovered Novels by Frances E. W. Harper.* Boston: Beacon Press, 1994.

Garrison, William Lloyd. *Thoughts on African Colonization, or an Impartial Exhibition of the Doctrines, Principles, and Purposes of the American Colonization Society.* Elibron Classics replica edition, Boston: Garrison & Knapp, 1832. Reprint, Adamant Media Corporation, 2003.

Gifford, Carolyn DeSwarte, ed. *Writing Out My Heart: Selections from the Journal of Frances E. Willard, 1855–1896.* Urbana: University of Illinois Press, 1995.

Graham, Maryemma, ed. *Complete Poems of Frances E. W. Harper.* New York: Oxford University Press, 1988.

Grimké, Sarah. *Condition of Women.* Ca. mid-1850s. In Bartlett, *Sarah Grimké,* 127–33.

———. *The Education of Women.* Ca. 1852–1857. In Lerner, *Sarah Grimké,* 77–91.

———. *An Epistle to the Clergy of the Southern States.* 1836. In Ceplair, 90–115.

———. *Letters on the Equality of the Sexes and the Condition of Woman, Addressed to Mary S. Parker, President of the Boston Female Anti-Slavery Society,* 1837. In Ceplair, 204–72.

———. *Marriage.* Mid to late 1850s. In Lerner, *The Grimké Sisters,* 301–9.

———. *Sisters of Charity.* Ca. 1852–1857. In Lerner, *The Grimké Sisters,* 289–96. Also cited from Lerner, *Sarah Grimké.*

Harper, Frances Ellen Watkins. *Iola Leroy, or Shadows Uplifted.* 2nd ed. 1892. Reprint, College Park, Md.: McGrath, 1969.

———. *Poems on Miscellaneous Subjects.* Philadelphia: Merrihew & Thompson, 1857. Reprint, Library of American Civilization collection. LAC 40118, poetry.

———. "We Are All Bound Up Together." *Proceedings of the Eleventh Woman's Rights Convention,* New York, May 1866. BCD, 217–19.

Harris, Ian, ed. *Edmund Burke: Pre-revolutionary Writings.* London: Cambridge University Press, 1993.

Jacobs, Harriet A. *Incidents in the Life of a Slave Girl: Written by Herself.* 1861. Reprint, ed. Jean Fagan Yellin. Cambridge, Mass.: Harvard University Press, 1987, 2000.

Jones, Beverly Washington. *Quest for Equality: The Life and Writings of Mary Eliza Church Terrell, 1863–1954.* Brooklyn, N.Y.: Carlson, 1990.

Lerner, Gerda. *The Feminist Thought of Sarah Grimké.* New York: Oxford University Press, 1998.

Loewenberg, Bert, and Ruth Bogin, eds. *Black Women in Nineteenth-Century American Life: Their Words, Their Thoughts, Their Feelings.* University Park: Pennsylvania University Press, 1976.

Lowance, Mason I., Jr., ed. *A House Divided: The Antebellum Slavery Debates in America, 1776–1865.* Princeton, N.J.: Princeton University Press, 2003.

Quarles, Benjamin. *Blacks on John Brown.* Urbana: University of Illinois Press, 1972.

Richardson, James. "Frances Wright's Establishment." *The Genius of Universal Emancipation,* July 28, 1827, 29–30. ODY Periodicals, APS II, year 35, microfilm 134.2, reel 1272–73 (1826–1839).

Richardson, Marilyn, ed. *Maria W. Stewart, America's First Black Woman Political Writer: Essays and Speeches.* Bloomington: Indiana University Press, 1987.

Ripley, C. Peter, ed. *The Black Abolitionist Papers.* Vol. 3, *The United States, 1830–1846.* Vol. 4, *The United States, 1847–1858.* Chapel Hill: University of North Carolina Press, 1991.

Robinson, Harriot H. *Massachusetts in the Woman Suffrage Movement.* Boston: Roberts Brothers, 1883.

Royster, Jacqueline Jones, ed. *Southern Horrors and Other Writings: The Anti-lynching Campaign of Ida B. Wells, 1892–1900.* Boston: Bedford Books, 1997.

Sklar, Kathryn Kish, ed. *Women's Rights Emerges within the Antislavery Movement, 1830–1870: A Brief History with Documents.* Boston: Bedford/St. Martin's Press, 2000.

Stanton, Elizabeth Cady, Susan B. Anthony, and Matilda Joslyn Gage, eds. *History of Woman Suffrage.* 2 vols. New York: Fowler & Wells, 1881. Reprint, Arno Press and the *New York Times,* 1969.

Still, William. *The Underground Railroad: A Record of Facts, Authentic Narratives, Letters, Etc., Narrating the Hardships, Hair-breadth Escapes and Death Struggles of the Slaves in their Efforts for Freedom, as Related by Themselves and Others, or Witnessed by the Author; Together With Sketches of Some of the Largest Stockholders, and most Liberal Aiders and Advisers, of the Road.* ("For many years connected with the Anti-Slavery Office in Philadelphia, and Chairman of the Acting Vigilant Committee of the Philadelphia Branch of the Underground Rail Road.") 1872. Reprint, New York: Arno Press, 1968.

Terrell, Mary Church. *A Colored Woman in a White World.* Washington, D.C.: Ransdell Company, 1940. Reprint, revised ed., Washington, D.C.: National Association of Colored Women's Clubs, 1968.

———. "The Duty of the National Association of Colored Women to the Race." *AME Church Review* (January 1900). In Jones, *Quest,* 139–50.

———. "First Presidential Address to the National Association of Colored Women." 1897. In Jones, *Quest,* 133–38.

———. "Lynching from a Negro's Point of View." *North American Review* 178 (June 1904). In Jones, *Quest,* 167–81.

———. "Peonage in the United States: The Convict Lease System and the Chain Gangs." *Nineteenth Century* (August 1907). In Jones, *Quest,* 255–73.

———. "A Plea for the White South by a Coloured Woman." *Nineteenth Century* (July 1906). In Jones, *Quest,* 239–54.

———. "Susan B. Anthony, the Abolitionist." *Voice of the Negro* (June 1906). In Jones, *Quest,* 231–38.

———. "What It Means to Be Colored in the Capital of the United States." *The Independent,* January 24, 1907. In Jones, *Quest,* 283–91.

Weld, Theodore Dwight, ed. *American Slavery as It Is: Testimony of a Thousand Witnesses.* 1839. Reprint, New York: Arno Press, 1968.

Willard, Frances Elizabeth. *Glimpses of Fifty Years: The Autobiography of an American Woman.* 1889. Reprint, New York: Source Book Press, 1970.

———. *Home Protection Manual: Containing an Argument for the Temperance Ballot for Woman, and How to Obtain it, as a Means of Home Protection; Also Constitution and Plan of Work for State and Local W. C. T. Unions.* New York: The Independent, 1879.

———. *How to Win: A Book for Girls.* New York: Funk & Wagnalls, 1886.

———. *Woman and Temperance or, The Work and Workers of the Woman's Christian Temperance Union.* 1883. Reprint, New York: Arno Press, 1972.

———. *Woman in the Pulpit.* Chicago: Woman's Temperance Publication Association, 1889.

———. *Writing Out My Heart: Selections from the Journal of Frances E. Willard, 1855–1896.* Edited by Carolyn DeSwarte Gifford. Urbana: University of Illinois Press, 1995.

———, assisted by Helen M. Winslow and Sallie Joy White. *Occupations for Women: A Book of Practical Suggestions for the Material Advancement, the Mental and Physical Development, and the Moral and Spiritual Uplift of Women.* New York: Success Company, 1897.

Wittenmyer, Annie. *History of the Woman's Temperance Crusade.* Philadelphia: Office of the Christian Woman, 1878.

Wright, Frances. *Altorf: A Tragedy . . . First Represented in the Theatre of New York, Feb. 19, 1819.* Philadelphia: M. Carey & Son, 1819. New Haven, Conn.: Research Publications, History of Women. Microfilm, reel 114, no. 749.

———. "Biography and Notes of Frances Wright D. Arusmont." 1844. In Wright, *Life, Letters and Lectures,* 5–44.

———. *Course of Popular Lectures, Historical and Political, as delivered by Frances Wright D'Arusmont, in various cities, towns and counties of the United States, Being Introductory to a Course on the Nation and Object of America's Political Institutions.* Volume 2. Philadelphia: Published by the Author, 1836. In folder 44, Celia Morris Eckhardt Papers, New Harmony Workingmen's Institute and Library, New Harmony, Indiana. Reprint, New York: Arno Press, 1972.

———. *A Few Days in Athens; Being the Translation of a Greek Manuscript Discovered in Herculaneum.* 1822. Reprint, New York: Arno Press, 1972.

———. "Geographical, Political, and Historical Sketch of the American United States" (Lecture 1, 1836), in *Course of Popular Lectures,* vol. 2, 25–49.

————. *Life, Letters and Lectures.* New York: Arno Press, 1972.

————. "Nashoba: Explanatory Notes, respecting the Nature and Objects of the Institution of Nashoba, and of the Principles upon which it is founded. Addressed to the Friends of Human Improvement, in all Countries and of all Nations." *New Harmony Gazette,* January 30, 1828, 124–25, February 6, 1828, 132–33, and February 13, 1828, 140–41 (continued in three different issues of the NHG).

————. "On Existing Evils and their Remedy, as Delivered in Philadelphia, on June 2, 1829." Lecture 7, 1829. In *Life, Letters and Lectures,* 101–16.

————. "On the Sectional Question—Southern Slavery." Lecture 3, 1836. In *Course of Popular Lectures,* vol. 2, 73–90.

————. "Origin and History of the Federal Party; With a General View of the Hamilton Financial Scheme." Lecture 2. In *Course of Popular Lectures,* vol. 2, 50–72.

————. *Supplement Course of Lectures, Containing the Last Four Lectures Delivered in the United States.* London, James Watson Publisher, 1834.

————. *Views of Society and Manners in America; in A Series of Letters from that Country to a Friend in England, During the Years 1818, 1819, and 1820, by AN ENGLISHWOMAN.* London: Longman, Hurst, Pubs., 1821. Reprint, ed. Paul R. Baker. Cambridge, Mass.: Belknap Press of Harvard University Press, 1963.

Wright, Frances, and Robert Dale Owen. *Tracts on Republican Government and National Education: Addressed to the inhabitants of the United States of America.* London: James Watson/Holyoake and Company, 1857.

Newspapers

African Methodist Episcopal Church Review
Anglo-African Magazine, Volume I—1859
Christian Recorder
Friend of Man
Genius of Universal Emancipation
Missionary Review of the World
National Anti-Slavery Standard
New Harmony Gazette/Free Enquirer
Union Signal
Woman's Journal

Annual Reports and Minutes

Annual Report of the National Association of Colored Women. University Publications of America microform.

National Association of Colored Women's Clubs, 1895–1992. University Publications of America microform.

National Woman's Christian Temperance Union. *Minutes & Annual Reports.* NWCTU section of the Temperance and Prohibition Papers Microfilm Collection.

Archival Collections

Columbia University Rare Books and Manuscripts Library. Lewis Corey papers. Unpublished manuscript on Frances Wright, ca. 1950.

New Harmony Workingmen's Institute and Library, New Harmony, Indiana.

Mary Church Terrell Collection Addition, Moorland-Spingarn Research Center,

Howard University, Washington, D.C.
Mary Church Terrell Papers, Library of Congress.
Weld-Grimké Papers, William L. Clements Library, University of Michigan, Ann Arbor.

SELECTED SECONDARY SOURCES

Abzug, Robert. *Cosmos Crumbling: American Reform and Religious Imagination.* New York: Oxford University Press, 1994.

———. *Passionate Liberator: Theodore Dwight Weld and the Dilemma of Reform.* New York: Oxford University Press, 1980.

Anderson, Bonnie S. *Joyous Greetings: The First International Women's Movement, 1830–1860.* New York: Oxford University Press, 2000.

Andolsen, Barbara Hilkert. *"Daughters of Jefferson, Daughters of Bootblacks": Racism and American Feminism.* Macon, Ga.: Mercer University Press, 1986.

Bacon, Jacqueline. *The Humblest May Stand Forth: Rhetoric, Empowerment, and Abolition.* Columbia: University of South Carolina Press, 2002.

Bacon, Margaret Hope. "By Moral Force Alone: The Antislavery Women and Nonresistance." In Yellin and Van Horne, *Abolitionist Sisterhood,* 275–97.

———. "'One Great Bundle of Humanity': Frances Ellen Watkins Harper (1825–1911)." *Pennsylvania Magazine of History and Biography* 113, no. 1 (January 1989): 21–43.

Baker, Jean H. *Sisters: The Lives of America's Suffragists.* New York: Hill and Wang, 2005.

———, ed. *Votes for Women: The Struggle for Suffrage Revisited.* New York: Oxford University Press, 2002.

Barry, Kathleen. *Susan B. Anthony: A Biography of a Singular Feminist.* New York: New York University Press, 1988.

Bartlett, Elizabeth Ann. *Liberty, Equality, Sorority: The Origins and Interpretations of American Feminist Thought: Frances Wright, Sarah Grimké, and Margaret Fuller.* Brooklyn, N.Y.: Carlson, 1994.

———, ed. *Sarah Grimké: Letters on the Equality of the Sexes and Other Essays.* With an introduction by Elizabeth Ann Bartlett. New Haven: Yale University Press, 1988.

Basch, Norma. "Equity vs. Equality: Emerging Concepts of Women's Political Status in the Age of Jackson." *Journal of the Early Republic* 3 (Fall 1983): 297–318.

———. *In the Eyes of the Law: Women, Marriage, and Property in Nineteenth-Century New York.* Ithaca, N.Y.: Cornell University Press, 1982.

Bederman, Gail. "Revisiting Nashoba: Slavery, Utopia, and Frances Wright in America, 1818–1826." *American Literary History* (2005): 438–59.

Belluscio, Steven. *To Be Suddenly White: Literary Realism and Racial Passing.* Columbia: University of Missouri Press, 2006.

Bensel, Richard F. *Yankee Leviathan: The Origins of Central State Authority in America, 1859–1877.* New York: Cambridge University Press, 1990.

Birney, Catherine H. *The Grimké Sisters: Sarah and Angelina Grimké, the First American Women Advocates of Abolition and Woman's Rights.* 1885. Reprint, New York: Haskell House, 1970.

Blight, David. *Race and Reunion: The Civil War in American Memory.* Cambridge, Mass.: Belknap Press of Harvard University Press, 2001.

Blocker, Jack S. *American Temperance Movements: Cycles of Reform.* Boston: Twayne, 1989.

Bolt, Christine. *Sisterhood Questioned? Race, Class and Internationalism in the American and British Women's Movements, c. 1880s–1970s*. London: Routledge, 2004.

Bordin, Ruth. *Frances Willard: A Biography*. Chapel Hill: University of North Carolina Press, 1986.

———. *Woman and Temperance: The Quest for Power and Liberty, 1873–1900*. Philadelphia: Temple University Press, 1981.

Boris, Eileen. "The Power of Motherhood: Black and White Activist Women Redefine the 'Political.'" In *Mothers of a New World: Maternalist Politics and the Origins of Welfare States*, ed. Seth Koven and Sonya Michel, 213–45. New York: Routledge, 1993.

Boyd, Melba Joyce. *Discarded Legacy: Politics and Poetics in the Life of Frances E. W. Harper, 1825–1911*. Detroit: Wayne State University Press, 1994.

Boylan, Anne M. *The Origins of Women's Activism: New York and Boston, 1797–1840*. Chapel Hill: University of North Carolina Press, 2002.

Brands, H. W. *Andrew Jackson: His Life and Times*. New York: Doubleday, 2005.

Bredbenner, Candice Lewis. *A Nationality of Her Own: Women, Marriage, and the Law of Citizenship*. Berkeley and Los Angeles: University of California Press, 1998.

Briggs, Laura. *Reproducing Empire: Race, Sex, Science, and U.S. Imperialism in Puerto Rico*. Berkeley and Los Angeles: University of California Press, 2002.

Bright, Charles C. "The State in the United States during the Nineteenth Century." In *Statemaking and Social Movements: Essays in History and Theory*, ed. Charles Bright and Susan Harding, 121–58. Ann Arbor: University of Michigan Press, 1984.

Brown, Elsa Barkley. "Negotiating and Transforming the Public Sphere: African American Political Life in the Transition from Slavery to Freedom." In *Women Transforming Politics: An Alternative Reader*, ed. Cathy J. Cohen, Kathleen B. Jones, and Joan C. Tronto, 343–76. New York: New York University Press, 1997.

———. "To Catch the Vision of Freedom: Reconstructing Southern Black Women's Political History, 1865–1880." In Ruiz and DuBois, *Unequal Sisters* (3rd ed.).

———. "'What Has Happened Here': The Politics of Difference in Women's History and Feminist Politics." *Feminist Studies* 18, no. 1 (Summer 1992): 295–312.

Brown, Mary Jane. *Eradicating This Evil: Women in the American Anti-lynching Movement, 1892–1940*. New York: Garland, 2000.

Burin, Eric. *Slavery and the Peculiar Solution: A History of the American Colonization Society*. Gainesville: University Press of Florida, 2005.

Carby, Hazel V. *Reconstructing Womanhood: The Emergence of the Afro-American Woman Novelist*. New York: Oxford University Press, 1987.

Carrigan, William D., and Clive Webb. "*Muerto por Unos Desconocidos* (Killed by Persons Unknown): Mob Violence against Blacks and Mexicans." In Cole and Parker, *Beyond Black and White*, 35–74.

Cash, Floris Barnett. *African American Women and Social Action: The Clubwomen and Volunteerism from Jim Crow to the New Deal, 1896–1936*. Westport, Conn.: Greenwood Press, 2001.

Chmielewski, Wendy E., Louis J. Kern, and Marlyn Klee-Hartzell, eds. *Women in Spiritual and Communitarian Societies in the United States*. Syracuse, N.Y.: Syracuse University Press, 1993.

Clifford, Deborah Pickman. *Crusader for Freedom: A Life of Lydia Maria Child*. Boston: Beacon Press, 1992.

Cohen, Lizabeth. *A Consumers' Republic: The Politics of Mass Consumption in Postwar America*. New York: Alfred A. Knopf, 2003.

———. *Making a New Deal: Industrial Workers in Chicago, 1919–1939*. New York: Cambridge University Press, 1990.

Cole, Stephanie, and Alison M. Parker, eds. *Beyond Black and White: Race, Ethnicity, and Gender in the U.S. South and Southwest*. College Station: Texas A&M University Press, 2004.

Collier-Thomas, Bettye. "Frances Ellen Watkins Harper: Abolitionist and Feminist Reformer, 1825–1911." In Gordon, *African American Women and the Vote*, 41–65.

Collier-Thomas, Bettye, and V. P. Franklin. *Sisters in the Struggle: African American Women in the Civil Rights–Black Power Movement*. New York: New York University Press, 2001.

Collins, Patricia Hill. *Black Feminist Thought: Knowledge, Consciousness, and the Politics of Empowerment*. New York: Routledge, 2000.

Connors, Robert J. "Frances Wright: First Female Civic Rhetor in America." *College English* 62, no. 1 (September 1999): 30–57.

Cott, Nancy F. *The Bonds of Womanhood: "Woman's Sphere" in New England, 1780–1835*. New Haven, Conn.: Yale University Press, 1977.

———. *The Grounding of Modern Feminism*. New Haven, Conn.: Yale University Press, 1987.

———. *Public Vows: A History of Marriage and the Nation*. Cambridge, Mass.: Harvard University Press, 2000.

———, ed. *No Small Courage: A History of Women in the United States*. New York: Oxford University Press, 2000.

Cutter, Barbara. *Domestic Devils, Battlefield Angels: The Radicalism of American Womanhood, 1830–1865*. DeKalb: Northern Illinois University Press, 2003.

Dailey, Jane. *Before Jim Crow: The Politics of Race in Postemancipation Virginia*. Chapel Hill: University of North Carolina Press, 2000.

Dailey, Jane, Glenda Elizabeth Gilmore, and Bryant Simon, eds. *Jumpin' Jim Crow: Southern Politics from Civil War to Civil Rights*. Princeton, N.J.: Princeton University Press, 2000.

Daly, John P. *When Slavery Was Called Freedom: Evangelicalism, Proslavery, and the Causes of the Civil War*. Lexington: University Press of Kentucky, 2002.

Davis, David Brion. *Inhuman Bondage: The Rise and Fall of Slavery in the New World*. New York: Oxford University Press, 2006.

Donovan, Brian. *White Slave Crusades: Race, Gender, and Anti-vice Activism, 1887–1917*. Urbana: University of Illinois Press, 2006.

Dorsey, Bruce. "Friends Becoming Enemies: Philadelphia Benevolence and the Neglected Era of American Quaker History." *Journal of the Early Republic* 18 (Fall 1998): 395–428.

Dray, Philip. *At the Hands of Persons Unknown: The Lynching of Black America*. New York: Random House, 2002.

Dreyer, Frederick A. *Burke's Politics: A Study in Whig Orthodoxy*. Waterloo, Ont.: Wilfrid Laurier University Press, 1979.

DuBois, Ellen Carol. "Ernestine Rose's Jewish Origins and the Varieties of Euro-American Emancipation in 1848." In Sklar and Stewart, *Transatlantic Antislavery*, 279–98.

———. *Feminism and Suffrage: The Emergence of an Independent Women's Movement in America, 1848–1869*. Ithaca, N.Y.: Cornell University Press, 1978.

———. "Taking the Law into Our Own Hands: *Bradwell, Minor,* and Suffrage Militance in the 1870s." In *Visible Women: New Essays on American Activism*, ed. Nancy A. Hewitt and Suzanne Lebsock, 19–40. Urbana: University of Illinois Press, 1993.

———. *Woman Suffrage and Women's Rights*. New York: New York University Press, 1998.

DuBois, Ellen Carol, and Richard Candida Smith, eds. *Elizabeth Cady Stanton, Feminist as Thinker: A Reader in Documents and Essays*. New York: New York University Press, 2007.

Earle, Jonathan H. *Jacksonian Antislavery and the Politics of Free Soil, 1824–1854*. Chapel Hill: University of North Carolina Press, 2004.

Edwards, Laura F. *Gendered Strife and Confusion: The Political Culture of Reconstruction*. Urbana: University of Illinois Press, 1997.

Edwards, Rebecca. *Angels in the Machinery: Gender in American Party Politics from the Civil War to the Progressive Era*. New York: Oxford University Press, 1997.

Edwards, Wendy J. Deichmann, and Carolyn De Swarte Gifford, eds. *Gender and the Social Gospel*. Urbana: University of Illinois Press, 2003.

Epstein, Barbara Leslie. *The Politics of Domesticity: Women, Evangelism, and Temperance in Nineteenth-Century America*. Middletown, Conn.: Wesleyan University Press, 1981.

Etcheson, Nicole. *Bleeding Kansas: Contested Liberty in the Civil War Era*. Lawrence: University Press of Kansas, 2004.

Evans, Peter B., Dietrich Rueschemeyer, and Theda Skocpol, eds. *Bringing the State Back In*. New York: Cambridge University Press, 1985.

Fabi, M. Giulia. *Passing and the Rise of the African American Novel*. Urbana: University of Illinois Press, 2001.

Faulkner, Carol. *Women's Radical Reconstruction: The Freedmen's Aid Movement*. Philadelphia: University of Pennsylvania Press, 2004.

Feller, Daniel. *The Jacksonian Promise: America, 1815–1840*. Baltimore: Johns Hopkins University Press, 1995.

Flexner, Eleanor, and Ellen F. Fitzpatrick. *Century of Struggle: The Woman's Rights Movement in the United States*. Enlarged ed., Cambridge, Mass.: Belknap Press of Harvard University Press, 1996.

Foner, Eric. *Forever Free: The Story of Emancipation and Reconstruction*. New York: Alfred A. Knopf, 2006.

———. *Free Soil, Free Labor, Free Men: The Ideology of the Republican Party before the Civil War*. New York: Oxford University Press, 1970.

Foster, Gaines M. *Moral Reconstruction: Christian Lobbyists and the Federal Legislation of Morality, 1865–1920*. Chapel Hill: University of North Carolina Press, 2002.

Foster, Lawrence. *Religion and Sexuality: The Shakers, the Mormons, and the Oneida Community*. 1981. Reprint, Urbana: University of Illinois Press, 1984.

Fox-Genovese, Elizabeth. *Within the Plantation Household: Black and White Women of the Old South*. Chapel Hill: University of North Carolina Press, 1988.

Freedman, Estelle B. "Race and the Politics of Identity in U.S. Feminism." In Ruiz and DuBois, *Unequal Sisters* (4th ed.), 1–14.

Freeman, Michael. *Edmund Burke and the Critique of Political Radicalism*. Chicago: University of Chicago Press, 1980.

Friedman, Lawrence J. *Gregarious Saints: Self and Community in American Abolitionism, 1830–1870*. New York: Cambridge University Press, 1982.

Gaines, Kevin. "Black Americans' Racial Uplift Ideology as 'Civilizing Mission': Pauline E. Hopkins on Race and Imperialism." In Kaplan and Pease, *Cultures of United States Imperialism*, 433–55.

Gerstle, Gary. "Liberty, Coercion, and the Making of Americans." *Journal of American History* (September 1997): 524–58.

Giddings, Paula. *When and Where I Enter: The Impact of Black Women on Race and Sex in America*. 1984. Reprint, New York: Amistad/Harper Collins, 2006.

Giele, Janet Zollinger. *Two Paths to Women's Equality: Temperance, Suffrage, and the Origins of Modern Feminism*. New York: Twayne, 1995.

Gilmore, Glenda Elizabeth. *Gender and Jim Crow: Women and the Politics of White Supremacy in North Carolina, 1896–1920.* Chapel Hill: University of North Carolina Press, 1996.

Ginzberg, Lori D. "'The Hearts of Your Readers Will Shudder': Fanny Wright, Infidelity, and American Freethought." *American Quarterly* 46, no. 2 (June 1994): 195–226.

———. *Untidy Origins: A Story of Woman's Rights in Antebellum New York.* Chapel Hill: University of North Carolina Press, 2005.

———. *Women and the Work of Benevolence: Morality, Politics and Class in the Nineteenth-Century United States.* New Haven, Conn.: Yale University Press, 1990.

Gordon, Ann D., with Bettye Collier-Thomas, eds. *African American Women and the Vote, 1837–1965.* Amherst: University of Massachusetts Press, 1997.

Gordon, Linda. "Voluntary Motherhood: The Beginnings of Feminist Birth Control Ideas in the United States." In *Mothers and Motherhood: Readings in American History,* ed. Rima Apple and Janet Golden, 423–43. Columbus: Ohio State University Press, 1997.

———, ed. *Women, the State, and Welfare.* Madison: University of Wisconsin Press, 1990.

Gordon, Sarah Barringer. *The Mormon Question: Polygamy and Constitutional Conflict in Nineteenth-Century America.* Chapel Hill: University of North Carolina Press, 2002.

Gordon-Reed, Annette, ed. *Race on Trial: Law and Justice in American History.* New York: Oxford University Press, 2002.

———. *Thomas Jefferson and Sally Hemings: An American Controversy.* Charlottesville: University Press of Virginia, 1997.

Gorrell, Donald K. *The Age of Social Responsibility: The Social Gospel in the Progressive Era, 1900–1920.* Macon, Ga.: Mercer University Press, 1988.

Gornick, Vivian. *The Solitude of Self: Thinking about Elizabeth Cady Stanton.* New York: Farrar, Straus and Giroux, 2005.

Graham, Maryemma. "Frances Ellen Watkins Harper." In *Afro-American Writers before the Harlem Renaissance,* ed. Trudier Harris and Thadious M. Davis, 164–73. Detroit: Gale, 1986.

Graham, Sarah Hunter. *Woman Suffrage and the New Democracy.* New Haven, Conn.: Yale University Press, 1996.

Green, Elna C. *Southern Strategies: Southern Women and the Woman Suffrage Question.* Chapel Hill: University of North Carolina Press, 1997.

Griffith, Elisabeth. *In Her Own Right: The Life of Elizabeth Cady Stanton.* New York: Oxford University Press, 1984.

Grossberg, Michael. *Governing the Hearth: Law and the Family in Nineteenth-Century America.* Chapel Hill: University of North Carolina Press, 1985.

Gusfield, Joseph. *Symbolic Crusade: Status, Politics, and the American Temperance Movement.* Urbana: University of Illinois Press, 1963.

Gustafson, Melanie Susan. *Women and the Republican Party, 1854–1924.* Urbana: University of Illinois Press, 2001.

Guy-Sheftall, Beverly. *Daughters of Sorrow: Attitudes toward Black Women, 1880–1920.* Brooklyn, N.Y.: Carlson, 1990.

Hale, Grace Elizabeth. *Making Whiteness: The Culture of Segregation in the South, 1890–1940.* New York: Vintage Books, 1998.

Hall, Jacquelyn Dowd. *Revolt against Chivalry: Jessie Daniel Ames and the Women's Campaign against Lynching.* New York: Columbia University Press, 1979.

Hamm, Richard. *Shaping the Eighteenth Amendment: Temperance Reform, Legal Culture, and the Polity, 1880–1920.* Chapel Hill: University of North Carolina Press, 1995.

Hamm, Thomas D. *The Quakers in America.* New York: Columbia University Press, 2003.

Hammand, Wendy F. "The Woman's National Loyal League: Feminist Abolitionists and the Civil War." *Civil War History* 35, no. 1 (1989): 39–58.

Harley, Sharon. "Mary Church Terrell: Genteel Militant." In *Black Leaders of the Nineteenth Century,* ed. Leon Sack and August Meier, 307–21. Urbana: University of Illinois Press, 1998.

Harley, Sharon, and Rosalyn Terborg-Penn. *The Afro-American Woman: Struggles and Images.* Port Washington, N.Y.: Kennikat Press, 1978.

Harper, Judith E. *Susan B. Anthony: A Biographical Companion.* Santa Barbara, Calif.: ABC-CLIO, 1998.

Hartog, Hendrik. *Man and Wife in America: A History.* Cambridge, Mass.: Harvard University Press, 2000.

Heineman, Helen. *Restless Angels: The Friendship of Six Victorian Women, Frances Wright, Camilla Wright, Harriet Garnett, Frances Garnett, Julia Garnett Perz, Frances Trollope.* Athens: Ohio University Press, 1994.

Hersh, Blanche Glassman. *The Slavery of Sex: Feminist-Abolitionists in America.* Urbana: University of Illinois Press, 1978.

Hewitt, Nancy A. *Women's Activism and Social Change: Rochester, New York, 1822–1872.* Ithaca, N.Y.: Cornell University Press, 1984.

Higginbotham, Evelyn Brooks. "In Politics to Stay: Black Women Leaders and Party Politics in the 1920s." In Ruiz and DuBois, *Unequal Sisters* (4th ed.), 289–302.

———. *Righteous Discontent: The Women's Movement in the Black Baptist Church, 1880–1920.* Cambridge, Mass.: Harvard University Press, 1993.

Hill, Patricia Ruth. *The World Their Household: The American Women's Foreign Mission Movement and Cultural Transformation, 1870–1920.* Ann Arbor: University of Michigan Press, 1985.

Hine, Darlene Clark. "'We Specialize in the Wholly Impossible': The Philanthropic Work of Black Women." In *Lady Bountiful Revisited: Women, Philanthropy, and Power,* ed. Kathleen D. McCarthy, 70–93. New Brunswick, N.J.: Rutgers University Press, 1990.

Hine, Darlene Clark, and Kathleen Thompson. *A Shining Thread of Hope: The History of Black Women in America.* New York: Broadway Books, 1998.

Hodes, Martha, *White Women, Black Men: Illicit Sex in the Nineteenth-Century South.* New Haven, Conn.: Yale University Press, 1997.

———, ed. *Sex, Love, Race: Crossing Boundaries in North American History.* New York: New York University Press, 1999.

Hoganson, Kristin L. *Fighting for American Manhood: How Gender Politics Provoked the Spanish-American and Philippine-American Wars.* New Haven, Conn.: Yale University Press, 1998.

Holt, Michael F. *The Rise and Fall of the American Whig Party: Jacksonian Politics and the Onset of the Civil War.* New York: Oxford University Press, 1999.

Humez, Jean M. *Harriet Tubman: The Life and the Life Stories.* Madison: University of Wisconsin Press, 2003.

Hunter, Tera W. *To "Joy My Freedom": Southern Black Women's Lives and Labors after the Civil War.* Cambridge, Mass.: Harvard University Press, 1997.

Ingle, H. Larry. *Quakers in Conflict: The Hicksite Reformation.* Knoxville: University of Tennessee Press, 1986.

Isenberg, Nancy. "'Pillars in the Same Temple and Priests of the Same Worship': Woman's Rights and the Politics of Church and State in Antebellum America."

Journal of American History (June 1998): 98–128.

———. *Sex and Citizenship in Antebellum America.* Chapel Hill: University of North Carolina Press, 1998.

Jeffrey, Julie R. *The Great Silent Army of Abolitionism: Ordinary Women in the Antislavery Movement.* Chapel Hill: University of North Carolina Press, 1998.

Jones, Beverly Washington. *Quest for Equality: The Life and Writings of Mary Eliza Church Terrell, 1863–1954.* Brooklyn, N.Y.: Carlson, 1990.

Jones, Jacqueline. *Labor of Love, Labor of Sorrow: Black Women, Work, and the Family from Slavery to the Present.* New York: Vintage Books, 1985.

Jordan, Ryan P. *Slavery and the Meetinghouse: The Quakers and the Abolitionist Dilemma, 1820–1865.* Bloomington: Indiana University Press, 2007.

Kaplan, Amy, and Donald E. Pease, eds. *Cultures of United States Imperialism.* Durham, N.C.: Duke University Press, 1993.

Kelley, Mary. *Learning to Stand & Speak: Women, Education, and Public Life in America's Republic.* Chapel Hill: University of North Carolina Press, 2006.

Kerber, Linda K. "A Constitutional Right to be Treated like American Ladies: Women and the Obligations of Citizenship." In *U.S. History as Women's History: New Feminist Essays,* ed. Linda K. Kerber, Alice Kessler-Harris, and Kathryn Kish Sklar. Chapel Hill: University of North Carolina Press, 1996.

———. "The Meanings of Citizenship." *Journal of American History* (December 1997): 833–54.

———. *No Constitutional Right to Be Ladies: Women and the Obligations of Citizenship.* New York: Hill and Wang, 1998.

Kern, Kathi. *Mrs. Stanton's Bible.* Ithaca, N.Y.: Cornell University Press, 2001.

Kerr, Andrea Moore. *Lucy Stone: Speaking Out for Equality.* New Brunswick, N.J.: Rutgers University Press, 1992.

Kessler-Harris, Alice. *In Pursuit of Equity: Women, Men, and the Quest for Economic Citizenship in Twentieth-Century America.* New York: Oxford University Press, 2001.

———. "In the Nation's Image: The Gendered Limits of Social Citizenship in the Depression Era." *Journal of American History* (December 1999): 1251–80.

Kissel, Susan. *In Common Cause: The "Conservative" Frances Trollope and the "Radical" Frances Wright.* Bowling Green, Ohio: Bowling Green State University Popular Press, 1993.

Knupfer, Anne Meis. *Toward a Tenderer Humanity and a Nobler Womanhood: African-American Women's Clubs in Turn-of-the-Century Chicago.* New York: New York University Press, 1996.

Kolmerten, Carol. *Women in Utopia: The Ideology of Gender in the American Owenite Communities.* Bloomington: Indiana University Press, 1990.

Kraut, Alan M. *Crusaders and Compromisers: Essays on the Relationship of the Antislavery Struggle to the Antebellum Party System.* Westport, Conn.: Greenwood Press, 1983.

Kunzel, Regina G. *Fallen Women, Problem Girls: Unmarried Mothers and the Professionalization of Social Work, 1890–1945.* New Haven, Conn.: Yale University Press, 1993.

Ladd-Taylor, Molly. *Mother-Work: Women, Child Welfare, and the State, 1890–1930.* Urbana: University of Illinois Press, 1994.

Larson, Jane E. "'Even a Worm Will Turn at Last': Rape Reform in Late Nineteenth-Century America." *Yale Journal of Law and the Humanities* 9, no. 1 (1997): 1–71.

Lerner, Gerda. *The Grimké Sisters from South Carolina: Pioneers for Women's Rights and Abolition.* 1967. Revised ed., Chapel Hill: University of North Carolina Press, 2004.

Lindhorst, Marie J. "Sarah Mapps Douglass: The Emergence of an African American Educator/Activist in Nineteenth-Century Philadelphia." Ph.D. dissertation, Pennsylvania State University, 1995.

Lopez, Ian Haney. *White by Law: The Legal Construction of Race.* Revised ed., New York: New York University Press, 2006.

Mancini, Matthew J. *One Dies, Get Another: Convict Leasing in the American South, 1866–1928.* Columbia: University of South Carolina Press, 1996.

Materson, Lisa Gail. *For the Freedom of Her Race: Black Women and Electoral Politics in Illinois, 1872–1932.* Chapel Hill: University of North Carolina Press, 2009.

———. "Respectable Partisans: African American Women in Electoral Politics, 1877–1936." Ph.D. dissertation, University of California, Los Angeles, 2000.

Matthews, Jean V. *Women's Struggle for Equality: The First Phase, 1828–1876.* Chicago: Ivan R. Dee, 1997.

Mattingly, Carol. *Well-Tempered Women: Nineteenth-Century Temperance Rhetoric.* Carbondale: Southern Illinois University Press, 1998.

Mayer, Henry. *All On Fire: William Lloyd Garrison and the Abolition of Slavery.* New York: St. Martin's Press, 1998.

Mayfield, John. *Rehearsal for Republicanism: Free Soil and the Politics of Antislavery.* Port Washington, N.Y.: Kennikat Press, 1980.

McCarthy, Timothy Patrick, and John Stauffer, eds. *Prophets of Protest: Reconsidering the History of American Abolitionism.* New York: New Press, 2006.

McDaniel, Donna, and Vanessa Julye. *Fit for Freedom, not for Friendship: Quakers, African Americans, and the Myth of Racial Justice.* Philadelphia: Quaker Press, 2009.

McFadden, Margaret H. *Golden Cables of Sympathy: The Transatlantic Sources of Nineteenth-Century Feminism.* Lexington: University Press of Kentucky, 1999.

McKay, Nellie Y. "The Girls Who Became the Women: Childhood Memories in the Autobiographies of Harriet Jacobs, Mary Church Terrell, and Anne Moody." In *Tradition and the Talents of Women,* ed. Florence Howe, 105–24. Urbana: University of Illinois Press, 1991.

Melish, Joanne Pope. *Disowning Slavery: Gradual Emancipation and "Race" in New England, 1780–1860.* Ithaca, N.Y.: Cornell University Press, 1998.

Midgley, Clare. "British Abolition and Feminism in Transatlantic Perspective." In Sklar and Stewart, *Transatlantic Antislavery,* 121–36.

Miller, William Lee. *Arguing about Slavery: The Great Battle in the United States Congress.* New York: Alfred A. Knopf, 1996.

Mitchell, Michele. *Righteous Propagation: African Americans and the Politics of Racial Destiny after Reconstruction.* Chapel Hill: University of North Carolina Press, 2004.

Morris Eckhardt, Celia. *Fanny Wright: Rebel in America.* 1984. Reprint, Urbana: University of Illinois Press, 1992.

Muncy, Robyn. *Creating a Female Dominion in American Reform, 1890–1935.* New York: Oxford University Press, 1991.

Murdock, Catherine Gilbert. *Domesticating Drink: Women, Men, and Alcohol in America, 1870–1940.* Baltimore: Johns Hopkins University Press, 1998.

Murrin, John M. "A Roof without Walls: The Dilemma of American National Identity." In *Beyond Confederation: Origins of the Constitution and American National Identity,* ed. Richard Beeman, Stephen Botein, and Edward C. Carter II, 333–49. Chapel Hill: University of North Carolina Press, 1987.

Neverdon-Morton, Cynthia. *Afro-American Women of the South and the Advancement of the Race, 1895–1925.* Knoxville: University of Tennessee Press, 1989.

Newman, Louise Michele. *White Women's Rights: The Racial Origins of Feminism in the*

United States. New York: Oxford University Press, 1999.

Newman, Richard S. *The Transformation of American Abolitionism, 1780s–1830s: Fighting Slavery in the Early Republic.* Chapel Hill: University of North Carolina Press, 2002.

Ngai, Mae M. *Impossible Subjects: Illegal Aliens and the Making of Modern America.* Princeton, N.J.: Princeton University Press, 2004.

Novak, William. *The People's Welfare: Law and Regulation in Nineteenth-Century America.* Chapel Hill: University of North Carolina Press, 1996.

Oakes, James. *The Radical and the Republican: Frederick Douglass, Abraham Lincoln, and the Triumph of Antislavery Politics.* New York: W. W. Norton, 2007.

———. *The Ruling Race: A History of American Slaveholders.* New York: Alfred A. Knopf, 1982.

Odem, Mary E. *Delinquent Daughters: Protecting and Policing Adolescent Female Sexuality in the United States, 1885–1920.* Chapel Hill: University of North Carolina Press, 1995.

Painter, Nell Irvin. *Sojourner Truth: A Life, a Symbol.* New York: W. W. Norton, 1996.

———. "Voices of Suffrage: Sojourner Truth, Frances Watkins Harper, and the Struggle for Woman Suffrage." In Baker, *Votes for Women,* 42–55.

Parker, Alison M. *Purifying America: Women, Cultural Reform, and Pro-Censorship Activism, 1873–1933.* Urbana: University of Illinois Press, 1997.

Parker, Alison M., and Stephanie Cole, eds. *Women and the Unstable State in Nineteenth-Century America.* College Station: Texas A&M University Press, 2000.

Pascoe, Peggy. *Relations of Rescue: The Search for Female Moral Authority in the American West, 1874–1939.* New York: Oxford University Press, 1990.

———. *What Comes Naturally: Miscegenation Law and the Making of Race in America.* New York: Oxford University Press, 2009.

Passet, Joanne E. *Sex Radicals and the Quest for Women's Equality.* Urbana: University of Illinois Press, 2003.

Perkins, A. J. G., and Theresa Wolfson. *Frances Wright, Free Enquirer: The Study of a Temperament.* New York: Harper and Brothers, 1939.

Perry, Lewis. *Radical Abolitionism: Anarchy and the Government of God in Anti-slavery Thought.* Ithaca, N.Y.: Cornell University Press, 1973.

Perry, Mark. *Lift Up Thy Voice: The Grimké Family's Journey from Slaveholders to Civil Rights Leaders.* New York: Penguin Books, 2001.

Peterson, Carla L. *"Doers of the Word": African-American Women Speakers and Writers in the North, 1830–1880.* New York: Oxford University Press, 1995.

———. "Literary Transnationalism and Diasporic History: Frances Watkins Harper's 'Fancy Sketches,' 1859–1860." In Sklar and Stewart, *Transatlantic Antislavery,* 189–210.

———. "Reconstructing the Nation: Frances Harper, Charlotte Forten, and the Racial Politics of Periodical Publication." *American Antiquarian Society* (1989): 301–34.

Pfeifer, Michael J. *Rough Justice: Lynching and American Society, 1874–1947.* Urbana: University of Illinois Press, 2004.

Pitzer, Donald E., ed. *America's Communal Utopias.* Chapel Hill: University of North Carolina Press, 1997.

Portnoy, Alisse. *Their Right to Speak: Women's Activism in the Indian and Slave Debates.* Cambridge, Mass.: Harvard University Press, 2005.

Quarles, Benjamin. *Allies for Freedom: Blacks and John Brown.* New York: Oxford University Press, 1974.

Renda, Mary A. *Taking Haiti: Military Occupation and the Culture of U.S. Imperialism, 1915–1940.* Chapel Hill: University of North Carolina Press, 2001.

Reynolds, David S. *John Brown, Abolitionist: The Man Who Killed Slavery, Sparked the Civil War, and Seeded Civil Rights.* New York: Alfred A. Knopf, 2005.

Richardson, Heather Cox. *The Death of Reconstruction: Race, Labor, and Politics in the Post–Civil War North, 1865–1901.* Cambridge, Mass.: Harvard University Press, 2001.

Roediger, David R. *Colored White: Transcending the Racial Past.* Berkeley and Los Angeles: University of California Press, 2002.

———. *The Wages of Whiteness: Race and the Making of the American Working Class.* 1991. Revised ed., New York: Verso Press, 1999.

Rueschemeyer, Dietrich, and Theda Skocpol, eds. *States, Social Knowledge, and the Origins of Modern Social Policies.* Princeton, N.J.: Princeton University Press, 1996.

Ruiz, Vicki L., and Ellen DuBois, eds. *Unequal Sisters: A Multicultural Reader in U.S. Women's History.* 3rd ed., New York: Routledge, 2000.

———. *Unequal Sisters: An Inclusive Reader in U.S. Women's History.* 4th ed., New York: Routledge, 2008.

Ryan, Mary P. *Cradle of the Middle Class: The Family in Oneida County, New York, 1790–1865.* New York: Cambridge University Press, 1981.

Salem, Dorothy. *To Better Our World: Black Women in Organized Reform, 1890–1920.* Brooklyn, N.Y.: Carlson, 1990.

Salerno, Beth A. *Sister Societies: Women's Antislavery Organizations in Antebellum America.* DeKalb: Northern Illinois University Press, 2005.

Salmon, Marylynn. *Women and the Law of Property in Early America.* Chapel Hill: University of North Carolina Press, 1986.

Samet, Elizabeth D. *Willing Obedience: Citizens, Soldiers, and the Progress of Consent in America, 1776–1898.* Stanford, Calif.: Stanford University Press, 2004.

Saxon, Martha. *Being Good: Women's Moral Values in Early America.* New York: Hill and Wang, 2003.

Schechter, Patricia A. *Ida B. Wells-Barnett and American Reform, 1880–1930.* Chapel Hill: University of North Carolina Press, 2001.

Schloesser, Pauline. *The Fair Sex: White Women and Racial Patriarchy in the Early American Republic.* New York: New York University Press, 2002.

Schwalm, Leslie A. *A Hard Fight for We: Women's Transition from Slavery to Freedom in South Carolina.* Urbana: University of Illinois Press, 1997.

Scott, Anne Firor. *Natural Allies: Women's Associations in American History.* Urbana: University of Illinois Press, 1991.

Sewell, Richard H. *Ballots for Freedom: Antislavery Politics in the United States, 1837–1860.* New York: Oxford University Press, 1976.

Shaw, Stephanie J. "Black Club Women and the Creation of the National Association of Colored Women." In *"We Specialize in the Wholly Impossible": A Reader in Black Women's History,* ed. Darlene Clark Hine, Wilma King, and Linda Reed, 433–48. New York: Carlson, 1995.

———. *What a Woman Ought to Be and to Do: Black Professional Women Workers during the Jim Crow Era.* Chicago: University of Chicago Press, 1996.

Sherman, Richard B. *The Republican Party and Black America: From McKinley to Hoover, 1896–1933.* Charlottesville: University Press of Virginia, 1973.

Sherr, Lynn. *Failure Is Impossible: Susan B. Anthony in Her Own Words.* New York: Random House, 1995.

Sklar, Kathryn Kish. *Catharine Beecher: A Study in American Domesticity.* New York: W. W. Norton, 1976.

———. "'Women Who Speak for an Entire Nation': American and British Women at the World Anti-slavery Convention, London, 1840." In Yellin and Van Horne,

Abolitionist Sisterhood, 301–33.

Sklar, Kathryn Kish, and James Brewer Stewart, eds. *Women's Rights and Transatlantic Antislavery in the Era of Emancipation.* New Haven, Conn.: Yale University Press, 2007.

Skocpol, Theda. "Bringing the State Back In: Strategies of Analysis in Current Research." In Evans, Rueschemeyer, and Skocpol, *Bringing the State Back In.* 3–37.

——. *Protecting Mothers and Soldiers: The Political Origins of Social Policy in the United States.* Cambridge, Mass.: Belknap Press of Harvard University Press, 1992.

Skowronek, Stephen. *Building a New American State: The Expansion of National Administrative Capacities, 1877–1920.* New York: Cambridge University Press, 1982.

Sneider, Allison L. *Suffragists in an Imperial Age: U.S. Expansion and the Woman Question, 1870–1929.* New York: Oxford University Press, 2008.

——. "Woman Suffrage in Congress: American Expansion and the Politics of Federalism, 1870–1890." In Baker, *Votes for Women,* 77–89.

Solomon, Barbara M. *In the Company of Educated Women: A History of Women and Higher Education in America.* New Haven: Yale University Press, 1985.

Stanley, Amy Dru. *From Bondage to Contract: Wage Labor, Marriage, and the Market in the Age of Slave Emancipation.* New York: Cambridge University Press, 1998.

Staudenraus, P. J. *The African Colonization Movement, 1816–1865.* New York: Columbia University Press, 1961.

Stauffer, John. *The Black Hearts of Men: Radical Abolitionists and the Transformation of Race.* Cambridge, Mass.: Harvard University Press, 2002.

Sterling, Dorothy. *Ahead of Her Time: Abby Kelley and the Politics of Antislavery.* New York: W. W. Norton, 1991.

——. *We Are Your Sisters: Black Women in the Nineteenth Century.* New York: W. W. Norton, 1984.

Stoler, Ann Laura, ed. *Haunted by Empire: Geographies of Intimacy in North American History.* Durham: Duke University Press, 2006.

Strong, Douglas M. *Perfectionist Politics: Abolitionism and the Religious Tensions of American Democracy.* Syracuse, N.Y.: Syracuse University Press, 1999.

Sullivan, Kathleen S. *Constitutional Context: Women and Rights Discourse in Nineteenth-Century America.* Baltimore: Johns Hopkins University Press, 2007.

Sutton, Robert P. *Communal Utopias and the American Experience: Religious Communities, 1732–2000.* Westport, Conn.: Praeger, 2003.

Swerdlow, Amy. "Abolition's Conservative Sisters: The Ladies' New York City Antislavery Societies, 1834–1840." In Yellin and Van Horne, *Abolitionist Sisterhood,* 31–44.

Taylor, Barbara. *Eve and the New Jerusalem: Socialism and Feminism in the Nineteenth Century.* Cambridge, Mass.: Harvard University Press, 1993.

Terborg-Penn, Rosalyn. "African American Women and the Woman Suffrage Movement." In Wheeler, *One Woman, One Vote,* 135–55.

——. *African American Women in the Struggle for the Vote, 1850–1920.* Bloomington: University of Indiana Press, 1998.

——. "Black Male Perspectives on the Nineteenth-Century Woman." In Harley and Terborg-Penn, *Afro-American Woman,* 28–42.

Tyrrell, Ian. *Woman's World, Woman's Empire: The Woman's Christian Temperance Union in International Perspective, 1880–1930.* Chapel Hill: University of North Carolina Press, 1991.

Underhill, Lois Beachy. *The Woman Who Ran for President: The Many Lives of Victoria Woodhull.* Bridgehampton, N.Y.: Bridge Work, 1995.

Van Burkleo, Sandra F. *"Belonging to the World": Women's Rights and American Constitutional Culture*. New York: Oxford University Press, 2001.

Van Deburg, William L. *Slavery and Race in American Popular Culture*. Madison: University of Wisconsin Press, 1984.

Varon, Elizabeth R. *We Mean to Be Counted: White Women and Politics in Antebellum Virginia*. Chapel Hill: University of North Carolina Press, 1998.

Venet, Wendy Hammand. *Neither Ballots nor Bullets: Women Abolitionists and the Civil War*. Charlottesville: University of Virginia Press, 1991.

Veysey, Laurence, ed. *The Perfectionists: Radical Social Thought in the North, 1815–1860*. New York: John Wiley and Sons, 1973.

Wald, Gayle. *Crossing the Line: Racial Passing in Twentieth-Century U.S. Literature and Culture*. Durham, N.C.: Duke University Press, 2000.

Ware, Susan. *Beyond Suffrage: Women in the New Deal*. Cambridge, Mass.: Harvard University Press, 1981.

Waterman, William Randall. *Frances Wright, 1795–1852*. New York: AMS Press, 1967.

Watson, Harry L. *Liberty and Power: The Politics of Jacksonian America*. New York: Hill and Wang, 1990.

Watson, Martha. *Lives of Their Own: Rhetorical Dimensions in Autobiographies of Women Activists*. Columbia: University of South Carolina Press, 1999.

Weiner, Marli F. *Mistresses and Slaves: Plantation Women in South Carolina, 1830–1880*. Urbana: University of Illinois Press, 1998.

Weisenfeld, Judith. *African American Women and Christian Activism: New York's Black YWCA, 1905–1945*. Cambridge, Mass.: Harvard University Press, 1997.

Welke, Barbara Y. *Recasting American Liberty: Gender, Race, Law, and the Railroad Revolution, 1865–1920*. New York: Cambridge University Press, 2001.

———. "When All the Women Were White, and All the Blacks Were Men: Gender, Class, Race, and the Road to *Plessy*, 1855–1914." *Law and History Review* 13, no. 2 (Fall 1995): 261–316.

Wellman, Judith. *The Road to Seneca Falls: Elizabeth Cady Stanton and the First Woman's Rights Convention*. Urbana: University of Illinois Press, 2004.

Wheeler, Marjorie Spruill, ed. *One Woman, One Vote: Rediscovering the Woman Suffrage Movement*. Troutdale, Ore.: New Sage Press, 1995.

———. *Votes for Women! The Woman Suffrage Movement in Tennessee, the South, and the Nation*. Knoxville: University of Tennessee Press, 1985.

White, Deborah Gray. *Too Heavy a Load: Black Women in Defense of Themselves, 1894–1994*. New York: W. W. Norton, 1999.

Wilentz, Sean. *Andrew Jackson*. New York: Times Books, 2005.

———. *Chants Democratic: New York City and the Rise of the American Working Class, 1788–1850*. New York: Oxford University Press, 1984.

———. *The Rise of American Democracy: Jefferson to Lincoln*. New York: W. W. Norton, 2005.

Williams, Carolyn. "The Female Antislavery Movement: Fighting against Racial Prejudice and Promoting Women's Rights in Antebellum America." In Yellin and Van Horne, *Abolitionist Sisterhood*, 159–78.

Winch, Julie. "'You Have Talents—Only Cultivate Them': Philadelphia's Black Female Literary Societies and the Abolitionist Crusade." In Yellin and Van Horne, *Abolitionist Sisterhood*, 101–18.

Witcover, Jules. *Party of the People: A History of the Democrats*. New York: Random House, 2003.

Yee, Shirley J. *Black Women Abolitionists: A Study in Activism, 1828–1860*. Knoxville: University of Tennessee Press, 1992.

Yellin, Jean Fagan. *Harriet Jacobs, a Life: The Remarkable Adventures of the Woman Who Wrote* Incidents in the Life of a Slave Girl. New York: Basic Civitas Books, 2004.

Yellin, Jean Fagan, and John C. Van Horne. *The Abolitionist Sisterhood: Women's Political Culture in Antebellum America.* Ithaca, N.Y.: Cornell University Press, 1994.

Zaeske, Susan. *Signatures of Citizenship: Petitioning, Antislavery, and Women's Political Identity.* Chapel Hill: University of North Carolina Press, 2003.

Zagarri, Rosemarie. *Revolutionary Backlash: Women and Politics in the Early American Republic.* Philadelphia: University of Pennsylvania Press, 2007.

Index

abolitionism, 65, 69, 141, 160; connections between temperance and, 126–27, 129, 148; immediate, 10, 12, 40, 62, 214; political, 72; rejection of, 62; Willard and, 141
Adams, John Quincy, 37
Addams, Jane, 211, 251n11
African Methodist Episcopal (AME) Church Review, 126–27, 130–32
Afro-American Council, 187
age-of-consent laws, 20, 154–55; and WCTU, 164–66
amalgamation. See racial amalgamation
American Equal Rights Association (AERA), 116, 119–21
American Anti-Slavery Society, 18, 76; Harper and, 101–6
American Revolution, 29, 158; betrayal of, 108; call for a new, 92; *History of the American Revolution,* 31; political inspiration from, 30–34; promise of, 25–27, 61; symbolism of, 55, 104; taxation without representation, 92, 124, 144
American Slavery As It Is: Testimony of a Thousand Witnesses (1839), 80–83
American Woman Suffrage Association (AWSA), 16, 85, 122
Anglo-African Magazine, 103, 115
Anthony, Susan B., 215; and black men's suffrage, 85, 121; and black women's suffrage, 168; National Council of Women, 134; NWSA and black women, 187–88; as political thinker, 7, 144; as women's movement historian, 8, 11, 26, 28, 119; Women's National Loyal League, 15, 70, 216
anti-clericalism, 9; critique of organized religion, 11, 37, 213; speakers, 55; Wright and, 6, 28–29, 52–53
anti-lynching, 7, 138, 198, 217; federal law, 17, 20–21, 126, 135; Terrell and, 185–87, 200, 210; and transatlantic reform, 6, 169–70, 192; Wells and,

169, 171–72, 175, 191–92; WCTU and, 21, 166–75. See also Ida B. Wells
Anti-Lynching Society of England, 192
Antioch College, 91, 181
antiracism, 12, 86, 200
antislavery; experiment, 41, 158, 213; movement, 12, 67, 98. See also abolitionism
Atlanta Constitution, 207

Baltimore, Maryland, 14, 97–100
Beecher, Catharine, 7, 144; and women's petitioning, 71; Wright and, 67
Bentham, Jeremy; intellectual influence of 6–8, 152; Wright and, 34, 47
Bethel Literary and Historical Association, 192
black clubwomen, 137–38, 185–86; as Christians 190, 193; local activism of, 17; and NACW, 22–23, 136–37, 189–93; and temperance, 126–27, 137; and WCTU, 126–27, 166–69
black men, 167; as citizens, 64, 110, 114, 135, 202–3; caricatured as intemperate, 129, 156; caricatured as rapists, 21, 114, 166, 173; disenfranchised, 123–24, 134, 195, 201, 206–7; violence against, 113, 173, 186; voting rights of, 111–13, 119–22, 215; and woman suffrage, 189, 215
black women, 166; citizenship rights of, 5, 22, 202–3, 215–16; class status of, 193–96; as domestic servants, 173, 196; double burden of, 5, 74, 83, 116–18, 188–89, 192–93; legal rights denied to enslaved, 81–82; as mothers, 193–97, 215; purity of, 81–82, 115, 193; rape of, 48, 50, 81, 166, 173, 186, 193; and self-help, 22–23, 137, 193, 195; separate organizations of, 7, 132, 137–38, 174–75, 189–93, 217; woman suffrage and, 117–24,

Woman's Convention Auxiliary
(National Baptist Convention), 190
Woman's Crusade, 143–44
Woman's Era, 190–92
woman's rights, 8–9, 236n32; critique
of marriage laws, 46, 74–75, 162–64;
Eleventh National Woman's Rights
Convention (1866), 116; Grimkés
and, 80, 89–90; Harper and, 115–16;
married women's property rights
and, 37; Wright and, 51–52
woman suffrage, 120–24; AWSA, 16,
85, 122; Harper and, 14, 99, 120;
Grimkés and, 14, 77, 94–95; and
literacy requirements, 131–32, 147,
167–68, 215; WCTU campaigns for,
19, 154, 157; Willard and, 145
women: citizenship and, 68, 145, 212;
cult of true womanhood, 139; and
Democratic Party, 158; and education, 32, 91; and Free Soil Party, 104,
142; as jurors 94; moral superiority
of, 14, 140, 162; as mothers, 84–85,
94, 145, 193; and petitioning, 70;
piety of, 93–95; political participation of, 65, 94–95, 105, 151, 214;
and Prohibition Party, 159–61;
property rights of, 37, 115–16;
public speaking of, 10, 12, 28,
67–68, 116, 199; purity of, 77, 95,
117–18, 139, 176; and Republican
Party, 141, 159, 162; rights of, 4, 10,
140; sexual purity of 51, 89, 162–66;
and Working Men's Party, 28
Women's International League for Peace

and Freedom, 23, 211
Women's National Loyal League, 15,
70, 216
Woodhull, Victoria, 7, 90, 155
working classes, 168, 194; as drinkers,
157; and Knights of Labor, 165–66;
Wright and, 53–55, 59–60
Working Men's Party, 10, 28, 56, 158
World's Anti-Slavery Convention
(London 1840), 84
World's Columbian Exposition
(Chicago 1893), 169, 190–91
Wright, Camilla, 25, 34, 36, 44- 45, 48,
54
Wright, Frances (D'Arusmont
1795–1852), 8–11, 82, 212; *A Few
Days in Athens* (1822), 34–35; *Altorf*
(1819), 25, 29, 35; antislavery and,
8–10, 32–33; and boarding schools,
58; education reform and, 31, 92;
education of slaves, 40, 45; equal
education and 11, 32, 44; free
thought, 11, 102; Hall of Science, 55;
at Lafayette's La Grange, 34–35; and
marriage laws, 37, 74, 90; mistreatment of slaves, 44–48, 52–54;
Nashoba, 9–10, 37, 39, 43–54, 61;
as political thinker, 27–31; public
lecturing and, 10–11, 28, 54–56,
67–68; state-level legislation, 28,
56–57; and states' rights, 27–30, 34,
38; *Views of Society and Manners in
America* (1821), 29–35, 55; woman's
rights and, 10–11, 46–47, 52
Wright, Henry C., 75–76, 78